FROM MOON CAKES TO MAO TO MODERN CHINA

FROM MOON CAKES
TO MAO
TO MODERN CHINA

AN INTRODUCTION
TO CHINESE CIVILIZATION

Zhu Fayuan, Wu Qixing,
Xia Hanning, and Gao Han

BEIJING MEDIATIME BOOKS CO., LTD.
CN Times Books, Inc.
501 Fifth Avenue
New York, NY 10017
cntimesbooks.com

Ordering Information: Quantity sales. Special discounts are available
on quantity purchases by corporations, associations, and others. For
details, contact the publisher at the address above. Orders by U.S. trade
bookstores and wholesalers. Please contact Ingram Distribution:
Tel: (866) 400-5351; Fax: (800) 838-1149;
or customer.service@ingrampublisherservices.com.

Grateful acknowledgment is made to Jiangxi People's Publishing House
for granting the exclusive global English-language rights for this work.

Editor: Jeannie Reed
Designer: Adam B. Bohannon

ISBN 978-1-62774-002-9

Printed in the United States of America

CONTENTS

INTRODUCTION xi

CHAPTER 1

The Origins of Chinese Characters 1
Chinese Writing and Chinese Language 4
Chinese Characters and Calligraphy 5
Using Consistent Character and Roadway Gauges 7
Four Treasures of the Study 8
The Dialects 10

CHAPTER 2

Names 12
Greeting Styles 13
Kinship Appellation 15
Chinese Zodiac 16

CHAPTER 3

The Traditional Calendar—The Agricultural Calendar 18
The Twenty-Four Solar Terms 19
The Spring Festival 21
Bringing in the New Year 22 • Dust Sweep 22
New Year Scrolls with the Character 福 22
Firecrackers 23 • New Year's Greetings 23
The Pure Brightness Day 23
Sweeping the Tomb 24
Tree Planting 25 • Flying Kites 25 • Swinging 25

The Dragon Boat Festival 25
Dragon Boat Racing 27 • Wearing Fragrant Pouches 27
Hanging Mugwort and Calamus Leaves 27

The Mid-Autumn Festival 27

The Double Yang Festival 29
The Festival of Ascending the Heights 30
Eating Double Yang Cakes 30
Appreciation for Chrysanthemums and Drinking Chrysanthemum Wine 30
Wearing Dogwood and Placing Chrysanthemums in the Hair 30
The Temple Fair 31

CHAPTER 4

The Emperors Yan and Huang 33
Da Yu Controls the Water 34
Pangu Creates the Universe 35
The Goddess Nuwa Makes Human Beings 37
Hou Yi Shoots the Suns 38

CHAPTER 5

The Cowherd and the Weaving Maid 40
Meng Jiangnu Weeps Down the Great Wall 42
Liang Shanbo and Zhu Yingtai 43
The Legend of the White Snake 44
The Legend of Mu-lan 46

CHAPTER 6

The Dragon 48
The Vicissitudes of the Dynasties 52
Minority Ethnic Groups 54
Family Ideology 56
Marriage Customs 59

CHAPTER 7

The Four Great Inventions 63

Papermaking 63 • Printing Technology 64 • Gunpowder 64 • Compass 65

The Abacus and Calculation 66

Post Roads and Relay Stations 68

The Sedan Chair 70

Horse and Carriage 72

CHAPTER 8

Yellow River Culture 74

The Silk Road 76

The Great Wall 77

The Terracotta Warriors 80

The Five Sacred Mountains 82

Lakes 84

CHAPTER 9

Lao Tzu 88

Chuang Tzu 91

Confucius 93

Mencius 96

Mo Tzu 99

Sun Tzu 102

Han Fei Tzu 104

CHAPTER 10

The Book of Songs 107

Poetry of the South 109

Han Fu 110

Han Yue Fu 112

The Records of the Grand Historian 113

The Book of Han 114

CHAPTER 11

The Yangtze River 117

Tea 120

Wine 122

Food 125

CHAPTER 12

Han Attire 129
Cheongsam 132

The Story of the Fan 134

Folk Arts and Crafts 136
Paper Cutting 136 • Embroidery 138

CHAPTER 13

Capital Cities 140

Palace Architecture 144

Temple Architecture 147
The Buddhist Temple 147

CHAPTER 14

Money 150

Medicine 152
Acupuncture 154 • Drugs 154 • Medical Texts 155

Chess 155

Martial Arts 157

Folk Theater 159
Musical Instruments 162

Painting 164

CHAPTER 15

The Great Books 168

Prose 170

Tang Poetry 174

Song Dynasty Poetry 176

Opera and Theater 179

The Novel 181

CHAPTER 16

Gardens 185

The Summer Palace 185 • The Mountain Resort 187
The Humble Administrator's Garden 189 • The Lingering Garden 191

Residences 192

The *Hutong* 192 • Courtyard Residences 193 • Enclosed Residences 194

Burial Rites 196

The Mausoleum of the Yellow Emperor 196 • The Tomb of Yu the Great 196
The Mausoleum of Emperor Qin Shi Huang 197
The Thirteen Ming Tombs 198

CHAPTER 17

Go 199

Primitive Religion: The Exorcising Dance 201

The Exorcism Culture 202

Beijing Opera 205

Kunqu Opera 207

Yu Opera 209

Huangmei Opera 211

Yue Opera 213

The Art of Dunhuang 213

Jingdezhen Porcelain 218

CHAPTER 18

Schooling 222

The Imperial Examination Culture 225

Collecting and Archiving Books and Documents 228

The Monastery Collections 230

Confucianism 231

Taoism 234

Metaphysics 236

Buddhism 237

Chinese Buddhism 238 • Tibetan Buddhism 240 • Theravada Buddhism 240

CHAPTER 19

A Dream of Red Mansions 241

Water Margin 243

The Romance of the Three Kingdoms 245

Journey to the West 248

CHAPTER 20

The New Culture Movement 251

Hu Shi 253

Lu Xun 255

Guo Moruo 258

Mao Dun 260

Ba Jin 263

Lao She 265

Cao Yu 267

APPENDIX: A BRIEF CHRONOLOGY OF CHINESE HISTORY 271

POSTSCRIPT 273

INDEX 275

INTRODUCTION

You can't watch a news program these days, read the business pages, or browse the travel section of most American Sunday papers without running into at least one mention of China. Usually, it's more than one. And, usually, it's more than a mention. And while we all read and we all watch and listen, most of us armchair travelers and U.S-based businesspeople have never actually been to China, haven't met many of her people, haven't experienced her culture . . . and, no, greeting the take-out guy at the front door doesn't count. So most of us really don't know much about this major trading partner, this up-and-coming engine of global growth, this home to a billion fellow global citizens.

And so—as is the case with all great nations—to understand China . . . to understand the nation best . . . we need to step into the palace of her culture and explore her rich history. Because acute insights about anything can't happen without a good, basic understanding. And so it is with Chinese civilization and history.

With this in mind, a group of scholars from China and America have put this book together as a kind of primer on all things China, from art and science to religion and society. From the Great Wall to no walls. They've tried to offer here a panoramic view of the totality of Chinese culture in all-too-brief chapters. The effort has been made to use only the most representative material, so as to introduce to the West the most typical aspects of Chinese civilization and life. For this reason, the authors hope that *From Moon Cakes to Mao to Modern China* is both accessible to its readers and spot-on informative.

And we hope as well that through this book people all over the world with an interest in China can find something to further pique that interest. The student, the traveler, the dreamer, the thinker, the businessperson— we hope all of you can find here something useful, if not also informative as well as entertaining. If reading this book is a happy experience and kindles in you an interest in Chinese civilization, if it can catalyze in you an unquenchable thirst for exploring China, our work will have been rewarded ten thousand–fold.

—EDITORIAL BOARD, *From Moon Cakes to Mao to Modern China*
January 1, 2013

FROM MOON CAKES TO MAO TO MODERN CHINA

Chapter 1

THE ORIGINS OF CHINESE CHARACTERS

Chinese, the world's oldest written language, is now in use by the largest of the world's populations. History tells us that Chinese writing emerged in the fourteenth century BCE, during the latter part of the Shang Dynasty, a period that gave rise to the preliminary form of written Chinese—Oracle Bone Script. The invention and application of Chinese writing not only stimulated the development of Chinese culture but has also had far-reaching implications for the development of world civilization. At present, many countries use written phonetic alphabets, but Chinese writing has retained the basic property of the ideogram. Therefore, since the form and structure of Chinese writing have not changed over the centuries, we are able to examine the life, society, customs and culture of the originators of the writing. This is a unique opportunity, as the written language forms of most other countries don't display such relationships.

Since ancient times, there have been numerous explanations for the birth of Chinese characters. The formation of characters by Cangjie is the best known and is referred to often in the ancient books. It is said that Cangjie was the historiographer of the Yellow Emperor. As legend has it, one day Cangjie saw a deity whose appearance was odd and whose face resembled a picture with writing on it. From this, it is said, Cangjie drew the image of that god, and so created the first Chinese characters. Ancient manuscripts also tell us that as Cangjie created the words, nature's mysteries were revealed, millet (grain) fell from the heavens and ghosts and gods cried and wailed in the night. Yet another legend says that Cangjie observed the tracks of birds and animals and found in them inspiration for his script.

While these are certainly beautiful legends, scientific evidence reveals that the true origin of Chinese characters was ancient drawings. Modern scholars agree that figures engraved on excavated artifacts are in all probability related to the origins of writing. Over six thousand years old, the Banpo archaeological site exhibits more than fifty written symbols. These are simple, trim and orderly and contain the essence of writing, and experts agree that they are most likely the very beginnings of Chinese writing. It is

Oracle Bone Script

also believed that one person could not have possibly conceived the entire system of Chinese writing. Ancient texts in general tell us that Cangjie is the architect of Chinese writing, but if in fact there was a man named Cangjie, he may have simply catalogued and promulgated the characters.

Besides the Cangjie theory for explaining the origins of Chinese writing and early pictographs, there are yet other explanations, including the theories of the knotted string and the Eight Trigrams, among others. Some scholars believe words were created by the inspiration of knotted string, a method the ancient Chinese used to record matters. Others say that the creation of written words relates to the Eight Trigrams in the *Book of Changes* (*I Ching*). Generally speaking, though, it is safe to say that the writing of Chinese is a product of history, requiring both internal and external conditions. The characters themselves and the writing syntax are all-inclusive. Furthermore, the emergence of Chinese writing tells us of the needs of people dealing with practical issues and long-term communal practices. The people began by engraving or drawing figures to record events, which eventually contributed to the foundation for the development of their language as a whole, forming the basis for a civilized society and leading to a great leap forward in human evolution.

When linguists explain the structure of Chinese words, they follow the criterion of the Six Methods, dividing the words into six categories: pictogram, ideogram, ideogrammic compound, phono-semantic, derivative cognate and phonetic loan.

The pictogram is the earliest example of character formation and resulted in the first written words. The pictogram character usually names a material object, the shape indicating what it represents.

The method of forming ideograms uses an abstract symbol in iconic form to create a word with more intent than that of the pictogram. Therefore, one is required to experience and observe carefully in order to comprehend an ideogram. There are two methods by which ideograms are formed. The first method uses a pictogram with combined symbolism as the basis for a word. For example, 本 (root) comes from the word 木 (tree); a horizontal line added at the bottom indicates where we find the roots. The roots or the trunk of the tree, referring to the foundation, or basis, symbolizes the literal meaning. The second method uses a pure symbol to indicate a symbol of something or its meaning.

The method of word formation using ideograms—the ideogrammic compound— joins two words to create a new, third word. For example, 明 (light) stems from 日 (sun) and 月 (moon), which bring us light. Another guideline to the way the ideogrammic compound works is to look at the relative position

The legend of Cangjie creating Chinese characters

of the symbols, as indicated in 旦 (dawn), signifying the sun rising on the horizon.

The phono-semantic method of word formation involves combining a character's phonetic aspect with a semantic element (radical), resulting in a significantly new word. For example, 爸 (father), contains 巴 (*bā*), the phonetic element. Statistically speaking, radical-phonetic characters account for about 90 percent of all Chinese characters today, making phono-semantics the most useful way to produce new words.

Further, while derivative cognates retain the same etymological roots, the phonetics changes among dialects. Later generations have employed the symbols and dialects for their own purposes in different ways, adapting character synonyms with different phonetics. For example, the character 豕 (shǐ: pig), later in other regions written as 猪 (*zhū*), and in yet others places as 彘 (*zhì*), involves the use of the pictogram 豕 to indicate "pig." With the addition of the phonetic symbols, *zhe* and *shi*, new words or mutually explanatory characters are formed. In this case, the meanings remain the same, but the pronunciation and character expression are slightly different.

The phonetic loan method of word formation uses homophones to create new words, which means that one spoken word can have two different meanings (rebus). This method of word formation is important in the history of Chinese writing—we see that moving from ideograph to phonogram is a key marker of development while also reflecting the transformation of the quality of the characters.

CHINESE WRITING AND CHINESE LANGUAGE

Written Chinese is the symbolic recording of spoken Chinese and the tool for creating literary works. Chinese writing and the Han Dialect are closely related and share a strong sense of space and time. The Han Dialect not only displays the similarities of ancient and modern Chinese but also interweaves many other different dialects. From the ancient Han Dialect to modern Chinese, the phonetics have changed considerably, and the vocabulary and grammar have also evolved immensely, yet the squared shape of the characters remains the same.

Chinese writing is a unity of form, sound and meaning. Words supply the vocabulary that in turn forms the syntax. Each character has three aspects: initial, final and intonation. In total, the Han Dialect contains twenty-one initials, thirty-nine finals and four tones. The Han Dialect has many homophones (some 3,755 words are in common usage, yet there are only four hundred sounds). Over many hundreds of years, the common people have created numerous insightful allegorical expressions using the same or similar sounds of different characters. This has become one of the Chinese language's great characteristics.

A unique two-part allegorical expression, *xiehouyu*, is a language usage created by a people to describe their life experience. It is commonly composed of two phrases, the first half being a vivid description and the second half containing a meaning that must be deciphered. This expression contains references to nature or daily life. In certain social environments, usually the first half is spoken, but the second is omitted intentionally so that others must infer the intended expression. *Xiehouyu* is a short, witty and vivid sentence. For example, in the expression "a stool of paper cannot work," work and sit sound similar in Mandarin. In the expression, "the Buddhist's house—wonderful," the Mandarin word for temple has the same sound as the word for wonderful. Some allegorical sayings have affiliations with Chinese traditional culture or historical figures, as in "Songjiang's military advisor—worthless"—because the counselor's name, "Wu Yong," sounds like the word "worthless," yet the characters are quite different.

Idioms and proverbs are another defining characteristic of the Chinese language. An idiom is a phrase with a fixed format, having been used throughout time and attributing to the descriptiveness of the written language. An idiom commonly consists of four words, such as 胸有成竹. This idiom literally translates to: bamboo grows from the chest, but the figurative meaning is: to have a well-thought-out plan. Unlike idioms, proverbs have no limitation on word number. They are created and popularized by the common people and are concise and comprehensive. Idioms compose a developed artistic language, and the discipline demonstrates the people's wisdom and experience. This is evidenced in the example: With rain brightens all four directions, without rain shines the tip of the heavens. English proverbs such as "Rome was not built in a day" don't follow strict rules of framework, but Chinese idioms are held to a four-word format.

CHINESE CHARACTERS AND CALLIGRAPHY

Calligraphy is the art of hand-writing Chinese characters. It is unique to China. Calligraphy involves techniques and rules of writing: how to hold the brush, brushstrokes, dotting, framing and layout (*i.e.*, distribution, order and composition). Along with the development of culture, calligraphy evolved from the use of brush pens for writing to include many more tools. For example, along the way, many different kinds of pens and colored paints came into use in addition to the traditional black ink.

Chinese calligraphy emphasizes brush technique. This art is composed of four parts: brush movement, the vigor of the stroke, the momentum of writing and the intended concept. The brush movement is the controlling of the brush. The brushstroke is the force of the writing. The momentum of the writing is the tendency and the kinetics of the line. The intended concept suggests sentiment, thereby revealing the inner spirit of the writer. Traditional calligraphy makes use of the character 永 to show the eight distinct types of strokes in regular script. The *Yongzi* Eight Ways refers to the eight different strokes of the character 永, each stroke representing a type of action. The strokes are affiliated with a movement: a bird flying, reining

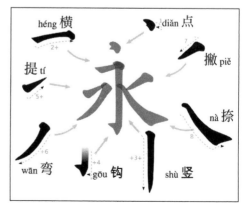

The Eight Ways of the character 永

in a horse, drawing a bow, kicking, whipping a horse, combing the hair, pecking for food and hanging meat, among other common movements.

The Oracle Bone Script is the first treasure in the history of Chinese writing. The script has variations of thickness, strength and speed. The stroke begins light and fast, there is thickness and heaviness in the movement, and the end is quick. Such is the rhythm of calligraphy. Inscriptions on bronzes and seals depict other styles of Chinese calligraphy. As compared with the Oracle Bone Script, the inscriptions on bronzes are much more robust and impressive, reaching a high standard.

The period of prosperity for calligraphy began during the Eastern Han Dynasty. During this time, specialists emerged: Cai Yi for *Li Shu* calligraphy (clerical style) and Zhang Zi for *Cao Shu* (grass style). *Li Shu* calligraphy set the standard for perfection. It was distinguished by the squared nature of the characters, the strict rules, and the tendency to write characters slanting downward and to the right. During the period of the Three Kingdoms, however, the popularity of *Li Shu* calligraphy declined, giving rise to *Kai Shu* calligraphy, which became the standard form of the art. Then, during the Jin Dynasty, a great number of master calligraphers emerged, the most important being Wang Xizhi, the Sage of Calligraphy. His preface to the *Poems Composed at the Orchid Pavilion* is praised as the greatest book of calligraphy under heaven.

The Sui Dynasty then brought together the warring states of the north and south, unifying China and enabling the latter Tang Dynasty to enjoy a comparatively peaceful and stable time. At this point, *Kai Shu* calligraphy had become fully developed in style, and so it served an important function of representing the past while ushering in the future of literary development.

Civilization in the Tang Dynasty was deep and profound, as China reached the highest peak of feudal culture. At this time, calligraphy entered a new era of splendor. *Kai Shu*, *Xing Shu* and *Cao Shu* calligraphy made vigorous strides in the new circumstances. The great masters of *Kai Shu* calligraphy include Ou Yangxun, Yu Shinan and Chu Suiliang. The *Cao Shu* masters, Zhang Xu, Huai Su, Yan Zhenqing and Liu Gongquan, were the most famous calligraphers of the period.

Song Dynasty calligraphy maintained the pace of progress, simultaneously developing a particular technique of writing, bringing forth a new attitude and giving people a new appreciation for the art. Calligraphers in this era included Su Shi, Huang Tingjian, Mi Fu and Cai Xiang.

Wang Xizhi's calligraphy

During the Yuan Dynasty, circumstances advocated a return to the ancients. The style of that time mimicked the calligraphy style of the Jin and Tang dynasties, with almost no innovation. The core figure of calligraphy in the Yuan Dynasty was Zhao Mengfu.

During the Ming Dynasty, the expert *Cao Shu* calligrapher was Liu Ji, while Song Sui was the master of *Xiao Kai* calligraphy. The preeminent calligraphers at that time were Zhu Ke, Zhu Yunming, Wen Zhengming and Wang Chong. By the late Ming Dynasty, calligraphy was romantic, free and unrestrained.

The movement took one step further during the Qing Dynasty, notably in the calligraphy of Zhu Fushan's *Eight Eccentrics of Yangzhou*, a collection of various works. The vivid and resplendent techniques in this work capture the eye and afford great insight into the culture of Chinese calligraphy.

USING CONSISTENT CHARACTER AND ROADWAY GAUGES

Before 221 BCE, there were many vassal states in China that often launched wars. Their inhabitants lived in chaos as their states fell apart. The Seven Warring States were the Han, Zhao, Wei, Chu, Yan, Qi and Qin dynasties. Of the seven, the Qin State was eventually declared the winner of all the wars, with Ying Zheng as its leader.

Ying Zheng became the first emperor of China and was given the title of First Emperor. From 230 to 221 BCE, Ying Zheng launched a massive war that destroyed the other six states. This time in Chinese history is known as the Qin Eradicate the Six States Period. Following 221 BCE, one country was established for the first time in China's history and was ruled by a uniform, multi-nation and centralized power called the Qin Dynasty (221–206 BCE). Ying Zheng believed that his contributions exceeded those of the ancient Three Sovereigns and Five Emperors, so he proclaimed himself First Emperor. He wanted the position to be hereditary, and so he declared himself as first in the succession.

After first unifying China, Ying Zheng implemented a series of laws and changes to society in order to maintain the unification of the Qin Empire, where much power was still entrenched in the feudal systems of various areas. The First Emperor therefore abolished feudalism and imposed a new national government. In order to avoid an insurgence by civilians, he ordered all weapons confiscated by the empire to be destroyed by melting or burning. To withstand invasions from minority factions, the First Emperor

The first emperor of China, Ying Zheng

implemented a great deal of manpower, materials and financial resources to build the Great Wall, not to mention the amount of time it took to build. Today, the Great Wall still rests on its original foundation; subsequent repairs were made on top of the original wall. The Great Wall is an extraordinary feat and a globally recognized symbol of China. Also, to control the thinking of the citizenry, the First Emperor implemented a policy of burning the books, so burying the Confucians. In addition, the laws were nationalized, weights and measures regulations imposed and the currency was standardized.

Among the Emperor's laws, one important regulation implemented a same-road-width policy. Before the unification, each state used a different style for writing, which made it inconvenient to communicate, but across China the width of roads also varied. So, after the unification, the First Emperor Qin ordered the states to use the same written character and track gauges. In the latter case, under the so-called same-road-width policy, a government standard was created for the width of roadways, and relay stations for post horses were constructed throughout the country along the roadways to allow for better communication between states. The roads built before unification varied in size, making it hard for vehicles to pass. As a result, the emperor decreed that same-width roads were to be built across the country and the axle length of carriages was limited to six feet. In this way, all vehicles could travel on all roads. One could say that this was China's oldest form of postal service.

In short, the policies of Qin the First Emperor, especially those mandating use of the same characters in writing and the same-road-width policy, established a firm foundation for maintaining a unified China for the next two thousand years. This unification mindset shines brightly in the spirit of every Chinese person.

FOUR TREASURES OF THE STUDY

Cultural Study, as it is called, emerged in the South and North dynasties of China (420–589). It emphasized a scholarly approach to the use of brush, ink stick, paper and ink stone, which are the four treasures of the study. Since most of the ancient literates could either write or paint—and some excelled at both—the inseparable brush, ink stick, paper and ink stone are the essential tools of the four treasures.

Four treasures of the study

The pen is the essential tool of writing. Among today's myriad pens, the writing brush is considered to be a Chinese innovation. Traditional writing brushes were not only the necessary writing tools for ancient literates but were also used to create a Chinese calligraphy that stands out as a unique form of writing. To see an ancient writing brush today, however, is a rarity, because the writing brush is delicate and difficult to maintain.

Black ink lent a feeling of simplicity and was indispensable to writing. The original writing tools allowed for the marvelous artistic concepts of Chinese painting to manifest. The world of black ink may seem tedious, but it is in fact richly nuanced. This art form is rarely used today.

Paper is one of the four great inventions of ancient China and has made an outstanding contribution to the dissemination of Chinese culture and history. Even the machine-made paper prevalent today evolved from the traditional methods, which produced the high-quality paper used in ancient paintings and calligraphy work.

The ink stone, also called an ink slab, was praised as the "hand" of the four treasures. In order to produce ink, water was poured into the ink stone, and the ink stick was ground on the ink stone. Ink stones are made of clay, mud, tile, metal, lacquer, porcelain and stone, among other things, the most common element being stone. The great demand for ink gave rise to many ink stone mines in every part of China.

The Lake brush, Anhui ink, Duan ink stone and fine Xuan paper are the finest examples of the four treasures of Cultural Study. Developed over the millennia, the four treasures represent the innovation and artistic capacity of the ancient artisans and numerous aspects of literacy development. Together, they are a gem of Chinese culture.

In addition to the four treasures, other literary tools included brush pots, brush racks, ink beds, ink cartridges, armrests, pen washers, book presses, water bearers, water spoons, ink drippers, ink stone boxes, seal pastes, seal cases, paper knives, seals and canisters. These tools, together with the four treasures, were the essentials of literary study.

THE DIALECTS

China is a multiracial, multilingual country with numerous dialects. Generally speaking, modern Chinese has seven major dialects.

The North Dialect is spoken in the Central Plains and vast parts of the northeast, northwest and southwest areas of China. This dialect gave rise to four secondary dialects that are spoken in Northeast China: the North River Dialect (Southwest Mandarin) and the Jianhuai Dialect (South River Mandarin).

The Wu Dialect, also known as the Jiangzhe Dialect, is spoken in the area south of the Yangtze River, which is made up of Jiangsu Province and the majority of Zhejiang Province. Shanghainese is the primary subdialect of the Wu Dialect.

The Xiang Dialect, also called Hunan Dialect, is spoken in the greater part of Hunan Province. The Hunan and Changsha dialects are the main subdialects here.

The Gan Dialect, also called Jiangxi Dialect, is spoken throughout Jiangxi Province, in the northwest Fujiang Province, in the eastern part of Hunan Province and in the southeast part of Hubei Province. The Nangchang subdialect is the most widely spoken Jiangxi Dialect.

The Hakka Dialect, also known as Kejia Hua or Ke Hua, is widely scattered but rather concentrated in the areas in which it is used. Hakka is found in the northeast region of Guangdong and the northwestern part of Fujian, Jiangxi, Hubei, Guangdong and Fujian, as well as in Sichuan, Guangxi and Taiwan. Most Chinese who live in Southeast Asia speak the Hakka Dialect. The primary subdialect is the Meizhou Dialect.

The Min Dialect (northern and southern Min dialects) is spoken widely, including in most of Fujian Province, the eastern part of Guandong, the Chaoshan area, the western part of Leizhou Peninsula, Hainan Province, the greater part of Taiwan Province and the southern part of Zhejiang. It is also widely dispersed throughout Southeast Asia by way of the Chinese communities in the regions there.

The Yue Dialect, also called Yueyu, Cantonese, Guang Fu and Bai Dialect, is spoken largely in Guangdong Province and the southeast part of the Guanxi autonomous region, as well as in parts of Hong Kong, Macao and North America. The Guangzhou dialect is the primary subdialect.

These seven dialects are a rough division of modern Mandarin dialects (not including the minority dialects). In reality, though, the situation is much more complex than this. Not only do northerners not understand the Cantonese and Fujian people's language, even people in Guangzhou within Guandong Province, the Meizhou people and the Shantou people, don't understand each other. The people of the Fuzhou district in Fujian Province, the Putian people and Amoy people, all do not understand each other's language.

The difference among the dialects nowadays is mainly in the sound, yet the diversity of the vocabulary is immense. Although the Jing, Jun and Tong districts are all neighbors, Beijing people say sweet potato (bai shu), while the people of Tongshan say red potato (hong shu) to mean the same thing. If you ask a young lady from Tiangjing, "Do you like to eat bai shu?," she will be confused and think, "How can people eat a white mouse? Quite disgusting!"(In the Tiangjin dialect, *bai shu*, 拼音，请填补 means white mouse.) So you see, there are great differences among the Chinese dialects, giving rise to even greater confusion.

Chapter 2

NAMES

As recorded in *Explaining Simple and Analyzing Compound Characters* (a second-century Han dictionary), the word, "surname" literally means "people give birth" but also means "from woman comes birth." Birth creates sound. It can be said that the word "surname" is a compound ideogram. The "woman" radical is part of the character, in addition to "birth," and designating a sound. Therefore, "surname" is a product of a maternal clan society, the character symbolizing a family's bloodline. Chinese surnames helped usher in the maternal clan society.

Chinese surnames originated in many different ways. First, in the maternal clan society, descendants took a mother's maiden name; therefore, many ancient surnames contain the radical for woman (女), such as: 姜, 姚, 姬. Second, in the age of antiquity, people's fondness for nature influenced naming. Common names included horse, ox and dragon. Third, surnames were created according to the nation of ancestry, for example Zhao, Song and Qin, among others. Fourth, some people were named after officials, as with Shangguan, Sima and Situ. Fifth, people took on their ancestors' titles of nobility, including the rank of king, marquis and official. Sixth, some were issued a name relative to where they were born and the scenery there. Examples are Dongguo (East Wall), Ximen (West Gate) and Liu (Willow Tree). Seventh, some inherited surnames by occupation. For example, people who made ceramics were appropriately named Ceramic (Tao). Eighth, others acquired surnames of famous ancients. For example, the Yellow Emperor's name was Xuanyuan, which later became a surname.

One or two characters, sometimes three, generally form a Chinese surname. A one-character name is called a single surname, while a two-character name is called a compound surname. Although there is no exact figure for how many surnames there are in China, more than five thousand surnames appear in Chinese historical documents. Today, there are about two hundred commonly used surnames. Zhang, Wang, Li, Zhao and Liu are the most common single surnames. Zhuge, Ouyang and Situ are examples of common compound surnames. Influenced by the Confucian teaching that we should respect our ancestors, Chinese people pay close attention to surnames. Changing the surname means changing your ancestor, and this is hugely humiliating. In modern Chinese novels, particularly in heroic war novels, a man will vindicate his own pride. In a daring act, the character will often say, "A great man will never change his surname. I am indeed so-and-so!"

Also, Chinese names have their own traditions and characteristics. Quite different from English names, Chinese surnames are placed before the given name, which is opposite to the way English names are expressed. 姓 is similar to an English speaker's family name passed down from generation to generation. 名 is the equivalent of an English first name, comprising one or two characters. A Chinese name often has a specific meaning, expressing a certain aspiration. Some names include the place and time of birth, and some contain reference to such natural phenomena as, Morning and Snow. Some Chinese names reveal hope or some kind of virtue, such as Loyalty, Righteousness and Belief. Still other names reveal a yearning for health, long life and happiness, for example Jian (health), Shou (long life) and Fu (fortune). Also, male and female names are different. Male names express prestige and fierceness, as in Hu (tiger), Xiong (hero) and Gang (strength). Female names are expressed by warm and beautiful characters, like Feng (phoenix), Yu (Jade) and Juan (graceful)

A Chinese name can also represent a person's place in the hierarchy of the family. For example, a name can include a character that represents seniority, while another character expresses the family name. In some names, a radical indicates family seniority in the clan. This is quite different from the English method of naming. Chinese also avoid as much as possible giving the name of an elder family member to a junior member, a taboo since ancient times.

GREETING STYLES

Greeting each other is the most common experience of everyday interaction. When we meet each other, we begin as a rule by paying our respects; but there are great differences in greetings between nationalities. Chinese greetings have their own classification, content, ways of showing appellation, basic courtesy, concrete meaning and unique characteristics.

First, Chinese greeting styles for expressing one's regards, for inquiring or for discussing are much like those in English. Nevertheless, Chinese ways of greeting are different from those of the West. For example, in English there is: good morning, good afternoon and good evening. But spoken Chinese does not contain such reciprocal greetings. Instead, often used is: *zao* or *ni zao*, meaning, "You got up quite early." Many greetings follow this simple format. These days, Chinese people more and more use "*Ni hao!*" to greet each other, particularly intellectuals and the cultured. There are also formal greetings showing honor and great respect. And in Mandarin there are phrases like "Where are you going?" and "Did you eat?" among other greetings of inquiry, revealing concern for the other person's well-being.

Second, in addition to cultural discrepancies and restrictions in language behavior regarding societal norms, the subjects of conversation are also different. English greetings use simple phrases, contain no specific information and show great respect, but they lack feeling and expression. In Chinese, many greetings are in the form of a question, and most questions inquire about the other person's daily struggles, giving people the feeling of amiable concern. Chinese often ask each other questions regarding age, income, marital status, health and popular topics of conversation, in addition to more specific items, in order to show consideration for the other.

The language of respectful greeting is a cultural characteristic, but each nationality has its own societal norms, standards of behavior and guidelines for social interaction. The differences in cultural backgrounds may bring about different standards, which are reflected in the nature of the questions. When Chinese people greet, they often use respectful speech and modest words, expressing respect and honor to their counterpart. This is a distinct characteristic of the use of Chinese language.

In addition to verbal greeting styles, Chinese also use a body language that has its own distinctive characteristics. The body languages of Chinese- and English-speaking countries show some commonality. Chinese, especially youthful men, will often nod among one another, or perhaps wave as a form of greeting. In former times, when Chinese people met they might bow or perhaps bow with the hands outstretched in greeting. Chinese greeting styles are generally rather implicit and reserved, even if people have been apart a long time. There is also a pat on the shoulder for comfort, or perhaps a handshake, but absolutely no kissing. And, generally, we rarely see men and women hugging each other. At most, they shake hands, but nothing more. In the West, on the other hand, physical contact is not uncommon in greeting in general nor between genders in greeting.

KINSHIP APPELLATION

Chinese people reside in their nationality, reflecting a language of complicated kinship appellation. The bloodline is taken very seriously. According to statistics, there are more than 230 words in Chinese pertaining to family appellation. In modern Chinese, there are just over sixty names dating back three generations. Following the collapse of feudalism, many titles reflecting hierarchy also vanished. In modern Chinese, the titles of appellation have been greatly simplified, but we still can see an obvious correlation to the ancestors' language of hierarchy.

The language of kinship status shows much respect for elders and reflects the ideas of honor, humility and order. The paternal grandfather is called *ye ye*, and the paternal grandmother is called *nai nai*. For each generation, the word "old" (*lao*) is added before the title to distinguish a generational difference. So, great-grandfather is called old grandfather (*lao ye ye*), and great-great grandfather is old-old grandfather (*lao lao ye ye*). For the younger generation there is "grandson" and "granddaughter;" adding "double" before the title expresses each generation, as in double granddaughter and double-double granddaughter. With respect to peers, a difference in age is emphasized. In one's own family, there are the titles "older brother," "younger brother," "older sister" and "younger sister," so as not to confuse status and rank. Titles like father's older brother, father's younger brother, sister-in-law and brother-in-law indicate one's rank in the hierarchy. There is a completely different system in English-speaking countries, the titles of siblings and other relatives being the same regardless of age difference.

Many more forms of address refer to distant relatives and distinguish clan bloodlines. These appellations have particular characteristics. One's title of rank corresponds to the mother's or father's side of the family, showing distinctiveness. For example, the parents of the father are called *zu fu* and *zu mu* (paternal grandfather and paternal grandmother), while the parents of the mother are called *wai zu fu* and *wai zu mu* (maternal grandfather and maternal grandmother). The brothers of the father are respectfully called *bo bo* and *shu shu* (father's older brother and father's younger brother). Uncles on the mother's side of the family are all called *jiu jiu* (maternal uncle); the order is denoted by adding a character to the beginning of the title, as in, big uncle (*da jiu*), second uncle (*er jiu*) and small uncle (*xiao jiu*), meaning brother-in-law, literally. In modern society the importance of ancestral relations is weaker, yet the extremely complex honorific language of the past has not completely dissolved. In villages in vast areas of China, the diverse titles of nobility are still in use.

CHINESE ZODIAC

The ancient Chinese correlated the time in which certain animals are active with the time in their own daily lives. Thus, twelve animals make up the twelve signs of the zodiac. In ranked sequence they are rat, ox, tiger, rabbit, dragon, snake, horse, ram, monkey, rooster, dog and pig.

Rat: 11 p.m. to 1 a.m. (called *zishi*). At this time, the nerves of the rat are strongest and it is most active.

Ox: 1 a.m. to 3 a.m. (called *choushi*). At this time, the ox has finished eating grass and is ruminating on the vegetation; it is slow and cozy.

Tiger: 3 a.m. to 5 a.m. (called *yinshi*). Ancient records reveal that, at this time, tigers are the most active and fierce, killing many people.

Rabbit: 5 a.m. to 7 a.m. (called *maoshi*). At this time, the sun is not yet exposed, the moon's radiance not yet vanished. In mythology, the Jade Hare is the only animal allowed in the Moon Palace.

Dragon: 7 a.m. to 9 a.m. (called *chenshi*). As legend has it, dragons congregate and make the rain at this time. In folklore, dragons are the major animals, therefore this time belongs to the dragon.

Snake: 9 a.m. to 11 a.m. (called *sishi*). It is believed that at this time snakes cannot harm people and are not crossing the walking paths. Rather, they are believed to stay hidden in the underbrush.

Horse: 11 a.m. to 1 p.m. (called *wushi*). According to Taoist teachings, when the midday sun is at the apex, the *yang* energy reaches the extreme, as the *yin* energy gradually increases, representing the point of *yin* and *yang* exchange. Generally at this time, all animals lie down to rest. Only the horse has the habit of remaining standing and never lying down to rest even when sleeping.

Ram: 1 p.m. to 3 p.m. (called *weishi*). It is said that at this time the ram urinates frequently and in this way cures itself of mental illness.

Monkey: 3 p.m. to 5 p.m. (called *shenshi*). At this time, the monkey likes to cry out in a most drawn out and resonating sound.

Rooster: 5 p.m. to 7 p.m. (called *youshi*). At this time, the sun sets in the mountains and the rooster returns to his roost for the evening.

Dog: 7 p.m. to 9 p.m. (called *xushi*). Dark night approaches and the dog guards the house. The dog watches with great vigilance, with the sharpest vision and hearing. At this time the dog can see things at great distances and hear very clearly.

Pig: 9 p.m. to 11 p.m. (called *haishi*). At this time the pig is intoxicated with sleep. Its snoring resounds, the muscles of its body twitch fiercely, producing meat the fastest.

Chinese zodiac

Not only do these twelve animals represent time periods throughout the day, but they also came eventually to represent a person's age.

There are many beautiful legends about the zodiac animals. According to one legend, in antiquity a person's memory was not great. For example, people often forgot their names, producing much confusion. The Jade Emperor's heart could not bear this, so he thought of a simple way to use the zodiac to determine one's age. One must only remember the twelve-year cycle as a definite way of calculating a person's age. So he issued a proclamation to all animals to come to his Heavenly Courtyard so that he could select the animals of the zodiac in order of their arrival. The dragon, tiger, rabbit and horse, animals of extraordinary ability and talent, often stopped as they traveled, although they were not late in departing. Slow but sure was the ox, plodding along at its own pace, day and night, not daring to stop for rest. Meanwhile the quietly cunning rat jumped on the ox's horn and slept. The ox would have been the first to arrive in the Heavenly Court had not the rat, seeing an opportunity, jumped from the ox's horn, so becoming the first in rank of the zodiac animals. Thus the ox became second in the hierarchy. Because of the pig's extremely slow walk, it was naturally last to arrive.

Chapter 3

THE TRADITIONAL CALENDAR—
THE AGRICULTURAL CALENDAR

The agricultural calendar is China's traditional calendar. It is divided into twenty-four solar terms and serves as a guide to agricultural activities. This calendar, used in vast areas of China, is known as the farming calendar. It is also referred to as the summer calendar, old calendar and Chinese calendar, but it is most commonly referred to as the lunar calendar. The calendar uses strict guidelines, following the waxing and waning of the moon. It also employs an intercalary month, to average the lengths of the solar years. The lunar and solar calendars make note of the relationship between *yin* and *yang*. Today, many Chinese all over the world, as well as North Koreans, South Koreans and Vietnamese, still use the agricultural calendar to calculate such traditional festivals as the Spring Festival, the Mid-Autumn Festival, the Dragon Boat Festival and the Pure Brightness (tomb-sweeping) Festival.

The agricultural calendar month and lunar calendar month have characteristics in common. The agricultural calendar month is 29.5366 days (29 days, 12 hours, 44 minutes and 3 seconds), while the lunar calendar has full months of thirty days and shortened months of twenty-nine days. There are, however, differences between the calendars. In the lunar calendar the full months and shortened months are arranged in specific order, while the agricultural calendar requires rigorous calculations. As a result, in the agricultural calendar there may be two consecutive full months as well as two consecutive shortened months. The first day of every agricultural month begins on the new moon (*i.e.*, the moon is between the sun and the earth, the dark side of the moon facing the earth). Since the lunar cycle is somewhat greater than twenty-nine days, for every one hundred months there are approximately fifty-three full months and forty-seven shortened months.

The lengths of the agricultural and solar calendars are similar. A twelve-month solar year has more days than a lunar year but lacks the thirteenth intercalary month. Ancient astronomers compiled the agricultural calendar such that specific days of the month mark the various phases of the moon. For example, on first day of the month the moon is dark, and then in about fifteen days the moon becomes full, completing its cycle. At the same time, the agricultural calendar, noting the seasons, adopted a metonic system of nineteen years and seven leap months. For every nineteen agricultural calendar years, there are twelve common years, each of which has twelve months, as well as seven leap years, each containing thirteen months. The months of the agricultural calendar comprise the same number of days as regular months (twenty-nine or thirty), but a leap month is added depending on the circumstances of the solar term.

The agricultural calendar is a substantial ancient Chinese contribution. Its main features are that any given day of the month embodies significant phases of the moon, and that it is made up of agricultural dates, including calculations of the tides (the tide being an effect of the moon's gravitational pull). This calendar, called *shixianli* (the state calendar), was instituted in 1645 and was officially used by the late Ming and early Qing dynasties.

THE TWENTY-FOUR SOLAR TERMS

The twenty-four solar terms were the special creation of the Chinese. This period reflects the changes of seasons, guides farming activity and affects the daily lives of thousands. The twenty-four solar terms are measured off by the position of the sun on the ecliptic (the orbit of the earth around the sun). The sun starts from the vernal equinox point (at this point, the sun's rays are perpendicular with the Equator) and advances 15 degrees during one solar term, circulating one cycle and returning back to the vernal equinox point. This is called one tropical year, adding up to 360 degrees, exactly twenty-four solar terms.

The twenty-four solar term calendar and the Gregorian calendar dates are of approximately the same year length. The first half of the year occurs around the 6th and 21st of every month (summer solstice), and the second half on about the 8th and 23rd. In the agricultural calendar, on the other hand, solar term dates are difficult to ascertain. The beginning of spring, for example, could begin one year as early as December 15, and the latest date could be January 15.

From the name "twenty-four solar terms," one can speculate that the divisions in the solar

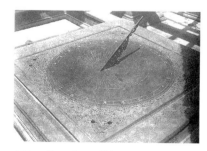

A Yuan Dynasty sundial

terms give sufficient consideration to the seasons, climate, seasonal vegetation and other natural phenomena changes. The beginnings of spring,
summer, autumn and winter, as well as the vernal and autumnal equinoxes
and the summer and winter solstices, reflects the seasons' change. These are
determined by divisions on the ecliptic, astronomical angles, the reflecting and turning point of the sun's altitude variation, thus differentiating
the four seasons. With astronomical angles, the first four are the starts
of seasons, and the later four are the turning points of the sun's altitude
variation.

Because China is a vast region with extremely distinct monsoon characteristics and various continental factors, the result is great differences
in the climate. As a result, the various regions' four seasons are different.
Minor heat, great heat, limit of heat, minor cold and major cold are five
solar terms reflecting degrees of temperature. Rain, grain rain, minor
snow and major snow are four solar terms indicating rain and snow precipitation, time periods and severity. Cold dew, white dew and descending
frost are the three solar terms regarding water vapor condensation and
appearance and essentially reflecting the process stemming from gradual
temperature decline: when the air temperature drops to a certain degree,
water vapor emerges and dew forms. As the temperature continues to
decline, the condensation increases as it gets colder. When the temperature
drops below freezing, water vapor turns to frost. Full grain and grain in
the husk are two solar terms indicating the maturing of domestic crops
and harvest time. The terms, awakening of insects and clear and bright,
reflect the occurrence of natural phenomena. In particular, the awakening of insects indicates the first thunderstorm from the heavens stirring
the underground insects from hibernation and indicating the return of
spring.

To help people to remember all this, a simple poem is often recited:

Spring rain brightens the valleys and the heavens,
The summer's grain in the husk reflects the heat,
Autumn's dew and cold, as frost descends,
Winter snow brings the major cold,
Every month, two terms are constantly changing,
At most differing one or two days.
The first half of the year arrives on the sixth and the twenty-first day
    each month,
The last half occurs on the eighth and the twenty-third day.

THE SPRING FESTIVAL

The Spring Festival is the first day of the agricultural calendar, also called Lunar New Year, and commonly referred to as the Chinese New Year. It is among China's most ceremonious and busy holidays, equivalent to the Western tradition of Christmas. Traditionally, the significance of the Spring Festival points to the beginning of the eighth day of the twelfth lunar month (*layue*), marking the *Laji* (ceremonial sacrifices). It is also held on the twenty-third day of the twelfth lunar month *Gizhao* (worship of the kitchen god) and continues until the fifteenth day of the first month, with New Year's Eve and New Year's Day being the climaxes. The last day of Layue is called New Year's Eve, the Eve of the Lunar New Year, and Year 30 (refers to the 30th of December in the lunar calendar). New Year's Eve serves as a watershed for two years. A common saying is, "One night connects two years, as the double hour separates two years."

Regarding the origin of the idea of the year, Chinese tradition has produced this interesting story:

In remote antiquity, there was a fierce and hideous beast called Year. When winter arrived, food in the mountains became scarce, prompting the beast to run down from the mountains, invade villages and injure people and domestic animals. Therefore, when winter arrived everybody was fearful, for the villages were not safe. And so many people moved to remote locations to avoid harm. As time passed, people discovered that, although Year was ferocious, it was afraid of three things: bright red, fire and loud noises, whereupon the people devised a clever countertactic. As winter arrived, indicating the time when the beast emerged from the mountains to enter the village, the villagers mutually agreed to protect themselves in various ways. The door to every house was to bear a large board painted red. At the village gate, many fires would burn. Nobody was to sleep at night, and in the house they were to beat gongs and play drums. Firecrackers were to be set off, and loud noises were to be made. Deep in the night, then, Year approached the village only to see bright fire and red everywhere and hear extremely loud noises. This frightened the beast and caused it to run back to the mountains. Since then, it has never dared to return. The next day at sunrise the whole village gathered, congratulating each other and wishing happiness. Afterwards, every year on this day, on each household door a red board was hung, fires were burned, gongs and drums were played throughout the night and firecrackers were set off. The next day, everybody wished each other happiness, celebrating his and her safety. Having come down from generations, these customs are reflected in the modern celebration of the Chinese New Year.

Bringing in the New Year

On New Year's Eve, everybody reunites with family to have a traditional dinner. This meal is eaten slowly by candlelight, beginning at *shen* (one of the twelve-hour periods) and lasting deep into the night, with family members coming and going at leisure. When the meal is finished, everybody sits in a circle under a lantern beside a stove, sharing stories of the passing old year and discussing the new one to come. The New Year's Eve overnight vigil signifies the driving away of evil, plague, sickness and epidemic and also expresses good fortune for the New Year. Ancient New Year's Eve celebrations signify two things: the elders bring in the New Year with the memory of years passed, cherishing the thoughts and the time remaining in their lives, while the younger generation brings in the new year so as to prolong the parents' bloodlines.

Dust Sweep

According to an ancient Chinese idiom, "On the twenty-fourth day of the twelfth lunar month (*layue*), brush off the dust and sweep the house." In Mandarin, the words "dust" and "old" are homophones, meaning the Spring Festival's Dust Sweep attempts to get rid of the old and bring in the new by sweeping everything old and unlucky out the door. Therefore, as the Spring Festival approaches, every family thoroughly cleans the house, washes all the utensils, washes the bedding and curtains, and sweeps to the six gates of the courtyard. Further, they brush away the dust, dirt and spider webs and dredge the irrigation ditches.

New Year Scrolls with the Character 福

New Year Scrolls, also called Spring Festival Couplets, Double Characters and Peach Symbols, are pasted on doorways in the spring. These are fine works of art that are concise, convey dualism and contain elaborate characters depicting this time of expressing happy wishes and desires. This ritual has given rise to a distinct form of Chinese literature. For every Spring Festival, whether in a city or in a rural area, every household attaches a big red scroll to the door to heighten the festive atmosphere. Some family members also place on the gates, walls and lintels the character *fu* (福) in various sizes. *Fu* refers to good fortune, good fate, protection and looking forward to a happy future and wishes granted. Embodying this spirit even more, some people tear down the scrolls to tell the world they have already achieved happiness and good fortune.

Firecrackers

Chinese people have a saying, "Open the door and light a firecracker." This indicates that as the first day of the New Year arrives, the first thing every household commonly does is open its door and light a firecracker, hoping the explosions will drive away the old and welcome the new. Firecrackers are a specialty of China. Also called *bao zhang, pao zhang* and *bian pao,* fireworks are found in over two thousand years of Chinese history. Over time, the uses of fireworks have become ever more extensive, and they have increased in variety and color. On every major holiday and at festive celebrations like weddings, building houses and opening businesses, one may see fireworks being used to express congratulations and wish good fortune.

New Year's Greetings

On New Year's Day, everybody gets up early, puts on new clothes and new hats and decorates him- or herself beautifully. Everybody then goes out and visits friends and relatives to wish them happiness and good fortune in the year to come. When expressing New Year wishes, the younger generation must first pay its respects to the older generation by bidding them longevity and good health. And the elders may prepare New Year gifts beforehand, wrapping money in red paper to give to the children. It is said that this money can subdue evil spirits. The meaning is derived from the idea that the words year, "sui," and evil spirit, "sui," are homophones. Receiving the money means the younger generation can pass safely through another year.

THE PURE BRIGHTNESS DAY

Pure Brightness Day was born twenty-five hundred years ago in China. It began, it is believed, during the Zhou Dynasty, when the emperors, generals and ministers offered sacrifices at tombs and left gifts. Later, this ritual was eagerly imitated by the commoners. On Pure Brightness Day, offerings are made to ancestors and the tombs are swept in much the same way as was done by previous generations, this having become a fixed and regular custom of the Chinese nation.

According to the Gregorian calendar, Pure Brightness Day (also called

Walking amid Greenery Day) takes place every year from April 4 to April 6. At this time, radiant spring sun and lush grasslands and forests constitute an opportune time to take a tour of spring (in ancient times called Stroll on the Grass). As a result, the ancients correlated Pure Brightness and Walking amid Greenery Day with traditional sporting activities.

Another famous yet still long lost ancient tradition like Pure Brightness Day is Cold Food Day. Cold Food Day, as the name implies, means that one refrains from using fire to cook meals, and eats only cold food. The original date for this observance is only one or two days from the Pure Brightness Day, so eventually the two days were merged. And as Cold Food Day in the present is referred to as Pure Brightness Day, the custom of eating unheated food is associated with both.

Local traditions of Pure Brightness Day are extremely abundant, including tomb sweeping, the planting of willows and other trees and hiking in the wilderness. There are various other social customs as well, like flying kites, swinging, playing *cuju* (ancient Chinese soccer), playing polo and other sporting activities. Therefore, this day encompasses offerings of sacrifice, sorrow and tears for departed relatives while sweeping the tombs, as well as an amusing tone that demonstrates an appreciation for nature, which makes the day an important festival.

Sweeping the Tomb

Commonly referred to as *shang fen*, this is a way to offer sacrifice to deceased ancestors. Many people of the Han ethnic group, as well as a few

minority groups, sweep their family's tombs for the Pure Brightness Festival. According to old custom, on this day, before noon, people bring the three lives (chicken, fish and meat), wine, tea, rice and paper scrolls to the foot of their ancestors' graves. In advance, they arrange the paper above the graves, using green and red paper cut into tassels. The tassels placed above the graves flutter in the wind, and so letting it be known that the tombs' occupants gave rise to later generations. At this time, prepared food, steamed wine and tea are placed before the tombs of close relatives. The relatives also burn ritual money and light firecrackers, ultimately kneeling with their heads to the ground (*kowtow*) in respect. In some places, on Pure

Sweeping the tomb

Brightness Day the family repairs the tombs or symbolically adds earth at the heads of the graves.

Tree Planting
Around the time of Pure Brightness Day, the spring's *yang* energy is quite prevalent, rain showers the earth, newly planted trees sprout tall and quickly grow and mature. Therefore, from ancient times China has practiced the custom of planting trees at this time. In 1979, the National People's Congress Standing Committee designated March 12 as China's Arbor Day. This encourages every citizen of the country to take an active role in the reforestation of the motherland and has become an extremely significant annual activity.

Flying Kites
During the Pure Brightness Festival, people fly kites during the day and also at night. For night flying, attached to the bottom of the kite or placed along the string are small multicolored lanterns that glitter like stars, and so they are called "divine lanterns." In ancient times, people would let their kites go soaring into the sky by cutting the strings, so their kites could fly to the ends of the earth. It was said that this removed sickness and calamity while bringing the kite flyer good luck.

Swinging
Swinging refers to moving through the air by holding on to a piece of leather rope. In ancient times, people tied the rope to a tree branch, then to a wooden peg and colored ribbon, thus making a swing. (These ancient swings differ from modern swings, which are made of two ropes attached to a seat.) It was felt that swinging not only promotes health but can also foster bravery and consciousness. These days, many are quite fond of swinging, especially young children.

THE DRAGON BOAT FESTIVAL

In the Chinese traditional calendar, May 5 is the day of the the Dragon Boat Festival. Also called *Duan Wu*, or *Duan Yang*, it began during the Spring and Autumn or Warring States Period and has a history of over two thousand years. There are many legends of its origins: to remember Wu Zixu, to commemorate the filial daughter, Cao Er, and to mark the practice of the Yue people of offering sacrifice to their ancient totems, for example. Among this folklore, the greatest impression is that made by the commemoration of Qu Yuan.

Qu Yuan was a chancellor to Emperor Huai of Chu during the Spring and Autumn Period. He pressed the people to make the military stronger and the country wealthier and advocated strongly to ally with the state of Qi in opposition to the state of Qin. Lord Zi Lan and others strongly opposed him, banishing him from the capital city and sending him into exile along the Yuan River in the Xiang Valley. While in exile, Qu Yuan wrote "Sorrow for Departure," "Asking Heaven" and "Nine Songs" to express his concern for his country and his people. These immortal poems have been of great influence (the Dragon Boat Festival is also called Poets Day). In 278 BCE, the Qin army breached the capital of the state of Chu. Seeing his motherland being invaded was like a knife in Qu Yuan's heart, and he produced the literary work "Embracing the Sand." Afterward, he committed suicide by throwing himself into the Miluo River, ending his life as a magnificent writer of patriotic poetry.

Legend has it that after the death of Qu Yuan the commoners of the state of Chu felt deep sorrow. One by one they went to the banks of the Miluo River to pay homage to the great Qu Yuan. Fishermen rowed their boats to the river surrounded the body of Qu Yuan to protect it. Some fishermen dropped rice balls, eggs and other food into the water for the fish, lobster and crabs to eat in so that they would not bite their beloved Minister Qu's body. As more and more people saw this, they imitated. An old doctor poured a bottle of yellow wine into the river so as to intoxicate the dragon fish, in an effort to preserve the remains of Minister Qu. Then, fearing that the dragon fish would eat all the food in the river, people wrapped rice in azalea leaves and tied them with a silk thread to feed the serpent. Later this developed into the modern *zongzi*. And now, each year on May 5, dragon boat rowing competitions, eating *zongzi* and drinking yellow wine are social customs in commemoration of Qu Yuan.

Zongzi

Dragon Boat Racing

China's observance of the Dragon Boat Festival is a grand celebration with all sorts of activities. One common custom is the dragon boat race. To pulsing rhythm drums, rowed boats in the shape of dragons, race for the amusement of the gods and the people. This festival is half-religion and half-entertainment, and it has broken the barriers of time and borders, having become an international sporting competition.

Dragon Boat race

Wearing Fragrant Pouches

It is said that children wear fragrant pouches on Dragon Boat Festival Day to avoid evil spirits and pestilence. The fragrant pouch is filled with cinnabar, realgar (arsenic sulfide) and fragrant herbs, bound together by a five-colored silk ribbon and button. The ornate pouches come in many shapes and sizes and may be strung together.

Hanging Mugwort and Calamus Leaves

A Chinese proverb says, "On Pure Brightness Day use a willow branch; on Dragon Boat Festival Day use a mugwort branch." For the Dragon Boat Festival, every family sweeps its rooms and courtyard and hangs calamus and wormwood leaves, traditional Chinese medicinal plants, on the gate lintel or in the main hall, in recognition of ancient customs.

THE MID-AUTUMN FESTIVAL

The Mid-Autumn Festival is the second-most important festival in China (following the Spring Festival in importance). This festival takes place on the fifteenth day of the eighth month on the Chinese traditional calendar, marking the middle of autumn, and hence the name. The traditional calendar contains four seasons, each season divided into three parts: *meng, zhong* and *ji*. Therefore, mid-autumn is also called Zhong Qiu Day. On the 15th day of the eighth month, the moon is much fuller and brighter than at other times of the year. In addition to the social custom of showing appreciation for the moon, people also eat moon cakes, baked in a shape resembling the moon. Therefore, this festival is also called the Moon Evening. On this night, people reunite with family and look into the sky to the moon for guidance. By means of the moon, people traveling in a distant place can send their thoughts and feelings to their relatives, and so the Mid-Autumn Festival is also called the Festival of Reunion.

The legends regarding the Mid-Autumn Festival are rich and abundant, like the myths of Chang'e flying to the moon, Wu Gan cutting down the laurel tree and the Jade Rabbit pounding the medicine. The Mid-Autumn Festival custom of paying homage to the moon comes from the story "Chang'e Flies to the Moon." According to ancient folklore, in the heavens ten suns appeared simultaneously, drying up and killing the crops and devastating the people. A hero named Hou Yi drew his divine bow and shot down nine of the suns, leaving only one sun to rise and fall for the benefit of the people.

Therefore, Hou Yi earned the respect and the admiration of the people, and many warriors yearned to learn his skills. But his disciple, Peng Meng, harbored evil intentions. One day, Hou Yi went to Mount Kunlun to seek a friend's guidance, coincidentally meeting the Queen Mother of the West and so asking her for a packet of immortal medicine. It is said that once this medicine is taken, one instantly ascends to heaven and becomes an immortal. Hou Yi accepted the medicine, but he did not wish to leave his beautiful wife Chang'e. Upon returning home, Hou Yi gave his wife the elixir and told her to hide it in a jewelry box on her dressing table, unaware of the watchful eye of the deceitful Peng Meng.

Three days later, Hou Yi led disciples on a hunt, but Peng Meng pretended to be ill and stayed behind. Soon after Hou Yi left, Peng Meng drew his sword and threatened Chang'e, to force her to hand over the immortal elixir. As she knew she was no match for Peng Meng. she turned desperately away, opened the box and swallowed the medicine. Immediately, her body began to levitate and, immortal now, she flew out the window to the heavens. In concern for her husband, she flew to the moon, the closest thing to earth.

As night descended, Hou Yi returned. On learning what had happened, he angrily drew his sword with the intention of murdering Peng Meng, but the traitor had already fled. Hou Yi beat his chest in sorrow and despair, looking to the night sky and calling out the name of his beloved wife. He noticed suddenly that the moon on this particular night was shining especially bright and had a silhouette resembling that of Chang'e. And so, totally determined, he pursued the moon, but to no avail.

Hou Yi desperately missed his wife. But at his wits' end and lacking an option, he ordered her favorite fresh fruit, pomelo, to be placed on the incense table at the rear of the garden as an offering. When the common people learned of this, they also decorated their altars under the moon, praying for the safety of the kindhearted Chang'e.

As well as paying homage to the moon during the Mid-Autumn Festival, a widespread custom is to eat moon cakes. As the proverb goes, "On the fifteenth day of the eighth month, as the moon is full, mid-autumn moon cakes are savory and sweet." Initially, moon cakes were used as an offering to the moon goddess. But people combined this practice with eating the cakes to reunite with family. At first, the cakes were made at home. Today, they are commonly produced by specialized bakeries. Not only is the filling

Moon cakes

delicious, but the moon cake is quite pleasing to the eye, boasting characters and intricate design sayings such as "Chang'e Flies to the Moon," "The Silver River's (Milky Way) Night Moon" and "Three Pools Reflecting the Moon."

THE DOUBLE YANG FESTIVAL

The traditional calendar's ninth day of the ninth month signifies a festival of Chinese antiquity—the Double Yang Festival. On account of the *Book of Changes*, six is said to be a *yin* number and nine a *yang* number. As a result, on this ninth day, the sun and the moon both embody the number nine, and so we have the Double Yang Festival, also known as the Double Ninth Festival.

The origins of the Double Yang Festival can be traced to before the Qin Dynasty. At that time, the ninth month was a time to harvest bumper crops and make offerings to the Celestial Emperor in connection with activities honoring ancestors. When the Han Dynasty arrived, owing to the influence of an ancient Taoist priest who beseeched medicine for immortality, people on this day began the customs of wearing dogwood (a kind of herb), eating herbal cakes and drinking chrysanthemum wine, in an effort to guarantee a long life. During the Tang Dynasty, the Double Yang Festival was made an official state holiday.

Today, the Double Yang Festival has been assigned a new meaning. In 1989, the Chinese Government decided to make this date Elder's Day. Combining modern tradition with the ancient Double Yang Festival, people show honor, respect and love toward elders, as well as offer them assistance.

The celebration of the Double Yang Festival involves rich and colorful activities. Common among these are outings, ascending an overlook to admire chrysanthemums, wearing dogwood, eating Double Yang cakes and drinking chrysanthemum wine.

Climbing to high places during the Double Yang Festival

The Festival of Ascending the Heights

Since antiquity, for the Double Yang Festival it is customary to climb to a high place, and this is referred to as the Festival of Ascending the Heights. The origin of climbing to high places bears much importance, especially as regards the elderly, because "high" takes on the added meaning of longevity. Hence, people believe that the Festival of Ascending the Heights can increase the life span. There are no provisions regarding where to climb, a mountain being the same as a lofty pagoda.

Eating Double Yang Cakes

According to historical records, there is no particular recipe for Double Yang cakes, also called flower cakes, chrysanthemum cakes and five-colored cakes. It is up to the baker's discretion. At dawn of the ninth day of the ninth month, parents place cakes on the foreheads of their children, wishing their children one hundred things high, with the original idea derived from the ancients. Exquisite Double Yang cakes made in the ninth month have nine layers, to resemble a pagoda. On top of each cake are two rams, in accord with the Double Yang concept (*yang* also means ram, a symbol of righteousness). In addition, some people put little red flags and candles on the tops of the cakes with the sayings "light the candle" and "eat the cake," which mean "ascend to the heights." The flag is a substitute for a dogwood twig.

Appreciation for Chrysanthemums and Drinking Chrysanthemum Wine

The Double Yang Festival occurs every year in the golden autumn, as the chrysanthemums are blooming. Following the tradition of the Double Yang Festival, it is customary to show appreciation for chrysanthemums and to drink chrysanthemum wine. This custom originated with the Jin Dynasty poet Tao Yuanming. Tao Yuanming is famous for having lived in seclusion with his poems, wine and love for chrysanthemums. Later generations imitated this, thereupon customarily showing admiration for chrysanthemums.

Wearing Dogwood and Placing Chrysanthemums in the Hair

The ancients believed that wearing dogwood deters disaster and calamity. They wore dogwood twigs on their arms, put them in fragrant pouches and stuck them in their hair (women and children especially did this, but in some places men did as well). Besides wearing dogwood, in some places it was customary to put chrysanthemums in one's hair.

The Temple Fair

The Temple Fair, also called Temple Market or Festival Place, is a custom related to the activities at Buddhist and Taoist temples, while also reflecting the people's widespread belief in development. In early times, the Temple Fair not only included many ritual offerings, it also followed economic development and the exchange of goods and services. As bazaars were gradually assimilated into the activities of religions, the fair became Temple Market, showing the great importance of townships. Some Temple Fair Festivals are held yearly, but others may be held a few days every month, with no particular guidelines regarding the dates. Wandering about a Temple Fair on New Year's Day is an indispensable custom for the Chinese, and each region's bazaar is somewhat different, with its own allure. The Dragon Dance, Lion Dance and riddles written on lanterns are just a few of the Temple Fair's traditional forms of entertainment.

The Dragon Dance is also called the Swing the Lantern Dance, or Dragon Lantern Dance. From the Spring Festival to the Lantern Festival, many regions have the custom of the Dragon Dance. The dragon is China's symbol for luck, respect, bravery and power. On festive days, people perform the Dragon Dance, praying to the dragon for protection, favorable weather and an abundant harvest. The Lion Dance is another form of Chinese traditional folk art. During every Lantern Festival and at other festive celebrations, the Lion Dance is quite popular. This custom originated from the time period of the Three Kingdoms and spread during the Northern and Southern dynasties, found in over one thousand years of history. Performers dress accordingly as lions and mimic the movements of the animal to the sounds

The Dragon Dance

The Lion Dance

of gongs and percussion instruments. The traditional belief is that the Lion Dance can drive away evil spirits.

Riddles written on lanterns are a distinct feature of the Lantern Festival, and there is an interesting story regarding its origins. According to folklore, in early times there lived a rich foreigner. Although his family was extremely wealthy, he was very rude. Everybody called him Smiling Tiger. He flattered those who were dressed in as fine garments as he, but he was autocratic and his behavior irrational toward the poor. One of the commoners he so treated was named Wang Shao. In order to twit Smiling Tiger, one year during the Lantern Festival, as people were hanging lanterns, on his own lantern Wang Sho wrote the riddle "The head is pointed, the body white as silver, having nothing nice to say. With eyes on the rear end, recognizing the clothes, but not the person." Smiling Tiger got the message and became very angry. He ordered his men to steal Wang Shao's lantern, but the men went to Wang Shao secretly smiling. Laughing, Wang Shao said, "Master, how can you say I offend you?" The irritated Smiling Tiger replied, "If this isn't to offend me, then whom?" Still laughing, Wang Shao replied, "Oh, my lord is suspicious! My poem is simply a riddle, the answer being a needle. Don't you think so?" Smiling Tiger thought for a minute and said, "No, it is not!" Glaring, embarrassed and with nothing left to say, he turned around and slipped away as the people in the area laughed heartily. Afterward, news of this event spread far and wide. So, for the next Lantern Festival many prepared their own riddles to amuse onlookers. Hence, these are called lantern riddles. Following this well-established custom, there are lantern riddle activities in various regions to this day.

Chapter 4

THE EMPERORS YAN AND HUANG

Throughout China's history it has been believed that two people were the primogenitors of the Chinese nationality: Yan Di (Fiery Emperor) and Huang Di (Yellow Emperor).

According to legend, in ancient times Yan Di was the chief of the Jiang tribe. It is said that when the mother of Yan Di was visiting Mount Hua, she saw a divine dragon and by him became impregnated. Upon returning home, she gave birth to Yan Di. As soon as he was born, Yan Di showed great intelligence. At three days old he could talk, and after five days he could walk. When he grew up he became a prominent leader of the tribe, with outstanding ability. Folklore tells us that he taught the people how to cultivate grains, becoming the founder of agriculture and earning the honorable title "God of Agriculture." He would also taste various kinds of plants to determine their medicinal properties and discover how to use them to treat illness. From this came the system of traditional Chinese medicine. Moreover, he built musical instruments, established markets and taught people to weave. These activities, among many others, gradually transformed the uncultured humans into a civil society. Because of the steady increase in the power of the tribe, Yan Di then guided the tribe to outward expansion, thereby greatly influencing each region, one by one. During the course of this expansion, the tribe of Yan Di began to clash with the equally powerful tribe of Huang Di. Finally, at a place called Hillside Spring, Yan Di had to concede victory to the tribe of Huang Di.

In ancient times, Huang Di was the head of the Ji tribe, born on the second day of the second month of the Chinese traditional calendar. It is said that one night the mother of Huang Di unexpectedly saw the aurora borealis, thereupon became pregnant, and consequently gave birth to Huang Di. After ten days he could speak, as a boy he was quick-witted and kindhearted, and as an adult he eventually became the leader of the tribe. Throughout Chinese cultural history, Huang Di plays an extremely significant role. He encouraged Cangjie to produce a character script that has developed into China's modern written language. His wife raised

The enormous statue of Emperors Yan and Huang

silkworms to make thread and manufacture clothes. He taught people how to build boats, vehicles and houses, making the lives of his people much more convenient. He created the Ten Heavenly Stems and the Twelve Earthly Branches with which to measure time. Under the leadership of Huang Di, the tribe became the most powerful tribe in the Central Plains of China, thus absorbing the entire region and unifying other tribes and establishing the basis of Chinese civilized culture.

Yan Di and Huang Di are Chinese culture's most illustrious leaders. They are revered by the Chinese people today as the founders of the humanities. Even today, the Chinese refer to themselves as descendants of Yan-Huang, expressing gratitude for their substantial contributions. People commemorate the two in many ways, in many places, and mausoleums and temples have been erected to show their great respect.

Completed in 2006, in Henan Province's Zhengzhou Prefecture's famous scenic area, is an enormous statue towering over the banks of the Yellow River. This statue's height is 348 feet, 26 feet taller than the Statue of Liberty in the United States and 20 feet taller than Russia's *The Motherland Calls*, making it the tallest statue in the world. This statue attracts Chinese people and descendants of the Fiery and Yellow emperors from around the world who come to admire and pay their respects. The two emperors are contained in the essence of the Chinese nationality as significant mark and symbol, each of the population being a descendant of either the Fiery or the Yellow Emperor.

DA YU CONTROLS THE WATER

As legend has it, a very long time ago, during the rule of Emperor Yao, the people often met with disaster and harm from floods. So Emperor Yao assembled the leaders of all the tribes to discuss how to manage the flooding. Finally, Gun was unanimously elected to tame the water. To do this, he decided to create mounds of earth to form a dam with which to resist rising water. In the end, though, the completed dam often burst from the flooding, and the people's suffering and calamity were as grave as before. So Gun's project to control the inrushing water was deemed a failure, and when Emperor Yao learned of it, he ordered Gun executed.

Decades later, Yu Shun inherited the king-ship of Yao. Once he ascended the throne, he too was determined to find a way to control the flooding. At this time, the son of Gun, Da Yu, was already an adult. Therefore Emperor Shun appointed Da Yu to continue his work toward controlling the flooding. At first, like his father, the son built levees to hold back the water. But not long after he finished the construction, the water rose and breached the

Yu mausoleum

levees. After countless defeats, and learning what was causing the floods, Da Yu eventually realized that flooding could not invariably be stopped. The solution was rather to pinpoint the times to fortify the levees by dredging canals. After realizing this, Da Yu immediately changed his strategy.

To begin with, Da Yu surveyed every part of the area, taking note of the tendencies of the river. When these became clear, he led his people to con-struct a drainage canal, so clearing a pathway for the river to the ocean. In doing this, Da Yu worked alongside his people. It is even said that he was so busy doing the job that he once passed his house three times without going in. This story has since been eulogized with the saying "passing the house three times and not entering." With such unremitting effort, at last Da Yu managed to successfully divert to the ocean the flow of the water from all over the country. As a result, people could once again cultivate their land with ease and not worry about the threat of a rising river.

By virtue of the accomplishment of controlling the flooding and so benefiting the people, in his old age Emperor Shun passed on the kingship to Da Yu. As a famous emperor in ancient times, since his death the son continues to be much praised by the Chinese people for contributing to the country's prosperity. In Zhejiang Province's Shaoxing Prefecture, at the foot of Mount Kuaiji, a tomb called Yu Mausoleum was built to commemorate Da Yu's glorious achievements. To this day, there are many visitors to the Yu Mausoleum who come to express reverence for this famous emperor.

PANGU CREATES THE UNIVERSE

How did the universe come into being? There is a legend in China, passed down by tradition, of how Pangu split the heavens from the earth to form the cosmos. Legend has it that long ago there was no sky, and the earth lacked substance, as the entire universe existed then as a gigantic egg. It is said that in this formless mass was a being who resembled humans by the name of Pangu. It is said that Pangu slept soundly in the egg for 18,000 years. Until one day he awoke into pitch blackness and could see nothing. Making every effort to escape, he broke open the egg, and something like egg white began floating upward and formed the sky, and something like yolk descended to create the vast earth.

So, having separated heaven and earth, Pangu felt much more comfortable. But the recently formed heavens frequently sank down, reconnecting themselves to the earth. Not wanting to return to the primal chaos of that large egg, with all his might Pangu started holding up the heavens with his hands and the crown of his head, his feet touching the ground. And every day, as Pangu supported the heavens in this way, his body grew, which caused the heavens and earth to become increasingly distant from each other, until finally they were separated forever. At this point, Pangu grew extremely tired and decided to rest for a while.

After lying down, though, Pangu would never rise again. His head became the Tai Mountain to the east; his abdomen formed the central Heng Mountain; his left arm in the south became what is also known as Heng Mountain (similar tones yet different characters). His right arm became Song Mountain in the north, and his foot formed the prominent Mount Hua in the west. The breath from his mouth also changed, becoming the spring wind, clouds and mist, and his voice became the thunder that shakes the heavens. His left eye became the burning sun, warming the earth every

day. The right eye became the brilliant moonlight that illuminates the people. His blood filled the rivers and lakes, his flesh became fertile land. The teeth, bones and marrow became gold, silver, copper and iron, as well as hard stone, smooth and full pearls, precious stones and jade. His skin and hair became the countless flowers, plants and trees, and the sweat of his body the dew and the rain. His hair and eyebrows became all the stars in the celestial sky, his muscles forming intersecting paths. Every kind of bird, beast, fish and insect embodied his spirit as a way of offering his entire body to the cosmos. The sun, moon and

Pangu creates the universe

stars in the heavens and the flora and fauna of the mountains and valleys together formed an orderly, dynamic universe.

Sacrificing his life to form the radiant universe, Pangu was revered by China's early ancestors as a god who brought us the cosmos as we know it. Later generations of Chinese often worshiped him and offered him sacrifices. Since ancient times, many regions have built temples in honor of Pangu. For example, Hunan Province's Xiangxiang boasts the Pangu Ancestral Hall. Every traditional calendar year, on the third day of the third month, masses of people congregate at the Pangu Ancestral Hall to pay their respects, displaying much gratitude to the unbounded cosmos and to nature, thanking the universe for everything it has bestowed and cherishing its innate qualities.

THE GODDESS NUWA MAKES HUMAN BEINGS

What is the origin of human beings on earth? From remote antiquity there is a legend about the goddess Nuwa, who created human beings. After the death of Pangu, there already existed in the cosmos a countless number of living things. But, unfortunately, humankind had not yet appeared on earth. After tens of thousands of years, a celestial goddess, Nuwa, appeared and created humanity. Her appearance was extremely odd. She had the head of a human and the body of a snake. Upon coming to earth, Nuwa discovered all around her only the beasts of the land and the birds of the air. Initially, these small creatures provided her with boundless happiness, making her feel exceptionally blessed. However, a long time passed and because the animals could not talk, when Nuwa wanted to express herself she could never find somebody to listen, and so she became lonely and depressed.

One day, as she was feeling bored, Nuwa used a twig to stir the moist clay that lay by her side, and at the will of her hands the earth was formed into a likeness of a human. Nuwa blew one breath into the clay figure and gave it life. She had formed not only a woman who could speak but also one who could understand her intentions. Nuwa thought this was interesting, but at the same time she did not want the woman to feel lonely too. And so she made a man and allowed the two to be partners. To see these two people side by side made Nuwa extremely happy and content, whereupon she continued to form many more people, until finally, becoming tired, she dipped her twig into the mud and threw it into the sky. The mud fell to earth, creating many more humans. In order for the new creatures to reproduce to create later generations, Nuwa allowed the men and women

The goddess Nuwa repairs the hole in the sky

to marry, and so began the human race. It is said that the humans formed by Nuwa's own hands became the upper-class society of later generations, and the humans she created with the twig became the lower-class peasants. No matter the case, though, because since the time Nuwa created mankind the earth's population has been allowed abundant opportunity and vitality.

But the joyful lives of the humans did not last long. One day, the earth and humanity suffered a sudden great catastrophe. The sky cracked, the earth split open, fires raged and unceasing floods threatened human beings with extinction. Nuwa didn't have the heart to witness the suffering and destruction of her beloved creations, so she refined a kind of five-colored stone and used it to repair the hole in the sky. At the same time, she used the mud from around the reeds to stop the inundating floods. With such great effort by Nuwa, the peace and tranquility humanity had known was restored.

In order to express their gratitude to Nuwa for her benevolence, humans bestowed on her the title, Mother Goddess Nuwa, honoring her as the creator of the human race, and all the nations offered her sacrifices. Moreover, because of this myth, Chinese people today have a profound sense about their land. When traveling great distances, people often take with them a bit of soil from their native place as a long-lasting memory.

HOU YI SHOOTS THE SUNS

It is said that in remote antiquity there were ten suns in the sky. On these suns lived ten birds named Crow, all the sons of the Celestial Emperor. Each day, one of the ten birds would emerge to do his task of providing light and radiant heat, while the other nine birds were elsewhere enjoying themselves and resting. Therefore, as daybreak approached, people on earth could witness the sun's ascent in the East, as a Crow appeared over the horizon to do his work.

For a long time, then, though there were ten Crows and ten suns in the sky, people on earth only ever saw one of each. By their grace the people scheduled work and rest, at sunrise tending the fields and at sundown sleeping, living with contentment. But one day, when the ten suns' mother was out for a time, the mischievous suns did a horrible thing. At dawn, all ten suns rose together in the sky. The Crows thought this was amusing, but the people on earth and all living things suffered a calamity. The ten suns hung there in the sky releasing an immense heat that quickly dried up the seas and killed hundreds of fish. This disaster caused a sea monster to come ashore and plunder the crops of the people, while all the forests on earth were set ablaze, burning many animals to death. The animals that did not die fled to the homes of people, desperate for food, and so the people and the livestock became the meals of the animals. Day after day the people were hungry and at the same time unable to endure the blistering hot weather, which was killing them.

Hou Yi shoots the suns

At this time there lived a young and handsome divine archer named Hou Yi, whose arrows were astoundingly accurate. On seeing the devastation on earth, he resolved to use his arrows to shoot down the troublesome Crows in the heavens. One day Hou Yi grabbed his weapon, packed his rations and set off on a journey. He climbed ninety-nine alpine mountains, forged ninety-nine rivers, passed through ninety-nine canyons and suffered untold hardships before finally reaching the East China Sea, where he climbed a supremely tall mountain. Atop the peak, Hou Yi drew his bow and arrow and aimed at the Crow in the middle of one of the suns, shooting it down into the East China Sea, thereupon eliminating one sun from the heavens. In this way, he felled nine Crows, so leaving only one sun in the sky. At this point, Hou Yi put down his bow, leaving the sun to prevail alone in the sky to benefit humanity.

Since then, this sun has risen every day off eastern China and has hung in the sky, warming the world and the people and enabling the seedlings to grow and all living things to survive. To express the wonder of Hou Yi's achievement, the story of Hou Yi shooting the suns is unfailingly passed on through the generations, forever etching the name of this hero in the minds of the people.

Chapter 5

THE COWHERD AND THE WEAVING MAID

In China, there is also an ancient and beautiful story of romance, reflecting the story of the love of Zhinu and Niulang.

As legend has it, in the heavens there existed a beautiful fairy named Zhinu, the Weaving Maid. She was the daughter of the heavenly courtyard's Queen Mother of the West. One day, Zhinu and a few companions sneaked out of the Heavenly Court and went to the world of the mortals, selecting the Jade Lotus Pond in which to bathe. Since they lacked freedom in the Heavenly Court, this sojourn was bringing them joy beyond comparison.

Near the Jade Lotus Pond lived a handsome young man called the Niulang (the Cowherd). Shortly after he was born into a peasant family, his parents had passed away, leaving Niulang to live with his older brother and his sister-in-law on a section of their land. But soon after, the sister-in-law expelled him from the family, giving him an old ox and a broken cart. Niulang and the ox became dependent on each other for survival, but in reality this old ox was a celestial immortal. To compensate Niulang for being truthful and benevolent, one day the old ox suddenly spoke like a person. It said, "Niulang, today you will go to the Jade Lotus Pond. There you will see some fairies bathing. Grab a set of their red clothing and conceal it. Those red clothes of the fairy will become your wife." On hearing this, Niulang was overjoyed. He arrived at the Jade Lotus Pond shortly after.

As the old ox had said, there in the Jade Lotus Pond frolicked a group of fairies. As they amused themselves, they paid no attention to Niulang snatching the red clothes and fleeing. Instead, as they frolicked in the pond they suddenly saw a human. One after another, they put on their clothes and ascended into the heavens. But Zhinu could not find her clothes, so she had to stay. At this moment, Niulang walked to her and returned the clothes and asked her to be his wife. The fairy saw that the cowherd was handsome and kindhearted, so she accepted his request and become his wife.

After marrying, the Cowherd and his new wife, the Weaving Maid, were bound by deep emotions and lived a fortunate and blissful life together. Several years after the wedding they had a son and a daughter, both very lovely. One day, Niulang came home and said to Zhinu, "The old ox has just died. While it was dying, it ordered me to skin it and said the skin can be used to fly to the heavens." On hearing this, into his wife's heart leaped an ominous premonition, and a mighty wind blew dark clouds that densely covered the sky. Immortals then appeared from the heavens to escort Zhinu back to the Heavenly Court. As Niulang saw the deities take her, anxiety filled his heart. He donned the ox skin, grabbed his children and left to pursue his wife. Using the ox skin to fly, he was

The Cowherd and the Weaving Maid

rapidly closing the distance between them when the Queen Mother of the West pulled a gold hairpin from her hair and drew a boundary between Niulang and Zhinu, thus forming the Celestial River (Milky Way). This heavenly river was unusually broad, and regardless of the great efforts of Niulang, there was no way to cross. The Celestial River would forever keep the lovers apart. Today we can still see them on either side of the Milky Way, where there are two relatively large stars. The Weaving Maid became Vega (in the constellation Lyra), and the Cowherd became the star Altair (in the constellation Aquila), where they remain side by side. Near Altair can be seen two smaller stars, the son and the daughter of Niulang and Zhinu.

Through all this, Zhinu could not see her husband and children, and so all day long her face was washed in tears, until finally the Queen Mother of the West promised her that every year on the seventh day of the seventh month she could meet with her family. And so, on that day a multitude of celestial magpies form a bridge in the heavens, connecting the two sides of the river. People call this the Magpie Bridge. It is on this bridge that the couple and their children are allowed to meet. And it is said that on the seventh night of the seventh month, in the event that somebody is under a vine of grapes, if he listens closely he will hear the faint sounds of Niulang and Zhinu speaking.

In China, with reference to this story, people traditionally call the seventh day of the seventh month of the lunar calendar Magpie Bridge Day, or Night of Sevens, in honor of the fidelity and romance of Niulang and Zhinu. In this, the Night of Sevens is similar to the West's February 14, the Chinese version of Valentine's Day.

MENG JIANGNU WEEPS DOWN THE GREAT WALL

Today, while most are familiar with the Great Wall of China, among the Chinese there is told the story "Meng Jiangnu Weeps Down the Great Wall." According to legend, during the period of the Qin Dynasty, the Meng household planted a melon in the garden. The vine grew to the neighboring Jiangnu house, producing a fruit. When the melon ripened, from within burst a young lady. She was named Meng Jiangnu and eventually became the mutual daughter of the two families. She grew up extraordinarily intelligent, of an honest character and with the adoration of the neighbors.

At that time, the First Emperor Qin was conscripting men to build the Great Wall. There was a scholar named Fan Xiliang, who constantly ran east and west in order to dodge the compulsory service. One day he was utterly parched and set out to look for water and arrived at the home of Meng Jiangnu. After her family understood the circumstances of Fan Xiliang, they expressed their sympathy and decided to harbor him in their house. Not long after, Meng Jiangnu's parents found Fan Xiliang to be extremely honest, handsome and learned, and so they resolved to allow their daughter to marry him. The two became a married couple with exceptional mutual love.

But after only three days of marriage, the authorities discovered that Fan Xiliang had avoided his obligatory service and arrested him, taking him away for forced labor. Seeing her husband apprehended, Meng Jiangnu felt great agony. Every day the tears flowed as she longed for her husband, and a year passed in futile waiting for him and with no information about him. Finally, Meng Jiangnu decided to go to the site of the Great Wall construction project to find her husband. Along the journey of three hundred miles, she was met with many trials and tribulations, but at last she reached the base of the Great Wall. She saw large numbers of servant workers there, some carrying heavy bricks on their backs, others lifting large stones and climbing up a high mountain with great difficulty. Their clothes were old and tattered and sweat soaked their backs. After several days of searching and making inquiries, Meng Jiangnu learned that her husband was dead and that his body was buried within the massive wall. Hearing this depressing news was like a thunderbolt from a clear blue sky. The widow was overcome with sorrow, weeping bitterly at the foot of the Great Wall for three days and three nights. As she cried, clouds obscured the sky, and the sun and the moon failed to shine. Then, suddenly, there was the sound of rumbling as 250 miles of the Wall collapsed to the ground, toppled by her tears.

The story "Meng Jiangnu Weeps Down the Great Wall" is very moving.

It denounces the cruel and unjust compulsory service in the era of Emperor Qin Shi Huang, while singing the praises of a young woman's love. In order to commemorate her, at the base of the Great Wall later generations built Meng Jiangnu Temple with a statue of her inside. Next to the temple is Waiting for Husband Rock, on which, legend says, Meng Jiangnu climbed to look far for her love.

LIANG SHANBO AND ZHU YINGTAI

In China there is a widely known legend that has been understood by all through the ages as a tragic romance. It is known as the legend of Liang Shanbo and Zhu Yingtai (The Butterfly Lovers).

During the Eastern Jin Dynasty, in the Zhejiang Province of Shangyu Prefecture, there lived a family named Zhu. Their daughter, Zhu Yingtai, was exceptionally beautiful and intelligent. As a child she took an interest in studying and wanted to go to Hangzhou to learn from the masters. Unfortunately, at that time girls were not allowed to attend school, so her parents refused the request.

Determined to receive an education, however, Zhu Yingtai set off for Hangzhou disguised as a man. En route, she met by chance an intellect from Kuaiji (present-day Zhejiang Province, Shaoxing Prefecture) named Liang Shanbo. It was like old souls meeting as they admired each other, until at last on the Thatched Bridge Pavilion they pledged an oath as brothers. Soon after arriving at Hangzhou, the two found themselves classmates at Wan Song Academy. They studied together there, as close as form and shadow, for three years and developed a deep emotional bond. Zhu Yingtai profoundly loved Liang Shangbo, from the outset unaware that she was a woman.

As their schooling ended and they had to return to their families, the two were reluctant to part. On part of their journey home, Zhu Yingtai unceasingly suggested her love for Liang Shangbo, but being an honest and considerate man, he still did not realize that Zhu Yingtai was a woman, much less a woman falling in love with him. Finally, with no better option, she lied and told him that in her family there was a younger sister that looked like him and would be willing to marry him. She said she greatly desired that he come to her

Liang Shanbo and Zhu Yingtai change into butterflies

family's manor so they could meet. In fact, this "younger sister" was Zhu Yingtai herself.

The two separated then, each going home. Because he was impoverished, Liang Shanbo was unable to visit the Zhu family in a timely manner to propose marriage. By the time he arrived he had come to realize that the "younger sister" Zhu Yingtai had spoken of was none other than she herself. By this time, though, her father had betrothed her to another. When Liang Shanbo learned of this, he felt great remorse and became gravely ill. Before his death he asked that his family bury him by the road that Zhu Yingtai would travel to be married, so he could see her as she passed.

Zhu Yingtai caught wind of this plea. On the day of her marriage, as the wedding procession approached the tomb of Liang Shangbo, Zhu Yintai went to the grave and offered sacrifices. She wept in affection for this man, her heart shattered. At this moment, the heavens delivered wind and rain as an impressive flash of lightning struck and split open the tomb. Zhu Yingtai then leapt into the grave, the tomb closing behind her, and was united with her lover in death. Afterwards, Liang Shanbo and Zhu Yingtai metamorphosed into butterflies, becoming a couple for all time.

Over a thousand years has passed, and their tale of romance endures. This classic romance is considered the *Romeo and Juliet* of the Orient. A violin concerto called *Liang Zhu* has become popular in the past several years at home as well as abroad.

THE LEGEND OF THE WHITE SNAKE

"The Legend of the White Snake" is a story that emerged during the Song Dynasty. It is said that long ago a white snake was captured in the claws of a black falcon. While the black falcon was preparing to eat the white snake, an old man named Xu saved the life of the snake. A millennium passed, and the white snake had become a demon, while among the descendants of the old man Xu was a handsome young scholar named Xu Xian.

In an effort to repay the old man for his life-saving grace, the white snake took the appearance of a human, naming herself Bai Suzhen. She looked everywhere for members of the Xu family, wishing to help them. In the course of events she met a similar green snake, named Xiaoqing, and the two proceeded together. In a

LEFT TO RIGHT: Bai Suzhen, Xiaoqing and Xu Xian

prophecy, Bai Suzhen saw Xu Xian among the descendants of the old man Xu, also foreseeing that on one particular day he would be going to West Lake in Hangzhou.

On that day, then, at the Broken Bridge, Bai Suzheng arrived at West Lake, had a chance encounter with Xu Xian, and there was born a mutual affection. Before long, the two were happily married and in love, and Xiaoqing became their servant. Bai Suzhen helped Xu Xian to open an herbal shop to treat the illnesses of the common people. Their treatments were exceptionally effective. In addition to not charging the destitute sick commoners, she also became greatly loved by the local masses for her skill. As their blessed life continued, Bai Suzhen became pregnant, the whole family becoming even more grateful. But as she was gradually forgetting that she was actually a white snake, disaster was coming slowly to the household.

One day, a monk from Jinshan Temple named Fahai arrived and informed Xu Xian that Bai Suzhen was actually a demonic snake. He refused to believe the monk. Later, Fahai told him to let her drink some yellow wine on the day of the Dragon Boat Festival, to try to turn her back into her original form. This time, Xu Xian listened to the words and secretly allowed his wife to drink the yellow wine. That night, Bai Suzhen changed back into a snake, frightening Xu Xian to his death. In an effort to save him, she went to the Celestial Courtyard to steal the plant of the immortals and so ultimately brought him back to life. Still, even after learning that his wife was actually a demonic snake, Xu Xian still profoundly loved her.

But Fahai had been ordered to capture Bai Suzhen. He therefore placed Xu Xian in detention at Jinshan Temple. Out of love for her husband, Bai Suzhen and Xiaoqing traveled to the Jinshan Temple to contend with Fahai. Fahai commanded the waters to inundate the Jinhan Temple, thus drowning the souls of many innocent people. Then Bai Suzhen, in violation of the edict of the heavens, gave birth to Xu Shilin. Yet again Fahai caught up with her and imprisoned Bai Suzhen in the Thunder Peak Pagoda in an effort to separate her from Xu Xian for eternity.

Eighteen years later their son, Xu Shilin, became a high-level scholar. He went to the Thunder Peak Pagoda and offered sacrifices to his mother. While he knelt, the Thunder Peak Pagoda collapsed, thus reuniting the entire family.

"The Legend of the White Snake" is a truly touching romantic story. It was not only circulated as a novel in China but

Thunder Peak Pagoda today, and West Lake

also adapted for many Chinese operas and television programs. In 1958, *The Legend of the White Serpent* was made into a Japanese animated film. The influence also reached France, as noted by French scholar Ru Lia's translation of the novel.

THE LEGEND OF MU-LAN

There is a widespread legend that a girl named Hua Mu-lan was born to a Chinese family during wartime long, long ago. At that time, an imperial edict ordered that each household should send a man to the battlefield to protect the country. In order to prevent her aged father and very young brother from going to the frontline, Hua Mu-lan determined to disguise herself as a man to take her elderly father's place in the army. So she bought a cavalry horse and packed her luggage in secret, then joined the emperor's troops, marching on to the frontline.

For twelve years on the battlefield, Hua Mu-lan lived and fought as a man without her identity being discovered. Thanks to her bravery on the front lines and her extraordinary fighting ability, she distinguished herself many times in battle. Because of her outstanding achievements, she was offered a government post by the emperor himself when the war was over. She turned down the position, though, and went home to live with her parents. Later, when former comrades visited her there, they were shocked to see her dressed as a girl.

Hua Mu-lan has been deeply respected as a courageous, witty and honest heroine for hundreds of years. During the Tang Dynasty she was deified as a goddess, and an emperor conferred upon her the posthumous title of "Filial and Valiant General." Her story has maintained its popularity for thousands of years. The famous *Collection of Yue Fu Poetry* compiled by Guo Maoqian during the Song Dynasty includes "The Ballad of Mu-lan," a folklore piece about the legend of Hua Mu-lan. Using only three hundred Chinese characters, the piece consists of concise language, and it ranks among the excellent narrative poems in ancient Chinese folk literature. Since then, Mu-lan's story has been made into plays, movies

Mu-lan

and a TV series. In particular, the film's influence has extended to America and the rest of the world.

Under the direction of Tony Bancroft and Barry Cook, Walt Disney Pictures released *Mulan* in 1998 in America, the story adapted into a quality cartoon for modern audiences. A small fire-breathing dragon called Mushu was added to the story to help Mulan win the war with his insightful remarks and superpowers. Then, in 2004, *Mulan II* was shot and directed by Darrell Rooney as a sequel to the 1998 film. In this film, the story goes that when Mulan and her fiancé, General Li Xiang, were about to be married, they were suddenly assigned a secret mission: to escort the Emperor's three daughters across the country to marry the king of Xiongnu for the sake of border peace. They all set out without delay, Mushu dragon and cricket going along. However, the three princesses found themselves upset by their arranged marriage because they were in love with others. As an advocator of female freedom, Hua Mu-lan decided to take a chance to help the girls escape their forced marriage. In fact, the Disney version of the story doesn't exist in traditional Chinese legends; despite the image transformation, though, both Hua Mu-lans share the same, risky, freedom-pursuing spirit.

The animated film *Mulan* and its sequel aroused such extensive attention in the U.S. that the American media extolled Disney for producing the Chinese-based story.

A poem goes:

Hua Mu-lan rose to fame in ancient China
because of taking her elderly father's place in the army
and her outstanding service in war,
while the Disney cartoon *Mulan II* is
a triumph of American and Chinese imagination.

The character Mu-lan has become one of the most recognizable symbols of Chinese culture worldwide, its unique charm sweeping the globe.

Chapter 6

THE DRAGON

Long (the dragon) is held in high esteem and plays a significant role in Chinese culture. In the Neolithic Age, the idea of the dragon germinated as a totem of the primitive human. Even today, the Chinese regard the dragon as an auspicious creature, and there are a variety of idioms about and allusions to dragon. The dragon has been firmly embedded in Chinese culture for thousands of years and is encountered across all aspects of Chinese society as well as in the awareness of the people. So the Chinese dragon is like the symbol of the Chinese nation, the emblem of the Chinese race, and the totem of Chinese civilization. Expressions like "posterity or descendants of the dragon" catalyze excitement, aspiration and pride within Chinese people.

What, then, was the dragon's original form? How did the concept come about? How did the image of the dragon and its cultural connotations evolve, and what role does it play in Chinese culture?

Ancient sources abound with ideas about the Chinese dragon. Some have suggested that it is a flying dragon without legs, looking like a soaring python. Others have suggested that the dragon has the appearance of a horse's head and a python's tail. Yet others have proposed, about its formation: its horns resemble those of a stag, its ears those of an ox, its head that of a camel, its eyes those of a rabbit, its neck that of a python, its belly that of a clam, its scales those of a carp, its soles those of a deer, its claws those of a hawk.

Later depictions of the dragon reveal that its image has undergone complex changes over time. The dragon image was continually enriched and developed gradually, as more totems were incorporated into it. Many scholars have done research into a prototype and from this has come a list of theories: Some have advocated that the dragon is a species of crocodile, others that it resembles a lizard, and some researchers feel it has the characteristics of a horse.

The theory of the python as the origin of the Chinese dragon, however, is the widely accepted one. This idea was first suggested by Wen Yi-duo in his famous work *An Examination of Fuxi* (a legendary ruler). He notes that every time after the python clan annexed another species, "they integrated his defeated enemy's emblem into their own. Such a myth explains why the dragon appears to have the attributes of various animals: the legs of fierce animals, the head of a horse, a hyena's tail, a stag's horns, a dog's claws, a carp's scales and tentacles."

Although the original image of the dragon was simple, the ancient Chinese began to depict their totem with more associations and imagination as their links to other tribes grew stronger. And so, after a long period of time, the figure evolved into a completely different dragon or totem.

According to type and posture, the dragon falls into the following categories: scaly flood dragon, horned dragon, hornless dragon, winged dragon, one-footed dragon, ichthyosaurus, one-head two-body dragon, double-headed dragon and firedrake, among others. In addition, its gestures are as rich and varied as these: sitting dragon, walking dragon, flying dragon, diving dragon, two dragons playing with a pearl of fire, dragon amidst clouds, and so forth.

As a common totem for all of the Chinese, the dragon is traditionally regarded as the god of wind, snow, rainfall and floods. From the point of view of geography, most Chinese regions feature a vast hinterland situated in a temperate climatic zone. Therefore, such advantages greatly facilitate the formation of a society founded on agriculture and animal husbandry and totally reliant on its natural environment and, in particular, on the climate. Timely wind and rain can bring good harvests, so each family can be well fed and well clothed. On the other hand, drought and flooding can cause farmers to miss a harvest and leave the land strewn with the corpses of hunger victims. As a result, the python-like dragon was worshiped as ruler of water-related weather phenomena and the source of all that was beneficial to communal wellbeing. For one thing, pythons are often found in deep, wet valleys, pools and swamps. For another, they like playing in water on rainy and hazy days and shuttling between forest and grassland. Therefore, they were deified as masters of water with the ability to summon wind and rain and to mount the clouds and ride the mist. In the beginning, the dragon was the totem of an ancient tribe. As time went on, the cultures of various nationalities blended during the process of intertribal warfare, population migration, mixed

Two dragons playing with a pearl of fire

residences and intermarriage. Different tribes came to be united under a common banner, and the dragon was adopted as a national totem.

With the establishment of a feudal society, emperors compared themselves to the dragon, thereby making it the exclusive symbol of imperial majesty. Chinese emperors thought they were the real dragons and the sons of the heavens. Thus, the emperor's ceremonial dresses were called dragon robes, the imperial cap the dragon crown, the throne the dragon seat, and the boats the emperors took were called dragon boats. The Chinese dragon is used as an emblem of the emperor's authority in many idioms, for example, "the dragon is indisposed" (the king is sick), "the dragon is in a great rage" (the reigning sovereign is angry), and "the majesty has a descendant of the dragon" (the throne has a newborn son). As a result, uniquely designed dragons can be seen on such Chinese royal buildings as the Imperial Palace, as well as on decorations and ornaments.

In modern times, belief in the dragon as the patron saint of the feudal rulers has faded without a trace. Among the people, however, dragon-related recreation customs have been passed down from remote times. The dragon has become a symbol of the spirit of the Chinese nation and has an important influence on all aspects of China's cultural traditions and social life. The dragon is widely used in denominating family names, pavilions, and even rivers and lakes. The dragon also plays an important part in Chinese festivals, like the dragon lantern show on the Festival of Lanterns and dragon boat races for the Dragon Boat Festival. The Chinese dragon in fact seems omnipresent, with a dragon star hanging high above the sky, a dragon vein lying deep in the ground, the dragon-horse being a beast, the dragon juniper a plant, even the dragon appearing in China's twelve zodiacs (symbolic animals used to designate years in the Chinese calendar). In addition, countless proverbs and idioms involve the dragon: "dragons rising and tigers leaping" (a scene of bustling activity), "like the flight of the dragon and the dance of the phoenix" (lively and vigorous calligraphy), "doughty as a dragon and lively as a tiger" (full of and vigor), "moaning of dragons and howling of tigers," "crouching tiger, hidden dragon" (undiscovered or concealed talents or experts), "as energetic as a dragon and a horse," and so on. In short, there are countless cultural phenomena associated with the dragon.

It is worth mentioning that the Chinese *long* (dragon) has features different from those of the Western dragon. In Chinese art, dragons are typically portrayed as an embodiment of massive virtues and unmatched qualities. They are fearless, staunch and chivalrous warriors. Much deification has been bestowed upon the dragon, ranging from the ability to prophesy to miraculous shapeshifting powers. The Chinese *Long* is a godlike creature, and Dragon Palace is a treasure house and a symbol of imperial authority. Meanwhile, since it is righteous and benevolent, the dragon will take any risk to bring rainfall to arid areas. In contrast to Chinese dragons, European dragons are considered an incarnation of an evil demon.

The Chinese dragon civilization prospers not only in China but also in many other regions and countries. The most compelling and numerous decorations are still the dragon ornaments in Chinese communities around the globe. The Chinese dragon is often utilized for decorative purposes on the eye-catching decorated archways at the

Dragon robe

entrance to Chinatowns. For example, 270 Chinese spectacular dragons are painted on the arch (a Chinese gate) on Seventh Street in Washington, DC's Chinatown. Walking in Chinatown, one cannot fail to notice a variety of dragon-style advertisements designed to attract customers, and one discovers dragon lanterns hanging everywhere. Overseas, buildings designed with traditional architecture have a unique style, partly because of the dragons on them. For example, dragon carvings can be seen on every part of the Confucian Shrine in Nagasaki, Japan; the entire building is almost covered with dragon carvings; even the stairway at the front of the temple uses dragon-design steps. Overseas, a lot of places are named after *Long*, like Dragon City in Australia, granite dragon gate in Malaysia, Dragon-Spring Cave in Iwate County, Japan. You can also spot small dragons if you're careful enough. For example, commemorative stamps with dragon patterns were issued in Italy and Japan.

In fact, the Chinese *long* has been involved in, undergone and witnessed the lengthy formative process of the Chinese nation, a process of harmonious integration. The Chinese people call themselves "descendants of the dragon," because they believe they've inherited the dragon-related cultural spirit. This doesn't mean they feel that they bear genetic similarities to the dragon. What it does mean is that the cultural ideology developed during the evolution of the earliest Chinese is similar to the essence that derived from the development of the dragon species. Both types of spirit emphasize harmony and tolerance, benevolence, living with nature and progress. Therefore, the Chinese people can be referred to as offspring of the dragon.

And such concepts as "descendants of the dragon" and "land of the dragon" have won worldwide recognition as the Chinese dragon culture has spread extensively.

THE VICISSITUDES OF THE DYNASTIES

In the time-honored traditions of China, variations in dynasties were fragmentary and complicated. The first order of business for each dynasty's founder was to establish a *guohao*, or official name.

The earliest dynasty dates back to the twenty-first century BCE, with the establishment of the Xia Dynasty. Because of Emperor Jie's brutality, he was overthrown by the military of Emperor Shangtang, thereby creating the second dynasty, the Shang Dynasty.

The last monarch of the Shang Dynasty was Emperor Zhou. His tyranny induced seething discontent, especially in Xiqi, where Ji Chang and his son Ji Fa led a revolt against Emperor Zhou and established the Zhou Dynasty (the dynasty Zhou and the Emperor Zhou are different characters).

In the Late Zhou Dynasty came the Spring and Autumn and the Warring States periods (770–221 BCE), when all of China was divided into vassal states, large and small. It wasn't until 221 BCE that Emperor Qin conquered and annexed the six major states, establishing China's first feudal dynasty, the Qin Dynasty.

Emperor Qin ordered the masses to build the Great Wall and to dig irrigation channels, exploiting the labor of the people for wealth, and this resulted in popular grievances. Coupled with the corrupt politics of the Qin Dynasty, the edicts resulted in Liu Bang leading a takeover and defeating Xiang Yu, in 206 BCE, and instituting the Han Dynasty. Ruling for more than four hundred years, this dynasty comprised the Western Han and the Eastern Han.

By the late period, there was more and more vying for supremacy, known as the famous Three Kingdoms Period. During this time, war raged everywhere and involved a struggle for authority by the warlords Cao Cao, Sun Quan and Liu Bei. Zhuge Liang and Zhou Yu each competed with courage and ability, filling brilliant chapters in China's history books.

The wars among the Three Kingdoms lasted more than half a century. Ultimately, the Wu and Shu states were overthrown by the Wei state. This in turn led to Sima Yan seizing power and establishing the Jin Dynasty, which ruled for more than 150 years. In 420, China once again entered a period of disunity, during the Northern and Southern Dynasties.

The Southern Dynasty experienced four smaller dynasties in succession: the Song, Qi, Liang and Chen, while the Northern Dynasty was occupied and ruled by the Wei, Qi and Zhou.

In 581, a man named Yang Jian ended China's then-divided situation, unifying north and south and establishing the Sui Dynasty, which lasted for only a brief time. The Second Emperor Yang Guang, whose reign was extremely brutal and corrupt, incited seething unpopular opinion. Consequently, Li Yuan, with the help of his son, Li Shimin, led the masses to topple the Sui Dynasty, establishing the Tang Dynasty in 618.

The Tang Dynasty was the most prosperous dynasty in the history of China. During this period, with great economic gains and a developing culture, China emerged as a great influence in the world. Even today, foreigners refer to Chinese abroad as people of the Tang.

During the An Shi Rebellion, however, a decaying Tang Dynasty unable to reform itself was finally crushed, consecutively giving rise to the five smaller states: the Later Liang, the Later Tang, the Later Jin, the Later Han and the Later Zhou, then continuing with ten small kingdoms: the Former Shu, the Later Shu, Wu, the Southern Tang, Wu Yue, Min, Chu, the Southern Han, the Southern Ping and the Northern Han. This historical period is called "The Five Dynasties and Ten Kingdoms."

In 960, in the Later Zhou period, General Zhao Kuangyin emerged wearing the robe of the emperor, and thus was the Song Dynasty founded.

The Song Dynasty frequently clashed with the Khitans, Nuzhen and Mongolians. Prioritizing literature ahead of warfare, the Song wished to live in peace. Later, treacherous court officials with power faced substantial corruption accusations. Ultimately, though, not able to withstand the increasing attacks of the Mongolians and having been conquered by Kublai Khan in 1279, China entered a new era, that of the Yuan Dynasty.

Regardless of which feudal dynasty we look at, the rises and falls of power throughout show a regular pattern in which we see corrupt politics in its later stages. As seen in the later period of the Yuan Dynasty, not only did the corruption cause the fall of the dynasty, but the Han people resented their country being ruled by foreigners, and this resulted in many military insurrections. Once, such a revolt succeeded under the leadership of Zhu Yuanzhang.

With the assistance of the writer Liu Ji and the military expertise of Xu Da, Zhu Yuanzhang overthrew the Yuan Dynasty in 1368, initiating the Ming Dynasty, which ruled for nearly three hundred years. But, again, with corruption in the courts, the Ming Dynasty was eventually defeated by Manchu, giving rise to the Qing Dynasty.

In the history of China, the Qing Dynasty marks a period of great prosperity, particularly during the reigns of emperors Kangxi, Yongzheng and Qianlong. During this time, politics, economics, culture and academics reached unprecedented heights.

The later period of the Qing Dynasty followed the usual pattern of corruption, however, which made the country vulnerable. Foreign aggressors took advantage of this and entered China, starting wars of both foreign and domestic factions and signaling a period of suffering and misfortune. Sun Yat-sen persuaded the people to oppose the emperor, resulting in the overthrow of the last feudal dynasty in the history of China and establishing the Republic of China, in 1911. After this, and after a long period of struggle against aggression and the country embroiled in civil war, the People's Republic of China (PRC) was established, led by Mao Zedong, in 1949.

As to the vicissitudes of the various Chinese dynasties, this popular poem has been passed down through the generations:

The Xia and the Shang, the Western Zhou
The Eastern Zhou contains two factions
The Spring and Autumn and the Warring States periods
Emperor Qin's unification, the two Han dynasties
The Three Kingdoms of the Wei, Shu and Wu
Followed by the Jin Dynasty
Northern and Southern Dynasties existing side by side
The Sui, Tang and the Five Dynasties
The Song, Yuan, Ming and Qing arriving later
Completing the rule of the imperial court

MINORITY ETHNIC GROUPS

China has been a united multiethnic country since ancient times.

After the PRC was established, the central government confirmed altogether fifty-six ethnic groups within the country. Because of the overwhelming predominance of the Han nationality, the other fifty-five are considered to be minority groups. The various groups are the Mongol, Hui, Tibetan, Uighur, Hmong, Yi, Zhuang, Bu, Korean, Manchu, Dong, Yao, Bai, Tujia, Hani, Kazakh, Dai, Li, Lisu, Kawa, She, Gaoshan, Lahu, Shui, Dongxiang, Nakhi, Jingpo, Kyrghiz, Tu, Daur, Mulao, Qiang, Blang, Salar, Maonan, Gelao, Xibo, Achang, Pumi, Tajik, Nu, Uzbek, Russian, Ewenki, De'ang,

Baoan, Yugur, Vietnamese, Tatar, Drung, Elunchun, Hezhen, Menba, Luoba and the Jinuo.

According to the fifth national census, taken in 2000, the top-five ethnic minorities in terms of population are the Zhuang (with a population of 17 million), the Manchu (10.68 million), the Hui (9.8 million), the Hmong (8.94 million) and the Uighur (8.4 million) people.

Each of China's ethnic groups is distributed throughout the country, cohabiting with others in small as well as in larger regions. The minorities live in regions of the Han, while the Han inhabit regions of ethnic minorities. Over the course of history, this pattern of diffusion has developed as each ethnic group has associated with the other, making mutual exchanges. The minority population, although few, is distributed widely, mainly throughout Inner Mongolia, the Uighur, Ningxia Hui, Guangxi Zhuang and the Tibetan autonomous regions, and the Yunnan, Guizhou, Qinghai, Sichuan, Gansu, Liaoning, Jilin, Hunan, Hubei, and Hainan and Taiwan provinces, Yunnan being the most diverse (with twenty-five different ethnicities).

China's ethnic minority areas are extensive regions abundant in natural resources. The surface area of grassland in China's minority regions amounts to over 1.16 million square miles, accounting for more than 75 percent of the country's grassland. China is well known for its five distinct regions of grasslands and grazing pastures. The forested area occupies roughly 21,800 square miles, or 43.6 percent of the country; and the volume of available timber is 185.4 billion cubic feet, or more than 55.9 percent of the nation's reserves. The hydroelectricity reserve is 446 million kilowatts, or approximately 65.9 percent of China's power consumption. Moreover, there are still vast amounts of mineral resources and plentiful flora and fauna, as well as the economic benefits of tourism.

The regional autonomy of ethnic minority regions reflects the government policy that links them. This was a major political decision. On May 5, 1945, under the leadership of the established Chinese Communist Party, the first provincial-level autonomous region was designated—Inner Mongolia. Later, the People's Republic of China established in succession: the Xinjiang, Uighur, Guangxi Zhuang, Ningxia Hui and Tibetan autonomous regions. Currently, for the fifty-five ethnic minority groups, forty-four autonomous regions have been established, occupying an area of about 64 percent of China's total land mass. The Chinese government continues to implement a policy of equality with regard to the ethnic groups' languages, systems of writing and religious beliefs. All are respected and protected by law.

Over the long history of the spread of ethnic minority groups, unique

Songkrang Festival of the Dai ethnic group

cultures have formed. In terms of social customs, for example, every ethnic group has a distinct method of production and way of life reflecting modern attitudes toward clothing, food and drink, residence, marriage, etiquette and funerary practices. With regard to diet, China has about ten ethnic minority groups that eat halal foods in accordance with Islamic tradition. Funerary practices that honor the deceased include such traditions as cremation, earth burial, water burial and sky burial. Also, among the various groups the New Year's Festival tradition is richly colorful. For example, the Tibetan regional calendar includes the Lasha Shonton Festival. Groups such as the Hui and the Uighurs hold Ramadan and Eid al-Azha festivals, while the Mongolians celebrate Nadam, the Dai have the Songkrang Festival, and the Yi ethnic group has the Torch Festival.

FAMILY IDEOLOGY

For the Chinese, the concept of family holds special meaning as the idea of a warm, safe household united as one. The family consists of a loving mother and a strict father, a virtuous wife and cosseted son. Everybody is familiar with the mountains and rivers, edible delicacies and beautiful historical legends of the hometown. From this love for family and one's birthplace, a feeling of pride in country is engendered. Both the Chinese who stay at home and those returning from abroad are truly the descendants of the Yellow and Fiery Emperors and have great respect for their motherland.

China is an extremely affectionate country, placing much emphasis on family and making the Chinese a very homebound nationality. Home, family affection and reunion weigh heavily in the hearts and minds of the Chinese. The reunification of the whole family continues to be a core tradition of Chinese culture. There are sayings such as "blood is thicker than water" and "every festival, I miss my relatives twice as much." (On the days when the Spring Festival, Pure Brightness Festival, Mid-Autumn Festival and the Double Yang Festival arrive, Chinese people all miss their relatives twice as much.)

The Spring Festival is China's most celebrated annual holiday. Every year on this day family members who work or study away from home make every effort to go home. Despite distance and economic hardship, much importance is placed on going home to reunite with family. Reunion is in fact the essence of the Spring Festival. Family members sit together around a steaming dining table with festive happiness and excitement. It might be said that this is the greatest characteristic of the New Year and proof of the deep love and affection people feel for their families.

The fifteenth day of the eighth month is the Mid-Autumn Festival, which also features the tradition of family reunion. Making use of the full moon, the entire family, old and young, sit at the table and listen to the words of the grandparents as the children laugh. Bathed in moonlight, everybody shares in this domestic bliss, which lives on in the psyche of every Chinese person. Therefore, the Mid-Autumn Festival has a special place in the hearts of the Chinese, reunion being a profound symbol of sentiment.

The Chinese have been influenced by Confucianism for thousands of years, and filial piety (孝) is regarded as a Chinese household's most important virtue. The Chinese will often say, "Of one hundred things, to be filial is the first," and "A filial son is a worthy grandson." Also commonly said is "Be forever filial." The idea of being filial is representative of Chinese culture and a core concept in the hearts and minds of the people. China has always been known as a country of etiquette, with society emphasizing love and affection for relatives, friends, life and birthplace, as well as advocating respect for elders and cherishing the young as a standard of ethics. Confucian ideology encompasses eight concepts to live by: filial piety, duty, loyalty, faith, courtesy, righteousness, honesty and humility. Among these, filial piety is deemed the most virtuous. It is often said, "A loving father and filial son means brotherly friendship and respect." This attitude is an embodiment of the thousands of years of cultural moral principles used to rear the young.

In a Chinese household, the opinions of the elders are greatly respected. It is often quoted, "The elder of the family is the treasure." and "A deaf ear to the elder's speech results in nothing to see to eat." The latter phrase is particularly used, reflecting the importance of the elder's guidance of the younger generation. The Chinese family also stresses the importance of a child's education and character development. Many proverbs demonstrate these ethics, such as "A child who steals a needle as an adult will steal gold."

For a Chinese person, great importance is attached to reunion, love, the virtue of filial piety and peace within the family. The most sought-after expectation is to be in a peaceful, happy home, working contentedly, the family and all things flourishing. People who cause too much intrafamily strife create the most regret. A Chinese poem says, "If the stem is born of the root, why should one prosper at the expense of the other?" Also, when there is a conflict in the management of household affairs, it is taboo to discuss the problem in the presence of others. Therefore, it is often said, "If the house is disgraced, one should not scatter gossip to the wind." Also said is, "Harmony is precious" and "Amiability makes you wealthy." These ideas are very important to Chinese individuals as well as greatly influential for social prosperity.

Thanks to the great influence of the feudal patriarchal system, the notion of the clannish family is emphasized. This advocates, "rightly treat the respectable and the humble, the elder and the young," paying attention to "the different ways one gets along with the respectable, the humble, the elder and the young." Also addressed is position within the family's hierarchy. It is regarded as impolite, for example, if a Chinese addresses an elder by name directly. In the Chinese feudalistic society, strict concepts led to the development of the feudal ethical code of the Three Cardinal Guides (ruler guides subject, father guides son, and husband guides wife) and the Five Constant Virtues (benevolence, righteousness, propriety, wisdom and fidelity).

To reiterate the concept of family, the household clan symbol is simply the family name. These have been recorded systematically since before the Han Dynasty. The culture formed by the family name exemplifies the prosperity and stability of the family. Recording genealogy is therefore a continuing activity within the Chinese culture and an important medium for conveying the importance of the idea of kinship. Seeking the root of one's ancestry is the foundation, and discovering the relationships of the parents lets the individual know that he is not at all alone in the world. At the same time, knowing that one's actions will not disrespect the ancestors, one's success then depends on the acknowledgement and of one's ancestry, and so a Chinese person understands humility and can see how to better deal with personal relationships. Therefore, Chinese people believe that genealogy is an extremely important matter.

In the time-honored tradition of China, there has continued the pursuit of prosperity and unification. Thus, in the eyes of a Chinese person, his or her family, although very important, is no more important than the country, especially in time of war. In wartime, larger numbers of gentleman display benevolence by defending the country and show love for country as family by abandoning a small family to look after everybody. For their country's safety they offer their lives, being a proud people. In China, family and country are interwoven. And as this civilization has spent over five thousand years united as one, sentiment for family and nation has not changed.

MARRIAGE CUSTOMS

Chinese people regard marriage as one of the top priorities of life, bringing much happiness to the clan, as the family's incense will continue to burn, and maintaining a stable society. Therefore, there are many distinct kinds of marriage customs, the ceremonies having complicated aesthetics.

The traditional Chinese wedding comprises Three Letters and Six Etiquettes.

The Three Letters are a request letter, a gift letter and a welcome letter.

1. The request letter is used as a formal agreement by the parents to allow the marriage.
2. The gift letter is a detailed list of prepared gifts, including a large gift.
3. The welcome letter is the letter welcoming the bride, used by the groom on the day of the marriage when he goes to the bride's household to take her to his home.

The Six Etiquettes refers to the six protocols of traditional Chinese marriage: *na cai, wen ming, na ji, na zheng, qing qi* and *qin ying*:

1. *Na cai* is referred to nowadays as a marriage proposal. In ancient Chinese marriages, strongly emphasized was the fate of the parents and the words of the matchmaker. Therefore, for a man and woman to get married, the man had to employ a matchmaker to go to the house of the intended bride to propose the marriage.
2. *Wen ming* is usually called *he bazi*. The man inquires about the woman's surname, birthday and time of day she was born to foresee good or ill luck.
3. With regard to *na ji*, also called *guo wending* and *xiao ding*: if the names and birth data are compatible, the matchmaker will be sent to the woman's family to offer small gifts.
4. *Na zheng*, or *guo dali*, means the man's family formally sends such betrothal gifts as money, bride cake presents and pastries.
5. *Qing qi* is what we today call selection day, the date of the wedding chosen by a fortuneteller as requested by the man's family.
6. Afterward, on the day of the wedding, the groom takes a four-wheeled carriage to greet the bride. This is called *qin ying* (welcoming the relatives).

The traditional Chinese marriage ceremony involves mainly the following customs:

◈ Exchanging age charts. If the names and birth data are shown to be compatible, after the proposal of the matchmaker the two families will exchange birth information as initial proof of engagement.

◈ *Guo wending* (sending small gifts). This is a prelude to *guo dali* (sending large gifts). This usually takes place one month before the wedding ceremony. The man's family chooses a propitious day to offer three things: domestic animals, wine and gifts along with the formal letter of engagement.

◈ *Guo dali* (sending large gifts). This, the grandest ceremony, takes place fifteen or twenty days before the marriage. The man selects a fortunate day to offer betrothal money and many other gifts.

◈ *An chuang* (installing the bed). Several days before the wedding, a particularly fortunate day is chosen, because a long and happy life requires a new bed to be moved to a suitable place. Later, before the wedding day, to ensure a long and happy life, the grandmother of the bride makes up the bed, readies the mattress, lays the sheets of the dragon and phoenix, and spreads on the bed delicacies the couple enjoys, such as jujube, cinnamon sticks, dried lychee, and red and mung beans.

After the bed is installed, nobody is allowed enter the bridal chamber or touch the bed until the new couple has entered the room on the wedding night. After the newlyweds enter the room, children can sit on the bed and eat the fruits. This is called *ya chuang* (pressing the bed), and enables one to obtain one hundred sons and one thousand grandsons. The bride's brothers are then allowed to make loud noises in the bridal chamber. From antiquity it has been thought that if the new couple is not noisy they will not expel evil, so the more noise, the more expelling and bringing of good luck to the marriage.

◈ Sending the dowry. After the *guo dali*, the bride's family must send a box (dowry) to the bridegroom's family no later than one day before the wedding ceremony. This box, large or small, indicates the status and wealth of the bride's family. In addition to precious stones and jewelry, the box may contain symbols of prosperity, such as scissors (symbolizing a pair of flying butterflies), candy (indicating sweetness), a wallet and belt (meaning wealth), a flower vase (indicating blooming riches and honor), a copper basin and shoes (meaning a happy and long life), as well as quilts with embroidered dragons and phoenixes, bed sheets and pillows.

◈ *Shang Tou.* On the eve of the wedding, the couple's families mutually select a good date and time (the man's family begins an hour earlier) for the *shang tou* ceremony. This ceremony must be presided over by a man from a good life and a woman from a good life (the families independently choose people from an older generation, or friends and relatives with healthy children and a happy marriage). The newlywed couple puts on pajamas. The bride's family selects a table near a window where the moon shines through, lights dragon and phoenix candles and incense, and using lotus seeds and jujubes makes three bowls of soup, putting six or nine pieces in each bowl. Fresh fruit, roasted meat and a chicken heart are included to pay homage to the heavens. The families of the man and the woman also provide a measuring tape, mirror, scissors and a so-called dragon head mirror and cut the measuring tape with the scissors. In order for the couple's brightness to last, the good man and woman chosen by the families then comb the couple's hair saying, "One brush for the hair, two brushes for mutual respect in old age, three brushes for many descendants, and four brushes for the four strips of silver on the upmost branches of the tree." The *shang tou* symbolizes the new couple's transition into adulthood.

✿ *Ying qin* (escorting the bride). In China, escorting the bride is the climax of the wedding ceremony. Accompanied by family, relatives and friends, the bridegroom will greet the bride with a bouquet of flowers. On arriving at her house, the groom must enter the door in order to receive the bride. But first he must pass a series of intelligence and physical stamina tests, and he must recite terms of endearment or love songs. Also useful for getting in the door is to give the older and younger sisters of the bride gifts or red envelopes with money, often 10 or 20 yuan each. When the sisters are satisfied, the groom can enter the house. When the groom has entered, the sisters give the brothers of the groom tea and cake, receiving them as guests. After the groom enters, the bride follows her older sister, or bridesmaid, as she is presented her to her father. Her parents then present the bride to the groom as a formal rite of a man and woman meeting.

The new couple will first kneel, express their gratitude to the heavens, and then offer their parents tea as they bow (*kowtow*). The bride then prepares two envelopes of money (*li shi*), representing prestige prosperity and benefit. After passing through the door, she presents them to her bridegroom's sister.

✿ *Chu men* (exiting through the door). After going outdoors, the bride's older sister or the maid of honor shields the bride from the sun with a red parasol, symbolizing a flourishing branch with leaves. The older and younger sisters walk side by side, looking up to the

The bride and groom bow to each other

sky. Rice (red and mung beans may be included) is then sprinkled by them over the parasol or tossed in the air to feed the Golden Rooster, so that the Golden Rooster will eat the food and not peck at the bride. The older sister then carries the bride on her back to the marriage sedan. It is said that the bride's feet should not touch the ground for fear of bad luck. Before entering the sedan, the bride bows to the friends and relatives as a show of respect.

❖ *Guo men* (crossing the entrance). After the bride leaves her house, she pays a formal visit the groom's household, paying respects to the paternal aunt, the parents and the elders of his family.

❖ *Sanzhao huimen* (in three days returning to the entrance). On the third day after the wedding ceremony, the new couple returns to visit the bride's parents, bringing roasted pork and other gifts as offerings to their ancestors. Sometimes they even live with her parents for a day before returning to the man's home.

Modern Chinese wedding ceremonies retain some aspects of traditional customs but have been simplified. Even as new styles of wedding ceremonies emerge, in general the wedding ceremony of the Chinese continues to embody grandness, happiness and liveliness. Friends, family and the community continue to compliment the couple and wish them well. Proverbs such as "live to old age in conjugal bliss" and "give birth to a child soon" are used to congratulate the newlyweds.

Chapter 7

THE FOUR GREAT INVENTIONS

China is an ancient country with a brilliant history of civilization. The four great inventions, papermaking, printing, gunpowder and the compass, are China's substantial contributions to science and technology, and all have had much influence on the history of human development in general. Karl Marx insightfully noted that the three inventions, of gunpowder, the compass and printing, mark the arrival of a bourgeois society. Gunpowder, in fact, literally exploded on society, crushing the knights of the cavalry. The compass not only opened world markets but also allowed for colonization. Printing became the new tool of learning and for recording scientific methods and advancements as well as having great influence on psychological development.

Papermaking

In the Eastern Han Dynasty (in 105), using as a basis the then-current technology, Cai Lun invented and popularized a new method of papermaking. This forever replaced the Oracle Bone Script of the Shang Dynasty, the Western Zhou's bronze inscription methods, and the bamboo writing slips, wood documents and thick writing silks of the Spring and Autumn Period previously used to record history. The contribution of papermaking enabled the Han Dynasty to begin to flourish in economics and cultural development.

Cai Lun invented a papermaking method

Cai Lun used tree bark, hemp fiber, rags and fishing nets. Employing a series of artistic and scientific processes, he pressed them together, duplicated them and then baked the material to create a plant fiber–based product that allowed for the manufacture of a significant amount of paper. Cai Lun presented the new paper to the Han Emperor. Upon receiving it, the emperor recognized the significance of the effort and proclaimed it under the heavens and on earth. Paper made by Cai Lun was officially called Caihou paper, in 105, considered by some to be the year in which modern paper was invented.

Printing Technology

Around the period of the Tang Dynasty, people invented a method of block printing. Its concrete procedures were: cutting and shaping wood blocks, then writing the characters in reverse on tissue paper and pasting the tissue to the wood block, and doing this for every character. Then a chisel was used to carefully carve the blocks so as to create raised-character blocks with each stroke visible. After an entire wood block was carved, a document could then be printed. When printing, one first brushed ink on the surface of the carving, then used white paper to cover the block. Then, using a clean brush, one lightly brushed the back of the paper. Finally, one pulled off the paper as a completed page. After several pages were printed consecutively, they were bound into a volume, eventually to become a book. Since this method of printing used carved wood, it was also called "woodblock printing."

Bi Sheng created clay movable type for printing

Printing during the time of the Northern Song Dynasty period was improved on by inventor Bi Sheng. Based on generations of experience and through trial and error, during the reign of Emperor Ren Zong (1041–8) he created clay movable type. This implemented typesetting, greatly increasing printing efficiency, and achieving a momentous revolution in printing.

Gunpowder

In attempting to concoct pills to ensure immortality, ancient Chinese alchemists invented gunpowder. While experimenting, they accidentally discovered that the right mixture of sulfur, saltpeter and charcoal quickly burned and even exploded as it was ignited. This, in fact, is the earliest known formula for gunpowder.

At the time, there was little interest in using gunpowder for military applications.

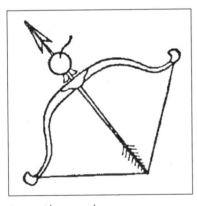

Arrow with gunpowder

Until the late Tang Dynasty and during the period of the Five Dynasties, the whole country was in rebellion. The originators of gunpowder, scholars from rich and honorable wealthy families, became destitute and homeless, and so they enlisted in the army. There they gradually developing a series of weapons that employed gunpowder. As the Song Dynasty arrived, most major cities had weapons manufacturing industries involving gunpowder. The military employed generous amounts of gunpowder with fire canisters and exploding arrows, but in the early days of gunpowder weaponry, the formidable power was limited. The hot new invention could not replace the old cold knife and sword. But after the middle of the Southern Song Dynasty, outstanding improvements were made in gunpowder artillery. And from that time on, and throughout the wars between the Song, the Jin and the Yuan, gunpowder was used more often.

Compass

The compass is a scientific instrument that uses a magnet and the polarity of Earth's magnetic field to indicate direction. The earliest compass to emerge was called a si nan (south pointer) and was commonly used during the Warring States Period. It is a carved naturally magnetic stone resembling a spoon that was balanced on a smooth chassis and surrounded by intervals of twenty-four directions. Pushed slightly, the needle would spin. When the rotations stopped, the longer end of the needle would be pointing south.

But the south-pointing compasses made with natural magnets were weak magnetically, and before the arrival of the Song Dynasty, people started using a method of artificial magnetizing, producing a north-pointing fish-shaped compass and the much more practical north-pointing needle compass. This was done by rubbing magnetite on a steel needle and using the magnetism created to point north. Later, a pan-indicating directional function was invented, this being the *luo pan* (compass), and so marking a significant stride in the history of compass development.

By the eleventh century, the compass had become a commonly used instrument for determining direction, greatly contributing to the development of ocean navigation.

The former compass—Si Nan

THE ABACUS AND CALCULATION

The abacus, a traditional Chinese calculating tool, is another significant invention of ancient China. It was in wide use in the world even before the emergence of Arabic numerals. The abacus has a history of more than six hundred years, the basis of the invention being the counting rods, which had already been in long use by the Chinese. In ancient times, people used these small sticks to calculate. The small sticks were called *suan chou*, and the method of calculation was called *chou suan* (rod calculation). But because of increases in development and production, using small sticks for calculation became unwieldy. As a result, a more advanced tool of calculation was invented—the abacus.

There are many different forms of abacus, and the materials to make them vary as well. Generally, they are made of wood or plastic, with a rectangular frame and an array of an equal number of counting beads. A horizontal rod in the middle divides the abacus into upper and lower sections, and there are straight rods down through the middle of the beads. Each rod containing the beads is commonly called a *dang*. Abacuses may have nine, eleven or fifteen rods. There are two beads above the horizontal bridge, each bead representing the number five. Below the bridge on each rod are five beads. The abacus used in finance has four beads below the bridge, each bead representing the number one.

There is a beautiful story regarding the history of the abacus. According to legend, during the reign of the Yellow Emperor there were no accountants. But after uniting the tribes, more and more material had to be accounted for. Every family and every household continuously had more things to count, creating much confusion with numbers and aggravating the emperor. Then a scribe in the emperor's palace discovered a way to use wild fruits to keep record of who killed what prey. But who expects such brightness for long—the various wild fruits after some time became rotten, throwing the accounts into chaos. Thereupon the scribe once again discovered a way of using different colored stones to keep track of the prey; this way there would be neither rot nor change in color. And so the scribe was happy, but the accounts were not rightfully safeguarded. One day, as the scribe was out on business, his son arrived with a group of children who were drawn to the pan with the beautifully colored stones. The curious children carelessly quarreled over the stones, causing the plate to fall and shatter, and the stones scattered everywhere. Once again, the accounts were ruined.

Having no alternative, the scribe crouched down to gather the stones. As he was doing this, his wife came in and said, "You should bore an eye through each stone and bind them with string; that way it won't be so confusing!" The scribe at once took out a dagger and carved a hole in each stone, and one by one strung them together. Each time there were ten or one hundred stones on a thread, a different colored stone was placed between the sets. This made it much easier to handle the financial records, enabling the scribe to know in his heart the workings of the numbers. After that there were no more fraudulent claims made from outside the palace doors.

As time went on, though, and in the wake of continuous production and forward development, the various types of prey increased, there were more and more skins and there was more variety, and so even more stones were needed. Again, the situation was troublesome and it quite vexed the scribe. When Empress Feng learned of this, she said to him, "To figure the accounts you need not use so many stones; just one hundred stones will be sufficient." Even though the scribe did not understand, Empress Feng continued, "For example, today's hunters brought back only five deer, and so you would push five stones on a bamboo rod. Tomorrow if they return with six deer, five plus six is eleven, so move one bead to the next rod. The number of beads will only be two, but in fact they represent the number 11. Each time you exceed the number ten or one hundred, simply advance one more place." The scribe then asked, "How do you record the number after advancing to the next place?" Empress Feng replied, "That's easy. Simply make a mark after advancing to the next place. For example, after adding up to the number ten, make a circle, after one hundred add two circles, after one thousand add three circles and after ten thousand add four circles. These can be called tens, hundreds, thousands and ten thousands." And so the scribe went home and made a large clay plate, gathered pearls from the belly of a tortoise, and bored a hole through each. Every strand represented ten, and as the numbers one to one hundred could be represented, he called his device the abacus. After this, it became much easier to record the numbers, giving rise to the tens, hundreds, thousands and ten thousands place values. No longer did one need so many stones.

The abacus, China's calculator, was invented five thousand years ago. Over time, continual changes have been made to the device, leading to today's method of calculation. The abacus proved fundamental to society, particularly in times of illiteracy. As long as people could understand the simple principles and operating rules of the abacus, everybody could use it. Therefore, in ancient times the abacus quickly spread to a wide area of China.

With continued use of the abacus, people summarized many computations as mnemonic devices, greatly increasing the speed of calculation. This method of calculation is called *zhu suan*, corresponding to four mathematical operations, collectively known as the laws of *zhu suan*. With regard to general calculation, the abacus can be much faster than the calculator, especially for addition and subtraction. When employed, the mnemonic devices determine which way to move the beads in relation to the problem. Calculations with the abacus are quick and convenient. Chinese stores commonly used this computing device. As the Ming Dynasty arrived, not only could the abacus perform the four basic rules of arithmetic (addition, subtraction, multiplication and division), it could also calculate land surface area and the dimensions of variously sized objects.

Because the abacus was simple to make, low in cost, and because of the easy mnemonic rules and the convenience of computation, it has been used throughout China, and also in Japan, Korea, the United States and regions of Southeast Asia.

Today we are in an age of modern computers, yet the ancient abacus still plays an important role. In China, in every type of industry there is still an abacus computation expert. Not only is the abacus convenient for math computation, it also helps to develop hand-eye coordination and using it serves as an exercise for the brain.

POST ROADS AND RELAY STATIONS

There are three types of ancient Chinese roads: the galloping road, the post road and the plank road. Of these, the post road was the most important as a passage for horse and carriage, opening up many opportunities for transportation and exchange.

Ancient post roads had several names—government road, plank road and salt road. The greatest difference between the post roads and the small intermountain roads was there was little need for necessary post road maintenance, they were more level and they were more accessible to horses and people. Rulers of successive dynasties used the post roads to send documents and transport tribute and they were the occasion for official inspections, as the use of the post roads become extremely prominent.

In ancient times, communication was undeveloped and information difficult to come by. The post road assumed the responsibility for transporting goods, moving people between distant places and delivering products and services, so helping to maintain the livelihoods of the people. At the sides of the roads, relay stations for post horses were set up. Passing carriages could stop there as well for replacement horses and vehicles. Post roads were ancient China's primary form of dry-land communication and transport.

They also served as military outposts, such as the famous Silk Road, the ancient Huguang post road, the Nanyang and Xiangyang roads, the Qinghao Passage and the ancient Mei Pass.

Post city of Jiming Mountain

Post roads and relay stations were used mainly to transmit orders, military intelligence and documents, to transport government officials, provisions, weapons, equipment, tribute, services and other goods. In addition, the relay stations provided much needed repairs for carriages, feed and fodder for horses, and lodging. When sending men with official documents and military intelligence, or possibly a government official en route, these stations provided a place of rest and a means to exchange horses. China is one of the first countries to have established efficient lines of communication and transportation. Although the history of the Chinese relay station dates back over three thousand years, not many of these cultural relics remain. Among the ones still standing is the famous Jiming Mountain station in Hubei Province's Huailai County. Another widely known structure, in the Yicheng district, is still intact.

Post stations were used in surveying the land and as checkpoints. Feudal officials used these stations when traveling on inspections. As goods and services were delivered, the direction of travel would depend on the postmark. The minister of war employed the postmarks with strict regulation. In particular, they were reserved for specific purposes, such as dispatching troops and delivering documents. All were required by the Ministry of War to display their passes so as to travel past the stations. Letter delivery by horseback also required the proper documents for the post stations. In case one needed to reach the capital of the country, or perhaps an outside area quickly, there was a form to complete. The bound document, called *ma shang fei di* ("on a horse flying"), would then travel 375 miles in a day. Documents marked as urgent traveled 250, or perhaps 375, the postmark indicating the time limit for delivery, but this method was not extensively used. In the Qing Dynasty the regulation of relay stations reached perfection, with punishable violations set by law. By the end of this period of rule, the relay stations began to be linked closely to information offices, eventually becoming one of the same.

Post stations in ancient China played a significant role and function. With the advent of post stations, communication was greatly expanded. The world of the stations involved every aspect of politics, the economy, culture, the military and the transmission of official decrees, leading to a high increase in the exchange of information. The relay stations of each dynasty had their own characteristics. The official seal was different, but the strict regulation and legal formalities were similar. Feudal monarchs used these stations to gather intelligence, collect harvest, issue commands and relay information, enabling a high level of feudal government control. At that time, the level of science and technology was restricted as compared with the speed and the amount of goods transported, but the strict level of organization and coverage compare favorably with modern-day communications and transport. It can be said that time has allowed for the development of the modern system based on the old relay station system, although, today, postal systems, highways, trade routes and the logistics of distribution have replaced the stations. On the periphery of the relay station there was also often an endless stream of horses and carriages and bustling activity, with the stations taking shape as busy little cities. In fact, there are several major cities in China today—for example, Shenyang, the capital of Liaoning Province—that owe their development to the presence of ancient relay stations.

THE SEDAN CHAIR

The sedan chair, formerly called the emperor's carriage, shoulder carriage, or yan zi, was in ancient times a unique means of transportation. According to historical documents, early types of sedan chairs were already prevalent in the Xia Dynasty. From the pre-Qin to the Jin dynasties, the ruling social class began using sedans for outings. Even though at the time their use was not widespread, a small segment of royalty increasingly employed them. In the Jin dynasty, Gu Kaizhi's painting *Admonitions of the Instructress to the Palace Ladies* vividly portrays a scene of Emperor Cheng of the Western Dynasty and imperial concubine Ban Jieyu on the same sedan chair.

Until the Tang Dynasty, the use of sedan chairs was generally reserved for royalty and for women, the elderly, invalids, and government officials.

During the Song Dynasty, sedan chair use became more widespread, and there were many new complicated designs. The well-known painting *Along the River During the Qingming Festival* depicts "main street" in the Song Dynasty capital city, Bianliang, with many sedan chairs in use. Even though they look like those carried by two people in the Han and Tang eras, the materials for later chairs were different. For example, hardwood was heavily relied on, and there were artistic decorative carvings, making the chair quite pleasing to the eye. During the Northern Song period, sedan chairs advanced yet another step in popularity.

As the later stages of the Ming Dynasty arrived, even the small landlords, as it was commonly said, preferred sedans to horseback. In the Ming and Qing dynasties, the

Wedding sedan

sedan chair developed so as to be carried by four or eight people. More and more aristocrats preferred the sedan as a means of transportation because there was less fatigue than riding in horse carriages, as the chair ride proved to be smooth, steady, and comfortable. During this period, sedan chairs became the principal means of transportation.

Generally, there were two types of ancient sedan chairs. One type had no curtain and was called the cool sedan, also the bright sedan or *xian* sedan. The warm sedan was equipped with a curtain and so was called a dark sedan. Different government sedans were manufactured with curtains of brightly colored cloth and curtained according to strict regulation. For example, in the period of the Ming and Qing dynasties, a common official could use blue or green wool to make the sedan curtain. So these were appropriately called the blue government sedan and the green government sedan. And as the sedans played different roles, they were named differently. The one used by the royal family was called a carriage sedan, sedans used by high government officials were called official sedans, and those used to escort brides to weddings were called wedding sedans.

There could be a few or many sedan chair porters, generally two to eight men. Among the common people, two carried a sedan. Government officials were allowed four to eight porters. Regulations set during the Qing Dynasty stated that officials of the third rank or higher could ride in a sedan with a pointed silver top and black curtains. Within the capital, four porters were provided, and in leaving the capital, eight men were used. Officials of the fourth rank and below could ride only in a small sedan with a tin roof carried by two people. The landlords and members of the gentry were obliged to ride in dark-painted sedans with flat roofs and black curtains. As well, there were other strict regulations regarding litters that reflected the hierarchy of feudal society.

HORSE AND CARRIAGE

With a history of at least three thousand years, the horse and carriage was another imperative mode of transportation in ancient China. Archeological evidence implies that during the Shang Dynasty two horses pulled most carriages. Toward the end of the Shang and the beginning of the Zhou Dynasty, a carriage pulled by four horses emerged. Evidence shows that the Shang Dynasty technology used in manufacturing horse carriages was relatively advanced. Carriages in the Zhou Dynasty were fundamentally the same as in the Shang period, but the structure was greatly improved on. For example, the shaft and the crosspiece became curved, more spokes were added to the wheels, and a roof was installed. The reins and mountings for the horses also developed. Leaving nothing to be desired, the Shang carriages increased the production of ornamentation, copper bells, copper spurs and various other parts. To make the carriages stronger, a number of crucial copper components were added. Wood linchpins were upgraded to copper, and the yolk carried copper reinforcement. Also used in manufacturing the carriages were lead, gold, silver, bone, shell, and animal skins, resulting in a myriad of fine detail.

Carriages of the Shang Dynasty were originally pulled by two horses, the number then gradually increasing to three, four and six. The two-horse cart was called a *pian*, and the three-horse carriage was referred to as a *can*. A carriage pulled by four horses was called a *si*.

The Western Zhou, Spring and Autumn and the Warring States periods were flourishing eras for the ancient Chinese chariot, lasting over a millennium. During this time, carriages were far stronger and ornamentation more luxurious than the carriages of the Shang Dynasty, reaching a new stage of perfection. Ancient carriages were not only employed for military purposes but also to escort royalty and were a clear indicator of power and status. This tradition continued until the final years of the Qing Dynasty where, in some northern cities, a commoner would not dare ride in a carriage without proper authority.

Interestingly enough, if we compare the spoke wheel of the war chariot from the Zhou Dynasty period with those of the Eurasian grasslands, Egypt and Southwest Asia, many similarities and even similarities in minor details are obvious. For example, the East and the West both used spoke wheels, adopting the technology to shape wood in a circle. The Pelham bit, the whip and other components are similar in manufacture, as technology spread to different regions. Methods of use and cultural restrictions are also interlinked, as all chariots were built under the jurisdiction of the ruling social elite, and the various kinds of chariots were viewed as reflecting various kinds of power. There were a few differences between the eastern and western regions' chariots, however. These were mainly in the physical dimensions of the body, the quality of the components, and the decoration, in part because of geographical distance and differences in cultural traditions.

Chapter 8

YELLOW RIVER CULTURE

The Yellow River is the second longest river in China and the fifth longest in the world. The headwaters originate in Lake Qinghai in the Kunlun Mountains, from which the river flows through nine provinces and autonomous regions: Qinghai, Sichuan, Gansu, Ningxia, Inner Mongolia, Shaanxi, Shanxi, Henan and Shandong. With a length of 3,395 miles and a drainage area of 290,000 square miles, the Yellow River is the mother river of China, producing one of the world's oldest and brilliant civilizations and one that would shape Chinese history.

The Yellow River culture occupies an extensive history. At the Xi Hongdu ruins, on the eastern bank of the Yellow River in Ruicheng County of Shanxi Province, there stone tools have been discovered that date back 1.8 million years. And so we know there was human activity even before that. At the Xi Hongdu site more than thirty stone artifacts were unearthed. To date, this is the earliest manifestation of humankind in China. But, whether existing or not during the time of the Three Sovereigns, the Xia, Shang or Western Zhou Dynasties, all civilizations emerged from the Yellow River Basin, the cradle of ancient Chinese civilization.

Beginning with the Xia Dynasty in the twenty-first century BCE, successive dynasties have established their capitals in the Yellow River Basin continuously for more than three thousand years. These are known in Chinese history as the Seven Ancient Capitals of China. Examples of these city centers are Anyang, Xi'an, Luoyang and Kaifeng.

As the capital of the Shang Dynasty, at Anyang (at that time under the jurisdiction of the Yellow River Basin) we find numerous oracle bone inscriptions. Some have been excavated, revealing the precursor of Chinese characters. Xi'an (containing Xianyang) is a well-known ancient capital encompassing a thousand-year period of history, serving as such since the times of the Western Zhou and Qin, Han and continuing to the Sui and Tang, totaling thirteen dynasties altogether. And in addition to the Eastern Zhou Dynasty moving its capital to Luoyang, the Eastern Han, Wei, Sui, Tang, the later Liang and the later Zhou dynasties all had once established

Luoyang as their capital, which is a history for this capital of over nine hundred years. And so it is known as the Ancient Capital of Nine Dynasties.

Located on the southern bank of the Yellow River, Kaifeng was established as the capital of the Northern Song Dynasty for over two hundred years. In this period of history, the political, economic and cultural center continued to be located in the Yellow River Basin. The middle and lower reaches of the Yellow River saw the country's earliest developments in science, technology, literature and art.

By 2000 BCE, bronze wares had already emerged in the Yellow River Basin. As the Shang Dynasty arrived, bronze-smelting technology reached a high level. Simultaneously, the smelting of iron began to develop, indicating a new level of productivity and development.

China's four great inventions are all products of the Yellow River Basin. From *The Book of Songs* to Tang poetry to Song prose and literary classics to a large number of cultural canonical texts, much literature has been produced in this region.

After the Northern Song Dynasty, although the economic center of the country gradually shifted from Yellow River area to the Yangtze River Valley, the Yellow River Basin and its lower plains still retained important status as regards economic and cultural development. The long cultural history of the Yellow River Basin is a rare and precious legacy for the Chinese. Not only is the Yellow River culture a jewel in China, but it has also made an indelible contribution to human civilization.

But in the wake of the glorious cultural history of the Yellow River, the area has increasingly faced major challenges, especially in modern times. Because of excessive development and environmental factors, the destruction of the ecology has been quite severe. Of all the major rivers in the country, the Yellow River is the most difficult to manage. The northwest region's barren Gobi Desert faces severe drought, as a large part of the river basin experiences semiarid to arid conditions. The northern reaches contain vast desert and see sandstorms and continuing damage to the water, as well as poor soil drainage. These factors have made for an extremely frail ecosystem, thus hindering the economic and social development of the Yellow River Basin.

Currently, management and proper development of the Yellow River is a top priority, to encourage sustainable social and economic development in the Yellow River Valley, in an effort to reinvigorate the once glorious Yellow River culture.

Hukou Waterfall on the Yellow River

THE SILK ROAD

The term "Silk Road" originated in German geographer Ferdinand von Richthofen's book *China—My Traveling Achievements*, written in 1877. The Silk Road was built by Zhang Qian to open the doors to Western regions during the Western Han period (202–138 BCE). The starting point was in Chang'an (the modern city of Xi'an), and the road continued by way of Gansu and Xinjiang to central and southwest Asia, finally reaching the Mediterranean Sea and so linking several countries (this route is also called the Northwest Silk Road, and it is different from two other routes also known as the Silk Road). Renowned for the westward transportation of goods, among which silk was the most influential, the route was called the Silk Road. The fundamental push to build it was during the two Han dynasties and it consisted of three passages: the southern, central and northern routes.

The opening and maintaining of the Silk Road has played a significant role in the exchange of both the material and spiritual cultures of China and the West. On this route, many cultural stories were exchanged between East and West. Long before Zhang Qian's route to the West, a great deal of silk had already been transported to the Western world. In ancient Rome, silk clothing had become fashionable attire for the aristocracy. Since it came from the East, silk was quite expensive, and Rome was spending massive amounts of gold to import silk. But because of its transparency, the Roman senate believed it offended public decency and so issued many orders forbidding the wearing of silk clothes. Yet the laws proved to be useless, as the desire for beauty proved irresistible. Today, on the Goddess Statue in the Pantheon and on the *Druidess of Bacchus* in the Naples Museum in Italy, one can see the elegant and beautiful silk clothing of the Greek and Roman periods.

Classic storytellers of the Roman Empire spoke of the silk-producing country of Seres, referring to China, and were greatly intrigued by Chinese silk. For quite some time, the people of Rome, and even Western scholars, were perplexed about how silk was actually produced. They believed, erroneously, that it was derived from trees, as ideas about raising silkworms and silk weaving technology did not reach the West until much later.

There has been, in general, a mutual national cultural exchange. As China bestowed exquisite and practical silk fabric on the Western world, each country in Europe

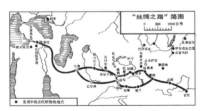

Silk Road map

returned the favor. According to ancient documents, the walnut, cucumber, shallot, coriander, pepper, poplar fruit, carrot and many other plant species went to China from Western regions. (These things in China begin with the word 胡 [hu], which refers to something coming from the north and the west minority groups. Later, the word was widely used to represent something brought in from abroad.) The documents also credit the envoy, Zhang Qian, for transplanting different species of plants from these regions. And beginning in the Han Dynasty, not only were plants imported from the West but also arriving were Roman glassworks, music, dance and acrobatics.

Along with the exchange of material culture, the spreading of spiritual cultures continued along the Silk Road. One of the world's three major religions, Buddhism, entered China as early as the final years of the Western Han Dynasty. Along the Silk road lie many Buddhist grottos, such as the famous Uch-Turpan Monastery in Kucha, the Mogao Caves in Dunhuang county, the Anxi Yulin Caves, the Wuwei Prefecture's Tianti Mountain, Yongjing County's Bingling Temple, Maiji Mountain in the Tianshui Prefecture, Cloud Ridge in the Datong Prefecture and Luoyang's Longmen (Dragon Gate). These sites reveal an integration of Eastern and Western art styles, the Silk Road bearing witness to the cultural exchange.

With its long history, the Silk Road has helped foster friendly relations, but the iron hoof of warfare also trampled on them there. People forget today the suffering while looking to link the East-West cultures. For the past few years, UNESCO has initiated a Silk Road research project, claiming the Silk Road is the path to dialogue. This project aims to positively promote exchange and cooperation between the East and West.

THE GREAT WALL

The Great Wall is an outstanding building achievement of the ancient Chinese and is included among the Seven Wonders of the World. Located in the northern part of China, the Great Wall reaches from Shanhai Pass in Hebei Province in the east to Jiayu Pass in Gansu Province in the west. It runs more than 4,100 miles (about 13,300 Chinese *li*) through seven provinces and several cities and autonomous regions, including Hebei, Beijing, Inner Mongolia, Shaanxi, Shanxi, Ningxia and Gansu. It is called the Ten-Thousand-*Li* Great Wall, which winds like a dragon across lofty mountains and passes through boundless grasslands and vast deserts until it faces the horizon of the endless sea.

According to historical documents, from the beginning of the Warring

States Period the construction of the Great Wall was a tremendous undertaking. Over twenty vassal states and feudal dynasties contributed parts to the structure. Currently, one can see the ruins of the Great Wall in many provinces, cities and autonomous regions, such as Xinjiang, Gansu, Ningxia, Shaanxi, Inner Mongolia, Shanxi, Hebei, Beijing, Tianjin, Liaoning, Jilin, Heilongjiang, Henan, Shandong, Hubei and Hunan. Among these areas, the Inner Mongolia section of the great Wall occupies over 30,000 *li* (about 9,320 miles). In the history of its construction, the Qin and Ming dynasties are especially noted.

After unifying the Six States, the First Emperor Qin began building the Great Wall. The millions of people who were employed to build the wall accounted for one twentieth of the country's population. The lack of machines during this period resulted in vast amounts of human power working under extremely arduous conditions. As a result, there were always people dying during the construction. This led to great resentment for the First Emperor's building project, as exemplified in the traditional story "Meng Jiangnu Weeps Down the Great Wall."

During the Ming Dynasty, northern invaders never stopped threatening the safety of the borders. Thus, throughout the two hundred years of the reign, the Ming Dynasty scarcely stopped working to defend itself. Of all the dynasties, these rulers spent the most time, initiated the largest engineering projects and built the largest defense systems. The Great Wall embodies China's ancient technology and building accomplishments as well as the wisdom and talent of the working people.

As time went on, the various states in power continued to build the Great Wall, mainly to deter military incursions by the minority groups in bordering regions. In theory, the Great Wall was a complex defense engineering project of ancient China to protect the people of the Central Plains and their economic and cultural development.

There still exist today several sections of the Great Wall. Badaling is located in the Yanqing area of the Beijing municipality. This particular section of the wall is the best-preserved and most complete section of the Ming Dynasty era work, being a typical representation of its construction. This was a significant mountain pass used for military affairs during the Ming Dynasty, in addition to being a major protective screen for the capital of Beijing. Ascending the Badaling section of the Great Wall, it is

The Great Wall

possible to "live high and look down"(an idiom). From here one has the best view of precipitous mountains and majestic beauty. Over three hundred major public figures have visited this section of the Wall, including Richard Nixon and Margaret Thatcher.

Shanhai Pass is the world-famous section of the Great Wall known as the entrance to the sea. Its overall length within the Great Wall is 16 miles. Included in this old twisting dragon is

The Jiayu Pass

the soul of China's flourishing reputation. The Jiayu Pass section of the Great Wall is the westernmost starting point of the Ming Dynasty building project. Built in 1372, during the five-year reign of Ming Emperor Hongwu, it is the best-preserved section of the Wall outside of city gates and served as an important stop on the Silk Road.

When compared with the other engineering projects of the ancient world, the Great Wall is unparalleled in terms of the time it took to complete, its tremendous size, the difficulty level of the construction and its cultural and historical significance.

The great democratic revolutionary pioneer of modern China Dr. Sun Yat-sen once commented on the Great Wall, "The most well-known project in China is the Great Wall . . . which is also a spectacle of the world." After visiting the Great Wall, former U.S. president Richard Nixon gave high praise, saying, "None but a great nation could make such a great wall."

As a marvel of human history, in 1987 the Great Wall was listed in the World Heritage Records. Not only does it embody a rich cultural heritage, it also provides a unique feature on the landscape. Nowadays, tourists from home and abroad are eager to climb the Great Wall, to experience the culture and to avail themselves of a view of the majestic mountains and rivers beyond. Often said with sentiment is the proverb, "One who does not visit the Great Wall is not a worthy person." Former British prime minister Howard Heath once said of his visit to the Great Wall, "China's past and future both have equal charisma . . . when I arrived at the Great Wall, I personally felt it to be far more spectacular than what I had previously seen in pictures, embroideries and paintings. To see the Great Wall is a spectacular sight."

As a symbol of China, the Great Wall stands forever on the ground of Shenzhou (the old name for China) and world civilization.

THE TERRACOTTA WARRIORS

In the spring of 1974, in the Lintong district of Xi'an City, Shaanxi Province, a local farmer was digging a well about a mile east of the of Emperor Qin Shi Huang's Mausoleum when he unearthed the ceramic head of a warrior. After further archeological excavation, it was realized that the tomb of the First Emperor and the Terracotta Warriors had been discovered, shocking the world.

At the request of the emperor, the First Emperor's Terracotta Warriors were buried in a layout of three pits. One pit contained only foot soldiers, and from east to west the pit measures 755 feet. The north-to-south width is 203 feet, and the depth is 16 feet, for a surface area of 153,500 square feet. The second pit included the cavalry, war chariots and soldiers (including archers). These special branches of the military were spread out over 64,600 square feet. The third pit was reserved for high-ranking officers, occupying 5,600 square feet. Altogether, over 7,000 terracotta figurines, one hundred war chariots, four hundred horses and over 100,000 weapons were buried. The Terracotta Warriors of the First Emperor is a grand scene, awe-inspiring, orderly in formation, and the grouping is testimony to the strength of the Qin army and its formidable weaponry.

These terracotta warriors and horses are exact copies of actual horses and figures. The terracotta figures vary in height from 5'9" to 6'5" and have well-proportioned physiques, made from molds of the bodies of actual officers of high rank in the Qin military. As with the different branches of the military, the warriors are categorized as foot soldiers, cavalry, crossbow archers and high-ranking officers. Foot soldiers in uniform carry bows and arrows on their backs. Most of the earth-made cavalry have one hand holding a halter and the other grasping a bow and arrow; they wear short pieces of armor, tight breeches and riding boots, ready to mount and go into battle at any moment. The crossbow archers are combat-ready, gazing ahead, some standing, some on one knee. The face of the officer is calm and composed, showing no fear, the demeanor of a great general. The terracotta horses stand roughly 5 feet high and are 6.5 feet long. They have large, fit bodies and well-developed muscles; their heads are held high; and the facial expressions reflect astuteness as quick battlefield steeds.

The Terracotta Warriors tell us of the First Emperor's great influence and the uniting of the powerful militaries of the Six States. The

The mausoleum of the First Emperor and the Terracotta Warriors

Emperor posthumously ordered the construction of these figurines at the expense of large amounts of labor power and financial resources, emphasizing his awesome influence during his lifetime and his absolute rule even after death.

The ruling Emperor Qin Shi Huang's posthumous status allowed for the making of the Terracotta Warriors and Horses, but in themselves these figures are of high artistic value. The figures were produced from molds of actual warriors and horses and reflect meticulous artistic skill. Their clothing and mannerisms, gestures and facial expressions are all unique. From these one can therefore determine if the statue is of an official or infantryman, or if it is the likeness of a foot soldier or a cavalry fighter. Here you will find the long-bearded veteran of the battlefield and the youthful warrior beginner. In sum, the First Emperor's Terracotta Army captures the distinct and intense characteristics of the era, not only enriching ancient Chinese culture but also holding a prominent place in the world history of art.

Crossbow archer

In 1961, China's State Council designated the Mausoleum of Emperor Qin Shi Huang a major cultural relic under state protection. In 1987, UNESCO listed the site on the World Heritage Records. An exhibition hall has been built over Pit No. 1, and the Museum of Emperor Qin Shi Huang's Terracotta Warriors and Horses now awes travelers from home and aboard.

The Terracotta Warriors has an allure that attracts people from all over the globe. Over

Terracotta warrior and horse

one hundred world leaders have come to the exhibit to see them. The first was Lee Kuan Yew, the founding Prime Minister of Singapore. On May 14, 1976, he praised it as "an astonishment of the world and the pride of Chinese nation." In 1985, while visiting the Terracotta Warriors and Horses for the second time, he left his written words, "This magnificent historical cultural relic implies a magnificent future." The former U.S. secretary of state Henry

Kissinger visited the site and remarked, "This is an unparalleled marvel of the world." Walter Mondale, former U.S. vice president, observed, "This is a genuine miracle, and all the people of the world should come here to see for themselves."

In 1978, then-mayor of Paris and former French president Jacques Chirac, said on visiting, "There are seven miracles in the world. The pits of the Terracotta Warriors and Horses are the eighth wonder of the world. As you would not visit Egypt without visiting the pyramids, you would not be regarded as having visited China without seeing the Terracotta Warriors and Horses." Since then, the international media has embraced his words of praise for the First Emperor's Tomb and Terracotta Warriors, which are now commonly regarded by the international press as the eighth wonder of the world.

The Museum of Emperor Qin Shi Huang's Terracotta Warriors and Horses can be compared to the pyramids in Egypt and the sculpture of ancient Greece, as they are all cultural treasures to the world.

THE FIVE SACRED MOUNTAINS

In ancient China people referred to the Central Plains portions of the east, south, west, north and central areas as having the "Five Sacred Mountains," namely, Eastern Sacred Mount—Mount Tai in Shandong Province, rising five thousand feet above sea level; Southern Sacred Mount—Mount Heng in Hunan Province, with a summit at 4,230 feet; Western Sacred Mount—Mount Hua in Shaanxi Province, at 7,070 feet; Northern Sacred Mount—Mount Heng in Shanxi Province, with an elevation of 6,617 feet; and the Central Sacred Mount—Mount Song in Henan Province, rising 4,724 feet above sea level.

Mount Tai, the first of the Five Sacred Mountains (also referred to as "the first mountain under heaven") is located in the center of Shandong Province, in the eastern part of China. Therefore, it is also referred to as the Eastern Sacred Mountain. Rich cultural connotation of the Ming and Qing dynasties is deeply rooted in the various styles of architecture at Mount Tai. In ancient times, Mount Tai was thought to be the Mountain of the Gods, one of the only mountains where emperors held sacrificial ceremonies. Many emperors through the ages paid personal visits to Mount Tai, where Buddhism and Taoism flourished. Throughout history, these royal visits contributed to the making of statues, temples and steles with inscriptions, leaving behind numerous cultural relics and historical sites. Personages of successive dynasties went to Mount Tai, praising the verses here that comprise more than one thousand poems. To be at Mount Tai is to step into a profound moment of Chinese history. The optimum time of year to visit Mount Tai is said to be March 11. Sightseeing here largely depends on four main spectacles—the sunrise, the jade sea of clouds, the glow of the sunset and the golden shores of the Yellow River.

Sunrise at Mount Tai

The Western Sacred Mountain, Mount Hua, lies within the boundaries of Huayin in Shaanxi Province, about 75 miles from Xi'an. The mountain consists of five main peaks: the Central Peak, the East Peak, the West Peak, the South Peak and the North Peak. From a distance, these five peaks resemble a lotus flower at the top of the mountain, giving it its name (in ancient China, *lian hua* referred to the lotus). It is also known as the strangest and most rugged mountain under heaven. In ancient times, many dignitaries came to Mount Hua to perform rites of sacrifice. These included Emperor Qin Shi Huang, Emperor Wu of the Han Dynasty, Empress Wu Zetian and Emperor Xuan-zong of the Tang Dynasty, who came to Mount Hua to conduct grand-scale sacrificial ceremonies. At the same time, Mount Hua is also a well-known Taoist site where one finds more than twenty Taoist temples. Since the Sui and Tang dynasties, poets such as Li Bai and Du Fu have written more than a thousand works about Mount Hua. April 10 is said to be the ideal time to visit. On the fifteenth day of the third month of the traditional calendar, large gatherings and celebrations take place in the temples as the sun rises over the mountain. The four seasons on Mount Hua produce a mystical and variable landscape. The different seasons can all be admired and are often referred to as Mount Hua clouds, Mount Hua rain, Mount Hua fog and Mount Hua snow.

The Southern Sacred Mountain, Mount Heng, is in Nanyue District of Hengyang City in Hunan Province. Because of the favorable climate conditions here, in contrast to that at the other four sacred mountains, the terrain is made up of deep forests and lofty bamboo. Throughout the year the site remains emerald green, displaying exquisite natural beauty, and so it has received the honorific "Great South Mountain." Mount Heng produces Clouds and Mist Tea, from a famous type of leaf known to the Tang Dynasty as Tribute Tea.

North Mount Heng of the Five Sacred Mountains is known as "the second mountain under heaven." It lies six miles south of the Hunyuan County seat of Shanxi Province and thirty-nine miles from Datong Prefecture. Mount Heng is the luxuriant mountain of modern Hebei Province. After

Shaolin Temple on Mount Song

the second reign of the Qing Emperor, jurisdiction shifted to Shanxi Province. Throughout history, successive emperors have come here to bestow their titles, including Qin Shi Huang, Emperor Wu of the Han, emperors Taizong and Xuanzong of the Tang Dynasty, and Emperor Zhenzong of the Song. Emperor Ming Taizu also came here to experience the divine essence. Mount Heng has also supported a long-standing tradition of Taoism. It is believed that here Zhang Guolao, a legendary Taoist sage, practiced the austerities required to become immortal. Mount Heng features many bizarre natural landscapes. Among these are the Bitter and Sweet Wells, located halfway up the mountain. The two wells are a yard apart, yet the water quality is poles apart. The water in one of the wells is sweet and cool, but in the other well the water is bitter and unfit to drink.

Central Mount Song is in the northwest of Dengfeng City in Henan Province. On February 13, 2004, UNESCO listed the mountain as an International Geological Park because of its undulating hills and oddly steep summits. In addition to the elegant nature and scenery here, there are also numerous places of historical interest. For example, a famous Buddhist monastery situated in Mount Song is known as Mount Song Shaolin Temple. Mount Song is also a place where kings and emperors through the ages made sacrifices. Of the Five Sacred Mountains, Mount Song has the most historical sites and cultural relics. Here we can appreciate the progress of China's eight-thousand-year history. Historic relics of the Yangshao and Longshan cultures, the Three Sovereigns and Five Kings, and the Xia Dynasty capital of Yangcheng can be found here.

Ancient emperors believed that on all Five Sacred Mountains immortals lived, so on being enthroned they paid royal visits to the mountains and conducted impressive sacrificial ceremonies. Therefore, the Five Sacred Mountains of ancient China are more than just famous summits. They also have rich historical and cultural implications.

LAKES

China is a country with many lakes, and more than 2,800 of these have areas of more than half a square mile. The total area of the lakes is 31,000 square miles. The freshwater lakes occupy roughly 14,000 square miles, accounting for about 45 percent of China's total lake area. The overwhelming majority of these are categorized as small-scale lakes. There are eleven famous lakes, with a total area of over 385 square miles. The largest freshwater lake is Poyang Lake, the largest saltwater lake is Qinghai Lake, and the greatest hypersaline lake is Qarhan Lake. Frog Lake in northern Tibet is 3.5 miles above sea level and is the highest saltwater lake in the world. It also happens to be in the vicinity of the highest freshwater lake in the world, Siling Co Lake, which is at an altitude of 3.3 miles. The Turpan Depression in Xinjiang holds the record as the world's lowest lake: Lake Aydingkol is 509 feet below sea level. Located on the border between China and North Korea, Tianchi Lake lies atop Baitou Mountain, the highest peak in the Changbai range. At 1,026 feet deep, it is the deepest lake in China.

China's most famous lakes include Poyang Lake and Dongting Lake, along the middle and lower reaches of the Yangtze River; Taihu Lake along the Yangtze River Delta; and the Huaihe River basin's Hongze Lake and Chaohu Lake. These lakes are the five largest freshwater lakes in China. There are also many saltwater lakes; the five largest in China are the well-known Qinghai Lake, Namtso Lake, Siling Co Lake, Lake Ulungur and Yamdrok Lake.

Poyang Lake, the most sizable freshwater lake in China, is located in the northern regions of Jiangxi. It empties into the Yangtze River by way of Hukou Falls and has inflows from the Gan River, Xiu River, Rao River, Xin River and Fu River. As a wetlands of global importance, Poyang Lake is the main reservoir of the Yangtze River and plays a crucial role in adjusting and retaining immense amounts of floodwater, protecting the biodiversity of the area. As one of the ten ecological protection areas in China, it is also an ecological area of global importance. It has been appointed by the World Wildlife Fund to play a key role in protecting regional and national ecological concerns. Moreover, the environment, water quality and climate here make it a suitable place for migratory birds to pass the winter, gradually leaving during the month of April. Today, the conservation district is home to over three hundred species and some one million birds. Among these species, fifty are rare breeds, making it the world's largest bird conservation district. Further, the largest flock of white cranes has been found living here. In 2002, the number of white cranes living through the winter in Poyang Lake was up to four thousand, accounting for 95 percent of the world's white cranes. Accordingly, Poyang Lake is called the World of the White Crane and the Kingdom of Rare Birds.

Poyang Lake becomes the world of the white crane

Dongting Lake was originally the largest freshwater lake in China, but in the last century the volume of the lake has decreased considerably, so that it is now China's second largest freshwater lake. Stretching over Hunan and Hubei provinces, the lake covers an area of 7,250 square miles, of which 1,060 square miles are natural lake, and embankments shape 463 square miles of an inner lake. In 1954, 1964, and the 1970s, three stages of construction to the lake's infrastructure allowed for water management and the creation of farmland. Since then, Dongting Lake has become one of China's most important regions of grain production and freshwater fisheries.

Taihu Lake, the third largest freshwater lake, is located in southern Jiangsu Province and the northern region of Zhejiang Province. It consists of a system of 180 interconnected lakes of various sizes. Together with the tributaries and outflow of rivers, the lakes form an integrated waterway, which makes it useful for shipping, irrigation and water-level adjustment.

Hongze Lake is China's fourth largest freshwater lake and is located at the lower reaches of the Haihe River in the western region of Jiangsu Province. It is a suspended lake in that the bottom is 13 to 26 feet above the Subei Plain in the east. The main tributary of Hongze Lake is the Haihe River, which has suffered from great floods since ancient times. So the history of the local people contending with rising waters is colorfully portrayed in stories and legends. Hongze Lake incorporates the Dujiangyan irrigation project, with a history of over two millennia, which was constructed almost entirely of columnar basalt. Maintained by successive dynasties, the project is 42 miles long as it twists and turns over the landscape, an aquatic version of the Great Wall.

Chaohu Lake is located in the central part of Anhui Province. Covering an area of 297 square miles, it is the largest lake in the province as well as the fifth largest freshwater lake in China. The major tributary rivers are the Hangbu River, Fengle River, Shangpai River, Nanfei River and Zhegao River, and by way of the Yuxi River flows into the Yangtze River. The lake is beneficial as a reservoir and is used for irrigation purposes. In addition, the lake's whitebait (similar to herring) is widely popular.

Qinghai Lake is not only China's largest inland lake but also the largest saltwater lake. It is located in the northeast part of Qinghai Province, and roughly thirty rivers surround the region. On the eastern shore of the lake lie two smaller lakes—Gahai Lake, a saltwater lake with an area of four square miles, and Erhai Lake, a freshwater body of 1.5 square miles. Every December, the surface of Qinghai Lake freezes over with ice eighteen inches thick, and it stays frozen for six months. Five small islands lie at the center of the lake, of which Haixin Mountain Island is the most sizable. Bird Island, located in the western part of the lake, covers an area of 1,184 square feet and is an ideal place for the habitat and breeding of over ten varieties of migratory birds, including the bar-headed wild goose, fish gull and the brown-headed gull, in all accounting for more then one hundred thousand birds. Currently, an environmental protection reserve area is being established on Bird Island.

In Tibetan, Namtso Lake means Lake of Heaven. It is the second largest saltwater lake next to Qinghai Lake. The water turns a deep azure color under a clear and cloudless blue sky, hence its name. Located north of Lhasa in Tibet, the lake borders the districts of Damxung and Baingoin. As the largest enclosed lake in Tibet, the primary water sources are precipitation and snowmelt.

In Tibetan, Reflecting Demon Lake refers to Siling Co Lake. As the second largest lake in Tibet, it is located in the border region between Baingoin County and Shenzha County. With an area of 633 square miles, the lake lies 2.8 miles above sea level, its greatest depth being 108 feet. The drainage basin occupies an area of over 17,580 square miles.

The Xinjiang Uighur Autonomous Region contains Ulungur Lake, which is located in the northern part of Junggar Basin. The lake is triangular in shape, with a width of 18.6 miles from south to north, and a length of 21.7 miles from east to west. The lake occupies an area of 319 square miles. With an average depth of 26 feet, it has long been known as the Gobi Sea, and it is well-known for its delicious Fuhai fish.

The pure and beautiful Qinghai Lake

Lake Yamdrok is situated on the southern bank of the Yarlung Tsangbo River in Nagarze County of Lhokha Prefecture. The lake covers an area of over 270 square miles and is 2.8 miles above sea level. The average depth is more than one hundred feet, and in some places it reaches twice that. The lake is fed by the surrounding snow-capped mountains and has no outlet. A dynamic balance is found between the melting snow and the evaporation of lake water, making Yamdrok Lake world-famous for its beautiful waters.

Yamdrok Lake

Chapter 9

LAO TZU

Lao Tzu was a native of Ku County (modern-day Henan Province's Lu city) in the State of Chu at the end of the Spring and Autumn Period. His given name was Er, and his surname was Li. As the story goes, he was born with white eyebrows and a beard, and so people called him Lao Tzu (old master). Lao Tzu assumed the responsibility of Keeper of the Archives for the royal court of Zhou. During this period, Confucius often consulted Lao Tzu about rituals. Later, after witnessing the gradual decay of the kingdom, Lao Tzu could not be found.

Lao Tzu is traditionally regarded as the founder the Taoist school of thought. His theory was further developed by Chuang Tzu. His book *The Way of Lao Tzu*, also called *The Book of Tao*, compiled and written in the early and middle stages of the Warring States Period, inaugurated the era of a now-ancient Chinese philosophy that has exerted an important influence from ancient to modern times on China's ideology and culture.

Lao Tzu's thinking mainly includes the following:

Tao (the way) is the basis of all living things

Lao Tzu created the philosophy of *tao*. He is regarded as the founder of the ontology of ancient Chinese philosophy in seeking a creator and the origins of the structure of the existing world. The *tao* is the foremost ideological concept of Lao Tzu. The character for *tao* appears seventy-three times in the book *The Way of Lao Tzu*, continually indicating profound meanings.

Tao is described as the myriad of all nature under the sky. "*Tao* gave birth to the one, from one came two, two birthed three, forming a multitude of all living things." Without form and content, *tao* is independent of all things, moving in cycles and by no means ceasing. *Tao* refers to not only the essence that is the material basis of the universe but also to the general laws and fundamental principles. Lao Tzu believed all things are in the process of changing and that it is impossible to perceive and acknowledge the *tao* eternally or at any given time. Lao Tzu's thinking embodies an unadorned dialectic. He believes that all living things are changing, contradicting, integrating and mutually transforming. He also says, "All things are of birth, birth itself is from nothing." He continues, "As all people recognize beauty under the heavens, the idea of ugliness exists. As virtue is recognized as virtue, this gives rise to wickedness. Existence mirrors nonexistence, difficultly achieves success, long and short test each other as high determines low. Sound becomes harmony, back follows front." He is also quoted as saying, "Calamity is dependent on fortune; in fortune lurks calamity."

Nature's laws of *wuwei* (inaction and action)

On the basis of *tao*, Lao Tzu proposes two key principles: the *tao* of the heavens and the *tao* of man. The *tao* of the heavens follows the laws of *wuwei*, or nature's inaction and action. The *tao* of humans relates to mankind allowing nature to take its course. These theories of natural law (sometimes referred to as heavenly law) and *wuwei* are the foundations of *taoist* thought.

Tao is the root of all things in nature, therefore humans, the earth and the heavens must follow the way of *tao*. But *tao* itself is not governed and acts on its own will, following the laws of nature. Here nature does not refer to nature in a physical sense but rather indicates involuntary action, which opposes human effort. Lao Tzu believed the heavens, earth and humanity follow the common law of the *tao* of nature, emphasizing that everything should accord with nature and obey the common code of humankind in all matters of the universe.

Since the *tao* of the heavens, nature and humankind follow this natural law, Taoism pursues the principal of nature without action (*wuwei*). Lao Tzu said, "*Tao* never acts; yet through it all things are accomplished." *Wuwei* does not mean that nothing is being done but rather indicates nature's unfaltering will to transform all living things in the course of time, so as to achieve action without action.

The notion of the *wuwei* of nature is demonstrated in modern political ideology in the idea of altruism. In relation to human philosophy, *wuwei* indicates selflessness and humility. Therefore, it leads one not to desire to know contentment. To be humble makes one capable of modesty. Lao Tzu advocated conduct to be modest and prudent, as well as yielding and weak. But yielding and weak are simply means of using the weak to overcome the strong.

The Political Ideology of a Small Country with a Small Population

Lao Tzu lived during the Spring and Autumn Period and was witness to the degeneration of feudal religious rights. His political ideology reflects his dissatisfaction and resentment of the social reality. He opposed violence

Lao Tzu

and theft and objected to justice by rule of law. He believed that the Confucian doctrines of righteousness, courtesy and knowledge could not resolve society's dilemmas. Therefore, to reinstate *tao* as the ruler was his fundamental goal. Lao Tzu opposed the endless catastrophes of war, having rather a praiseworthy belief in human ideology. He surmised that a small number of greedy rulers with inadequate resources were the leading faction in war; therefore, to overcome the disaster of war, people must avert their appetite for expansion if they are to fundamentally improve humanity. Certainly, he was not opposed to a righteous war, yet he reminded the monarchs not to go to extremes. Even though one may stand up and be righteous, one must not admire conflict and allow his character to become warlike. This, in Lao Tzu's view, would be dreadful. And so, although the war may prevail, there must be sympathy for the victims at the funerals.

While criticizing social reality, Lao Tzu paints the picture of an ideal society in a small country with a small population. To his mind, one need not use people as tools but rather allow them to die in defense of their homes and not relocate them to other regions. He believes that despite the fact that sedans exist, one need not ride in them; that while there may still be weapons, they need not be brandished; and that one should return to tying the rope for its intended use. People should be content with their food, pleased with their clothing, satisfied with their homes and take pleasure in their daily tasks. The neighboring countries may hear each other's roosters and dogs until death without ever associating with them. In Chinese intellectual history, Lao Tzu is the first thinker to criticize overall and speak against unreasonable politics, and at the same time offer a conception of an ideal society.

Lao Tzu and his taoist thought have exerted a lasting influence on China, and his philosophy became an important philosophy, coexisting with Confucianism. In ancient China, when an intellectual or minister of the state was at a low in his career or personal life, he would often seek guidance and comfort from Lao Tzu's principles. The philosophy of Lao Tzu not only still exists in China, but it has also had extensive influence throughout the world. With the passage of time, people have more and more come to recognize the value of his ideas about inaction and respect for natural law.

CHUANG TZU

Chuang Tzu (369–286 BCE) was given the name Zhou and was a native of the State of Song in the Warring States Period. A well-known thinker, philosopher and writer, he was the chief spokesman for Taoism. He promulgated and developed the philosophical thought of Lao Tzu, becoming the founder of the Chuang Tzu School of Thought during the pre-Qin Dynasty era. His theory encompassed almost every aspect of the social life of the time, but for its fundamental aspects he reverted to the philosophy of Lao Tzu. Successive generations have called them together, "Lao Chuang," their credos collectively known as the Lao Chuang Philosophy.

Chuang Tzu inherited and continued with development of the knowledge of Lao Tzu and Taoist thinking, forming his own distinctive philosophical ideology marked by a unique style of study and writing. He considered Tao as surpassing all space and time and of an infinite noumenon, existing in all living things and omnipresent. Its current form is within all things; it is the origin of the myriad of the heavens and natural law. On the politics of *wuwei*, in order for humanity to survive, Chuang Tzu advocated a return to a plain and simple coexistence. He wrote, "The heavens, the earth and myself are born of the same, thus all living things and myself are one," as he contemplated spiritual boundaries and advocated an unfettered peaceful consciousness.

In Chuang Tzu's opinion, the real essence of life is involuntary nature. Therefore, one need not instruct and regulate but rather erase matters, disregard measures, neglect intention, and resist opportunity and distinction. Such being the case, there is no use of politics to disseminate the idea of propriety and righteousness. This governed advice and education creates a phony person, Chuang Tzu believed, and therefore we need to abandon it.

Maintaining that benevolence and righteousness, as well as differentiation between right and wrong, were a punishment upon the people, Chuang Tzu attacked the righteousness of the ruler concept and the rule of law. He sharply criticized propriety, law, authority and power. His incisive view suggests concise criticism, as in the quote, "As long as the sage never dies, the bandits will excessively plunder." And "A small thief is put to death, but he who steals a country is a monarch."

With regard to humankind's way of life, Chuang Tzu upheld nature and advocated a spiritual condition of "coexistence with the heavens and the earth and myself as all living things." Furthermore, he believed the utmost frontier in human life is to be free and content, with unconditional spiritual liberty, and he placed blame on material goods and hypocritical fame. The thoughts and allegations of Chuang Tzu exerted a profound influence on later generations and became a precious spiritual wealth of information in the history of human thinking.

Founded in taoist thought, Lao Chuang philosophy is the only philosophical ideology that can stand as an equal beside Confucianism and Buddhism as one of the great theoretical frameworks of ancient China.

Chuang Tzu's influence on later generations is not only present in today's philosophy but also in modern literature. His political claims and philosophical thinking are by no means dull and dry preaching. His writing contains vivid images and wit in humorous fables, which he makes alluring by throwing off restraint in the sea of literature. His book reads like a collection of folklore tales. Created with great imagination, these fables are inspired by strong artistic intent.

The structure of Chuang Tzu's articles is quite idiosyncratic, as well. In general, it is loose and always elicits unexpected feelings. The style of his writing is his own, changeable and without limit. At times, sections of his works are arranged as he wished and seemingly unrelated, but one finds the ideas to be embodied from beginning to end. The syntax is quite pliable, things are written in sequence or in reverse, perhaps long or short, using vivid words and minuscule details. In addition to irregular rhyme, the writing style is full of lavish expression and innovation.

Chuang Tzu preserved his moral integrity during his lifetime and lived a poor reclusive life, inheriting and developing the Taoist ideology of Lao Tzu. He was not only a philosophical master but also a talented literary virtuoso. In *Butterfly Dream* he does not separate dream from reality. He once had a wonderful debate with Huizi, asking him, "How do you know whether the fish is happy?" It is said that upon the death of his wife Chuang Tzu sang songs accompanied by drumming on a bowl.

In a fluent and free writing style and with the use of vivid images, and stemming from a unique imagination and a broad-minded temperament, the work of Chuang Tzu gives readers a feeling of transcending worldliness and of lofty sweetness. He develops a school of his own in the history of

Chinese literature. His syntax structure breaks away from the style of quotations and signifies the development of pre-Qin prose to a mature level. It is often said that *The Book of Chuang Tzu* represents the highest achievement of pre-Qin Dynasty prose.

Chuang Tzu wrote a book of over ten thousand words called *The Book of Chuang Tzu,*

Chuang Tzu

which attests to the fact that philosophical ideology and literature in China prospered at a profoundly high level during the Warring States Period. The work is a treasure among the Chinese classics. Therefore, Chuang Tzu is not only a famous thinker in the history of philosophy but also a brilliant literary figure of China. Whether on philosophical ideology or literary language, he has exerted a deep and profound influence on thinkers and writers in China and is of high stature among them.

CONFUCIUS

During the Spring and Autumn and Warring States periods, there emerged in China a philosopher and educator named Confucius.

Confucius, whose surname was Qiu and given name was Zhongni, was a native of the State of Lu (now part of Shandong Province). When he was three years old, his father died of illness. His mother then relocated, bringing him to the imperial city of Qufu, the capital of the state. Both could depend on each other, yet they experienced a life of poverty. At about the age of thirty, Confucius started a private school. He is is said to have risen to the position of Justice Minister of the State of Lu around the age of fifty. But before long, because of the political turbulence in Lu, he was forced to leave the state after three months in his position. This prompted him to travel with his students to other states and he lived fourteen years in exile. In his later years, he returned to the State of Lu and spent the remainder of his life lecturing and compiling ancient texts.

Confucius spent most of his life in the field of education as a famous teacher in ancient China. It's been said that he once had over three thousand students, among whom seventy-two were men of prominent achievement. Confucius started private schools, changing the government standard, and had great influence on education in China. He compiled six books, including: *The Book of Poetry, The Book of History, The Book of Rites, The Book of Changes, The Book of Music* and *The Spring and Autumn Annals.* These classics were his teaching materials as he worked to preserve the developing Chinese culture.

In his forty years as an educator, Confucius accumulated much teaching experience. He expressed many thoughts and propounded principles on education and instruction that have great significance today. For example, his belief in teaching students in line with their ability implies adopting different methods of teaching in light of the various dispositions of students. Teaching without discrimination means that regardless of whether a student is rich or poor, a sage or a simpleton, the individual should be treated like all the others, irrespective of background. Confucius also expected teachers to be insatiable in learning and teach with tireless zeal, meaning one should never feel content in learning or fatigued in teaching. He earnestly practiced what he advocated—when his students didn't understand, he always patiently explained until they could fully comprehend. Another conviction of Confucius was that if three of us are walking together, then one should be my teacher. He advised people to be modest, believing that when a group is walking together, one can most certainly learn from the others.

Confucius was not only a great educator but also a great philosopher, his thoughts reflected in *The Analects of Confucius*. Most likely completed during the initial stage of the Warring States Period, after his death, the book was arranged and compiled from the recollections of his disciples and their students. The contents touch on many aspects of life, including philosophy, politics, economy, education, literature and art, and the book is a classic Confucian text.

The core of Confucianism is benevolence, and this word appears 108 times in *The Analects of Confucius*. It was used often by his followers. The benevolent love for others—to love a person is the origin of benevolent thought—is the nucleus as well as the ultimate goal.

Benevolence in politics is demonstrated as moral behavior. From within his heart, a ruler must love the people and establish a benevolent government that is in the best interests of the subjects. Teaching without discrimination, ensures that anybody, despite financial status, has the right to an education. In modern times, benevolence also refers to *zhong* (loyalty), *shu* (kindheartedness), *xiao* (filial piety) and *ti* (fraternal love). Being loyal means being faithful and honest. Kindheartedness is the doctrine of tolerance and forgiveness as put forth in *The Analects of Confucius*. These are exemplified by the following: putting oneself in the place of another; wishing to establish oneself while seeking also to establish others; and not doing to others what you would not have done to you. All of these concepts instruct people to stand in somebody else's shoes, to consider, show compassion, understand and help others. Filial piety refers to respecting one's parents and elders. Fraternal love relates to love and respect for brothers and fathers. Confucius believed that filial piety and fraternal love are the foundations of benevolence, asking, "How can a person who doesn't love his or her family love others?" So it can be seen that the benevolence Confucius spoke of is a kind of altruism toward the masses, in the realm of ethics translating to putting others before oneself. Confucian thoughts are revealed in *The Book of Rites*, Commonwealth of the State:

> All men love and respect their own parents and children, there is caring for the old, duties for adults and education for the youth. There is means of support for the widows and widowers, the disabled and all who find themselves alone in the world. Every man and woman has a distinct role in society.

Then how can we achieve benevolence? Confucius preached, "Restrain yourself and

Confucius

return to the rites; do not look at what is contrary to propriety; do not listen to what is contrary to propriety; do not speak about what is contrary to propriety; and do not act in any way that is contrary to propriety." This propriety is not as we know it today but rather an etiquette, a general criterion for the way people should regard others and for their actions and speech, diet, dress and living conditions, so as to conform to the social norm. Propriety implies having the ability to get to the root of a problem and help people to discriminate between right and wrong and disgrace and honor, the heart filling with virtue. Furthermore, propriety is pliable and does not rely on enforcement but rather the strict self-regulation of one's own heart.

The whole of society could be in harmony if everybody, from monarch to commoner, abided by the law and behaved discreetly. And so the core of propriety is using proper titles: namely, clarifying the ranks as regards status, privilege, responsibility and accepted code of behavior. Confucius further said, "Let the ruler be the ruler, the minister be the minister, the father be the father, and the son be the son." In other words, every title contains certain implications that constitute the essence of the duties for each. The ruler, minister, father and son should follow their respective paths, thus maintaining the key social order of Chinese feudal society. Confucius always judged people's thoughts and behaviors by *yi* (righteousness), which in essence means conforming to propriety. Without propriety, one's actions are not just.

When Confucius passed away, every dynasty thereafter held memorial ceremonies and constructed temples honoring him throughout the land.

During the Western Han Dynasty, Emperor Gaozu Liu Bang held for the first time the Tai Lao (grand sacrifice), an enormous ceremony that offered sacrifices to Confucius, the heavens and the Yellow Emperor. In feudal times, this became known as the Three Kingdoms Sacrifice.

During the Western Han Dynasty, Confucianism became the orthodox cultural belief system, and it remained so for over two thousand years of feudal society in China, greatly influencing the ideology, lifestyle and values of Chinese citizens.

In recent years, the world has seen a fever of cultural development of Confucianism, Chinese nationalism and tradition. There are over 140 Confucius Institutes in fifty countries thus far. During the International Culture of Confucius Festival in 2005, a grand global memorial ceremony was held. On June 23, 2006, the Confucius Educational Award, set up by UNESCO and in the name of Chinese government, was offered in the city of Qufu in Shangdong Province, the hometown of Confucius. It was the first time that an international award has been named after a person of Chinese nationality.

MENCIUS

Mencius (372–289 BCE), whose given name was Ke and whose courtesy name was Zi Che or Zi Ju, was a great thinker in ancient China and one of the main promulgators of Confucianism during the Warring States Period. *The Book of Mencius* is the expression of his opinions, compiled and edited by Mencius and his students. The work focuses on his words, political opinions and actions with regard to Confucianism. Mencius continued with and developed Confucian thought, becoming a master. He was called the Second Saint, Confucius being the first. Confucius and Mencius were called jointly Kong-Meng. Mencius's theory was based on *The Analects of Confucius*, and conveyed the idea of benevolent governance while advocating the moral rule of a country. In the Southern Song Dynasty, Zhu Xi combined *The Book of Mencius, The Analects of Confucius, The Great Learning* and *The Doctrine of the Mean* to produce *The Four Books*. From then until the Qing Dynasty, the contents of *The Four Books* was essential to the imperial examination.

When Mencius was three years old, his father passed away, leaving his mother to raise him through many hardships. She was very strict with her son. Still, many interesting stories have been passed down over thousands of years about how she moved their household three times to provide him with a better environment in which to learn. Her weaving talent is also a subject of folklore. In later generations, through these stories she became a paragon for mothers raising children.

The thinking of Mencius can be summarized as follows:

1. The idea of the citizen

"The citizen is most precious, the state is second and the monarch is of least importance." Mencius' ideals insist that a ruler ought to protect the populace and ensure people's rights. He also endorsed the overthrow of tyrannical regimes.

2. The theory of benevolent governance

Mencius inherited and further progressed the Confucian idea of moral governance, developing the doctrine of benevolent governance, which became the core of his political ideology. In order to ease the tension of social contradiction and safeguard the long-term benefits of the feudal governing class, he applied the principles of *qin-qin* (amiability) and *zhang-zhang* (eldership) to politics.

In some regards, Mencius strictly differentiates the ruler from the class that is ruled, believing, "Those rule who labor with the mind; those who work with physical strength are ruled." He lays out a fixed system of hierarchy, from the rightful emperor to the common people, in accordance with the doctrines of the Zhou Dynasty. He compares the relationship between the ruler and the ruled to that of parents and their children, proposing that a ruler should care for the people's suffering, and the people should respect the ruler as their parents. Mencius believed this to be an ideal political system. If the ruler governs the state by benevolence, he is fully supported by the people. But if a ruler neglects the life and death of his subjects or imposes oppressive rule, he must be overthrown. The concrete substance of benevolent governance is quite comprehensive: it includes economics, politics, education and the unification of the country, becoming one thread in the framework of the life of the citizen.

Mencius maintained that the treatment of a populace is extremely important and bears the weight of the rise and fall of a nation. He attached great importance to ambition as well as to opposition by the people and used many historical events as examples. This concept elaborated on the crucial importance to a country's gains and losses. He said, "Benevolent government must first create geographic boundaries." Mencius advocated the dividing of cropland and implementing an equal-field system, which would be based on a feudalistic natural economy. Each family of every

Mencius

household would be given a small agricultural base, thus forming a system of serfdom labor and taxation. A family would be given a plot of five *mu* (one-fifth of an acre), with one hundred *mu* completing a field, so as to allow for self-sufficiency in food production and clothing. Mencius believed that "The way of the people is this: if they have a certain livelihood, they will have a fixed heart. If they have not a certain livelihood, they will not have a fixed heart. As long as people have permanent property and land designated for them to live on, they will live in peace and work happily, and only then will they not break criminal laws or perpetrate outrages."

In Mencius' opinion, once the material life needs of people are guaranteed, the government can establish schools and educate them on filial piety, civic duty and just conduct, guiding them to be kindhearted. Thus, the positive moral styles of *qin-qin* and *zhang-zhang* are exemplified in his words, "The work of one's duty lies in what is easy, while people seek after what is difficult."

Mencius also advocated benevolent governance by a ruler to secure the support of his people, this giving him the advantage of unparalleled rule. Mencius felt that this benevolent governance resides with rulers who have merciful hearts. He said, "Ancient kings were merciful, therefore their governments were also merciful." He believed a ruler should have a store of great sympathy and kindheartedness. He maintained that, in general, one should be affectionate to parents and benevolent to people and to "Honor the elderly as one's own aged parents and care for the children of others as we do our own." In politics, the policy of benevolence is an embodiment of kindheartedness.

Mencius weaves ethics and politics into a solid fabric, emphasizing virtue and accomplishment as the fundamentals of just governance. He also said, "The root of the kingdom is in the State, the root of the State is in the family, the root of the family being the individual." The theory of "Self-cultivation, Family Harmony, State Governance and World Peace" as discussed in *The Great Learning* was developed from the thinking of Mencius.

3. Moral ethics

Mencius generalizes ethics into the four categories of benevolence, righteousness, propriety and knowledge. He says there are five kinds of human relationships. He says, "Between father and son there should be affection;

between ruler and subject, righteousness. There should be an allowance for differences between husband and wife, a proper order among old and young, and there should be fidelity between friends." He believed that among the concepts of benevolence, righteousness, propriety and knowledge, the former two are most important and are the foundation of filial piety and fraternal love. Filial piety and fraternal love, in turn, are the fundamental ethics on which are based a good relationship between father and son, as well as among brothers. Mencius considers that if each person in society is tolerant of the other through benevolence and righteousness, a credible guarantee will be provided that the feudal system will remain stable and the country unified.

In order to clarify the origins of these moral ethics, Mencius proposed the idea of the innate goodness of the individual, believing that, although there are different social classes, the human characteristics remain the same. He adds, "Thus, all things which are the same in kind are like one another; why should we doubt man to be the solitary exception? The sage and we are of the same kind." While discussing general human nature, Mencius equates the status of the ruler and the ruled, keeping up with the historical trend of slave emancipation and the social transformations of the era. His was an in-depth understanding of the intensity of human thought and a tremendous boost to the development of ethical ideology.

MO TZU

Mo Tzu (ca. 468–376 BCE), whose given name was Di, was a native of Teng-zhou in Shangdong Province. A well-known thinker during the Warring States Period, he was the founder of a system of education called the Mohist School. He spoke about indiscriminate love, nonaggression, esteem and frugality. His thoughts were handed down in the book bearing his name, Mo Tzu. The book consists of two sections: one combines the words and actions of Mo Tzu with the expressions of his thinking, representing an earlier stage of the Mohist School; the other comprises six chapters, generally known as the Six Teachings or the Six Disciplines, which stress epistemology and logic, as well as a great deal of natural science, and representing a later stage of the Mohist School. The influence of the Mohist School was as great as that of Confucius at the time, and, like Confucianism, it was regarded as an orthodox school of thought.

The main ideology of Mo Tzu includes the following:

Indiscriminate love and nonaggression
Indiscriminate love embodies equality and humanity. Mo Tzu requires that the ruler and subjects, father and son, and brothers get along with each other equally. "One should love others as one loves oneself." He believed that the existence of torment, insult and arrogance between the strong and weak, rich and poor, noble and humble is due to the fact that they do not mutually love each other.

The will of the heavens and spirits
Advocating the will of the heavens and the existence of spirits is another distinguishing feature of Mohist thought. Mo Tzu believes that one aspiration of the heavens is to love people unconditionally. He says "No matter young or old, noble or humble, all are subject of the heavens" and "The heavens love the people deeply." Mo Tzu also points out that if a ruler disobeys the will of the heavens, he will be punished, whereas if he is in compliance he will be rewarded. Not only did Mo Tzu firmly believe in the existence of spirits, he also thought that spirits punish the deceptive but reward the benevolent ruler and aristocrat. Mohism embraces the concept of human rights and places restrictions on monarchy, which is a main tenet of this philosophy.

Identification with the superior and the virtuous
Identification with the superior means that common man and ruler should respect the intention of the heavens, creating a righteous government. Identification with the virtuous requires the selection of virtuous people as officials and rulers. Mo Tzu proposes that a king should choose people of high moral standard, and common people should obey the administration of the king. Furthermore, he suggests that rulers understand the conditions or feelings of the masses so that kindness will be rewarded and violation punished. He requires rulers to pay more attention to the virtuous and place the talented in important positions, neglecting the unworthy. Mo Tzu pays much attention to the identification of the virtuous, which is considered the core of good governance. He strongly opposes nepotism and supports nominating ethical people without prejudice. He suggests, "Officials will not likely always be noble, and people will not likely be forever humble."

The economy of expenditures and funeral rites
The economy of expenditures is an opinion emphasized by Mohists, who strongly opposed the extravagance of rulers and aristocrats. They were especially opposed to the custom of the ceremonial funeral favored by Confucians. They believed that rulers and aristocrats should live thrifty

and simple lives like that of Yu the Great (Da Yu) of ancient times. Mo Tzu required that his adherents practice what they advocated in this regard.

A key contribution to Mohist philosophy is epistemology. Mo Tzu maintains that cognition is based on what one sees and hears. In his view, judgments of the existence or nonexistence of things should not depend on individual assumptions or solely the perceptions of others. He emphasizes taking indirect or direct experiences and social effects as a guide, while also striving to overcome subjective prejudice. With regard to the proper names of things, he feels they should be not just in name but also in reality. He also suggests that the validity of epistemology is seriously limited. Mo Tzu feels that a belief in the existence of spirits and demons is based on the idea that some people say they have seen them.

As an important pioneer in the framework of logical thinking in ancient China, Mo Tzu adopted deductive methods to establish and demonstrate one's own ideas of politics and ethics. He is the first in the history of Chinese philosophy to employ the ideas of debating, classification and reason, proposing that debating be addressed as a special field of study. Although the idea of argument proposed by Mo Tzu refers to the techniques of debating, to debate one also needs to understand the classification of and reason for objects and ideas. Therefore, debating belongs to a category of logical analogy and argument. Mo Tzu also applies analogical methods to lay bare an opponent's self-contradiction. Owing to Mo Tzu's ideas regarding enlightenment, Mohism has become established as a tradition that respects reason and was the first complex system of logic in ancient China.

Mo Tzu also contributed a great deal to science and technology. For example, as regards the theory of the cosmos, he believes that the universe is a continuous macrocosm and that any individual or part is an integral component. He proposed the concept of space and time existing as continuous and endless, and consisting of the smallest units. Among these, the infinite embodies the non-finite, and continuation embodies non-succession.

In the field of mathematics, Mo Tzu is the first scientist in Chinese history to use a high level of reasoning to address mathematical computation. He presents a series of propositions and definitions in mathematics with great

Mo Tzu

abstraction and preciseness, as, for example, the definitions of multiplication, equivalence and squares.

With regard to physics, Mo Tzu's research involved the subdivisions of mechanics, optics and acoustics, giving rise to the concept of inertia. He made many important discoveries and summarized some of the main theories of physics.

In the field of mechanical engineering, Mo Tzu was a master machinist who spent three years meticulously manufacturing a wooden bird capable of flight. An expert in making carts, he could build a cart in one day that had a load capacity of thirty *dans* (1.7 tons) of stones.

SUN TZU

Sun Tzu, a well-known military expert in Chinese history, is called the forefather of military strategy. His surname was Sun and his given name Wu, his courtesy name being Changqin. Later generations addressed him respectfully as Sun Tzu, or Sun Wu Tzu. His father was an aristocrat and well-known general of the state of Qi during the Spring and Autumn Period. Sun Tzu composed *The Art of War*, which is known as the earliest military book in the world. It laid the foundation for Chinese military science.

The Art of War consists of thirteen chapters and five thousand words. Each chapter is concerned with a different theme, but they are all interconnected so as to reveal a series of patterns in military affairs and form a complete theory of military strategy. With separate and interrelated themes for each chapter, the book put forth a series of general military rules and is a comprehensive study of military affairs.

The chapters are as follows:

1. "Laying Plans" addresses the possibility of going to war. Sun Tzu postulated that war is a matter of a country's life and death. Moral law (*tao*), heaven, earth, the commander, and method and discipline are the essential deciding factors of battle.
2. "Waging War" deals with how to advance in conflict and advocates for rapid victory. Even more praiseworthy is the author's assertion that captives should receive preferential treatment, because in this way the enemy is even more quickly defeated.
3. "Attack by Stratagem" emphasizes the strategy of assault to achieve victory in battle. The author writes, "Knowing the enemy and yourself will get you unscathed through a hundred battles."

4. "Tactical Dispositions" relates to achieving complete victory by taking advantage
   of material conditions. Sun Tzu says that
   the advantages of material conditions are
   based in military expenditure, the amount
   of supplies, the number of soldiers and the
   balance of power.
5. "Use of Energy" stresses defeating the enemy
   by combined effort. Sun Tzu advocates using
   advantageous situations to defeat the enemy,
   for example by a surprise attack or ambush.
6. "Weak and Strong Points" deals with how
   to be flexible in time and knowing when to
   initiate an attack. Sun Tzu maintains that it
   is vital to gain dominance by enticing the
   enemy and by understanding the situation in the enemy camp, as well as
   by concealing one's own situation while also noting the regular patterns
   of troop movements. He advocates exploiting the enemy's weaknesses
   and errors to crush him. Avoiding the strong and attacking the weak
   can thus achieve victory.

Sun Tzu

7. "Maneuvering an Army" deals with the importance of taking advantage
   of certain situations to achieve a favorable position. Sun Tzu says that
   one must refrain from hasty decisions about advancement and should
   understand the trends of the territory, be familiar with the roads and the
   topography and employ adept guides, thus deceiving the enemy. Also,
   planning fortifications and the dispersal of troops must be accomplished
   in light of different conditions and the enemy's position, morale and
   military strength.
8. "Variation of Tactics" elaborates on the importance of flexibility in com-
   manding. Sun Tzu believed this to be the basis for best determining the
   comprehensive pros and cons of ordering movements. This approach
   has the potential to threaten, subdue and perplex the enemy, as well as
   to entice them.
9. "The Army on the March" deals with the importance of organizing and
   deploying an army and observing and gathering enemy intelligence, as
   well as rallying the officers and soldiers.
10. "Classification of Terrain" stresses the relationship of various terrains to
    military courses of action.
11. "Nine Situations" deals with nine distinct battlefields and the correspond-
    ing requirements.

12. "Attack by Fire" relates to the targets, category, combustible materials and atmospheric conditions needed to carry out the assault.
13. "The Use of Spies" talks about the importance of the underlying principles of espionage.

The Art of War has not only been influential in China, it has also been translated into several languages and is widely available around the world. The famous French statesman and military expert Napoléon Bonaparte, after his defeat at Waterloo, came across *The Art of War* and lamented, "If only I had seen *The Art of War* by Sun Tzu twenty years ago, history would have a different ending." These days, in Vietnam, Korea, Japan, Israel, the United Kingdom, Germany and Russia, military experts avail themselves of this book. In the preface to the English-language version, the well-known British strategist Sir Basil Henry Liddell Hart comments that the ancient Chinese military strategy of twenty-five hundred years ago is useful for waging war in the modern era.

Besides the importance it places on military affairs, *The Art of War* now lends itself to other arenas, especially to that of business administration, as the financial market itself is a war without weapons. The Japanese entrepreneur Ohashi Takeo points out in his book *A Complete Collection of Military Tactics Management*, "Adapting the ideas of Chinese military science to instruct on the management of business is still far more reasonable and effective than the methods of business management in the United States." And the American economist Richard M. Hodgett remarked that "Many principles and theories disclosed in *The Art of War* by Sun Tzu are indisputably valuable."*

HAN FEI TZU

Han Fei (ca. 280–233 BCE), also called Han Fei Tzu, was native of the State of Han in the late Warring States Period and a well-known philosopher, thinker and writer. He was also a great contributor to the Legalist school of philosophy. Although he often stuttered, he was quite adept when it came to writing. Moreover, he continued to develop the Legalist ideology of Xun Tzu and at the same time adopted the theories of previous Legalist doctrines. By comparing experiences of success and failure of political reform in different states, he was able to present a combined theory of law, method and the wielding of power. Having compiled a large amount of

Legalist thought, Han Fei Tzu wrote to the king of the state of Han several times, to make suggestions on political reform. His suggestions were not adopted, however, and so he determined to write books to expand on his theories, in an attempt to be reputable and famous.

Ying Zheng, the emperor of the State of Qin, attached great importance to Han Fei's thoughts and admired his ideas. So Emperor Ying Zheng wrote a letter to the emperor of the State of Han, asking him to send Han Fei on a diplomatic mission to the State of Qin. Legalist doctrine then served as the theoretical basis for the first unified, centralized state power in the history of China. But while in the state of Qin, Han Fei met with misfortune. Prime Minister Li Si arranged to have him imprisoned, and this resulted in his death. His fifty-five articles were passed down in his works, *Han Fei Tzu*.

During the pre-Qin era, the Legalist school attached great importance to law, opposing the rituals advocated by Confucianism. The Legalists were famous for advocating rule by law in governance, proposing a series of theories and methods that contributed immensely to the study. Their accomplishments included probing the relationships between basic themes such as origins, nature, the effect of law and the social economy. They also discussed the demands of the era, the power of a nation, the virtue of ethics, social customs, the natural environment and the population and personal relationships.

Legalist School philosophers believed that if good does not prevail, then evil will do harm, and that it is human nature to avail oneself of advantages to avoid calamity. Moral standards mean nothing when people face such choices. Therefore, a ruler should encourage people with benefits and honors. For example, significant rewards such as awarding official positions should be made to all who distinguish themselves in action, so that they will inspire soldiers and generals to take courage in battle. This is one of the reasons why the Qin army was so powerful. The ideology of humanity of the Legalist School of thought played a significant role in the Qin State's process of unifying China.

The Legalist School opposed the conservative ideal of returning to the ways of ancient times, proposing vigorous reform instead. The Legalists claimed that as history moves forward, all laws and social systems should develop with the times. Maintaining that reverting to ancient times or to diehard conservative attitudes is not acceptable, Shang Yang (a famous reformer of the Warring States Period) said, "The ancient laws do not conform to modern society's standards." Han Fei further developed Shang Yang's opinion and wrote, "Society would be led to chaos if the government

Han Fei Tzu

didn't change with the times." He even satirized the conservative Confucians as fools guarding a tree stump lying in wait for rabbits (waiting idly for opportunities).

As three representatives of the Legalist School, Shang Yang, Shen Dao and Shen Buhai all attached great importance to law, to the wielding of power, and to method as inseparable concepts with different features. Han Fei, by means of ancient fables, combined the three concepts, summarizing the success and failure of monarchs in ancient times. He clarified the theory of systematically governing by law, expressing his ambition and opinion.

Law is an indicator of a robust legal system; the wielding of power points to the authority and influence of a monarch as the sole leader of the military; method, in this circumstance, is the act of propagating law and maintaining rule by the issuance of tactics and strategy so as to preserve the hierarchy. The thinkers also stressed the importance of political awareness and preventing rebellion.

But the Legalist philosophy also has its disadvantages, including exaggerating the impact of law and advocating harsh tactics for governing the state by not only administering harsh sentences for petty crimes but also employing superstitious laws. The neglect of benevolence and righteousness, which were strongly advocated by Confucianism, is considered to be one of the leading causes of the collapse of the Qin Dynasty.

Chapter 10

THE BOOK OF SONGS

The Book of Songs is the first collection of ancient musical works in China, comprising 305 poems collected from various parts of the country. Dating back to the early Western Zhou Dynasty (eleventh century BCE) and to the middle of the Spring and Autumn Period (sixth century BCE), more than five hundred years separate some of the poems. Originally called simply *Poems*, or *Three Hundred Poems* in the pre-Qin Dynasty, the compilation is listed as the first of the Five Classics by Confucius and was given the honorific of *The Book of Songs* by Confucians during the Han Dynasty.

The Book of Songs was originally a collection of song lyrics, embellished with musical composition and divided into three categories: "Airs of the States," "Courtly Songs" and "Hymns."

The ballads of different regions, comprising fifteen distinct folkloric song types—namely, "Airs of the States"—consists of 160 entries that occupy over half the book. "Courtly Songs" and "Hymns," when compared with "Airs of the States," seem to be a breath of fresh air and are vivacious, as is the opening ballad, "The Crying Ospreys," which is written with passion and youthfulness. "Meng" is a poem that describes the grief of a woman after being abandoned by her husband. "Jiangnu" is another work about romantic love.

"Courtly Songs" is a collection of music starting with the State of Zhou period. These are orthodox songs and formal music sung by the nobles in the court or at banquets. According to the type of music, "Courtly Songs" is divided into thirty-one "Greater Courtly Songs" and seventy-four "Lesser Courtly Songs." In "Lesser Courtly Songs," a few entries are folk songs, but for the most part these are the works of aristocratic scholars and were performed in common celebrations. "Greater Courtly Songs" are used in grand ceremonies and large banquets.

"Hymns" is a collection of anthems used as prayer offerings during imperial sacrifices to ancestors and gods. This section of the book is divided into thirty-one Zhou Praises, four Lu Praises, and five Shang Praises, totaling forty, all works of the literate aristocracy.

The Book of Songs marks a splendid point of origin for the history of

Chinese poetry. Its rich and plentiful content includes epic sagas, poems of sarcasm, narratives, love songs, songs of war and carols, as well as various songs of the laborers. The songs reflect many aspects of the Zhou Dynasty era, including labor and love, military conflict, oppression, customs and marriage and deal with every aspect of life. For example, in "Greater Courtly Songs" the poem "Sheng Min" tells of the birth of Hou Ji to King Wu of Zhou, who overthrew tyrant Zhou of Shang. The book is a reflection of the Zhou Dynasty culture and helped in the development of the literary history of other states.

In terms of technique of expression, the selections in *The Book of Songs* are mostly four-character based, with the structural repetition of phrases and stanzas rhyming at the end of every line or every other line, to strengthen the expression of emotions. A great artistic effect is achieved with only several changes of words in each stanza. In addition, three literary devices, *fu*, *bi* and *xing*, are often employed in *The Book of Songs*. *Fu* indicates directly expressing one's emotions in great detail; it is the most basic way of expression. *Bi* is the English equivalent of metaphor. Many poems in the book employ metaphor in various ways. For example, in "Meng" (common people), the flourishing and withering of the mulberry tree is used to reflect the vicissitudes of love between husband and wife. *Xing* is used to invoking images other than the subject matter and is often used at the beginning of a poem or in the first stanza of a poem.

The Book of Songs was a brilliant beginning for Chinese literature. Owing to its rich content and high achievement in ideology and art, the book has status today in Chinese and world cultural history. It set the precedent for brilliant traditional Chinese poems, which exerted an indelible influence on literature in later times. As early as the Spring and Autumn Period, *The Book of Songs* was already widespread, and it has been used as teaching material by aristocrats in China for thousands of years. In *The Analects*, Confucius says, "A person who doesn't learn *The Book of Songs* will not know how to speak." He also taught his students by quoting from the book.

Of the Five Classics—*The Book of Songs*, *The Book of History*, *The Book of Changes*, *The Book of Rites* and *The Spring and Autumn Annals*—Confucius and his disciples used *The Book of Songs* as a textbook for their students. Even when the first emperor of the Qin Dynasty issued a decree to burn all the volumes, the contents of the book continued to be spread by scholars by word of mouth. The book has also had great influence outside China, having been introduced to Japan, Korea and Vietnam at an early time. Since the beginning of the eighteenth century, versions in French, German, English and Russian have also emerged.

POETRY OF THE SOUTH

Poetry of the South, also called *Songs of Chu*, was one of the folk song styles of the Chu State, created by the poet Qu Yuan in the late Warring States Period. At the end of the Western Han Dynasty, Liu Xiang compiled sixteen works by Qu Yuan, Shong Yu, Xiaoshan, Dongfang Shuo, Wang Bao and Liu Xiang, who wrote in the style of Qu Yuan and Song Yu and created great works. Liu Xiang named the compilation *Songs of Chu*, and later Wang Yi added his "Nine Thoughts." Ultimately there were seventeen works, called collectively *Poetry of the South*. Because of the style of the representative work by Qu Yuan, "Sorrow for Departure," *Songs of Chu* set the style for the region. As the first collection of romantic poems, it exerted heavy influence on the literature that followed, and it not only marked the start of the writing of rhymed prose but also exerted an effect on the prose writing of the dynasties to come. *Songs of Chu* was the start of a positively romantic poetry style in China.

The *Songs of Chu* is mainly works by Qu Yuan and Song Yu. These encompass the rich flavor of the local culture and the literary style, dialects and rhymes of the Chu area. *Songs of Chu* deals with history and customs, the natural landscape, and the stories of local people through historical stories, fairy tales and local customs.

The totality of the work is the basis for the *Poetry of the South*. *Songs of Chu* is therefore a vital part of Chu culture, combining both local features and traits of central China.

One of the main authors of *Songs of Chu*, Qu Yuan, created the immortal masterpieces "Sorrow for Departure," "Asking Heaven," "Nine Songs" and "Nine Elegies," among many others. Qu Yuan (ca. 339–278 BCE), whose given name was Ping, was the earliest patriotic poet in the history of Chinese literature. Given a threat to Chu from the powerful State of Qin, Qu Yuan argued for reform in the government and alliance with the wealthy state of Qi in the east against the State of Qin in the west, to ensure the safety of Chu. Yet the King of Chu was surrounded by the self-absorbed, who had accepted bribes from Qin's envoy and so not only dissuaded the King from taking Qu Yuan's advice but also had him removed from office. Moreover, when King Chu Xiang acceded to the throne, Qu Yuan was

Qu Yuan

banished in exile. Helpless in saving his own country and viewing his ambitions through the prism of reality, he drowned himself in the Miluo River. In the major work by Qu Yuan, "Sorrow for Departure," the political lyric reflects the poet's advanced ideals, his unremitting striving for reality, and an ambition coupled with frustration and depression. Passionate and imaginative, the lyric embodies the poet's unswerving loyalty to his homeland and his firm determination to seek a higher consciousness.

Rich with local flavor, *Songs of Chu* was developed on the basis of folk songs of the Chu area by means of copying and compiling. Owing to differences in geography and language environment, the Chu area had from ancient times developed a unique style of music and singing called the Southern Feng. The area had a long history characterized by the popularity of sortilege, and local people paid sacrifice to the heavens by hymns and dances. Volumes of mythology have been preserved in the list of songs, which evoke the first grand religious atmosphere. The songs all have a distinctive high pitch, yet what emerges is a deeply profound color because of the style. And so the popularity of *Songs of Chu* is closely connected to the edification of folk music and local culture in the Chu area.

Songs of Chu is also the product of the influences of both the northern Chu culture and the northern central Chinese culture. After the Spring and Autumn and Warring States periods, the State of Chu, which had long been considered a barren state, became increasingly stronger. In the process of frequent contact with northern states in communication with central China and contending for hegemony, an extensive exchange of culture had been promoted between south and north, as well as with central China. As a result, the great poet Qu Yuan and his extraordinary poems of splendor, *Songs of Chu*, were able to flourish.

Playing an important role in the history of Chinese poetry, the appearance of *Songs of Chu* begins another volume of Chinese songs after *The Book of Songs*. Later generations entitled *The Book of Songs* and *Songs of Chu*, respectively, *Feng* and *Sao*. *Feng* refers to the culture of the fifteen vassal states, represented in *The Book of Songs* with realism and spirit. *Sao* refers to *Li Sao* (the poem "Sorrow for Departure"), which magnifies the true romanticism of Chu poetry. *Feng* and *Sao* became the two schools of thought embodying the realism and romanticism of Chinese classic poetry.

HAN FU

Han fu (Han rhapsody) refers to the Han Dynasty–era rhymed prose that combined elements of poetry and style and elaborated on themes. In its literary form, the vivid description of objects and the diverse content were expressions of great aspiration. *Han fu* covered mainly five kinds of content: the rendering of palaces and cities; the description of the king's hunting expeditions; the narration of travel experiences; the expression of emotion; and commentary on various animals, birds, grasslands and forests. The first two kinds of content are typical *Han fu* works and became representative of a new literary form in Chinese literature after *The Book of Songs* and *Songs of Chu* were made public. *Han fu* also became the most popular literary form of the time. During the four hundred years of the two Han dynasties, scribes generally adopted the form, which became the fashion of the times and a key component of Han literature.

Han fu consisted of Greater *Han fu* and Lesser *Han fu*. Greater *Han fu* rhapsody is also known as Lisao-style rhapsody. It is grand in scale, with an extensive framework and marked by majestic vigor and a flowing diction that formed long masterpieces. Jia Yi, Mei Cheng, Sima Xiangru and Yang Xiong were the masters in the Western Han Dynasty; Ban Gu and Zhang Heng were representatives of *Han fu* in the Eastern Han Dynasty. Among these artists, Sima Xiangru, Yang Xiong, Ban Gu and Zhang Heng are known as the four masters of *Han fu*. Developing the useful and discarding the useless of Greater *Han fu*, Lesser *Han fu* with its shorter length and comely literary grace focused mainly on the realities of society and the natural surroundings. Zhao Yi, Cai Yong and Mi Heng were the masters of Lesser *Han fu*.

Han fu, especially Greater *Han fu*, enjoys a high place in Chinese literary history, despite the shortcomings of the ornate rhetoric, the fact that it attends to trifling things and neglects the essentials, and the fact that it lacks emotion. Still, it occupies a significant place in Chinese literary history. To begin with, Greater *Han fu* describes palace courtyards, the king's hunting grounds and great cities, describing and eulogizing vast areas of land, rich products, prosperous cities and the governing achievements of the State of Han. Moreover, the ruler in this form was endowed with positive significance, indicating cultural and military achievements. Also, although Greater *Han fu* boasts a strange flowery rhetoric, certain achievements were made in terms of rich vocabulary, the use of language and sentence structure, and improving on the means of rendering images through words. Furthermore, in the historical context, the prosperity in the two Han dynasties spoken of in Rhapsody promoted the formation of distinct ideas in Chinese literature. From the beginnings of *The Book of Songs* and *Songs of Chu* to the Han Dynasty and the development of *Han fu*, literature and learning in general began to move apart. As there was more recognition of literary characteristics, the ideology became increasingly transparent.

HAN *YUE FU*

Han *Yue fu*, a form of Chinese poetry of the Han Dynasty, is poetry that was collected by *Yue fu* officials. Some of the poetry is songs and their musical scores, devised for ceremonial court occasions by the rulers to honor their ancestors, similar to the hymns in *The Book of Songs*. Another characteristic of this form is the music passed down through the generations, called *Yue fu* ballads.

Yue fu poetry is classified according to the different forms of music in it. In the one-hundred-volume *Collection of Yue Fu Poetry* by Guo Mao-qian of the Song Dynasty—so far the most integrated poetry collection on record—is the work from the Han Dynasty to the Five Dynasties. This work assigns *Yue fu* to twelve categories. Most prevalent are the following:

1. songs in temple, used by the aristocratic intellectuals for sacrifice ceremonies;
2. songs for drum and pipe, also called cymbals songs, introduced by northern minority groups at the beginning of the Han Dynasty and mainly used as the military music of the day;
3. *xianghe* ballads, for the most part folk songs and ballads passed freely among commoners (*xianghe* refers to a way of singing, and included a combination of silk and bamboo instruments along with the voices); and
4. various songs, yet another form whose musical scores have been for the most part lost and so can't be traced back to their origins.

Most Han *Yue fu* songs are preserved within the styles of *xianghe*, songs for drum and pipe, and various songs; among these, *xianghe* is the most common.

Most of the over forty ballads of Han *Yue fu* are works of the Eastern Han Dynasty, kept in the *Collection of Yue Fu Poetry*, reflecting the social realities and people's lives at the time. With keen language expressing feelings of love and hate, the ballads tends to be realistic in style, exposing resistance against class exploitation and oppression, criticizing war and compulsory service, protesting feudal Confucian ethics and marriage, and singing the praises of great love for the common people.

Like the *Book of Songs*, Han *Yue fu* is a genre of ballads from ancient times. Different from the romanticism of *The Book of Songs*, however, Han *Yue fu* marks the beginning of the realist style. In Han *Yue Fu*, for example, women as subject matter became important. Using common language to create a work of art relevant to everyday life, there were five emphasized topics: using a narrative; portraying a character in the finest detail; eliciting a character's temperament; creating a completely interwoven plot; and vividly describing particulars and so reaching a high plane of thought and meaning. These are five distinct languages of poetry that played an important role in the development of Chinese writing styles.

"The Roadside Mulberry" and "The Peacock Flies Southeast" are examples of Han *Yue fu* ballads. The latter is the longest narrative from ancient China. This and "The Ballad of Mu-lan" are known as the two pearls of *Yue fu*.

THE RECORDS OF THE GRAND HISTORIAN

The Records of the Grand Historian is China's first comprehensive history book written in biographical style. It was praised by later generations as a "great work of historians without the rhyme of 'Sorrow for Departure.'" It records three thousand years of Chinese history, from Emperor Huang Di to Han Dynasty Emperor Wu, and includes 130 pieces with 526,500 words. The book comprises five parts, including twelve Basic Annals, eight Treatises, ten Tables, thirty Genealogies and seventy Biographies. The Basic Annals depict the reigns of various emperors, recording the emperors' words, deeds and achievements while in power by succession. Biao is a brief timeline of events involving personages in history. Treatises record and narrate system development, the laws of astronomy, music, military science, social economics and aspects of the delta culture. Genealogies is a descriptive record of the succession of feudal offspring and inheritance in the dynastic aristocracies. Biographies is a collection of essays outlining important figures in history.

The Records of the Grand Historian was compiled between 104 and 91 BCE and was much admired by a great scholar, Dongfang Shuo. In the book he refers to himself with three characters as the Grand Scribe or *Tai Shi Gong* (太史公). *Tai Shi* refers simply to his official position, and *Gong* is an honorific. *The Records of the Grand Historian* at first had no fixed title; it was also called *The Records of the Grand Scribe* and *The Book of the Grand Scribe*. *The Records of the Grand Historian* was the generic term used from the beginning of the Three Kingdoms Period, eventually becoming the famous *Book of the Grand Scribe*.

Sima Qian

The author of *The Records of the Grand Historian* was Sima Qian (145–90 BCE), also called Tzu Chang, a well-known historiographer and literary master of the Han Dynasty. Before writing about a historical character or event, he first did in-depth research using historical documents. It is with a precise and earnest writing style that he created his histories. In his twenties he left Chang'an, capital of the Western Han, and began his traveling and investigation into historical relics. He crossed numerous great mountains and rivers, broadening his vision and opening his mind while learning many anecdotes about historical figures, the local folk customs and the economies. Ban Gu, a historian in the Han Dynasty, thought highly of Sima Qian's anthropologic approach and his full and accurate recording of historical events, eulogizing his objectivity, his use of reliable historical fact, and his practical and realistic recording. This was a golden achievement for Sima Qian in that what he wanted to reflect was true history while providing historical reference for feudal rulers. He selected historical figures according to their practical conduct rather than social status or official position. For example, he wrote great volumes of biographies about the wanderings of knights, and about merchants and doctors, and he introduced extremely worthy people of the lower class. In his heart he felt that these people had noble, desirable attributes.

The Records of the Grand Historian was the first Chinese history book written in the style of biography and interweaving politics, economics, nationality, and culture while carrying on the age-old historical tradition of precise, realistic writing. The work had extensive influence on the fiction, drama, biographical literature and prose of ancient times. It is a great monument in both Chinese and literary history.

THE BOOK OF HAN

After *The Records of the Grand Historian* came another history classic, *The Book of Han*, written by Ban Gu (32–92). Born in Fufeng Anlin (the northeast part of Xianyang City in Shanxi Province), the author was a genius who could compose writings as early as the age of nine. He studied extensively the Nine Schools of Thought as he grew up. *The Records of the Grand Historian* records Chinese history until the early years of Emperor Wu of the Han Dynasty at which time many attempted to continue in this manner of writing.

Yet Ban Gu's father, Ban Biao, was not satisfied with these and wrote sixty-five articles for *The Records of the Grand Historian Post Biography*. After his father passed away, when in his twenties Ban Gu set about collecting and finalizing his father's manuscripts, determined to succeed in his father's cause and finish a continuation of *The Records*—compiling *The Records of the Grand Historian Post Biography*. Not long after publishing his work *The Book of Han*, somebody in the court lodged an accusation against him of "conspiring to alter national history," he was put in jail, and all the books in his home were confiscated. Later, Ban Chao, his younger brother, explained to Emperor Ming of the Han the intention of his brother in compiling and writing the book. Local officials also gave Ban Gu's manuscript to the emperor. Understanding the situation, the emperor appreciated the talent of Ban Gu, summoned him to the division of records and appointed him an official in charge of proofreading historical documents.

The style of *The Book of Han*, as compared with *The Records of the Grand Historian*, reflected changes. *The Records of the Grand Historian* is a general history, while *The Book of Han* records dynastic history. Basic Annals in the former became simply Annals in *The Book of Han*. Treatises became Records. And the content on the meritorious ministers in Genealogy was folded into the Biographies section. Other historical books hereafter followed these changes in style. *The Book of Han* includes twelve Annals of emperors, eight Tables, ten Records and seventy Biographies, altogether one hundred pieces, divided into 120 volumes by later generations and mainly recording a history of 230 years, from the first year (206 BCE) of Emperor Gao Zu of the Han Dynasty to the fourth year of Di Huang of Wang Mang (the year 23). It is another milestone among the historical classics produced after *The Records of the Grand Historian*.

Discussing and comparing imperial edicts was the main point of *The Book of Han*. Also included were many biographies of minority groups. The book also included new content: *The Record of Criminal Law*, *The Record of the Five Phases of Philosophy*, *The Record of Geography* and *The Record of Art and Literature*. The evolution of the legal system and some concrete regulations were systematically set forth for the first time in *The Record of Criminal Law*. *The Record of the Five Phases of Philosophy* systematically recorded the natural calamity phenomena from the Spring and Autumn Period to the end of the Western Han Dynasty. In *The Record of Geography*, county and district partitions, history, evolution and the registered permanent residences of the time were recorded. Moreover, records on local products, the situation regarding economic development, and folk customs were especially attractive entries. Textual research on the origins of various academic schools can be found in *The Record of Art and Literature*, in which a catalogue of books was preserved, books that were recognized as the earliest existing in China. In addition, *The Record on Agriculture and Commerce*, with more detailed content, was evolved from Pingzhun Shu. It consisted of two volumes. The first volume dealt with the agricultural and economic situations and the second with commerce and the monetary situation, and the specialized economy of the time.

Although *The Book of Han* contains orthodox feudal ideology, it marks a new compilation style of employing the history of dynasties while sequentially recording biographies. It includes a wealth of material, as many important historical documents have been preserved here, thereby playing an important role in Chinese historiography.

Chapter 11

THE YANGTZE RIVER

The Yangtze River Valley and Yellow River Basin are the birthplaces of Chinese ancestry. Existing in ancient times, they form the cradle of Chinese culture and civilization, embodying material and spiritual civilization.

The Yangtze River is the longest river in China and the third longest in the world, shorter only than the Amazon and the Nile rivers. Originating from the north of the Tanggula Mountain Range on the Qinghai Tibetan Plateau and the southwest side of Shaanxi and the snow-capped mountain of Geladandong, the Yangtze River crosses three major regions of China. Stretching across the southwest, central and eastern regions, it pushes its way through eleven provinces, cities and autonomous regions of Qinghai, Tibet, Yunnan, Sichuan, Chongqing, Hubei, Hunan, Jiangxi, Anhui and Jiangsu and finally flows into the East Sea at Shanghai. The Yangtze River is nearly four thousand miles long, some five hundred miles longer than the Yellow River. The entire river valley area is 695,760 square miles, accounting for 18.75 percent of China's land. The drainage area is 386,870 square miles larger than that of the Yellow River. In this region, generations of Chinese people gradually shaped a unique culture through diligence and wisdom.

At one point, only the Yellow River Valley and its culture had been regarded as the cradle of Chinese civilization. In fact, however, history has since shown that the Yangtze River is also an origin of Chinese cultural development. Just as the Euphrates and Tigris gave birth to Babylonian culture and the Indian and Ganges Rivers produced India's culture, both the Yangtze and Yellow River cultures should be considered the root of Chinese heritage.

The Yangtze River culture has a long history. In the Yangtze River Basin, in May 1929, a fossil known as Yuanmou Man was unearthed in Yuanmou County of Yunnan Province. According to the scientific evaluation, Yuanmou Man lived roughly 1.7 million years ago, making this the earliest primitive human discovered thus far in China, living about one million years earlier than the better-known Peking Man, whose fossils were uncovered in the Yellow River Valley. In addition, the excavation of historical ruins of the Yangshao culture, which can be traced to five thousand to seven thousand years ago, reveals the earliest culture in the Yellow River Valley. Correspondingly, the Hemudu culture, representing the civilization of the Yangtze River Valley, originated some fifty-three hundred to seven thousand years ago. The splendid primitive culture discovered in Yangshao and Hemudu is strong evidence that both the Yangtze River Valley and Yellow River Valley are the cradles of the Chinese civilization.

The discovery of the Sanxingdui has significance in the history and culture of the Yangtze River Valley. Sanxingdui is located in Nanxing Town, west of Guanghan city, at the upper reaches of the Yangtze River. The name *Sanxingdui* refers to three earth mounds found on the Chengdu Plain. The three mounds have been described as three gold stars, hence the name, Sanxingdui (Three Star Mounds).

In the spring of 1929, a peasant named Yan Daocheng found a piece of bright-colored jade while digging a ditch. This was the catalyst to the discovery of a mysterious ancient kingdom. Eventually, in 1986, the two Shang Dynasty sacrificial pits were unearthed. Archaeologists brought to light thousands of cultural relics including bronze wares, jade articles, ivory, cowry shells, pottery and gold plates.

Many of the mysterious ancient Shu treasures are bizarre and impressive. Some of the striking finds are:

❖ First, the world's earliest and largest bronze holy tree, a 12'7" bronze tree constructed in sections and divided into three parts from root to top, with three branches in each section. Fruit grows on the nine branches, and nine birds perch exquisitely on the tips of the branches. An uncanny dragon twists downward on the trunk.
❖ The second piece is a bronze human figure. The striking statue is 8'7" tall and weighs 397 pounds. It is the oldest and most complete life-sized standing human statue in the world.
❖ The most overwhelming find is that of a large bronze head, 25 inches high, with giant protruding eyes, and ears spaced 54.5 inches apart; this is the world's largest bronze head.

These treasures are unprecedented rarities in the spiritual realm. In addition to these artifacts, many invaluable articles have been found, including lustrous gold staffs and jade articles carved with mysterious patterns.

According to experts, Sanxingdui was built at the latest in the beginning of the Shang Dynasty. The archeological discovery aroused worldwide attention and the site was hailed as the world's ninth wonder. Meanwhile, the historical site is of great archaeological significance in determining the age and the stage of development of ancient society. Traditionally, historians regarded the Yellow River as the mother river where Chinese culture began and gradually diffused throughout China. Yet, the discovery of Sanxingdui provides important factual evidence that civilization in western China in the ancient state of Shu goes back at least five thousand years. Such evidence defies the traditional theory that the Yellow River was the sole "cradle of Chinese civilization," supplanting this idea with the reality that the Yangtze River and the Yellow River cultures were the origins of Chinese civilization.

Yangtze River

There was a difference, though. The Yellow River culture flourished in terms of human progress, while the Yangtze River culture was on the fringes, of marginal status. The Yangtze River civilization eventually achieved the same vital position as Yellow River culture, however, after the era of the Wei, Jin, and Southern and Northern dynasties.

During this period, residents of the Yellow River Basin were forced to migrate to the Yangtze River area because of natural disasters and frequent warfare. The Yangtze Valley, especially areas of the middle and lower reaches, experienced rapid economic development in the Sui and Tang dynasties. The second expansive growth in the southern region occurred after the An Shi Rebellion as many refugee Northerners fled to the south. Immigrant communities cropped up in present-day Jiangsu, Anhui, Jiangxi, Hubei and Sichuan provinces. The third tide of population migration occurred in the Song, Yuan and Ming dynasties. Northerners settled in almost every town of the central and lower reaches of the Yangtze River.

In the process of several population influxes, the Yellow River culture gradually merged into the Yangtze River society, making for a giant leap forward in the development of Yangtze civilization. The beautiful and rustic countryside of the south inspired many northern scholars to create prose of spiritual influence. At the same time, northern-style architecture and decorative fashions began to spread throughout the south. Cultural fusion contributed immensely to the improvement of the Yangtze River culture, which in turn had a positive impact on Chinese civilization.

In modern times, the social transformation in the Yangtze River Valley is more progressive than that of the Yellow River Basin.

It is said that the Yellow River is the traditional region of government politics, while the Yangtze River region is the model of vigorous commerce.

The Yangtze River Valley in Southeast Asia is in fact the origin of China's early development, of which Shanghai is a modern metropolis.

Yangtze River culture still shows ever-increasing vigor and vitality. The region covers only one fifth of the total land, yet the agriculture yields can feed nearly one third of the population and accounts for one half of the industrial and agricultural sectors' capital. As time goes on, the Yangtze River civilization will be playing an increasingly prominent role.

As well, in recent years Yangtze River culture has sparked much enthusiasm among academic circles at home and abroad. The First International Symposium on Yangtze Culture and Chu Culture was held in Hubei Province at the end of the twentieth century, preceding the International Symposium on Sanxingdui Culture and Yangtze Civilization hosted in Sichuan in October 2003. In addition, the publication of the Research Library of Changjiang Culture undoubtedly stimulated intense interest among people around the globe.

TEA

The Chinese always have on hand the seven necessities: firewood, rice, oil, salt, soy sauce, vinegar and tea. Among these, tea is of great importance in daily life.

China is the birthplace of tea, thus it was the first country to produce and drink tea.

According to several sources, the discovery of tea can be traced to approximately 2737 BCE to 2697 BCE, the period of the Three Sovereigns and Five Emperors. When it was discovered, tea was used as an herbal medicine. During the late Western Han Dynasty, tea was a high-quality beverage revered by monks, royalty and dignitaries. During the period of the Three Kingdoms, drinking tea in the royal court became common practice. Chinese tea evolved from a palace delicacy to a common beverage during the Jin and Sui dynasties.

It was not until the early Tang Dynasty, however, that the custom of drinking tea spread across China. During this era, the art of tea drinking gradually shifted from a crude style of quenching the thirst to drinking in a refined fashion, enjoying small sips to appreciate the subtle allure of the tea. The Sage of Tea, Lu Yu, was the great contributor to this transition, which marked a significant event in the history of the tea culture. His book *The Classic of Tea* is a proof of the emergence of the Chinese tea society. *The Classic of Tea* is a historical integration of the natural connotation and human value of drinking tea. Lu Yu, the initiator of the science of tea, incorporated Confucian, Taoist and Buddhist philosophy into his works. During the Tang Dynasty, another factor affected the development of the art of tea: the rise in popularity of Zen meditation.

Tea-planting area in Zhejiang Province

Because drinking tea was known to improve one's mental performance while also quenching the thirst of the spirit, the monasteries advocated tea drinking. The tea ceremony during the Tang Dynasty was of three varieties: the tea ceremony of the royal court, the monastery tea ceremony and the literati tea rite.

In the Song Dynasty, professional tea-tasting associations emerged, such as the official Social Soup and the Buddhist Thousand Beings Society. Emperor Zhao Kuangyin of the Song Dynasty was extremely fond of tea. At that time, an office was established in the royal court to manage the different grades of tea and develop a system of etiquette for drinking it. Tea was listed as the prime gift from the emperor to encourage the ministers, manifest his love and care for relatives and strengthen relations with foreign countries. Tea drinking customs were particularly lively among the common people. Neighbors would offer tea to express their best wishes to a family who planned to move. *Yuanbao* tea was commonly offered to a guest upon entering a home. Tea was also considered an important betrothal gift. On the wedding day it was customary that the couple serve their parents tea. The newlyweds would then share a cup of tea before entering the bridal chamber. Such interest in tea on the part of the common people initiated the tea selector culture and important competitions, the tea being judged on a variety of attributes ranging from the quality, color, and fragrance of the leaves to the participants' art in tea selection. Tea-making methods, such as steaming, pan drying and baking, made great strides. Tea sets were made in diverse styles, varying textures and fascinating designs.

The art of tea experienced significant changes in tea type and drinking method during the Ming and Qing dynasties. From the time of the Tang

Dynasty, loose tea became the basis for growth, and it became the norm in the Ming and the Qing dynasties. Loose tea was passed down through the generations and is the primary form of tea served today. The Ming Dynasty's loose-leaf, pan-fried method was primarily used for green tea but also was used with the teas from flowers. The number of tea types grew in the Qing Dynasty. In addition to green tea and the flower teas, oolong, red, black, white and many other types emerged, thereby establishing China as a master of tea.

All the world's tea tree growth, brewing methods and drinking customs came from China. It is estimated that Chinese tea spread abroad some two thousand years ago. In the fifth century (Northern and Southern dynasties), Chinese tea began to be exported to Southeast Asia and other parts of Asia. In the ninth century, a Japanese monk brought tea seeds to Japan, which began the Japanese custom of tea drinking. In the tenth century, Mongolian trade caravans brought Chinese brick tea via Siberia to remote areas of central Asia.

Early in the fifteenth century, the tea trade further spread when Portuguese traders came to China. In 1610, Chinese tea went to West Europe on a Dutch merchant ship, reaching Eastern Europe after 1650, then to Russia and France. By the seventeenth century, tea had arrived in the Americas. In the early part of the eighteenth century, Chinese tea was adopted by the upper class in Britain as a luxury gift, and drinking black tea became the fashion there. Since the eighteenth century, the British East India Company has reaped huge profits from a large-scale trade in Chinese tea. Some 1.45 million *piculs* (32 tons) of Chinese tea was exported to England in 1880, accounting for 60 to 70 percent of total tea export volume. By the nineteenth century, Chinese tea could be found around the globe. It is now consumed all over the world.

Today, twenty-one provinces (autonomous regions, municipalities) and 967 counties are China's large tea producers. These are found in four main tea areas: the southwest region, the southern region and the areas south and north of the Yangtze River. There are ten immensely popular teas, namely: West Lake's Dragon Well Tea, Spring Snail, Wuyi Stone Tea, Anxi's Iron Goddess, Tunxi Green Tea, Qi Men Red, Xinyang's Fur Tip, Silver Needle Tea, Pu'er Tea and Yunnan Black Tea.

WINE

While the Chinese tea culture is famous for its time-honored history, its wine culture in no way pales by comparison. In the thousands of years since the start of civilization, alcohol has permeated nearly every aspect of Chinese social life.

Throughout China in ancient times, cereal grains were primarily used in fermentation. The base of China's economy is agriculture. The prosperity of the wine business therefore depends on the bounty of the grain harvest, the state of society, political-economic activity, and the intimate bonds forged by cultural traditions. In ancient Chinese books, the legend of Ape Wine is recorded. Of course, it doesn't say that apes themselves brewed wine. The record rather tells of apes and monkeys collecting fruit. The fruit that was not eaten fermented and produced cider. Therefore, China's earliest "wine" imitated nature's masterpieces of fruit cider and fermented milk.

In Chinese antiquity, cereal grains were used to produce yellow wine. Also called rice wine, this belongs to a category that occupies an important position. It is among the world's three major brews: yellow wine, grape wine and beer. Made from unique brewing techniques, yellow wine has become the model for and representative of Oriental wine making. Yellow wine takes its name from its yellow color, hence the literal translation. But there are certainly other distinct hues of yellow wine, including black and red, so one cannot comprehend it only by name. Yellow wine is produced with the raw materials of grains, using a wheat or barley starter, or possibly rice and sugar, to start fermentation. In Northern China, millet is the major ingredient, while in South China rice is preferred. In modern times, rice wine is commonly used in translations to mean yellow wine.

In ancient times, wine was seen as divine, and so the process of making it was a serious matter. In classical antiquity, wine was a necessity in ceremonial sacrifices. Ancient rulers viewed wine as an "important matter of the state, for sacrifice and military affairs" and inseparable from ceremonial use as a libation to heaven, the deities and the ancestors to express reverence. In times of conflict, wine was used to boost the warriors' morale before they went into battle.

Wine drinking was not only an aspect of the conduct of state affairs but also an inalienable part of human life, and so came about great diversity in the customs of drinking wine.

In China there is a custom of drinking wine at weddings. Joyful wine or *xijiu*, is often synonymous with the wedding ceremony, so partaking in the *xijiu* may be considered as part of the wedding. In fact, almost every stage in a wedding involves wine. In fact, wine plays such a role in these occasions that it has taken on appellations: there is daughter wine, the union wine cup, welcoming wine, send-off wine, banquet of relatives wine and homecoming wine.

Early wine workshop

Also, the important annual Chinese festivals involve social wine-drinking customs, such as having calamus wine for the Dragon Boat Festival, chrysanthemum wine for the Double Yang Festival and New Year's Wine on New Year's Eve.

Full moon wine (or hundred days wine) is drunk during a full moon and shortly after the birth of a child. Banquet tables are arranged with wine, and friends and family are invited to jointly congratulate the family. Normally, those joining the feast bring gifts or red envelopes to show their regard.

Generally the fiftieth, sixtieth and seventieth birthdays are called the elders' grand birthdays, for which feasts are hosted by the children or grandchildren of the elders and that are attended by friends and relatives. At these, *shoujiu* is served.

In rural areas of China, on the day when construction is completed—a new house is built—or there is a major event in the life of a citizen, a banquet is commonly held at which Shangliang wine is served. On the day a family moves to a new location, a feast will be prepared and housewarming wine served to celebrate and to praise the deities and ancestors, to avoid misfortune.

Opening-business wine or bonus wine is served when a store is opened, when a boss treats employees to a feast, or perhaps at the end of the fiscal year as stock dividends are awarded.

Robust wine, also called farewell wine, is used at banquets honoring friends about to embark on long journeys. In times of war, before the troops were to execute dangerous and life-threatening missions, military officials would commonly offer a cup of robust wine.

Confucianism, the core of traditional Chinese civilization, deals with the manner of drinking and focuses on an etiquette of self-restraint and compliance.

The Chinese people are hospitable and at banquets will commonly serve *quan* wine. Not only is this accompanied by a variety of entertainment but a series of wine games is held and songs are sung, as well.

Over the millennia of the evolution of the wine culture, many amusing anecdotes have evolved as well. Long-told tales are of lakes of wine and forests of meat, describing unbridled debauchery; there are also the stories of "The Wine Master," "Lu Wine of Handan," "The Feast of Hongmen," "The First Han Emperor Beheads the White Serpent," "Wenjun Danglu," "Steamed Hero Wine," "The Seven Sages of the Bamboo Grove," "Pure Wine Makes the Sage," "The Eight Drinking Immortals" and "Dismissing the Military Hierarchy Using Wine Cups."

From ancient times, wine has enjoyed an affinity with literature and art and it has spurred the making of invaluable works in painting, opera, other music forms and in richly colorful classical narratives.

FOOD

Cuisine is a central part of the Chinese food culture. Regional cuisines have taken shape after long histories of evolution under the influence of geography, environment, climate, available local products, eating habits and other factors. After several thousand years of creative and cumulative effort, Chinese cuisine is among those unequaled in the world. The most influential and representative regional variations are the Lu, Chuan, Yue, Min, Su, Zhe, Xiang and Hui Cuisines, commonly known as the Eight Great Cuisines.

Lu (Shandong) cuisine ranks as first among the Eight Great Cuisines. Since the Song Dynasty, Shandong cuisine has become representative of northern Chinese cooking. During the Ming and Qing dynasties, Lu cuisine entered the imperial court in the form of rare royal delicacies. In the modern era, it has evolved to include the local flavors of the Jinan and Jiaodong regions. Characteristics of Shandong cuisine are a distinct aroma, fresh and tender ingredients and simple taste, with special attention paid to broth and to milk soup. Clear soup is rather thin, while milk soup is creamy and white. Jinan cuisine involves the cooking techniques of popping, roasting, deep frying and stir-frying, among other famous methods. Typical courses in Shandong cuisine include Nine-turned Large Intestine, Crackling Soup, Roasted Oysters and Bird's Nest Soup. Jiaodong dishes mainly involve seafood and feature delicious, refreshing, pure and light tastes. Braised Whelk with Brown Sauce and Steamed Red Porgy (fish) are highly recommended.

As one of the Eight Great Chinese Cuisines, Sichuan has a long history. It is recorded in history books that Sichuan cuisine dates to the States of Shu and Ba in ancient times. Sichuan-style dishes took shape from the late Qin Dynasty to the early Han period and saw rapid development in the Tang and Song dynasties. Sichuan evolved into one of the major cuisines with the native flavors of China's Ming and Qing dynasties, as Sichuan restaurants were opened around the world. Traditional Sichuan cuisine is typified by the dishes of the cities of Chengdu and Chongqing. It is sour, sweet, tingling, spicy, savory and oily, and there is a concentrated taste,

Mapo Tofu

with particular attention paid to seasonings. Inseparable from the style are the three peppers (chili, black and Chinese prickly ash) and fresh ginger root. The universally enjoyed spicy and tingling flavor has given rise to the saying, "One dish exhibits one flavor, one hundred dishes offer one hundred different tastes." The Sichuan culinary art boasts many cooking techniques, including roasting, baking, dry frying and steaming. Famous Sichuan dishes are Braised Dry Bead Curd Shreds, Stewed Eel, Chicken with Special Hot Sauce and Mapo Tofu.

Yue cuisine, short for Guangdong cuisine and one of the main cooking styles in China, comprises the Guangzhou, Chaozhou and Dongjiang cooking styles. Guangdong cuisine has taken on its own three distinctive characteristics:

1. A variety of ingredients is used, including animals that fly, crawl and swim.
2. Special attention is paid to an intensive selection of ingredients, elaborate techniques and a substantial variety of dishes for banquets and meals. The chefs excel at fusing the appeal of delicacies from all over China and are innovators in the culinary arts.
3. Emphasis is placed on quality and taste. Guangdong flavor is rather light, with an emphasis on the fresh, tender, crisp, smooth and aromatic qualities.

Famous dishes are Roasted Suckling Pig, the Dragon and Tiger Battle, Taiye Chicken, Stewed Grain Worms, Boiled Dog Meat, Five-Colored Shrimp and Stewed Snake and Cat with Chrysanthemum Flowers.

Fujian cuisine originated in Minhou County of Fujian Province. There are three types: Fuzhou, South Fujian and West Fujian, with slight differences among them. Fujian cuisine has four qualities:

1. An emphasis on fine slicing techniques so that the result is reputed to be as thin as paper.
2. The Fujian people are particular about soup, of which there are many variations.

3. Clear, refreshing, delicious and light flavors that make for a slightly sweet-and-sour taste.
4. Exquisite culinary techniques that include stir-frying, steaming and stewing.

Some of the appealing Fujian dishes are Buddha Jumping Over the Wall, Chicken with Bamboo Shoots, Three-Stewed Sea Cucumbers, Fried Scallops, Sliced Chicken in Bird's Nest Soup and Lychee Pulp.

Jiangsu cuisine originated during the Southern and Northern dynasties and became as famous as Zhejiang cuisine after the Tang and Song dynasties. It was recognized as a distinct regional style during the Ming and Qing dynasties, enjoying the same status as the Sichuan and Guangdong cuisines at the time. Huaiyang cuisine, one branch of Jiangsu cooking, was once common in the imperial courts and is now commonly served at Chinese state banquets. Jiangsu cuisine consists of the styles of Jiangsu-Yangzhou, Suzhou-Wuxi, Nanjing-Xuzhou dishes. The slicing techniques are delicate, and much attention is paid to cooking temperature. The flavor of Huaiyang cuisine is known for being not too spicy but not too bland. And the food is light, fresh and sweet and of a delicate elegance. Cooking techniques are stewing, roasting, baking, simmering and stir-frying. When preparing the food, strict attention is paid to color and shape as well as to the four seasons. Famous dishes are Clear Fire Soup, Shark Fin Stuffed Duck, Squirrel with Mandarin Fish, Watermelon Chicken and Salted Duck.

Zhejiang cuisine comprises the specialties of Hangzhou, Ningbo and Shaoxing. As a whole, the Zhejiang cuisine tradition is noted for its own local characteristics. The four main signatures of the style are:

1. Small, fresh and unique ingredients are meticulously selected.
2. The cuisine specializes in stir-frying, deep-frying, braising, quick frying, steaming and roasting.
3. Food color and texture are preserved, and the chef lets the inherent qualities of the food emerge.
4. Special attention is paid to the meticulous shaping and elaborate designing of the food, so it is extremely elegant in appearance.

This cuisine is noted for its West Lake Fish in Vinegar Sauce, Dongpo Pork, Fried Shrimp

West Lake Fish in Vinegar Sauce

with Dragon Well Tea, Beggar's Chicken, Dachang Fish Soup and Popping Cuttlefish Rolls.

Hunan cuisine consists of a variety of local dishes from the Xiangjiang River valley, the Dongting Lake area and the Western Hunan mountain area. The Hunan people are quite fond of hot pepper. And so goes the saying, "Jiangxi natives don't fear hot peppers; Sichuan locals fear them even less; and the Hunan people fear to be without them." Hunan cuisine is characterized by thick and pungent flavors, including hot and spicy, numbing and spicy, fresh and spicy, hot and sour and bitter and spicy. "General Tso's Chicken" is the hottest item on Hunan cuisine menu. Hunan food has five characteristics: there is a wide selection of ingredients; there are abundant tastes and flavors; there is fine workmanship in the cutting; various kinds of seasonings are used; and the cuisine employs a variety of techniques. Typical courses include Dong'an Chicken, Spicy Chicken, Stewed Shark Fins and Brown Sauce, Puffed Tripe Soup, Lotus Seeds in Rock Sugar Sauce and Spotted Butter Fish.

Anhui cuisine mainly deals with the local flavors of Huizhou and other areas along the Yangtze and Huai rivers. Chefs in Anhui Province are expert especially at cooking delicacies from the mountains and the sea. The highly distinctive characteristics of Anhui cuisine rely on several factors:

1. Strict selection of ingredients from local resources. (With the changing of the seasons, Anhui's abundant mountains support many treasures of wild game.)
2. Control of the cooking flame so as to achieve the desired texture, aroma and degree of cooking.
3. The prevalence of popular cooking methods, such as roasting, stewing, smoking and steaming, that also makes this style distinctive.
4. Particular attention is paid to the supplemental value of food, using food as medicine and focusing on raising a healthy body while retaining the local flavor.

The dishes are categorized according to nutritional value. Popular Anhui dishes include Braised Masked Civet, Fuliji Roasted Chicken, Stewed Ham and Bamboo Shoots, Braised Pheasant with Snow Vegetables, Gourd Duck, Salted Mandarin Fish, Stewed Soft Shell Turtle with Ham and Maofeng Anchovies.

Chapter 12

HAN ATTIRE

Han attire, or *Hanfu*, refers to the clothing worn by the ethnic Han before the Qing Dynasty. This type of dress was designed and made popular by the Han Dynasty, hence the name. Han attire is easily identifiable because of its unique characteristics, such as the Y-shaped cross-collar (left over right), the absence of buttons, and a string or a belt for fastening, giving the garments a relaxed yet elegant feel.

Han attire included both formal dress and common clothing. Generally, the formal outfit consisted of an upper and a lower garment (the lower garment in ancient times was a skirt). *Shenyi* (informal wear) was made by stitching the upper and lower sections together but also included a shorter jacket. Among these, the court dress with upper and lower garment became the most formal attire and was reserved for emperors and officials of the highest rank. The closed, full-body garment was informal dress for various other officials and scholars. The short coat, shirt and skirt were favorites of women, while laborers wore short upper garment and trousers.

Accessories and hair ornaments were also important to *Hanfu*. In ancient times, Han men and women wore their hair in a bun and held it in place with a hairpin. Men traditionally adorned their heads with coronets, turbans and caps. Women combed their hair in various styles and wore all kinds of hair ornaments, such as pearls, flowers and hairpins with pendants. Also in vogue was stylized hair in the area of the temple and the use of veils.

Jade girdle ornaments were another unique feature of Han attire.

Han attire for men fell into two categories, according to the features. One type of dress was representative of the clothing popular during the ancient Qin and Han dynasties. It included a large overlapping lapel, crossed collar, wide sleeves and extensive wraps. Such attire was in vogue through the Shang, Zhou, Spring and Autumn and Warring States periods, the period of the Three Kingdoms, the two Jin dynasties, the Southern and Northern dynasties, the Sui, Tang, the Five Dynasties and the Song, Yuan and Ming dynasties and influenced countries such as Japan and Korea. (The kimono in Japan was modeled after this style.)

The other style of *Hanfu* was the closed, round-collared robe, which was worn during Sui and Tang dynasties. It was also prevalent during the Five Dynasties, as well as during the Song, Yuan and Ming dynasties. (Such clothing also greatly affected the styles in Japan and Korea.)

In the early styles of Hanfu, the one-piece clothing style (*shenyi*) of women and men were similar, but garments later incorporated styles shorter in length. For millennia, Han Chinese clothing has retained its simple and elegant style despite the changes in dynasties. The fashion of the Ming Dynasty was a long coat and was basically the same as that of the Western Han Dynasty except for some minor details. The styles of garments during the Spring and Autumn and Warring States periods were those of the Shang Dynasty, with only slight alteration. Garments of the Spring and Autumn and Warring States periods embodied a more relaxed style than those of the Shang period. The sleeves were flared, and the collars were of varied sizes. There were no buttons; a belt cinched the clothing at the waist, and some belts had jade ornamentation. People in the following Qin Dynasty adored the color black, so black became a common hue for the clothing of that time, but the style of the overlapping lapel (from left to right) was retained.

Informal wear for men in the Han Dynasty fell into two categories: diagonal body-wrapping robes (*quju*) and garments with straight lapels (*zhiju*). *Quju* robes evolved from the long coat popular during the Warring States Period and into the Han Dynasty. Yet, as the Eastern Han period arrived, few wore full-body garments. Straight-lapel gowns could be worn in everyday life, but they were not suitable for formal occasions. During the Qin and Han dynasties, the styles of *quju* robes were similar for men and women. These consisted of a long, one-piece slender robe that often dragged and had a diagonal lapel. The lower section flared out and concealed the feet as one walked. The sleeves were flared and the cuffs were commonly decorated with trim. The collar was low-set so as to expose the underlying garments. All the layers of clothing were being worn at once, as many as three layers, and each layer had to be revealed. These three layers were known as the three main garments.

Straight-lapel garments for men and women emerged in and were in vogue through the Western Han Dynasty. These could not serve as formal attire, because ancient trousers had no crotch, and so trouser legs reached only to the knee. Also, a belt was worn around the waist. This style of crotchless pants was worn around the house, while long robes covering the entire body were worn in public in the belief that exposing one's trousers in important situations was disrespectful. Later improvements in undergarments led to the emergence of crotched trousers. The fashion of the Eastern Han

Dynasty and thereafter regarded the traditional long robe as superfluous and the style was abandoned.

By and large, men's coats were distinctive for their broad sleeves during the Wei and Jin periods and the Southern and Northern dynasties. This type of layered men's clothing was greatly loved and admired even into the Southern Dynasty. Dresses for ordinary women inherited the style from the Qin and Han dynasties. The fashion of the time consisted mainly of slender and form-fitting blouses or short jackets with loose sleeves accompanied by long pleated floor-length skirts that completed the elegant look of the woman. Round-collared robes with narrow sleeves were the uniform for officials throughout the Tang Dynasty, but ceremonial clothing was worn on significant occasions. The style of ceremonial dress

Shenyi (informal wear) and *ruqun* (short jacket)

was adopted from the former Sui Dynasty and consisted of conical or flat cap, wide-buttoned sleeves, a petticoat, and a jade-adorned belt. A *ruqun* (short jacket) was the major style for women in the Tang Dynasty. Beginning in the Sui period, women wore short jackets that featured narrow sleeves and tight, long skirts. The waistband was set very high, sometimes up to the underarm area, and a ribbon connected to the back complemented the beauty of the female shape. Compared to the early Tang era, *ruqun* styles were broader and more relaxed in the mid-Tang Dynasty, but it was fundamentally the same fashion.

Since ancient times, China has been renowned as a country of formal dress and etiquette because of its rich culture of attire. And so *Hanfu* (hat and clothes) has gradually become a cultural symbol of the long and rich culture of China.

Men's *quju*

Women's *quju*

Under the rule of the Manchurian Qing Dynasty, an order was issued to have all the men shave the front of the head in order to strike a blow against the self-respect of the Han people. Moreover, the entire system of attire was changed, altering the appearance and politics of dress of the Han people and burying the Han traditional attire for the next three millennia. Nevertheless, traditional Han attire has a distinctive appeal that has written a brilliant chapter in the history of China. Even today, the unique style is admired around the world.

Cheongsam

The *cheongsam* is a style of clothing that developed from Manchurian attire. During the Manchurian period of minority rule, women wore a traditional long gown, modeled after the garb of the Manchu women. The *cheongsam* was labeled *qipao*, after the Manchurian social group *qiren* (referring to the eight banners).

Because of improvements to the *cheongsam* in the early twentieth century, it reached the height of popularity in the 1930s, when it became known worldwide as the Chinese dress. This was in fact the golden age of the *qipao*. From its birthplace in Shanghai, it rapidly became the fashion in almost every part of the country and the standard of dress for all Chinese women. The female socialites of Shanghai were quite socially active, and during the 1930s they embraced luxury and the modern waves of fashion. Soon afterward, for the entire country the *qipao* was the choice attire of Chinese women. Further, Shanghai revered the Western lifestyle to such an extent that a Western-influenced *cheongsam* came on the scene. This style broke the mold of the traditional aesthetic, creating a more slender, voluptuous look, emphasizing the beauty of women and becoming a fresh, distinguishing fashion among Chinese women. After several years of modification and improvements, the *cheongsam* has become a fashion complementary to American women.

The traditional dress of China, *qipao*, is constructed using traditional materials such as silk and brocade. Commonly worn with the hair wrapped in a tall bun, the dress well suits the flowing, melodic beauty of the Chinese woman, like a natural, unrestrained painting accompanied by poetry. This emerged in modern times as a warm and virtuous look, attractive, lucid and elegant, matching the temperament and standard of fashion of the first half of the twentieth century, as East-West aesthetic ideas were exchanged and interwoven. And so the breathtaking charm of the Orient propelled a popular classic style into the iconic fashion of today.

There is a wide range of *qipao* styles. There are button lapels, pipa-style lapels, slanting lapels, double lapels, high-collared, low-collared, no-collared, long, short, with or without sleeves, possibly a slit on the side of various lengths, as well as custom fitting tailored to the height of the individual—all of which serves to make each unique. The changes in *cheongsam* style that took place during the first half of the twentieth century were mainly to the sleeves and the lapels, yet the fundamental pattern and certain distinct features endured. *Qipao* is now recognized as the epitome of classic Chinese women's attire. Despite thousands of fashion trends, fashion designers still look to this classical treasure for inspiration.

The exterior of the *qipao* most commonly features a large lapel that overlaps from left to right, in either a full-buttoned or half-buttoned style, a standing collar with a button, and a slit on one side. The garment is generally cut from one piece of material. The opening on the side is a distinct trait of the *cheongsam* but is not a required feature. There are slits on both sides, and the upper and lower sections of the dress are approximately the same size. The collar and cuffs are adorned with meticulous decoration, which are fine examples of the complex handicrafts of embroidery, embedding, inlay and coiling. In modern times, the *cheongsam* has entered an era of three-dimensional design. It has become more form-fitting in the waist and back, with added Western-style sleeves, or sleeves not so long as previous. The fine embroidery patterns are even more exquisite than meticulous hand-worked embroidery that took hours.

Cheongsam reached the peak of its popularity in the 1930s and 1940s, but in the wake of the Communist Revolution, the general populace regarded elegant clothing in a completely different way. The leisurely and wise virtuous female image represented by the *cheongsam* gradually lost its status in that atmosphere. Then, during the 1980s and 1990s, the *cheongsam* as uniform emerged. Women began wearing them as greeters for businesses promotions, in ceremonies, as entertainers and as waitresses. Since the 1990s, people have been taking yet another look at the *cheongsam* after society's aesthetic ideas about the ideal female image underwent more drastic changes. The *cheongsam* became appropriate for the fashionably tall, slender feminine physique, once again attracting new attention.

Qipao is the traditional dress for the modern Chinese woman, but the true traditional Chinese clothing is the Han attire. This style has undergone several changes over time, but, more importantly, its popularity has spread

Diversified styles of *cheongsam* in 1930s China

throughout the modern world. The *cheongsam* has a definite historical value. Moreover, it has retained its value as elegant fashion. Though some of the modern styles may lack content, some regions have preserved their elegant folk art styles and these are bound to increase in worth, as they are greatly admired.

THE STORY OF THE FAN

In ancient times, the folding fan was called the *jutou* fan, *san* fan and *zhedie* fan. The names refer to the two ends of the fan folding together. The slats of the fan were typically constructed of bamboo or ivory, with a paper or silk covering. The three components of a folding fan are: the slats, the leaves and the face. Generally, the slats of an ordinary fan were made of bamboo, with paper annealed to the face. In addition, more elaborate fans were adorned with famous paintings and calligraphy. Extremely high-quality folding fan slats and leaves were generally made of ivory, and many featured extremely intricate carvings. Rare masterpieces like these were invariably painted or etched by famous artists.

The folding fan emerged before the Song Dynasty but its use was not widespread. As the Song Dynasty arrived, the production of folding fans reached considerable heights. This was a trend that continued throughout the Ming Dynasty, as the emperor issued an edict that all artisans should replicate the *gaoli* fan of Korea, drawing from foreign influence to develop a Chinese version. The Ming and Qing eras were the golden age for the folding fan. Using fine, rare materials and exquisite techniques, various artistic forms were expressed on the slats, creating a unique style admired by many. Every inch of such a fan embodies the heart and soul of the artist and incorporates an elaborate overall arrangement. The face is adorned with scenic mountains and rivers, birds, flowers or scenes of activity involving people and expressing an elegant, classical rhetoric and spiritual intensity.

In the early stages of fan making, nobles of the Ming Dynasty used folding fans commonly made of bamboo and silk. Later, the imperial court issued an edict that every year numerous exquisite fans were to be manufactured and presented as tribute to the emperor. This practice gained increasing momentum among the palace of the Ming Dynasty.

The selection of materials used to produce the fans became more and more refined and the creation skillfully innovative. Fan slats were made of ivory, hawksbill tortoise shell, fragrant sandalwood, agar wood and Lady Palm, as well as other types of wood. Refined techniques of fan making included spiral gold inlaying, etched lacquer ware and lustrous stain. Various designs and patterns were carved on the slats, exhibiting exceptional and wonderful artisanship.

During the Yongle period of the Ming Dynasty, Emperor Zhudi prompted a tide of fan manufacturing, ordering that great numbers of fans be made. On the face of these fans was inscribed classical poetry, and they were given as gifts to his ministers.

At one time the folding fan was quite rare but later became typical fashion. Literary and refined scholars wrote verses expressing friendly analogies and metaphors in calligraphy on fans. Carrying a fan in hand was an indication of nobility and refinement.

The folding fan continued to evolve, reaching the pinnacle of perfection during the Qing Dynasty. During the Ming and Qing dynasties, the production of masterpieces in the Jiangnan region began, and on these fans scholars expressed their romantic passion with intricate design. Their classical works depicted the scenic beauty of the Jiangnan region and the heavy romantic atmosphere of river culture. They incorporated poetry and landscape paintings. By means of the folding fan, these talented works were and continued to be displayed in imperial palaces, official residences, boudoirs, common households and abroad, retaining their intrinsic value and receiving a tremendous boost in prestige.

Various types of fans were produced using different materials, and the fans were named accordingly. The spring fan or autumn fan was made with many light slats. The fragrant fan was doused with perfume. Travelers made use of the boot fan, as it was easy to conceal in the boot for later use. Another type of fan was the *qiaolang* fan, whose face was made of a transparent muslin such that one could see through it. There was also a type of fan called a three-faced fan that opened from the left and the right because the face was made of three distinct panels. In the middle of one of the panels was a painting of the Spring Palace.

In addition, fans produced by particular manufacturers and different artists were named accordingly, such as the *Huang shan, Cao shan, Pan shan, Chuan shan* and *Qingyang shan*. The folding fan varied in ornamentation and practical use; the material and craftsmanship determined its use.

It is recorded that the earliest fan business was Hangzhou's Fangfeng establishment. This family grew wealthy from generations of producing and selling fans. Within the walls of Hangzhou City they purchased a villa secluded by flowers, trees, bamboo and rocks. Their hundred-slat fan is one of the ancient classical fans still produced today. Although its slats surpass a hundred pieces, this fan looks small and dainty and is painted in

A folding fan painted with birds and flowers

antique color tones. Chengdu, Nanjing and other regions are also well known for fan manufacturing.

The folding fan is far less practical than the cattail leaf fan for its cooling ability. Yet the Chinese folding fan has grown beyond the realm of functionality, bearing distinguished art that represents the beauty of life. It is commonly believed that the folding fan was brought to China from Japan. After the Japanese fan arrived in China during the Song Dynasty, it quickly generated widespread interest in imperial households and among scholars, gaining the favor of literary artists. On their early contact with the Japanese fan, artisans in Zhejiang Province quickly absorbed its merits. They adopted Lady Palm, mottled bamboo, ivory, boxwood and sandalwood to produce the fan ribs. Artisans also carved poems, pictures of figures, landscapes, flowers and birds on the slats. They adorned the fans with such pendants as jade accessories and fringe, creating rich, artistic treasures for the world. Today, China is the world's largest producer and exporter of folding fans, which have found their way to several countries.

FOLK ARTS AND CRAFTS

Folk arts and crafts have played a significant role in China's five thousand-year history and retain a strong essence of life as well as distinguishing features. A great variety of art forms enrich the scope of folk crafts, including paper cutting, embroidery, fabric printing, batik dying, kite-making, ceramics, wood cutting, shadow theater, clay sculpture and New Year painting. Often, the artisan is employed to create commodities with a high practical value. Still other craftsmen emphasize ornamental value as they produce the artwork used for marriage ceremonies and festivals. Paper cutting and embroidery are two widely acknowledged excellent examples of Chinese artistry.

Paper Cutting
Paper cutting refers to the traditional method of making handicrafts by cutting paper with scissors to form different patterns. Materials utilized for this popular art range from common paper to gold and silver foil, tree

bark and leaves, cloth and leather. Paper cutting is one of the oldest Chinese handicrafts and has a close relationship with Chinese festivals and marriage ceremonies. At these times, people paste paper cuts on walls, windows, pillars and mirrors to enhance the festive atmosphere and as prayers for good luck and fortune. Regional styles with distinct local character have emerged all over China. In particular, the paper cuts in Gaomi of Shandong Province and Foshan of Guandong Province are unique for their outstanding characteristics. Generally speaking, the artistic style of the northern Chinese paper cut is straightforward, bold, honest, simple and concise. In the south, it's more exquisite, refined and delicate and often incorporates humorous subject matter. As a reflection of cultural folklore, such subjects include "Eight Immortals Crossing the Sea," "One Hundred Years of Lotuses," "The *Qilin* (unicorn) Carrying Its Son," and "Rats Marrying Off Their Daughters."

The art form of paper cut emerged in the sixth century. During the Tang Dynasty, the paper cut evoked the soul of the social customs of the time and circulated among the common people, reaching high levels of achievement as complete intricate works of art were created.

The technology of making paper experienced great improvement in the Song Dynasty, as different colors of paper were introduced, thus stimulating the popularity of paper cutting. Paper-cut designs were commonly used as decoration on gifts and placed on windows, lanterns and tea cups. Among the masses, during the Song Dynasty the popularity of paper cutting grew. In the Jizhou district of Jiangxi Province, artists discovered a way to incorporate a type of paper cut and ceramics, using a delicate glaze and kiln-firing process to form a kind of ceramic. Common images popular among the people included donkey, ox, horse, ram and other shadow puppet animals. Carved human images completed the shadow theater cast. During the Ming and Qing dynasties, the art of paper cutting was immensely popular and reached its peak. The public expanded on the use of paper-cut patterns as bright floral designs. These were applied to lanterns and fans as decoration as well as integrated with embroidery. The use of machinery to cut the patterns also began. Even more common, this art form has been extensively applied as household decor to create an appealing social environment. People adorn wooden gates, windows and cabinets, as well as canopies. Paper cuts are tremendously popular for festive events.

In addition to the professional male artisans who emerged during the Northern Song Dynasty, among the common people in rural villages many highly

Rats Marrying Off Their Daughters

skilled women excelled at this art. In fact, paper cutting is a traditional skill in China typically long practiced by women. Similarly, the art of paper cutting was also commonly studied by women from an early age. They learned the craft from their elders or older sisters. The methods include the face cut, double cut and drawn cut and the results portray an appreciation for nature's birds, beasts, flora and fauna. The skill travels from one's heart, as great expression is revealed with scissors. Like ivy on a tree, the art of paper cutting, has retained its vigor and vitality from ancient times, even today having symbolic meaning and being of practical and aesthetic intent.

Embroidery

The embroidery of ancient times was known as *zhenxiu*, which used brightly colored thread to stitch decorative designs on textiles and was a pioneer in the field of visual arts. Traditionally practiced by women, it was referred to in the past as *n'hong* (female needlework). Excellent examples of surviving Chinese handmade embroidery exemplifying exquisite balance have been excavated in Hubei and Hunan provinces. These artifacts date to the Warring States Period and the periods of the two Han eras. Embroidery of the Tang and Song dynasties is characterized by the fine and even distribution of thread and vivid color. Also prevalent at the time were embroidered calligraphy and precise decorative patterns. The works commissioned by the Ming and Qing royal palaces are quite unique. Simultaneously, there was further development in the skills among the common artisans, giving rise to four distinct regional styles—Su, Yue, Xiang and Shu—all with their own styles and everlasting charm, with the techniques passed down from one generation to the next.

Su embroidery, made popular during the Song era, has a long history. At that time, in the city of Suzhou in Jiangsu Province emerged an embroidery and clothing district that produced much artistic work. During the Ming Dynasty, *Su* embroidery continued to develop its distinct attributes, thus expanding its influence. The Qing Dynasty allowed for a mature phase—embroidery for the royal courts came mainly from the hands of *Su* needle workers, and styles among the masses also became abundantly colorful during this time. *Su* embroidery has been widely regarded as fine, distinct and elegant. Beautiful designs, quiet colors, brilliant luster, agile stitching and meticulous work give birth to lifelike images. The criteria for this style can be summarized in eight words: balance, luster, orderliness, distribution, harmony, arrangement, thinness and density.

Numerous stitching methods were developed for *Su* work but mainly used were the straight stitch, backstitch, crouching and laid work, the cross stitch and the satin stitch. *Su* embroidered pieces fall into two major categories: one includes commonly used items such as quilts, pillowcases, clothes, theater costumes, rugs and cushions; the other strives for aesthetics and includes work such as wood-framed designs, hanging scrolls and standing screens. Embedded in the work are a range of subjects including flowers, plants, animals, human personas, landscapes and calligraphy.

Su embroidery

Yue embroidery, also called *Guang* embroidery, contains complex and arranged compositions of dazzling rich color, well-distributed materials, numerous types of stitching and continuous flowing lines. *Yue* embroidery is found in many brilliant works. Greatly admired are wall scrolls and hanging and standing screens. Items in everyday use include decorated quilts, pillowcases, bed covers, shawls, scarves, valances and embroidered garments. These typically include images of birds and flowers and much ornamental design. Frequently depicted are the phoenix, peony flowers, cranes, apes and deer. Chickens, geese and other such creatures are also often seen together within a frame.

Xiang embroidery comes from areas around the Changsha Prefecture of Hunan Province. Early works of *Xiang* embroidery give prominence to the decoration of things in daily use. Later this form evolved to be used to create brilliant works of art. Distinctive qualities of Xiang embroidery include the use of velvet thread (without wool) and delicate weaving patterns, which produce genuine works of art. Frequently used was the popular blue tint of traditional Chinese paintings and deep multicolored thread, and there was an emphasis on contrast, intensely lifelike imagery and a bold, unconstrained style.

Also called *Chuan* embroidery, *Shu* embroidery is the general term for embroidery originating in the areas surrounding Chengdu in Sichuan Province. *Shu* needlework is done with soft satin and brightly colored silk as raw materials. Designs on *Shu* embroidery include landscapes, people, fish, birds and flowers of all sorts. Various methods of *Shu* include the crotch stitch, *yun* stitch, slanted stitch, rotating stitch, chain stitch, tent stitch and the plaited stitch—in fact, there are over one hundred types of stitches. The work is found on things such as quilts, pillow cases, clothing and shoes. *Shu* embroidery is characterized by its distinctly vivid quality, bright colors, the use of three dimensions and meticulous, dense stitching that is flat and even.

Chapter 13

CAPITAL CITIES

The capital cities that emerged in the early wake of nation building are numerous.

It is estimated that there have been about two hundred Chinese capitals since ancient times. Among the capitals of the various dynasties, Beijing, Xi'an, Luoyang, Kaifeng, Nanjing, Hangzhou, Anyang and Zhengzhou are the most famous, known as the Eight Great Ancient Capitals. The capitals are noted for governing vast regions. The number of years a city was occupied by a dynasty was a determining factor in its overall impact on the historical record.

Beijing, the capital of the People's Republic of China, is the center of modern China's politics, economics, culture, transportation and tourism. It is one of the world's greatest historical and cultural cities, as well an ancient capital. Beijing was a strategic city during the slave-owning Yan and Ji periods. It was the provincial capital of the Liao Dynasty and the seat of the governments of the Jin, Yuan, Ming and Qing. On both ground level and underground, Beijing has an abundance of preserved cultural relics, and it is known around the globe as having been a significant city over the course of history. This ancient city has a time-honored tradition, a history of over three thousand years. Currently in Beijing there are Tiananmen Square, the Monument to the People's Heroes, the Memorial Hall of Chairman Mao, the Forbidden City, North Sea Park, the Temple of Heaven, the Summer Palace, the Thirteen Tombs of the Ming and the Great Wall, as well as the ruins of early peoples and numerous relics of revolutionary and cultural significance.

Xi'an, in ancient times called Chang'an, is located on the Guanzhong Plain in the southern regions of the Weihe River. As the capital city with the longest history, former regimes that chose Xi'an their capital included the Zhou, Qin, Han, the Western Jin Dynasty, pre-Zhao Dynasty, pre-Qin, Late Qin, the Western Wei Dynasty, Northern Zhou Dynasty, the Sui and the Tang Dynasty. As a world-renowned ancient capital, Xi'an boasts many cultural relic sites. Among these, the most famous are: Fenggao of the Western Zhou, Epang Palace of the Qin Dynasty, Chang'an City of the Han Dynasty, the Palace of Tang, the Giant Wild Goose Pagoda, the Small Wild Goose Pagoda, in addition to the bell and drum towers of the Ming Dynasty and the Stele Forest. The surrounding area is also the location of Emperor Qin Shi Huang's mausoleum, the Terracotta Warriors, the ancient walls of Xianyang and the ruins of the Banpo Neolithic Village.

In 139 BCE, renowned ambassador and traveler, Zhang Qian, led a detachment of troops on a diplomatic mission. For the first time, they traveled from Chang'an to the Western Regions, visiting the Loulan, Guizi and Yutian regions, establishing what history recognizes today as the Silk Road. This road passed through Central Asia, reaching the lofty Pamir Plateau and connecting to Southwest Asia. For several centuries, the route played an important role in promoting the cultural communication between China, India, Rome and Persia. The great inventions of the Chinese, including silk, gunpowder, paper and printing, were spread to the West via this route. At the same time, Buddhism, Nestorian Christianity and Islam were introduced to China, as the Silk Road served as a bridge in the form of amiable communication between China and the outside world.

Luoyang, formerly called Yi Luo, part of Yuzhou in ancient times, takes its name from its location on the verdant slopes of the ancient Luoshui River. The eastern portion of the city is connected by the Zhengzhou Prefecture, the Pingdingshan, and Nayang prefectures to its south; Sanmenxia in west, and the Jiaozuo Prefecture to its north, and it is divided by the Yellow River. Luoyang was a famous capital city for nine dynasties, and so there are many historic sites such here including the most famous, in the southern region of the city—The Longmen Grottoes. In the eastern portion lies White Horse Temple, the first Buddhist temple in China. This area also boasts the ruins of the ancient cities of the Han, Wei, Western Zhou, Sui, and Tang periods, as well as the many ancient Tombs of Guanlin. Luoyang itself is a historic and cultural relic, being one of the four largest capitals of ancient China, with tourism now being important to its growth. Thirteen dynasties and regimes chose Luoyang as their capitals, in succession: the Xia, Shang, Western Zhou and Eastern Zhou Periods, the Eastern Han, Cao Wei Dynasty, Western Jin Dynasty, Northern Wei, Sui, Tang and Later Tang, as well as the Later Jin period. The city is remarkable for its thousand-year history as a capital city, second only to Xi'an.

Kaifeng, in ancient times known as Bianliang, is located in the central region of China. Situated on the banks of the Yellow River, it has played an extraordinary role in Chinese history and is considered the cradle of Chinese civilization. The city has an established tradition of more than twenty-seven hundred years. Kaifeng served for a time as the Capital of Seven Dynasties, including the Wei State of the Warring States Period, the Later Liang period of the Five Dynasties, the Later Jin Dynasty, the Later Han period, the Later Zhou, the Northern Song and Jin dynasties. A great number of cultural relics and historic sites are found in the area, including the Iron Pagoda, the Fan Tower, the Dragon Pavilion, the Terrace of King Yu, the Daxiangguo Temple and the Northern Song's Bianliang City Ruins. Kaifeng city enjoys a superior location, temperate climate, bountiful resources and convenient transportation. It has experienced remarkable development in education, advancements in technology, and a prospering economy, and so it has become a major tourist attraction whose doors are open to visitors.

As one of the eight celebrated capitals, Nanjing has been described as where tigers crouch and dragons coil, in reference to its strategic location. Known as the Jingling ancient imperial state, Nanjing has been a regal state since ancient times and bears a brilliant cultural heritage. To date, the city has been occupied in succession by the Wu Dynasty, the Eastern Jin, Song, Qi, Liang, Chen, Northern Tang and Ming dynasties and the Taiping Heavenly Kingdom. It was also the seat of the Republic of China. Spanning more than 455 years of history, Nanjing is commonly referred to as the Capital of the Ten Dynasties. Within its borders are a variety of historic and cultural heritage sites, including Yuecheng, the Ruins of Jilin, the Tomb Carvings of the Six Dynasties, the Two Imperial Mausoleums of the Southern Tang Dynasty, the Ming Dynasty City Wall Ruins, the Mansion of the Prince of the Taiping Heavenly Kingdom and Dr. Sun Yat-sen's Office and memorial at Zhong Shan Mausoleum. The scenery in this city is exquisite. There are undulating hills in the southeast, flowing rivers in the northwest and lush trees within the city walls—more than forty-eight scenic wonders in all. The culture of the area is fascinating, as well. To imagine ancient times and the numerous fluttering flags in the Qinhuai district of the city tells one of the grace and beauty of the inhabitants of Nanjing and reveals a sense of fascination with the regal state of Jiling.

Hangzhou is another of China's ancient capitals. The Qin Dynasty invested in establishing Qiantang County, which became the city of Hangzhou in the Sui Dynasty. It was the capital city of the Wu and Yue states during the period of the Five Dynasties and became the temporary capital of the Southern Song Dynasty. Hangzhou is a city renowned around the world for tourism, as visitors come to see the many ancient cultural

Dr. Sun Yat-sen's office

relics, such as the West Lake Lingyin Temple, the Temple of Yuefei and the Six Harmonies Pagoda, among many others. The West Lake is undoubtedly the best-known feature of Hangzhou. Often quoted is, "In heaven there is paradise; on earth there is Suzhou and Hangzhou," elaborate praise for a brilliant city throughout the ages. Su Dongpo, a talented writer of the Song Dynasty, wrote, "Among the thirty-six western lakes under the heavens, Hang-

Hall of Supreme Harmony in the Forbidden City

zhou contains the greatest." West Lake is surrounded by cloud-capped hills on three sides and a landscape of beautiful mountains and rivers bordering the city walls on the fourth.

It is said that the natural beauty of Hangzhou is as great as that of a beautiful woman with or without makeup, as it bridges the natural beauty of the landscape and all living things.

Hangzhou's scenic beauty blends naturally with its cultural traditions. In this scenic area are: ancient gardens, pavilions, pagodas, springs and gullies, grottoes, inscriptions carved on a stele cliff faces, bead curtains, jade belts, willow trees and bridges, the West Lake Lingyin Temple, the Six Harmonies Pagoda, Feilai Peak, the Temple of Yuefei, the Xiling Pass, Dragon Well, and Tiger-running Spring, the most frequently visited attractions. These marvelous scenes of lush mountains and clear waters have attracted generations of scholars, as well. It was once said, "Among all the sights to remember in Jiangnan, Hangzhou is the most memorable!"

The city of Anyang is home to the famous Oracle Bone Inscriptions and the birthplace of *The Book of Changes*. Anyang's history as a capital city dates from the Shang Dynasty, when King Pan'gen moved the seat of the government to Anyang in 1300 BCE (today's suburbs of Anyang). The city served as the capital city of the Shang Dynasty for 254 years, home to eight dynasties and twelve emperors. Excavation of this area has uncovered the earliest evidence of writing in China—the Oracle Bone script—in addition to the world's largest bronze tripod vessel, Simuwu. The city is also part of many ancient folklore tales, such as "Dayu Controls the Water," "King Wen Consults the Changes," "Fuhao's Request," "Su Qin Pays His Respects," "Xi Menbao Governs the Ye District" and "The Mother-in-law Gives a Tattoo." Under way now are efforts to preserve Anyang's many cultural relics. Within its borders there are eight major sites under state-level protection and thirty-two cultural relic sites under provincial-level protection. A long history and resplendent culture has left an invaluable historical and cultural heritage in Anyang.

Zhengzhou was one of the capitals of the Xia and Shang dynasties, as well as the capital of the Guan, Zheng and Han vassal states. Research in this area has revealed evidence of the eight thousand-year-old Peiligang culture, a Dahe village dating back over five thousand years and numerous relics of Prince Qin, as well as the Dragon Mountain site. A long history has left a rich cultural heritage in Zhengzhou. The city boasts more than fourteen hundred cultural places of interest; among these, twenty-six are national heritage conservation sites. The Songshan Scenic Area is one of forty-four key scenic areas and a national model of scenic interest and tourism. Shaolin Temple, honored as the grandest temple under the heavens, is located at the base of Songshan Mountain. The world-renowned Shaolin art of *kung fu* originated at this temple. There are also many distinct structures here, such as China's earliest observatory, Zhougong's Observation Deck and the Star Observation Terrace of the Yuan Dynasty. Also here is one of China's four ancient academies, the Songyang Academy of the Song Dynasty, and the Zhongyue Temple, the largest existing Taoist structures in China. Scattered around Zhengzhou and the surrounding area there are also the sites of ancient cities, civilizations, tombs, ancient architecture, old mountain passes and the ruins of battlefields. The city has been the birthplace of many great historical figures, including Lie Zi, Zi Chan, Du Fu, Bai Juyi and Gao Gong. Located in the hinterland of the central plains, Zhengzhou is an important city and a major transportation hub along the newly established Eurasian Continental Bridge.

PALACE ARCHITECTURE

Beginning with the construction of the royal palace of the Qin Dynasty, architecture has been an important part of Chinese society. The palace is where the monarch and royal family resided. As a show of the emperor's prestige and rule over all things under the heavens, the architecture of ancient palaces was dignified and awe-inspiring. The palace was generally designed in two main sections, front and back. The front portion was where the emperor dealt with the politics of the dynasty. In the back section were the living quarters for the ruler's concubines and wives. Between these was the main palace section, built on a north-south central axis, the sides symmetrical. Courtyards were positioned one after another, and the royal halls of the palace were endless, traversing vast areas of the precise and stately building.

The central portion of the palace was dominated by a vast roof of gold and jade in glorious splendor (an idiom of the day) and there were pillars of vermilion-painted wood, grand entrances and broad white marble floors.

The great roofs of the palaces are not only very beautiful but also served to safeguard the buildings. Layer upon layer of eaves and roof horns are curved so as to divert rainwater from the building, thereby protecting these wooden structures. The meaning of the birds and beasts decorating the roofs is shrouded in mystery today, but they did serve as pivoted fastening points and prevented the rotting that comes from precipitation. The roof of the palace was commonly decked out with gold-tinted glazed tiles. This color evoked the idea imperial power and so was reserved exclusively for the royal family.

Using large amounts of timber to build a palace was a fundamental characteristic of Chinese architecture. The roof beams, pillars, doors and windows were made of wood and painted a rich vermilion color, symbolizing happiness and wealth. In some parts of a palace there were paintings of dragons, phoenixes, flowers and plants and seas of clouds. The bright colors not only added to the palace splendor but also served to waterproof the walls and resist termites. The Hall of Supreme Harmony in Beijing is the largest wooden palace in China.

Pure, thick white marble was the basis of the flooring and the foundation of the imperial palace. The Palace Museum in the Hall of Supreme Harmony, as another example of a palace's use of marble, is constructed of three floors of white marble, the stele and the steps carved with exquisite dragons and various kinds of decorative designs. The main hallways used by the emperor were carved of immense stones into ocean waves, floating clouds and raging dragons, altogether a spectacular sight.

For thousands of years, the emperors did not hesitate to use their kingdoms' labor, materials and financial resources to build their expansive palaces. The pity is that most of that splendid architecture was destroyed by fire during the wars. Also, many palaces were burned in conjunction with the emperors' passing. The Forbidden City in Beijing is today the most preserved and intact of the royal structures.

The Beijing Imperial Palace, also called the Forbidden City, arose during the Ming and Qing dynasties and was the residence of twenty four emperors. There are numerous grandiose halls here. It is one of the largest and the most intact ancient buildings, and it is ranked number one among the world's Five Great Palaces (France's Versailles Palace, Buckingham Palace

The Temple of Heaven

The Summer Palace

in London, the United States' White House, and the Kremlin in Russia being the other four.) The palace incorporates Chinese traditional classic styles and Eastern patterns and is indispensable to reminding us of the heritage of China. In 1961 it was named a national historic cultural relic.

The Temple of Heaven occupies an area of 1.05 million square miles, vaster than the Forbidden City. Double walls form inside and outside altars that surround the area. The main sections are the Hall of Prayer for Good Harvests, the Imperial Vault of Heaven and the Earthly Mount. The wall of the ancient altar was square in the southern portion and round in the northern part. This symbolized the roundness of the heavens and the squared nature of the earth. The Earthly Mount altar is in the south, the Hall of Prayer for Good Harvests altar in the north. Both rest on a north/ south axis but are separated by a wall. In the area of the Earthly Mount Altar, one finds the Earthly Mount and the Imperial Vault of Heaven. At the Altar of Prayer for Grain there are the Hall of Prayer for Good Harvests, the Hall of Imperial Zenith and the Gate to the Hall of Annual Prayer. The rational layout of the Temple of Heaven and the beautiful, meticulous construction have made this building famous around the world. This was the palace where the Ming and Qing dynasty emperors offered sacrifices to heaven and prayed for grain production in the region. This installation is the largest group of ancient sacrificial structures in modern China and a treasured heritage of world architecture.

In addition to the Imperial Palace and the Temple of Heaven, the Summer Palace and the Old Summer Palace boast two more famous royal court architecture styles in historic China. The Summer Palace features the most well-known landscape garden in China, with green mountains and sparkling rivers. Also here are lofty pavilions and meandering corridors, all resplendent and magnificent. The Summer Palace enjoys a high reputation in China and among foreign countries in terms of the landscape. And here, too, is the Long Corridor, the most extensive corridor in the country, connecting distant mountains and nearby waters and extremely artistic in nature.

TEMPLE ARCHITECTURE

China is a country of many religions. There is the native-born Taoism, and there are the foreign beliefs, including Buddhism, Islam and Christianity. The various religions all have their own distinct architectures. The Taoists build what are called palaces or monasteries. Buddhism is housed in temples pagodas and grottoes. Islam has the mosque and Christianity the church, each religion determining its building style. Yet, despite the foreign religious architectural style influences, the religious structures in China retain much Chinese influence.

The Buddhist Temple

Buddhist temples are generally built in the mountains, far from the racket of the city. In the most scenic areas of China we find monasteries, the most famous being the Four Sacred Mountains of Buddhism, namely, Mount Wutai, Emei Mountain, Mount Jiuhua and Mount Potala, each with a celebrated temple.

Buddhism arrived in China from India, but China's Buddhist structures are quite different from their Indian counterparts. India's temples use the minaret as the center. China adopted this building practice but placed the palace hall at the center. The overall arrangement of the temple, the design of the hall and the construction of the roof all imitated these features in the palace of the emperor, making for a distinctive attribute of Chinese Buddhist architecture.

Chinese temples are commonly built on a north-south central axis and are of symmetrical design on either side. Generally, the shrine built on this axis includes the monastery gate, the Emperor's Heavenly Palace, the Hall of Great Strength, the Preaching Hall and the Hall of Buddhist Scriptures. Also included on either side of the main hall are drum towers, adjoining palace halls and the monks' living quarters. The architecture of the temple is splendid and grand and evokes in the mind a magnificent, stately feeling. The Luoyang White Horse Temple and Heng Mountain's Suspended Temple are typical of this type of construction.

White Horse Temple is located 5.6 miles east of the city of Luoyang. The north side is backed by Qi Mountain, and the Lou River flanks the south. Ample evergreen and cypress trees make for a solemn environment and cast protective shadows on the lush vegetation and vermilion-painted walls. Housed in the rectangular courtyard are the Hall of the Heavenly Emperor, the Hall of the Great Heroes, the Hall of One Thousand Buddhas, Guanyin

Pavilion and the Pilu Pavilion. Of these, the main structure is the Hall of the Great Heroes. In addition to visiting tourists, many Buddhists make the journey from within China to pay their respects here.

As the first official Buddhist temple in China, White Horse Temple was commissioned by the Han Emperor Liu Zhuang in accordance with the demands of Buddhism and in admiration of the traditional architecture. After the establishment of this temple, the Buddhist influence grew, deeply influencing the thoughts and lives of many. Later, Buddhism spread abroad from China, to Vietnam, Korea and Japan, among others, where the Chinese influence was felt. Therefore, White Horse Temple is referred to as Buddhism's Ancestral Courtyard.

Within the borders of Shanxi Province is the Suspended Temple, on the lofty northern sacred Mount Heng. As if suspended among the clouds, this temple embodies the great wisdom and techniques of ancient artisans. The Suspended Temple is on a precarious cliff and looks over a deep ravine. The temple is of distinct design and was made with building methods rarely seen. The Suspended Temple was built halfway up the mountain on the west side of the Golden Dragon Valley, twenty-two miles south of Huanyuan County. It is today the only wooden temple in China situated on a cliff overhang. It was first built during the Northern Wei period, then consecutively restored during the Tang, Jin, Ming and Qing dynasties. The temple faces Mount Heng, and a screen of jade green vegetation is at the rear. The endless stone stairs here lead to a magnificent aspect of Mount Heng.

Wutai Mountain in Shanxi Province is one of the most famous holy Buddhist sites in China. There are many Buddhist structures on Wutai Mountain. To date, fifty-eight ancient buildings have been preserved. Among these are the most well-known South Meditation Temple and the Light of the Buddha Temple. From north to south, the South Meditation Temple measures 197 feet, and the east-west length is 168 feet. The temple was built during the Tang Dynasty over a three-year period, beginning in 782. In recognition of its four distinct wonders—the statues, murals, calligraphy and architecture—the South Meditation Temple has been called a gem of the world. The Light of the Buddha Temple was renovated continuously throughout various dynastic periods. Situated halfway down the mountain, it features three levels of courtyard, each enclosing a palace hall, a main chamber, residences and other structures. The Light of the Buddha

The Suspended Temple at Mount Heng

Temple was given an earthly aspect, the pillars, arches, gateways and walls having only a flowery green tint. As prescribed, these have been painted vermilion.

The Great Buddha Palace in Tibet

Chinese temple architecture differs from region to region, each nationality having its own distinctive style. For example, the Lamaism temples each contain a Great Buddha Palace and a Hall of Buddhist Scriptures, built in relation to the particular mountain location. The Tibetan temples were built of earth, timber and stone, with timber being the main material. The Halls of Buddhist Scriptures have three floors. The thick walls are of brick and stone mortar, and the windows are extremely small, making for an ascetic tone. The Potala Palace in Lhasa, Tibet, is one of the most prominent temples of China. It is of the typical architectural style of the Tang Dynasty and was made using the artistic building methods of Nepal and India. It has become a major tourist attraction for both Chinese and foreign visitors.

Chapter 14

MONEY

China was among the first countries to use money, and its currency has been in use in China for at least four thousand years.

Before the advent of currency, people mainly used the barter system, but this proved to be a difficult system, and so a form of monetary exchange emerged. China's earliest currency was introduced during the Shang Dynasty (seventeenth to eleventh century BCE), this at first being mainly cowry shells. In the later period of the Shang Dynasty, bronze, shell-shaped coins heralded the start of the minting of Chinese coins. Although used as currency for the Shang, these were not widely circulated. As the Spring and Autumn Period arrived (770–476 BCE), minted bronze coins become the common currency. Throughout the Spring and Autumn and the Warring States periods (770–221 BCE), every state issued a different type of coin. Among these, the state of Chu issued the *ying yuan*, China's earliest form of gold currency. There is evidence to suggest that China was among the earliest nations to adopt gold as a form of exchange.

In 221 BCE, Emperor Qin Shi Huang unified China and standardized the currency, stipulating gold to be the metal of highest value and the lesser-value bronze coins to be used for daily circulation. Further, bronze coin manufacturing was regulated such that only circular coins with a hole in the middle could be produced, so giving China's currency a basic shape. This style was in use for over two thousand years, until the final days of the Qing Dynasty.

In the first year of the reign of the Han Dynasty (338), minted coins began bearing the name of the emperor's reign. This type of currency is called *Han xing*, as the first production clearly indicated the first year of the reign of Emperor Li Shou.

The Tang Dynasty (618–907) saw ancient Chinese society at the peak of perfection. The continuing development of politics, economy and culture in turn triggered changes in the currency. The Tang Dynasty stopped naming coins by weight and mass, the value no longer calculated by these measurements. The coins for circulation were renamed the *tong bao*. Among these was the *kai Yuan tong bao*, which was in use for over three hundred years as the main coin in circulation during the Tang period. Also during the Tang era there arose a type of paper money called *fei* currency. Merchants made massive amounts of money in the form of coins, but it was inconvenient and unsafe to bring the coins home, and so a different mechanism of exchange needed to be developed. An institution was created that kept half a receipt, the merchant holding on to the other half, to indicate a withdrawal or deposit. Merchants could then go home safely and easily with financial records. *Fei* currency was quite similar to the use of personal checks today.

Kai Yan Tong Bao coin

Coins minted during the Song Dynasty surpassed those made earlier in both quantity and quality. The most-used material for the coins of the Northern Song period was copper. During the Southern Song Dynasty, iron coins were prevalent. (At the same time, silver also played an important role in the development of money.) One of the most significant events was the birth of *jiaozi*, the earliest paper note in the world. Paper currency became increasingly useful, and it was also known by a variety of names, including *kuaizi* and *guanzi*. Paper bills first emerged in Sichuan during the Northern Dynasty and the currency was named using the local dialect. *Jiaozi* was first used only among a few merchants but this currency eventually replaced the copper and iron coins. Afterward, the government of the Northern Song established offices to handle transactions involving *jiaozi*. During the Southern Song Dynasty, state-issued *kuaizi* and *guanzi*, similar to *jiaozi*, were put into circulation and became the dominant forms of currency of the day.

The high point in the use of paper money in ancient China came during the Yuan Dynasty, although silver remained a standard form of exchange. (The silver ingot, called *Yuan bao*, originated in the Yuan Dynasty.) Early in the time of the Yuan government, at one point copper coins were banned. Although later in that period, a few types of copper coins were minted, the amount was still far less than previously. The paper note became the dominant form of currency (while silver money remained as and accounted for a large proportion of the wealth).

The Ming Dynasty was vigorous in its issuance of paper currency, called *chao*. In the early period of this dynasty, only *chao* was used for exchange, and copper coins were not in circulation. Later, money became a mixture of copper coins and *chao*. Eventually only one kind of paper bank note was issued, the Great *Ming bao chao*. Also, silver issued by the Ming Dynasty became legal tender and was used for large business transactions, while the paper *chao* notes were used for smaller transactions. All the currency in circulation at that time was collectively called *Tong bao*.

During the Qing Dynasty, small amounts of silver were used for frequent business transactions. At the onset of the Qing Dynasty, the over two-thousand-year-old method of minting coins evolved into a casting process. During the later period, the Chinese emulated the machine minting processes of other countries.

Further, imported silver coins were made popular during the Qing Dynasty and the Republic of China. They were imported from Spain during the Wanli period of the Ming Dynasty (1573–1620) but were not extensively circulated until the Qing era. During the reign of Dao Guang (1821–50), the Taiwan and Fuzhou regions mimicked coins of foreign origin, producing the *yin bing*. The Guangdong area minted silver coins called Guangxu *yuanbao* in the fifteenth year of the reign of Guangxu (1889). Other regional mints were then established and produced similar coins. In the second year of the reign of Xuan Tong (1910), the Qing government issued regulations on the monetary system, establishing silver as the standard coin metal. But the Xinhai Revolution occurred, so the system was not officially adopted.

In 1912, the first year of the Republic of China, souvenir coins were issued in honor of the founding father, Dr. Sun Yat-sen. In 1914, silver coins were minted bearing the likeness of former Emperor Yuan Shikai on one side. Among ordinary people this coin was referred to as the Yuan *datou*. In 1935, the Nationalist Government enacted currency reforms prohibiting the circulation of silver coins.

After the People's Republic of China was established, the People's Bank of China collected and exchanged the remaining outstanding silver at a fixed rate, as the circulation of silver was now illegal.

The Chinese people take pride in the history of China's money, particularly in the paper money that emerged during the Song Dynasty, as this ushered in a new era of currency production around the world. The Chinese paper *jiaozi* outdates the earliest Western paper currency by five hundred years. (Swiss Bank notes arrived on the scene in 1661.)

MEDICINE

Traditional Chinese medicine, also referred to as *Zhong Yi* and has thousands of years of history. During the Warring States Period (221 BCE), a systematic work of medical theory appeared entitled *The Yellow Emperor's Internal Classic*. Since then, Chinese medicine is the only medical system in the world that has continued in its original form, and today it continues to play a vital role in treating disease.

As a unique medical system in China, Chinese traditional medicine has made significant contributions to medical science. Some even call it the fifth great invention of China.

While Chinese medicine focuses on the body, it also views the body as part of nature, and so the anatomy alone is not studied. The, Chinese approach attaches great importance as well to the relationship between disease and state of mind, living conditions and environmental factors, especially changes in the weather. In clinical treatment, Chinese medicine opposes the idea of simply treating the head for a headache and the foot for foot pain, emphasizing instead a complete understanding of the root causes of the disease at hand and treating it accordingly. At the same time, Chinese medicine regards the body as an organic whole. It does not address the disease symptoms alone. Instead, it closely inspects the whole body and makes correlations between affected areas and internal organs, meridians (energy channels), the blood and bodily fluids. In pharmacology, Chinese medicine emphasizes the compatibility of medicines when prescribing. One example of this approach is that the kind of medicine prescribed depends on the individual traits of the patient. Attention is also paid to the properties of the medicines and the proper ratios of mixtures. Chinese medicine and its doctrines use modern scientific observation and methods that result in a profound understanding.

Over the years of the development of Chinese medicine, a series of unique diagnostic and treatments have come to be summarized. These are commonly referred to as observation, listening, questioning the patient and feeling the pulse.

Diagnosis by observation refers to examining the body, the complexion and the shape and coating of the tongue. In this way, the location and nature of a disease can be pinpointed in accordance with changes in the above-mentioned areas. This method is also referred to as inspection diagnosis.

"Listening" means that the doctor identifies the sounds and smells of the patient, in addition to the condition and changes in the voice. So this is also known as listening and smelling.

"Questioning" is simply interviewing the patient and family regarding the onset and development of the disease, as well as understanding the current symptoms and conditions relevant to that disease.

Feeling the pulse, also called touching, refers to taking the patient's pulse and probing the skin, hands, abdomen limbs and other parts of the body in order to diagnose a disease.

Among these four observations, feeling the pulse and probing are unique to Chinese medical diagnosis. This focus on the pulse tells us that doctors in ancient China had mastered pulse conditions and their relationships to various parts of the body including the heart, blood and blood vessels, the rate of circulation of the blood, breathing, and pulse frequency. Understanding all of these demands great knowledge of anatomical physiology. The idea of diagnosing the pulse and probing the body spread to neighboring countries (including Japan and Korea), spread to Arab regions in the tenth century and reached Europe in the seventeenth century.

Acupuncture

Acupuncture is a primary mode of treatment in traditional Chinese medicine and an in-depth methodological system. Its advantages lie in curing disease without the need for medication. Instead, the patient is pierced with needles in areas that correspond to other areas of the body. (Heat may also be used to stimulate particular regions to combat illness; this method is known as moxibustion.) According to ancient medicine and meridian theory, each part of the body is filled with main and collateral channels of blood vessels and energy channels, which regulate the flow of qi (气) and blood (血). These relate to functions of the organs and blood and connect the upper and lower parts of the body as well as its internal and external functions. The acupuncture points are the monitors of the meridian networks, and so stimulating them plays a significant role in regulating the meridian systems. Acupuncture therapy has a clear and obvious effect in treating illness. Many foreign scholars regard China as the motherland of acupuncture therapy. The practice is not uncommon in the West today.

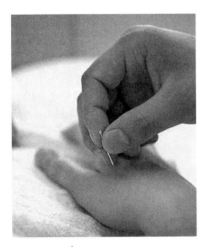

Drugs

Chinese pharmacists through the ages have studied and recorded more than three thousand plants, animals and properties of minerals and the efficacy and uses of them as medicine. From these materials as ingredients, different types of curative mixtures, pills, powders, ointments and pellets are made. Chinese traditional therapeutic formulas are referred to as *zhongyao*.

Acupuncture therapy

Medical Texts

Many famous Chinese medical works have been preserved over the ages. One such book is *Shennong's Herbal Classic*, completed during the Eastern Han Dynasty. This is the first specialized work in the world on the study of medicine, outdating European books on the subject by at least sixteen centuries. *The Treatments for Typhoid and Other Complicated Diseases*, written by Zhang Zhongjing during the Eastern Han Dynasty, is another early specialized classic on pharmacology, written hundreds of years before *The Canon of Medicine* by the Persian medical scientist Avicenna. Another groundbreaking text emerged during the Song Dynasty, *Record of Washed Grievances*, compiled by Song Ci. It is the world's first compilation in forensic science. During the Ming Dynasty, Li Shizheng published a work entitled *Compendium of Materia Medica*, which is celebrated as Oriental medicine's dictionary. It has therefore been published in several languages. These famous indispensable works have enabled the science of Chinese medicine to be handed down intact from generation to generation.

Throughout the history of Chinese medicine, there have been many famous doctors, such as Hua Tuo, Bian Que and Zhang Zhongjing. Of the two, Hua Tuo of the Eastern Han Dynasty was the first to administer general anesthesia. (It was not until 1805 that a Japanese surgeon, Hanaoka Seishu, used datura flowers as an anesthetic, and this is acclaimed as a pioneering achievement in the history of anesthesia.) The fact is, however, that this great undertaking occurred much later than the work of Hua Tuo.

CHESS

Xiangqi, or Chinese Chess, is a unique invention of the Chinese. Its long history originates from the Warring States Period. After a period of development, the modern form of Chinese Chess appeared during the Northern Song Dynasty. The game consists of thirty-two pieces and a chessboard containing a river boundary. The pastime continued to be popular in the Southern Song Dynasty.

Xiangqi is played by two opponents whose objective is to kill or capture the enemy's general (checkmate). Generally, the player with the red pieces moves first. Each player moves in response to the other, on separate lines, and this goes on until there is victory, defeat or a draw. Each player moves one piece from the point it occupies to another intersecting point of lines. A piece can be moved onto a point occupied by an opponent's piece, in which case the enemy piece is captured and removed from the board. A

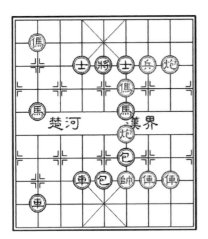

Chinese Chess

move and a response made are called a round. Chinese Chess is an ideal game for enriching cultural life, cultivating personality and perseverance, boosting intelligence and improving one's capacity for dialectical analysis.

Chinese Chess uses thirty-two pieces, red and black, each player starting with sixteen pieces of the same color. The opponents have similar pieces that are divided into seven categories and placed on opposite sides of a board. The red side has one king and two: guards, ministers, chariots, knights and cannons, in addition to five soldiers (pawns). The black pieces are a general, two pieces each of advisors, elephants, knights, chariots and cannons, as well as five soldiers. All the pieces in the same category perform the same functions.

The chess pieces are played placed on a distinctive board, a rectangle nine parallel lines wide by ten lines long. This makes a total of ninety intersecting points on which the pieces are placed to form a square grid. The center of the board is an empty space between the fifth and sixth horizontal lines, called a river boundary. The river is the dividing line between the opposing sides. An area with two diagonal lines connecting opposite corners and intersecting at a center point and forming a matrix is called the nine points of the palace. To record competitions and study strategy, a notation system is used that describes absolute positional references. The positions on the board are numbered one to ten, from closest to farthest away; the digits one to nine are used for the files from right to left. Both values are relative to the moves of the players. The black and red pieces are placed on the appropriate intersecting points for the start of a game. Each move toward the opponent is recorded as an advance; a withdrawal is retreat. If the forces are equal, the play is called balanced.

Soon after the People's Republic of China was founded in 1956, Chinese Chess was listed as a national sport. The statewide chess competition categories today are men's singles, men's team, women's singles and women's team. The best players are awarded titles by the Chinese National Sport Committee. These include Chess Grandmaster and Distinguished Grand-master.

In November 1978, the Asian Chinese Chess Federation was launched via the concerted efforts of foreign players and people from various regions of Southeast Asia. Its membership has since expanded to include players from the Philippines, Malaysia, Thailand, Singapore, Indonesia, China, Brunei, Hong Kong and Macao. Hong Kong tycoon Huo Yingdong was once the president. The Preparatory Committee of the Chinese Chess Federation was set up in Beijing in 1988, and this encouraged the further development of traditional Chinese Chess. The first World Chinese Chess Championship was held in Singapore in 1990.

Recent years have seen vigorous growth in the popularity of Chinese Chess. Chess leagues and clubs are found throughout the world, and Chinese Chess associations have been established in many countries, including the United States and France. Chinese Chess, along with Western (international) chess, enjoys immense popularity as a pastime in many countries in Europe and the Americas.

MARTIAL ARTS

The martial Arts, or wushu, also known as kung fu, consist of a number of fighting styles developed over the centuries in China. Martial arts are one of the chief representatives of traditional Chinese culture. The movements in martial arts include the kick, punch, throw, hold and thrust. Among these, the thrust is emphasized. By mastering these techniques, one learns self-defense with the bare hands or by using special weapons and restricted movements.

Two main components of *kung fu* are hand-to-hand combat and a series of skills and techniques. The practice takes the form of a series of predetermined movements done in a linear way. The combinations of attack and defense movements are greatly admired and a spectacle to see.

Wushu can be practiced solo, in pairs or by groups, barehanded or armed with ancient Chinese weapons. Among the many styles are *changquan* (longfist), *nanquan* (Southern Fist), *tai chi chuan, Xingyiquan* (shadowboxing) and *baguazhang*. The weapons are the knife, sword, staff, spear, double broadsword, double rapier, nine-section whip and three-section truncheon. There are three distinct types of sparring: hand-to-hand, with weapons and barehanded while the opponent is armed. Group exercises involve hand-to-hand sparring and armed combat. The many routines and movements not only show off combative and defensive skills but have as well an aesthetic value. *Wushu* is a popular form of barehanded fighting.

Over thousands of years of evolution of Chinese martial arts, some unique features gradually developed. For one, the practice emphasizes physical and mental harmony. Chinese *kung fu* practitioners follow the philosophical ideal that the body and mind are an inseparable, integral system. They believe that *wushu* is by no means limited to external movement but also involves the full exercise of the internal temperament, mental attitude and potential of the combatant. So, as well as exercising the body, the spirit is also trained. The three fundamentals of *wushu* are the practice of thought, the flow of *qi* and the body's capacity for strength. Much attention is also paid to harmonious social relations.

Traditional Chinese schools of martial arts often deal with the study of martial arts not just as a means of self-defense and mental training but also as a system of ethics. Although different groups of martial artists have their own characteristics and practices, moral character and etiquette are held in great esteem by *wushu* masters. The values stress cultivating generosity and tolerance for the sake of a stable and orderly society. Every school has a set of precepts to preserve the dignity of the teacher, to propagate goodwill and to avenge evil. The master will test the virtue of the potential pupils before he accepts them as disciples. Within Chinese *wushu* there is a martial morality that is a criterion for evaluating *wushu* competitions and related events.

Another characteristic of *wushu* is the importance of the harmony of man and nature, and this is recognized by many martial arts masters. In their view, humans have an intrinsic relationship with the universe and can draw inspiration from the laws of nature so as to create different styles of fighting. For example, martial artists have developed the Snake Fist style by imitating the movements of snakes.

Among the Chinese martial arts communities, the Shaolin Monastery is prominent. Located at Mount Shaoshi (at Song Mountain), west of the city of Zhengzhou, in Henan Province, in the Dengfeng district, the Shaolin Temple has a long history. It was built during the Northern Wei Dynasty in the nineteenth calendar year of the reign of Emperor Taihe. During the early period of the Tang Dynasty, the thirty monks of the Shaolin Temple fought on behalf of Li Shimin, the king of the state of Qin, to defeat the self-appointed emperor, Wang Shichong. After Li Shimin was enthroned, he awarded the Shaolin Temple large grants of land and money to expand the temple complex. During the period, then, the Shaolin Temple witnessed explosive growth, and Shaolin *kung fu* was greatly improved on and developed, thanks to the substantial support of the imperial court.

The Chinese believe that all *kung fu* under the heavens originates at the Shaolin Temple. In 1982, the film *Shaolin Temple*, starring Jet Li attracted thousands of *wushu* fans from around China as well as abroad, and this resulted in scores of visitors to the Shaolin Temple and the growth of the practice of Shaolin martial arts. Moreover, Shaolin *kung fu* has captivated the attention of more and more people in other nations. There are Shaolin *kung fu* associations in over forty countries, including the United States and Germany. Shaolin temples are established in accordance with the traditional training and skills of the Shaolin monks and are warmly received by the locals.

Shaolin monks practicing *kung fu*

Another traditional Chinese martial art popular in China is *tai chi chuan* (supreme ultimate fist). *Tai chi chuan* is a collection of motions that temper force with mercy, and the practice is conducive to good health as well as self-defense, owing to its perfect balance of forcing and yielding. *Tai chi chuan* training has proved effective in clearing away obstructions in the body, synchronizing the heart and blood flow, nourishing the viscera and strengthening the muscles and bones, among other beneficial results.

Most modern styles of *tai chi chuan* trace their development to at least one of the five traditional schools—the Chen, Yang, Wu Hao, Wu and Sun styles. *Tai chi chuan* is quite common in China. In public places one often sees people practicing this martial art. In other parts of the world, including Europe, the Americas, Southeast Asia and Japan, the art has been received and accepted as a form of exercise and is enjoyed as such by many. Rough statistics indicate that in the United States alone more than thirty books on *tai chi chuan* have been published. And there are *tai chi chuan* associations and groups in several countries.

Chinese martial arts have also greatly influenced motion pictures. The displays of *kung fu* by stars such as Bruce Lee, Jackie Chan and Jet Li are widely admired by Hollywood and by moviegoers around the world. Many viewers elsewhere also appreciate Chinese *kung fu* on the silver screen.

FOLK THEATER

Folk musical theater (quyi) is a general term used to describe speaking and singing performances. It is a tradition of oral literature and song. Over time, these art forms have greatly evolved into distinct styles. Oration and song are the major artistic devices of folk musical theater. According to surveys, there are some four hundred varieties of theater still in vogue all over China. Among the various types of folk musical theater that have been passed down, the widely popular and influential forms include comic dialogue, short sketch, storytelling, ballad singing, monologue storytelling, *kuai ban* and duets.

Chinese comic dialogue originated in Beijing and became popular in all parts of the country. It is generally believed that the comic dialogue originated during the Qing Dynasty. An art form that amuses by telling jokes or doing comic Q&As, comic dialogue is presented mainly in the Beijing dialect, although in different parts of China local dialects are also used. There are three main types of comic dialogue: the monologue, crosstalk and group banter. In the monologue form of comic dialogue, one actor performs and tells jokes. In the crosstalk comic dialogue, there are two performers, and three or more actors perform in a group, banter-style, also called *qun huo*. The artistic devices employed in crosstalk are primarily speaking, imitating, teasing and singing. Speaking refers to telling jokes, guessing lantern riddles and performing tongue twisters. Actors also emulate the sounds of birds and animals as well as the actions, speech and facial expressions of peddlers, opera singers and various other characters. Teasing involves the actors joking with each other. Singing refers to the vocalizing of traditional peaceful songs. Over its long evolution, a list of famous actors have worked with Chinese comic dialogue, including Hou Baolin, Ma Sanli, Ma Ji, and Jiang Kun. Chinese comic dialogue enjoys great popularity not only in China but abroad as well, especially the form of imitation. At the end of 1989, Canadian Mark Rowswell (Chinese name Dashan) honored his teacher, the famous performing artist Jiangkun. He went on to perform on many stages in China and on television, and so his name became a household word.

The short sketch form of comic dialogue deals with brief dialogues and performances. Using distinctive spoken languages as a basis, it is often improvised and includes a complete understanding of and exact imitations of characters and their languages. As a type of impromptu performance, the short sketch requires that the actor embody everyday life experiences and express them using a common language. The comedic scene is the most common form of short sketch. A more recent genre of Chinese comedy arose in the early 1980s. Given a dramatic inheritance and growth in the appreciation of the merits of drama, crosstalk, dance duets and short plays, Chinese comedy has broadened its horizons. Several famous players have done funny acts, most notably Zhao Benshan and Chen Peisi.

Storytelling is called *pingci* in the north, northeastern and northwestern parts of China. In southern China it is called *pinghua*. This is an oral form of literature created by the early Chinese. In the early days of storytelling, an actor sat at a table with a fan, a wooden gavel and a block of wood. The gavel was used to strike the block, indicating the start of the performance and intermission. The gavel was also used to remind the audience to be quiet and to get their attention, thus reinforcing the theatrical effect. The performers usually wore traditional gowns as they recited and commented on ancient folklore. Development during the middle of the twentieth century, however, led to the abandoning of the tables, folding fans and gavels, actors started standing, and they routinely did not wear gowns. Monologue storytelling is mainly performed with the northern dialect as the basis; the Beijing dialect of Mandarin serves as the standard tone. Since monologue storytelling is spoken, the third-person narrative is mainly used in telling the story. Shan Tianfang is a prime example of a famous performer of monologues.

Ballad singing, also referred to as Suzhou *pingtan*, is the general name for Suzhou storytelling using lyrics in the Suzhou dialect. It is an ancient and graceful artistic form of describing and singing. In this form of storytelling, an actor performs on a stage describing historical romances and chivalrous heroes. Another lyrical form involves two actors singing to the accompaniment of a *pipa* (lute), and sometimes it is one actor playing an instrument and singing. The ballads often involve love stories from legendary novels and folk tales. As ballad singing is mainly performed in the Suzhou dialect, it is a flexible artistic form of speaking and singing. This art is celebrated by many as the most beautiful vocal art in China, and it is quite pleasing to the ear.

Monologue storytelling, developed in Beijing and Tianjin, involves oration mainly in the Beijing dialect, with drum accompaniment. Before 1946, there were many different names for this performance art. After folk musical theater guilds were established in Beijing in 1946, *jingyun dagu* became the official name. The accompanying instruments involved are mainly the three-stringed *sanxian* and the four-stringed *sihu*. In certain situations, the *pipa* (lute) is also played. Performers create rhythms by beating drums and wooden percussion instruments. This form of theater emphasizes singing short songs in the Beijing dialect.

Kuai ban started out as a type of singing and performing by beggars in the street. Then it developed over time as a result of the work of inventive actors. Common performances of *kuai ban* consist of actors standing on stage while keeping rhythm with bamboo clappers and singing rhyming lyrics. *Kuai ban* emphasizes creating improvisational lines. An actor must be well versed in impromptu work and able to articulate thoughts without hesitation. These demands mean that a performer has to be quite talented.

Duets, also called *bengbeng*, originated in the three northeast provinces of China. People in these regions, especially farmers, are fond of the duet. It is a form of theater that involves speaking, singing, dynamic music and lively dance. *Bengbeng* has been around for about two hundred years. The duets are mainly presented in this way: a man and a woman in brightly colored clothing hold folding fans and handkerchiefs. They step, sing and dance side-by-side as a story is revealed. The singing is uninhibited and humorous, with the libretto easily understood in the language. The duets are marked by a fine sense of humor and are breath of fresh air, full of the vivid colors of life. Of the many well-known duet song-and-dance performers, Zhao Benshan is one of the most famous.

In sum, many forms of Chinese folk musical theater have arisen to enrich the lives of the people. Moreover, given their abundant cultural connotations, these forms of musical performance are also appealing to foreigners.

Musical Instruments

The ancient Chinese invented a great number of musical instruments with various designs and characteristics, All of these produce beautiful and rich melodies. They are pleasing to both the eye and mind and so are greatly admired. Chinese musical instruments are able to express both subtle feelings and complicated changes in emotion. The Chinese folk instruments popular today are the reed pipe, the bamboo flute, the zither, the long zither and the two-stringed *erhu*.

The reed pipe, also called the bamboo *xiao*, is an ancient instrument. It is made of bamboo and is blown directly into. Along with the bamboo flute, it has a long history and belongs to the same family of musical instruments. The timbre of the reed pipe is a gentle and round tone that lends an air of seclusion. When played in the night, its warm and beautiful sound is moving. Performers in China are commonly referred to as *chuixiao* or *pinxiao*. These names reflect the belief that only individuals of high moral sentiment can play the reed pipe. For this reason, ancient scholars greatly admired this instrument. Much later, the reed pipe was introduced abroad, where its music was also well received. At the International Exposition in London in 1896, and in Panama in 1913, the Chinese *yuping* reed pipe was awarded gold and silver medals, respectively, marking the first times a Chinese musical instrument won world prizes.

The bamboo flute, also called a *dizi*, is made from a single section of bamboo. The sound is made by holding it horizontally and blowing into the side. The bamboo flute has a fairly long history in China. Sima Qian's *Records of the Grand Historian* from the Han Dynasty makes mention of this flute. The bamboo flute has distinct ethnic features and produces a bright warm sound that is enjoyed by many. For this reason, this flute is celebrated outside China as an amazing musical instrument with invaluable ethnic qualities. The bamboo flute is common throughout China, and many musicians who can play this flute live in rural areas.

The *guzheng*, or zither, is an extremely ancient Chinese stringed instrument. According to *The Records of the Grand Historian* by Sima Qian, the *guzheng* was fairly popular in the state of Qin during the Warring States Period. In 1979, in the city of Xianyan in Guixi County of Jiangxi Province, an archeological discovery was made of a *guzheng* in a group of tombs, proving it had passed the test of time. During the Tang and the Song dynasties, the *guzheng* typically had thirteen strings; later, varieties of sixteen, eighteen, twenty-one and twenty-five strings were developed. Today the *guzheng* has gener-

Zither

ally twenty-one strings. The typical technique for playing the *guzheng* is to use the thumb, index finger and middle finger of the right hand to pluck the strings and play the melody. The left hand is manipulated to control the variation of tone and the pitch of the strings. The range in sound of the *guzheng* is extremely wide, allowing for a beautifully colored tone, and so it has been regarded as the king of musical instruments and the piano of the Orient.

The *guqin*, also called the heptachord or long zither, is one of the most ancient of Chinese plucked stringed instruments. It enjoyed great popularity during the period of Confucianism and has continued to influence the Chinese upper class for the last three thousand years. The name, *guqin*, literally meaning ancient stringed instrument, was coined in the early twentieth century. This instrument is usually 3 *chi* long and 6.5 *cun* (47–49 inches), symbolizing the three hundred and sixty-five days in a year. The *guqin* originally had five strings. Later, the number increased to seven, and so it was called the seven-stringed *quqin*. The tone of the *guqin* is peaceful and elegant. In order to achieve an ideal mood for artistic creation, performers are required to meld the outdoor surroundings with a peaceful state of mind. In ancient Chinese society, the *guzheng*, Chinese Chess, classic literature and painting were regarded as essential to cultivating the personality of literati and scholars. Moreover, for thousands of years people of such stature have traditionally favored the *guzheng* as an instrument of great subtlety and refinement. Today, the sounds produced by the *guzheng* are a symbol of the soul and essence of Chinese music. One particular piece of *guzheng* music has been recorded and pressed on a gold-plated record that is aboard the

United States spacecraft *Voyager*. And so the music is sounding day and night through boundless space, yearning to make intimate acquaintances throughout the universe. On November 7, 2003, UNESCO headquarters in Paris issued its second list of representative works of the oral and non-material legacy of mankind, and the *guzheng* was on that list.

The two-stringed *erhu*, one of the most common bowed string instruments, first heard during the Tang Dynasty, is still played today and so has enjoyed a history of over one thousand years. It arose among the ancient nomads of northern China and was known throughout the region as the *huqin*. The tradition of the *huqin* continued throughout China during the Ming and Qing dynasties, and it became a primary instrument for theater performances. As the modern era arrived, the instrument was renamed *erhu*. With an elegant and mellow timbre, the *erhu* can be used to express lonely, exquisite and almost lyrical emotional tones, much like the human voice. Throughout China, well-known erhu music includes a composition by Abing (Hua Yanjun) entitled *The Moon's Reflection on the Two Springs*. This work is deeply emotional and has a unique timbre and expressive force as the strings sing to the hearts of millions. This composition has fascinated not only the Chinese people, it has also earned a great reputation in international music circles. The world-famous Japanese conductor Seiji Ozawa commented, "I should kneel down upon listening."

For their unique regional characteristics and ethnic flavor, Chinese musical instruments offer the world a unique aesthetic in music rich in Chinese cultural connotations.

PAINTING

The classical art of Chinese painting in ancient times had no particular name. It was generally known as *danqing*, and this referred mainly to paintings on loosely woven silk and fine paper that were mounted on scrolls that were hanged or rolled up. As the modern era arrived, in an effort to differentiate between Western painting and the traditional Chinese style, the former became Western oceanic painting and the latter Chinese painting or National painting. The tools used for traditional Chinese painting are the paintbrush, ink, traditional water-based paint and special paper or silk. Using traditional artistic styles and techniques, painters create outstanding visual works.

Chinese paintings can be categorized according to the materials used and the means of expression. Ink-and-wash paintings depict people. So-called landscape paintings are of mountains and rivers. Bird-and-flower-style paintings are, appropriately, of animals. With its deep-rooted ideological implications, Chinese painting reflects the social ideologies and aesthetic tastes of the Chinese people. It also represents the artists' understanding of nature, society, politics, philosophy, religion, morality, literature and art.

Ink-and-wash painting is a distinctive form of traditional Chinese painting. It makes use of water-based ink (*shuimo*). The style developed in China during the Tang Dynasty and continued during the period of the Five Dynasties, also enjoying great popularity during the Song and Yuan. Throughout the Ming and Qing dynasties and then into the modern era, the style became even more refined. Having mastered the brush, an artist can produce rich strokes with abundant layers of saturation and a wide range of colors. Wang Wei of the Tang Dynasty believed these paintings to be divine, and later generations were of the same opinion. Ink-and-wash paintings have long occupied an important position in the history of Chinese art.

Renwu hua are basically paintings of people. These figure paintings, in short, *renwu*, are a major form of Chinese art, and they emerged earlier than landscape art and paintings of birds and flowers. They generally include Taoist and Buddhist art, paintings of official women, portraits and paintings of social customs and historical events. The painters make every effort to portray the distinct characteristics of the individual, to render a vivid, life-like appearance of both body and spirit. Often depicted in the wash of ink is a residence—the embodiment of the social atmosphere—or a gracefully moving body. The objective of ancient Chinese caricature paintings is to depict an image that is spiritually vivid. Gu Kaizhi was a master of this style during the Eastern Jin Dynasty.

As another type of Chinese painting, landscape painting, is also known as "mountains and waters." Landscape paintings primarily illustrate such natural scenery as mountains and rivers. Landscape painting developed gradually during the Wei and Jin dynasties and the Northern and Southern dynasties. But figure paintings were still popular in those times, and so the landscape style served mostly as background. Distinct landscape styles did not emerge on a grand scale until the Sui and Tang dynasties, the period

A painting by Mi Fu

of the Five Dynasties and the era of the Northern Song. Many famous painters did landscape work during these periods, including the well-known father and son, Mi Fu and Mi Youren.

The Yuan Dynasty turned to freehand brushwork to convey meaning, allowing a correct ideology to guide practical work, emphasizing the technique and beauty of the brush and ink and opening the door to innovation. During the Ming and Qing dynasties, and to this day, the genre of landscape painting has seen further development by using contemporary features.

Birds-and-flowers painting is a Chinese style named for its subject matter: plants and animals. The birds-and-flowers genre focuses on expressing the aesthetic relationship between man and nature in a romantic way. Through the depiction of plants and animals, artists reflect their own thoughts and feelings about the spirit of the times and the state of society. Paintings in this genre reflect the distinctive features of foreign paintings with similar themes. Famous artists in this style include Zhu Da of the Qing Dynasty and Wu Changshuo in modern times.

Chinese national paintings have characteristics particular to China and show the great contrasts between Chinese and Western paintings. Chinese paintings put an emphasis on romantic charm, whereas Western paintings attach importance to the representation of form. To contrast them, the differences between Chinese and Western paintings can be described as follows:

1. The brushstrokes that make Chinese paintings distinctive are used throughout, while such strokes are not common in Western paintings. In Chinese paintings, painters use brushstrokes to represent objects and motion, while Western painting is primarily concerned with the representational and classical methods. As seen at a glance, Western styles of painting pay close attention to material objects, while, in the Chinese tradition, this is not necessarily the case.

2. Chinese painting does not emphasize perspective as much as Western painting does. Typical of Western painting are stereoscopic objects represented on the plane, as the style strives to depict real objects. To achieve this, perspective must be emphasized. Chinese painting, on the other hand, does not typically do this and is not constrained by perspective. Chinese painters go as far as their imaginations will take them.

3. Classical Chinese painting does not fully express anatomy, while the Western painting of figures is strongly associated with the physique. Western portraits typically strive to portray a genuine human anatomy, while artists doing traditional Chinese painting focus on the posture and traits of their subjects rather than their sizes and dimensions. So this

genre of symbolic art, as opposed to realism, was adopted in China to achieve a sense of spirit rather than common likenesses.

4. Western painting emphasizes the background, whereas Chinese painting does not always do this. Typically, Chinese paintings do not reach to the edges of the canvas. For example, a plum blossom may be painted in the middle of a piece, seemingly suspended in mid-air, and around it are wide, blank margins. This is by no means the way of Western realist paintings, as here every object requires a setting. For example, fruits are painted with desks or tables as background. Figures are depicted indoors or in open fields. Commonly, there is no blank space on the canvas of a Western painting. Also, in the West, emphasis is placed on true rendering and on the obvious qualities of the subjects. This is not so with Chinese painting. The portrayal of a setting is systematic in classical Western painting, based on a theory regarding outward appearance and resemblance. Conversely, Chinese paintings strive to capture the spirit of the subject, and the artists opt to omit what they see as trivial matters; in Chinese painting, themes are highlighted.

5. Most of the themes of Chinese paintings are of nature, whereas the human subject is usually the major theme in classical Western paintings. Before the Han Dynasty, this was also the case, but landscape painting began to take center stage during the Tang Dynasty. So far, in fact, landscape painting has been the most important style of Chinese painting, while since the days of ancient Greece portraits have been the major theme in the West. During the Middle Ages, artists generally focused on portraits of religious figures.

The style of Chinese classical painting is distinct as an art form, especially as it has developed into modern times and the modern work has inherited the traditional skills and techniques of classical art.

Chapter 15

THE GREAT BOOKS

The Four Books is a compilation of representative Confucian essays. *The Four Books* includes *The Analects of Confucius*, *The Book of Mencius*, *The Great Learning* and *The Doctrine of the Mean*. The Five Classics refers to *The Book of Songs*, *The Book of History*, *The Book of Rites*, *The Book of Changes* and *The Spring and Autumn Annals*.

 The Analects of Confucius records the words and deeds of the great ideologist, Confucius, and his disciples. Confucius, whose given name was Qiu and courtesy name, Zhong Ni, lived between 551 and 479 BCE in the State of Lu (present-day Qufu in Shandong Province) during the Spring and Autumn Period. He was a great thinker, statesman and educator and the founder of Confucianism. Confucius had significant influence on Chinese culture and ethics. Completed by his disciples during the early period of the Warring States era, *The Analects of Confucius* is one of the classic works of the Confucian school. It deals with philosophical, political, economic, educational and literary issues.

 The Book of Mencius is a written account of the thoughts and actions of the philosopher, Mencius (372–289 BCE) and his students. He was also known by his birth name, Meng, and the courtesy name, Ziyu. He was from Zou County (today the southeastern city of Zoucheng in Shandong Province) and lived during the middle of the Warring States Period. He was a great ideologist, politician, educator and advocate for Confucian ideology.

 Prior to the Southern Song Dynasty, *The Great Learning* was originally one chapter in *The Book of Rites* and had not been published separately. The work is said to have been written by Zeng Can (505–434 BCE), a disciple of Confucius. During the Southern Song Dynasty, Confucian scholar Zhu Xi took the chapter "The Great Learning" from *The Book of Rites* and rearranged it to make it an integral masterpiece among *The Four Books*. Moreover, Zhu Xi considered *The Great Learning* to be the most significant of *The Four Books*.

 The Doctrine of the Mean was also originally part of *The Book of Rites*. It was not published on its own before the Southern Song Dynasty. It is said that the grandson of Confucius, Zisi (483–402 BCE), compiled the work. During the Southern Song Dynasty, Zhu Xi withdrew the section from *The Book of Rites* and included it among *The Four Books*.

The Book of Songs—in the early Qin Dynasty period called *Poetry* or *Three Hundred Poems*—is the first anthology of Chinese poems. It is a collection of 305 poems written over a period of five hundred years, from the start of the Western Zhou Dynasty to the middle of the

The Four Books and the Five Classics

Spring and Autumn Period. Sources indicate that the work was edited by Confucius. *The Book of Songs* contains three types of songs: *feng*, *ya* and *song*. Feng is local music and collected folk songs. *Ya* is music intended for nobles. And *song* is the accolade used during temple ceremonies. The book is commended as an encyclopedia of ancient society, mirroring social reality and containing glimpses of ordinary life.

The Book of History, in ancient times called *The Book*, received its present title during the Han Dynasty. It is the earliest compilation of documented records of events from the days of ancient China. Recorded in this book are the times of the emperors, Rao and Shun, and coverage until the Eastern Zhou era, telling a history of more than fifteen hundred years. The contents of this book are mainly ancient imperial proclamations and conversations between emperors and ministers. There are two versions of *The Book of History*: the modern language format and the ancient Chinese version.

The Book of Rites is an anthology of articles written by Confucian scholars from the Warring States Period to the Qin and Han dynasties. The book deals with their interpretations of the ancient text, *Etiquette and Ceremony*. However, *The Book of Rites* overshadows *Etiquette and Ceremony* in its influence because it is a much more in-depth report. There are two adaptations of *The Book of Rites*. One version was written by Dai De and consisted originally of eighty-five chapters. Today there are only forty known chapters, *The Classic Rites of Da Dai*. The nephew of Da Dai went on to compile another version comparable to the modern *The Book of Rites*, which contains forty-nine chapters selected by Dai Sheng. It is known as *The Classic Rites of Xiao Dai*.

One of the most important texts of ancient China, *The Book of Changes* is revered as an early leader in classic literature. *The Book of Changes*, also referred to as *The Changes of the Zhou*, was completed during the Zhou Dynasty. It contains 24,070 Chinese characters. *The Book of Changes* is composed of two parts, the script and the commentary. The commentary is written to explain and expand on the meanings of the script. As a manual of divination, *The Book of Changes* is a summary of life experiences and growth. It uses abstract symbolism to interpret the phenomena of the cosmos and the laws of nature. In modern times in the West, it is known as the *I Ching*.

The Spring and Autumn Annals was originally a general term for the official chronicles of every state during the pre-Qing period. With the passage of time, though, only the official chronicle of the State of Lu stayed intact. The text of the *Annals* was compiled by various scribes from the State of Lu. It is believed that it was arranged, revised and given particular meaning by Confucius, thereby becoming a classic work of Confucianism. *The Spring and Autumn Annals* is the ancestor of Chinese chronological historical texts and documents the 242-year history of the State of Lu. The sentences are short, and there is little effort at composition, but when read aloud it is heard to be of a disciplined and prudent quality. By the careful use of word and allusion, Confucius, writing in the *Annals* style, expounded his political ideals and propositions in *The Spring and Autumn Annals* by using as examples historical figures and events. Therefore, this work was classified by later generations as a classic that delivers profound thought via the use of sublime words. Moreover, this book had a great impact on the development of chronological historical records and the literature of later times.

After the Southern Song Dynasty, *The Four Books* and the Five Classics became required textbooks of Confucianism and basic matter for the imperial examinations. In particular, the service exams of the dynasties after the Southern Song Dynasty required that scholars have a good command of *The Four Books*, which led to their popularization. In ancient times, *The Four Books* and the Five Classics were held in extremely high regard, similar to the status elsewhere of the Bible and the Koran.

The classics have had extensive influence on Chinese social norms, interpersonal communication, social civilization and self-development. Even today, *The Four Books* and the Five Classics convey great philosophical implications and strong ethical values. There is also an ever-expanding authority abroad for this classic piece of literature, and it is highly ranked among the world's heritage.

PROSE

The Eight Classical Chinese Prose Masters of the Tang and Song dynasties was a general term used to describe the eight main representatives of prose writing. They included Han Yu and Liu Zongyuan of the Tang Dynasty. The

Song period gave rise to the three Su: the father Su Xun, the elder brother Su Shi and the younger brother Su Zhe. Other prominent authors of the Song Dynasty were Ouyang Xiu, Wang Anshi and Zeng Gong. At the onset of the Ming Dynasty, Zhu You selected and edited the essays of these eight literary giants into *The Works of the Eight Masters*. Shortly thereafter, Mao Kun arranged and compiled their writings and called the collection *Prose of the Eight Masters of the Tang and Song Dynasties*. From then on, later generations referred to these writers as the Eight Masters.

Han Yu (768–824) was born in Heyang (today's western region of Mengzhou city, Henan Province). He was also known as Han Changli because his ancestral home was the city of Changli in Hebei Province. He was a litterateur, philosopher and cultural leader of the Tang Dynasty. As one of China's finest essayists, he ranks first among the Eight Great Prose Masters. Han Yu underwent a series of setbacks in attempting to pass the imperial examination and enter political life. This was due to his reverting to the old ways of thinking and advocating the orthodox Confucian ideology. He started the Ancient Literature Movement of the Tang Dynasty and led a revolution against the popular formal prose style. He insisted that literature should be a carrier of ethics to serve as meaningful guidance to later generations. His writing is compiled in *The Collected Works of Chang Li*.

Liu Zongyuan's (773–819) ancestral home was Hedong, hence his pen name, Liu Hedong. Born in the city of Changan during the reign of Zhenyuan, he was a renowned imperial graduate, eminent ideologist and literary master of the Tang Dynasty. As one of the Eight Great Masters, Liu Zongyuan opposed the then-current literary circles and worked in an ornate and intricate style while advocating unadorned and fluent essays. His popular works are contained in *The Anthology of Liu Hedong*.

Ouyang Xiu (1007–72) was born in Mianyang, Sichuan Province. As a statesman, writer, historian and poet of the Northern Song Dynasty, he called himself "The Drunkard." He was a reformer in both politics and literature and a strong supporter of the Qingli Reformation instigated by Fan Zhongyan. During the Northern Song era he was

Liu Zongyuan's calligraphy

Ouyang Xiu

an innovative leader in the classical prose movement. He was also a patron of younger talents, and Su Shi and his sons, Zeng Gong and Wang Anshi, were all his students at one time or another. During his time as a writer, his poems, lyrics and various essays were extremely popular. His influential ideological thinking and euphemistic expression made him one of the great masters of the Tang and Song eras in the genre of reformed prose. His famous works are compiled in *Collected Works of Ouyang Xiu*. After his death, he was buried in the ancient capital of Kaifeng in Xinzheng County (today's Henan Province).

Su Xun (1009–66) was a famous essayist born of a literary family. He and his sons, Su Shi and Su Zhe, are known as "the Three Su's of Meishan" of the former State of Mei (modern-day Meishan in Sichuan). Su Xun was an expert essayist, especially with regard to political commentary. His prose was remarkable for its fluency and vigorous penmanship. Famous selected works of Su Xun are bound in *The Collected Works of Jiayou*. Legend has it that Su Xun did not begin to study until he was twenty-seven years old, yet he achieved great strides in literature after decades of hard work.

Su Shi (1037–1101) was a writer, poet, essayist, artist and calligrapher of the Song Dynasty. He was often referred to as Su Dongpo. The fifth son of Su Xun, he was born in Mei Shan, in Sichuan Province. During the second year of the reign of Jiayou, he and his younger brother, Su Zhe, both passed the highest level of the imperial examination. In the second year of the Yuan Feng era (1079), Su Shi introduced the controversial and critical style of *wutai* poetry, for which the government sentenced him to exile. He compiled famous masterpieces, as exemplified by the anthology *Seven Works of Dongpo*. Su Shi's literary theory was in line with that of Ouyang Xiu, but the he emphasized originality, expressive force and the artistic value of literature. The essays of Su Shi are easy to understand, fluent, unstrained and passionately written. Following Ouyang Xiu, Su Shi was another leader in the literary circles of the Northern Song Dynasty. He associated with and mentored many scholars during his lifetime and had had a profound effect on the development of Chinese literature in his day as well as in years to come. Su Shi is a rare genius in Chinese literature and art.

Su Zhe (1039–1112), one of the Three Su's, was a native of Meizhou, near Mount Emei in what is now Sichuan Province. He appealed to atone for his imprisoned brother, Shu Shi, who had been found guilty by the government of offensive writing. He offered to forfeit his official post. As a master writer, Su Zhe was greatly edified by his father and his brother. He advocated cultivating and disciplining one's capacity for greatness, believing the effectiveness of an article depends on the education the author has received. His most popular writings are represented in the *Collected Works of Luancheng*.

Wang Anshi (1021–86), also known as Wang Jinggong, was a native of Linchuan (present-day Fuzhou city of Jiangxi Province). He was also known as Mr. Wang of Linchuan. He was a remarkable politician, philosopher, litterateur and reformer during the Northern Song Dynasty. In the third term of the Xi Ning era (1069), Wang Anshi came to power as a prime minister and introduced and advocated socioeconomic reform policies. He was not only a prominent politician and ideologist but also a remarkable literati who placed great significance on the social function of literature and on writing to serve society. Wang Anshi regarded practicality as an element fundamental to literary creations. His works mirrored social abuse and contradiction, with an emphasis on politics. His essays and poems have been compiled in the *Wang Linchuan Anthology*.

Zeng Gong (1019–83), came from Nanfeng, Jiangxi Province, and was a scholar of the Northern Song Dynasty. He is classified as one of the eight great literary masters of the Tang and Song dynasties. His political performance would come to pale in comparison with his literary philosophy and development. As an advocate of moral values, he stressed benevolence and honesty. He was one of the supporters of the Northern Song's new prose reform movement and is known for his outstanding essays. In these he followed the example of Sima Qian, Han Yu and Ouyang Xiu, promoting the literary works that illuminated ethics. His articles had a strong impact on writers of later generations. Some essayists, such as Wang Shenzhong and Tang Shunzhi of the Ming Dynasty, and Fang Bao and Yao Nai of the Qing Dynasty, sanctify Zeng Gong's works to a great extent. His most prolific writings can be found in the collected works, *Yuanfeng Leigao*.

The works of the Eight Great Masters of Prose are the epitome of literary achievement during the Tang and Song dynasties as well as brilliant examples of Chinese classic literature.

Wang Anshi

TANG POETRY

Tang dynasty poetry refers to lyrics written during the Tang Dynasty, often considered the Golden Age of Chinese poetry. Tang poetry is one of the brilliant literary heritages of China. It spans a history of over a thousand years and is still widely known today. *Three Hundred Tang Poems*, compiled by Qing scholars, was for many years a household anthology of poems.

In fact, many poets emerged during the Tang Dynasty. Records tell us there were twenty-three hundred famous authors at the time. Further, there are still many yet to be discovered. The poets' work is preserved in the *Complete Poetry of the Tang*, which contains more than 48,900 poems. The styles of Tang poetry are diverse. The ancient style of verse basically includes five- and seven-character poems, while the modern style falls into two categories: four-line and eight-line poems, both of which can be further subdivided into five- and seven-character poems. The modern style of poetry has strict and comprehensive rules and formats, and so it is also called metrical verse.

There are four main classifications of Tang poetry: early, flourishing, middle and late Tang poetry. At the beginnings of Tang poetry, the art of literature was reformed and became more vigorous, due in large part to the influence of the Four Talents: Wang Bo, Yang Jiong, Lu Zhaolin and Luo Binwang. In addition to these writers, there were many more poets, such as Chen Zi'ang, Shen Quanqi and Song Zhiwen. The styles and fundamentals of Tang poetry took shape in the early stages of its development. Poets of the period, known as the flourishing Tang era, enjoyed a golden age. This was in part due to a wise reign, a prosperous economy and the prevailing strength of the civilization. A number of gifted poets emerged during this time, pushing the development of poetry to its pinnacle by producing a wide range of compositions. At that time, descriptions of fields, rivers and mountains, as well as wars amidst borders, accounted for a large part of the subject matter. Li Bai, the Immortal of Poetry, and Du Fu, the Sage of Poetry, were also very active during this period. In the middle and late periods of the Tang Dynasty, though the splendid pinnacle of society had passed, the writing of poetry continued, and there emerged Han Yu, Liu Zongyuan, Li He, Bai Juyi, Yuan Zhen, Liu Yuxi, Du Mu, Li Shangyin and Wen Tingyun. Their poems are artistic recountings of the decline in prosperity of the Tang and of a high artistic caliber, and so they are accorded prominent status in the history of Chinese literature.

Li Bai and Du Fu, the two greatest poets of the Tang Dynasty, were called by later generations the Immortal of Poetry and the Sage of Poetry, respectively. These two poets hold outstanding positions in the history of poetry and appealed greatly to poets of later ages.

Li Bai (701–62) was born in Longxi (now Gansu Province). A celebrated romantic poet in the Tang Dynasty, he created many works. "Gazing at the Waterfall of Lu Mountain" is one of his classics. His poems are characterized by distinctive features. First, his poetry has a strong sense of passion. Li Bai had a broad range of emotions and despised the concepts of love and hate. He would drink and sing to his satisfaction and feel jubilant, laughing sardonically. But he would also vent his grief and indignation by wild railing and wailing. Second, his poems brought his incredible imagination into full expression. An inspiration would hit him like lightning, but soon afterwards his drive would unexpectedly escape him like a gust of wind. The range of subjects of his poems was wide, covering historical figures, astronomy, geography and illusory myths. Lastly, Li Bai often expressed his unruly emotions in an extravagant way. For example, he wrote, "My white hair streams back thirty-thousand feet long," to describe deep grief.

The Immortal of Poetry, Li Bai

Du Fu (712–70) was born in Gong county of Henan Province into a family of scholars. His paternal grandfather was Du Shenyan, a noted poet. Epic works created by Du Fu are "Three Officials" and "Three Separations." Du Fu is an exemplary realist poet in the history of Chinese literature, many of his poems mirroring the social outlook of the once-prosperous Tang Dynasty. Du Fu's ideological sentiment sparked the conscience of many outstanding intellectuals of the day. Despite physical suffering, he had great sympathy for the common people

The Sage of Poetry, Du Fu

and in his poems exposed the sharp line between exploiter and exploited. His political inclinations served as a model for traditional men of letters.

Du Fu wrote heartfelt poems with rich social content, sincere enthusiasm, deep indignation and solemnity. His lifelong effort to achieve perfection of his distinct style was greatly admired by poets of later periods. He inherited and carried forward the tradition by opening and studying "ten thousand scrolls." His language is everlasting, but he never stopped trying to refine his own writing style. He was particularly skillful at composing both ancient-style and modern-style verse. So he is honored by being called "the Sage of Poetry." His former residence, known as Du Fu's Thatched Cottage in Chengdu, Sichuan Province, is still well preserved by historians and a place where people visit and show respect.

Tang poetry is nearly synonymous with Tang literature because of its astonishing literary value. In the history of Chinese literature, Tang poetry is an unparalleled style from which generations of poets have drawn to enrich and improve their own writing. Further, Tang Poetry has become a symbol and a fundamental element of traditional Chinese culture.

SONG DYNASTY POETRY

Song dynasty poetry represents the literary achievements of the Song Dynasty and is compared in ancient literature with poetry of the Tang. As a literary form that is accompanied by music, Song poetry is also called as folk-song poetry. It originated in the Sui Dynasty and took its form in the Tang, reaching a peak in the Song era. More than twenty thousand poems by 1,330 poets have been compiled in the *Complete Collection of Song Poems*. The sheer number of poems shows us the prosperity in which Song artistic works were written. Song poetry utilizes distinct forms of verse, for example, *man jiang hong* and *xi jiang yue*, which decide the format. Lyric writers had to produce words that complied with the rhythm and arrangement of the music.

The many famous poets of the Song era include Yan Shu, Yan Jidao, Liu Yong, Su Shi, Zhou Bangyan, Li Qingzhao, Xin Qiji and Jiang Kui.

Yan Shu (991–1055), a former Song dynasty poet, was born in Linchuan, Jiangxi Province. More than 130 works by this poet were compiled into *Pearl and Jade Verses*. Under the influence of Southern Tang poet Feng Yansi, Yan Shu's lyrical poems reflect the tastes of the affluent, conservative literati with their graceful language and sweet rhythms. A line from "The Silk-Washing Brook, "The flower has no alternative but to fall, just like the return of the swallows. . . ." is one that lingers in the memory.

Yan Jidao (ca. 1040–1112), the seventh son of Yan Shu, was himself a celebrated poet. He created more than two hundred entries in the compilation *Poems of the Hills*. His verses have great artistic value because his poems are endowed with sincere and sorrowful sentiment and reach to the level of high art. It is said that his poetry can sway the hearts of the people. In the world of Chinese poetry, Yan Jidao and his famous father are known as the Two Yans.

Liu Yong (987–1053) native of the Wuyi Mountain region of Fujian Province, was one of the greatest writers of the Northern Song era. His "Bells in the Rain" is representative of the body of his work. In his young adulthood, Liu Yong lived in large cities and brothels, and so his writing mainly revolves around interaction and love affairs with female singers and prostitutes. His poetry fascinated people of all ranks, from the prostitute to the emperor, because of its local and colloquial style. It was said that anyplace there were inhabitants one could find singers who could sing Liu Yong's verses. Liu Yong's *Collection of Musical Pieces* consists of more than two hundred poems.

Su Shi (1037–1101), native of Mei Shan in Sichuan Province, was an eminent poet of the Northern Song Dynasty. His 340 poems took on a broader social outlook than the poems that focused almost entirely on sentiment. Su Shi has a unique status in the world of Chinese poetry. He transformed the traditional styles of the late Tang and Five Dynasties, developing a bold and unrestrained style. He also made significant contributions in the form of thematic extension and poetic innovation. His prominent works "My Darling Slave" and "The Moon Festival" are regarded as showcasing this unrestrained style. He and another great writer, Xin Qiji, are together known as Su Xin.

Zhou Bangyan (1056–1121) was known in Hangzhou city, Zhejiang Province as an excellent poet during the Northern Song Dynasty. He excelled at musical interpretation and had a strict sense of poetry. His lyrics express the love between man and a woman with artistic and elegant language. Zhou Bangyan was extremely influential during the Song Dynasty period. In the final years of the Northern Song era, his unrestrained artistic works were immensely popular. His works are typified by the collection *Qingzhen Poetry*, also known as *Poems of Jade*.

Li Qingzhao (1084–1155) was a native of Jinan city in Shandong Province. She came from a family known for literary talent, was a primary artist during the Northern and Southern Song eras and one of the first great female poets in Chinese literature. Her early lyrics mainly recount the lives of aristocratic girls and express their loneliness and longing for love, while the style of her later poetry expresses fallen destiny and deep melancholy. Li

Li Qingzhao

Qingzhao's lyrics are created from a distinct female perspective. She said there was a great difference between the writing of lyrical poetry and the writing of prose. One of her most prominent poems is "Sound, Sound, Slow." The collection of her masterpieces is *Poems of Washed Jade*. Li Qingzhao is the only female poet in Chinese history to have a crater of the moon named after her.

Xin Qiji (1140–1207) was a talented and notable poet during the Southern Song Dynasty. His ancestral home was Jinan in Shandong Province. Throughout history, he has been paired with the great writer Su Shi, known as Su Xin. He and Li Qingzhao are collectively known as the Two Greats of Jinan. Xin Qiji's poetry is brimming with enthusiasm, vehemence, solemnity and emotionality and is executed in a bold, unrestrained style. His stunning lyrics are regarded as the dragon of Song poetry. He further extended the themes of prose using the fundamentals of Su Shi, thereby enhancing the status of poetry as a literary form.

Jiang Kui (1155–1221) was born in Poyang of Jiangxi Province. He was a famous poet and composer of the Southern Song Dynasty. He was orphaned in childhood and housed by his older sister during his adolescence. He cherished music, literature and calligraphy. His words were of a primarily desolate tone, and he wrote in an elegant style that differed from that of the traditional schools of writing. In addition, he marked his lyrics with a kind of ancient Chinese musical notation. As these are the only well-preserved musical documents with Song lyrics, they have significant cultural value. The collection of his works is *Songs of Jiang Baishi* (Jiang Kui's nickname).

The poetry of the Song Dynasty is a large and brilliant diamond in the crown of ancient Chinese literature. The style is highly praised as the most beautiful of all Chinese poetry. Even today it catches the attention, giving readers great enjoyment and triggering much appreciation for the art.

OPERA AND THEATER

Yuan opera refers to the Chinese opera of the Yuan Dynasty. Its categories are Yuan opera and Yuan mixed theater, which together comprise the main body of literature of the Yuan Dynasty. Yuan opera, Tang poetry and Song lyrics are the three most significant accomplishments in Chinese literature. However, Yuan mixed theater far exceeds Yuan opera in achievement and influence, and so some include the opera in the category of mixed theater.

Yuan mixed theater reached the apex of its popularity in the latter half of the thirteenth century. As a new and complete form of drama, Yuan mixed theater had its own distinct sophistication and strict format. Chinese opera evolved by combining music, dialogue and dance in one stage performance. Also, many scripts were produced featuring a perfect mixture of rhymed verse and prose, systematically integrating drama and literature.

Yuan mixed theater was known for integrity and meticulous composition. The performance generally consisted of four acts and an interlude. Although each production always had four acts, a second interlude was sometimes included. The so-called *zhe* was similar to the act of a modern play. A script contained four acts with suites of music and the portrayal of the conflict and the natural resolution with the passage of time. Among the performances of Yuan mixed theater, in addition to the four acts a *zhe* or prelude was often used to explain the circumstances of the plot and summarize the story. Often, a *zhe* was inserted between acts.

Yuan mixed-theater roles included *dan* (female character type in Chinese opera), *mo* (middle-aged man in classical opera), *jing* (actor with a painted face) and *za* (miscellaneous cast). *Zheng dan* referred to the leading female role and *wai dan* was the second lead. *Mo* included the main male part, *zheng mo*, and the secondary role of *fu mo*. *Jing* were roles for which the actors wore makeup and chosen for their ability to provide comic relief. *Za* was the collective term for the rest of the cast. These included such roles such as *gu* (the official) and *jia* (the emperor). In Yuan mixed theater, only the major leading roles had librettos. In the latter case, *dan ben* was the term used to describe the libretto of the *zheng dan* (lead female). A prime example of this was *The Injustice to Dou E*, which consisted of the female leading role. The leading male character's libretto was called *zheng mo*, as for example the leading male role in *Autumn in the Palace of the Han*.

In Yuan mixed theater, there was also *binbai*

Illustrations from *Autumn in the Palace of the Han*

and *kejie*. Binbai, also called *binshuo*, was the dialogues and monologues other than for the leading roles. *Kejie*, also referred to as *ke*, included the singing and actions of the other performers. In terms of Yuan opera, *ke* referred to four main things: stage blocking, the performers' facial expressions, acrobatic fighting and dance. Often, stage effects were also included in a performance.

Many extraordinary playwrights and works of art arose in the prosperous age of Yuan opera. Among these were Guan Hanqing, Ma Zhiyuan, Zheng Guangzu and Bai Pu, all of whom were honored as the Four Great Yuan Playwrights.

Born at the end of the Jin Dynasty or the beginning of the Yuan Dynasty in Dadu (today's Beijing), Guan Hanqing is regarded as having been the leading playwright of the Yuan Dynasty. Much of his history is unknown. According to some records he played an active role in theater development from 1210 to 1300 in Dadu and visited such regions as Hangzhou. Guan Hanqing was a productive writer who created over sixty operas, only eighteen of which remain. His most famous work is *The Injustice to Dou E*. Guan Hanqing had immense influence on later generations. On the planet Mercury is a crater named after him.

Ma Zhiyuan (ca. 1250–1323) was another celebrated playwright of Dadu (today, Beijing) during the Yuan Dynasty. His style of script was distinct in that he was adept at turning simple and natural words into fine-tuned sentences that vividly delineated characters. His representative work, *Autumn in the Palace of the Han*, is praised as one of the great classics of Yuan drama. As well, Ma Zhiyuan was an expert composer of music and the authority of the Yuan period. Today, more than 130 of his lyrical works have been preserved. His best work, *Autumn Thoughts*, is poetic and picturesque and creates a lasting impression.

Zheng Guangzu was a native of Xiangfen county of Shanxi Province. Although it is unclear exactly when he lived, he was a well-known playwright of the Yuan Dynasty He wrote eighteen theatrical scripts. Among them, *A Young Lady's Departed Soul* is his masterpiece. His dramas revolve mainly around two themes: the love stories of young men and women and historical legends.

Bai Pu (given name, Heng) was born in 1226. By 1306, although he was still living, his whereabouts were unknown. He came from an official family. His father was a graduate of the imperial exam and became an office holder. Bai Pu's celebrated composition, *Rain on the Paulowina Tree*, depicts the romance between Emperor Li Longji and his consort, Yang Yuhuan. The play had great influence on Hong Sheng's *The Palace of Eternity*, a noted Qing Dynasty work.

The four great tragedies of Yuan drama are Guan Hanqing's *The Injustice to Dou E*, *Rain on the Paulowina Tree* by Bai Pu, Ma Zhiyuan's *Autumn in the Han Palace* and *The Orphan of the Zhao Family* by Ji Junxiang. Classified as the four greatest romance plays are: *The Pavilion of Moon-Worship* by Guan Hanqing, *Romance of the West Chamber* by Wang Shifu, *Over the Wall on a Horse* by Bai Pu and *A Young Lady's Departed Soul* by Zheng Guangzu.

Yuan Dynasty theater was an extremely dramatic artistic form with distinctive and traditional Chinese cultural traits. In his book *The History of Song and Yuan Drama*, Wang Guowei acclaims Yuan opera as China's most natural literature.

After the Yuan era, drama continued to develop, and later playwrights scored enormous achievements following the peak of flourish of the Yuan Dynasty. The Ming Dynasty, for example, saw the work of Tang Xianzu, who gained immortality as the dynasty's most gifted playwright for his plays *The Legend of the Purple Hairpin*, *Handan Dream*, *Southern Branch Dream* and *Peony Pavilion*. The quartet has been dubbed *Four Dreams at Linchuan* because Tang Xianzu was a Linchuan native and met the characters from his major works in dreams.

Tang Xianzu and his *Four Dreams* hold an outstanding position in and have had an enormous influence on the history of Chinese drama. Particularly, *Peony Pavilion* has been performed for four centuries and is warmly received to the present day. It was said that a female reader, Yu Erniang from Loujiang city, was moved so deeply that she was in great sorrow every day and last died from this tragic story. Today, as one of a popular repertoire, *Peony Pavilion* is often staged on college campuses. Since the early twentieth century, Tang Xianzu's plays have been translated into many languages and are performed by non-Chinese artists. The writer is praised as the "Shakespeare of the East" and his renowned body of work demonstrates the significant role of Chinese opera on the world dramatic stage.

THE NOVEL

The Ming and Qing dynasties were prosperous periods for the novel in China. From the beginning of the Ming Dynasty, novels served as a literary form, discussing social functions and being of academic value. Breaking the dominance of orthodox verse, the novel form achieved a position in literary

Luo Guanzhong

history equal to that of the poems of the Tang Dynasty, the lyrical works of the Song Dynasty and the musical scores of the Yuan Dynasty. In the Qing Dynasty period, the classical Chinese novel reached its zenith and then began to decline in popularity. Later, the world saw the beginning of the era of the modern novel.

A number of varied collections of novels emerged during the Ming and Qing eras, typified by China's Four Great Classic Novels, including *Romance of the Three Kingdoms*, *Water Margin*, *Journey to the West* and *Dream of Red Mansions*.

Romance of the Three Kingdoms, by Luo Guanzhong, was among the first ancient Chinese novels and is of enormous historical influence. It is widely known in China as one of the four brilliant classic literary works. The novel is based on the history of the three kingdoms of Cao Cao, Liu Bei and Sun Quan (respectively known as the states of Wei, Shu and Wu) and their struggle to reunite the empire in the third century. Using a broad historical background, the book takes place during a complex era of bitter politics and war. A major artistic component of *Romance of the Three Kingdoms* is the depiction of the human experience of war. The superbly written novel presents graphic descriptions of large and small battles, has a fascinating plot line and depicts blood on the gleaming knife. Among the stories, "The Battle of Guandu" and "The Campaign of Redcliff" are effective in portraying the kind of warfare that frightens the heart and moves the spirit.

At the same time, *Romance of the Three Kingdoms* is populated by more than two hundred vivid characters, the most notable being Zhuge Liang, Cao Cao, Guan Yu and Liu Bei. Zhuge Liang is the embodiment of a "virtuous councilor" who is endowed with incredible curiosity and impressive strategic insight. Cao Cao is a treacherous warlord who is the embodiment of an ambitious but cunning and cruel ruler. Guan Yu is revered by later generations for his loyalty and courage. Liu Bei is the author's idea of an emperor who embraces universal benevolence and respect for the wise and who has the wit to know his subordinates and assign them jobs commensurate with their abilities.

The military and political strategies discussed in *Romance of the Three Kingdoms* exerted an ever-widening influence on later generations. It is the greatest and most influential work among the historical novels and has had an immeasurable impact on Chinese literature as well as on the lives of the people because of its endless charm and ever-increasing popularity.

Even today it sheds light on human talent, military strategy and technology and political science. The novel has also been well received and admired among foreign readers. As early as 1569, *Romance of the Three Kingdoms* was introduced into Korea. By 1635 it was included in the collections of Oxford University in England. Since then, it has attained an influence of global proportions, and there are versions in Japanese, English, French and Russian.

Water Margin was either written by Shi Nai'an alone, in the Ming Dynasty, or completed through the combined efforts of Shi Nai'an and Luo Guanzhong. With brilliant craft and writing, the book talks of the full development of a peasant uprising from its inception—including the rise of a rebel group at Liangshan—through its defeat. Through descriptions of the darkness and corruption of the feudal society, *Water Margin* fully examines a commonly cited theme of the authorities forcing the people to rebel. The novel is noted for an appealing plot and effective revelations about the characters' personalities. Some of the literary images, such as those of Li Kui, Wu Song, Lin Chong and Lu Zhishen, have become household words. *Water Margin* employs common, concise, vivid and expressive dialogue, making it one of China's first novels to use native folk dialect. Also, the novel has exerted its influence beyond Chinese literature and society to reach other countries around the world. Among the many English translations, *All Men Are Brothers* by Pearl S. Buck, written in the mid- to late 1920s, was the first. It was published in 1933 as the first complete English translation and became an instant hit in the United States. *Outlaws of the Marsh* is another, relatively good English version, translated by Sidney Shapiro, an American Jewish scholar of Chinese nationality.

Journey to the West was written by Wu Cheng'en during the Ming dynasty. It tells the story of Xuanzang, a Buddhist monk of the Tang Dynasty, and his disciples, Sun Wukong (Monkey King), Zhu Bajie (Pigsy in some English translations), Master Sha Wujing and the White Dragon Horse. They endure eighty-one trials in an effort to reach the Western Paradise to obtain sought-after Buddhist scriptures. The author creates a supernatural world of gods and demons and the reader experiences his bold and free imagination. *Journey to the West* is the pinnacle of the classic Chinese novel and is considered one of the masterpieces of romanticism in world literature. The *Encyclopedia Americana* says it "renders an enchanting world where rich social content and brilliant thinking are inseparably blended." The *Encyclopédie française* describes it as a humorous and clever book that "is a pleasure to read." Since the start of the nineteenth century, this classic has been translated into more than a dozen languages, including Japanese, English, French, German and Russian.

A Dream of Red Mansions, completed during the Qianlong period of the Qing Dynasty, is at the peak of Chinese classical realist novels. The book consists of 120 chapters, the first eighty of which were written by Cao Xueqin, the remaining forty by Gao E. Told through the characters, Jia Baoyu, Lin Daiyu and Xue Baochai, the novel is a tragic tale of romance and marriage in a time of the declining fortunes of a large royal family. The story unfolds at the collapse of feudal society and the beginning of the trend toward democratic ideas. The great success of *A Dream of Red Mansions* is in part attributable to the fact that its characters have distinct personalities. Its success also lies in its intricate plot, detailed descriptions and elegant language. The novel has more than 480 characters, dozens of whom are highly individualized. At the same time, characters such as Jia Baoyu, Lin Daiyu, Xue Baochai and Wang Xifeng, have become unforgettable, stunning images. Cao Xueqin's flawless language gives us convincing and vivid characterizations. Not only does each character have a unique appearance, each also has a distinct voice and emotions. In sum, *A Dream of Red Mansions* is highly applauded as an outstanding artistic achievement among the novels of the Ming and Qing eras, and it has had a great impact on Chinese literature and society. This influence has spurred international research and review, called Redology, which is dedicated to commentary on the novel. The book is not only a great artistic Chinese work but also a rare world literary gem. It not only enjoys high prestige in China, with a circulation totaling more than one million there, but it has also spawned a large number of popular journals in various countries. The novel has been translated into over ten languages, including English, French and Russian. *A Dream of Red Mansions* has gradually become a spiritual wealth being shared by people around the world.

In addition to the Four Great Classic Novels, relatively famous stories of the Ming and Qing periods include the anonymously authored novel *The Golden Lotus*, the Qing Dynasty's *Strange Tales of a Lonely Studio* by Pu Songling and Wu Jingzi's *The Scholars*.

The novels of the Ming and Qing periods play an indispensable role in the history of Chinese literature and culture. In specific, the Four Great Classic Novels have all been adapted for television, and through this medium they have been made an enduring treasure.

Chapter 16

GARDENS

China has a time-honored tradition of landscape gardening. As early as the Western Zhou Dynasty, royalty and aristocracy had begun to construct gardens. During the Qin and Han periods, more and more country residences were built, including the famous ancient Chinese gardens of Epang Palace (Qin Dynasty) and the Shanglin Garden of the Han. Chinese gardens serve as both entertainment facilities and living spaces. Most are distinguished by the integration of hills and forest within the residential areas of a city. These landscape parks do not simply present natural settings; they reflect the artistic sensibilities of classical Chinese landscape paintings and poetry, creating a backdrop that summarizes the essence of the environment's innate beauty while using a slightly impressionistic approach. The design of classical Chinese gardens is based mainly on natural landscape features integrated with such man-made structures as palaces, pavilions, corridors, buildings, terraces and multistory towers, as well as artificial interpretations of nature. All reflect the zeitgeist of the various historical periods, especially within the artistic realm of famous ancient Chinese classical poems, verses and paintings. Chinese classical gardens are world renowned, the most famous being the Summer Palace, the Mountain Resort, the Humble Administrator's Garden and the Lingering Garden, also known as the four great classical gardens of China.

The Summer Palace

The Summer Palace lies nine miles northwest of Beijing. It served as the imperial gardens of the Qing Dynasty, a place for royalty to escape the summer heat. The picturesque scenery is made up of springs, marshes, jade green mountains and flowing rivers. The construction of the imperial gardens here began in the eleventh century. In the fifteenth year of Emperor Qianlong's reign during the Qing Dynasty (1750), the garden was expanded and it became known as the Garden of Clear Ripples. The garden was unfortunately ransacked and burned by Anglo-French allied forces in 1860. In 1888, the Empress Dowager Cixi appropriated the military allowance of the

Chinese navy to rebuild the grounds; this cost over thirty million ounces of silver, and the work took more than ten years. The finished project was once again called the Summer Palace. By the end of the Qing Dynasty, the total area of the garden was more than four square miles. Such a vast and exquisite royal garden is a rarity in the world.

The Summer Palace is home to Longevity Hill and Kunming Lake. Three quarters of the garden is water. There are more than three thousand buildings, including palaces, pagodas, temples, corridors and terraces surrounding the hills and lakes. The structures, mountains and lakes reflect and balance one another. Each is placed in such a way that it is in harmony with the overall scene and the feeling of the garden.

There are four major scenic areas in the Summer Palace: The eastern-most part has the Eastern Palace Gates. This part was used by the emperor for political activities and as a place of temporary residence. It houses the Hall of Benevolence and Longevity, home to elegant dormitories, theatrical stages and courtyards. It was also used for meetings with ministers and visiting officials. The Hall of Jade Ripples started off as Emperor Guangxu's palace residence but shortly after became his prison. (One can still see the towering wall that blocked his passage.)

Along the front face of the lofty Longevity Hill are most of the structures. The entire scenic area is based on two perpendicular lines with a central axis. The east-west axis contains the famous Long Corridor. From the middle promenade of the Long Corridor, in succession on the north-south axis are the Gate of Dispelling Clouds, the Cloud-Dispelling Hall, the Garden of Harmonious Virtue and the Tower of Buddhist Incense, the center of the garden. From here, the buildings are meticulously symmetrically distributed to resemble a myriad of stars surrounding the moon.

In the most northern part of the scenic landscape, past the lakes and mountains, there are few structures among the plentiful trees and twisting pathways. The tranquil style here is in sharp contrast to the luxurious area before one gets to the mountains. A group of Tibetan structures and buildings characteristic of the water villages of Suzhou in southern China is set in a compact layout, each with its own wit and beauty. Three quarters of the area of the Summer Palace is water, no body of which is more visible than

The Tower of Buddhist Incense

the front lake, with its infinite waves. There are mountains in the west, and most of the buildings are clustered in the north. At the lake is a causeway lined with peach trees and willows. There are also six distinct styles of arched bridges along with three islands housing classic structures. The exquisite Seventeen Arch Bridge stretches over the lake. Not only is it a pathway to the middle of the lake, but it also makes for an unforgettably picturesque setting.

The main building of the Summer Palace is the Tower of Buddhist Incense on Longevity Hill, which is built on a foundation 69 feet high. The pavilion is 131 feet high and features eight faces, three floors and four series of eaves. Inside the pavilion are eight huge Ceylon ironwood pillars. The structure is complex and built in the ancient classical architectural style. Cloister and horn kiosk are common in the garden. The Long Corridor of the Summer Palace, at 2,388 feet, is the longest corridor in the world. More than fourteen thousand paintings line the corridors, vividly depicting traditional lore, flowers, birds, fish and insects. The splendid Kouru Pavilion with its eight series of eaves is on the eastern shore of Kunming Lake and is the largest of its kind in China. Also in the area is the richly carved and vividly ornamented Marble Boat, immense in size and matchless in beauty.

The Summer Palace features various kinds of garden styles from different regions. It is the quintessence of classical Chinese architecture and is often referred to as the museum of Chinese gardens.

The Mountain Resort

The Mountain Resort is also named Chengde Palace or the Rehe Traveling Palace. It is located in the northern part of the city of Chengde, along a narrow valley on the west bank of the Wulie River in Hebei Province about 143 miles from Beijing. It was once used by Qing Dynasty emperors as a summer resort and a place for conducting state affairs.

Construction of the Mountain Resort began in the forty-second year of Emperor Kangxi's reign, during the Qing Dynasty (1703), and continued through three generations of emperors: Kangxi, Yongzheng and Qianlong. It was eventually completed in the fifty-fifth year of Emperor Qianlong's reign (1790), after eighty-seven years of building.

The Emperor Kangxi discovered in his travels to northern China that Chengde was not only excellent terrain, pleasant in weather and beautiful in scenery but also a gateway for the emperors to the cradle of the Qing Dynasty. Moreover, it was a place on mainland China that overlooked the interior and enabled the emperors to keep an eye on Mongolia. And so Emperor Kangxi decided to build a palace here. In the forty-second year of his reign (1703), large-scale construction began. Lakes were dredged and new roads and

The Mountain Resort

palaces were built. In the fifty-second year of his reign (1713), thirty-six scenic areas and the wall around the resort were completed. During the reign of Emperor Yongzheng, construction was suspended, to resume in the sixth year of the reign of Emperor Qianlong (1741). The project was finally finished in the fifty-seventh year of Emperor Qianlong's reign (1792). Along the way, thirty-six more scenic outposts and eight outer-lying temples were added to the original plan, forming a resort of spectacular scale that housed unique imperial gardens. Originally, the Mountain Resort was called the Rehe Traveling Palace. The name was changed when Emperor Kangxi carved "The Mountain Resort" into the Meridian Gate.

Compared to the Forbidden City in Beijing, the Mountain Resort is a work of simple elegance. It adopts the innate qualities of natural landscapes, incorporating the scenic attributes of the southern and northern frontiers of China. It remains the largest ancient imperial palace in existence in China. The Mountain Resort is divided into four sections: palaces, lakes, plains and mountains. The palace section is on the south bank of one of the lakes. The terrain here is flat and even. This area, where emperors managed state affairs and held celebrations, also functioned as a temporary living palace for the emperor. It covers an area of about twenty-five acres and comprises four groups of buildings: the Main Palace, the Pine Crane Temple, the Palace of Ten Thousand Swaying Pines and the Eastern Palace.

The lake section is situated to the north of the palace area. Islands included, the lakes occupy an area of 106 acres. Eight islands divide the lakes into different regions, each having distinct elevations, and there are smaller lakes strewn randomly throughout. The ripples on the surface of the clear water recall a utopia, with an abundance of fish and rice (more specifically, the remote southern Yangtze River area). In the northeast corner lies the famous crystal-clear Rehe Spring. The flatland section is situated at the foot of mountains, with the lake section to the north. Within this vast terrain are countless gardens of trees, a stable for horses, jade-colored plants, lush forests and boundless pasture.

The mountain section occupies four fifths of the grounds in the north-west part of the Mountain Resort. An undulating chain of mountains forms ravines that are interspersed with multistory pavilions and temples. There are many bodies of water in the southeastern area and many mountains in the northwest. This is the embodiment of China's geography.

Outside the confines of the grounds, magnificent temples and grandiose manor houses form a cosmos that encircles the Mountain Resort. This ring around the resort is a symbol of national unity and the centralization of authority. The Eight Outer Temples are distributed in the north, at the foot of the mountains, occupying more than a hundred acres. Originally, there were eleven temples. Remaining today are the Temple of the Potraka Doctrine, the Temple of Happiness and Longevity, the Temple of Universal Bliss, the Temple of Universal Peace, the Temple of Far-Reaching Peace, the Temple of Universal Charity and the Shuxiang Temple. All are built of gold and jade, making for splendor.

The Humble Administrator's Garden

The Humble Administrator's Garden is located along Northeast Street in the city of Suzhou. It is the largest of its kind in the area and one of Suzhou's four famous gardens as well as a chief representative of the northern Chinese garden. In the years of the Tang Dynasty, it was the private villa of poet Lu Guimeng. After the arrival of the Yuan Dynasty, it became Dahong Temple.

During the reign of Emperor Jiajing in the Ming Dynasty (1522–66), an administrator named Wang Xianchen, frustrated with his career in office, returned to Suzhou. He purchased the temple and employed the famous landscape artist, Wen Zhengming, to design the garden. After sixteen years, the task was completed. The lord named the garden "the Humble Administrator's Garden" after a verse in the poem "Idle Life" by Pan Yue of the Western Jin Dynasty: "Water the garden, sell the vegetables; offering meals morning and night . . . this also serves as the humble man's politics." Not long after the garden was finished, Wang Xianchen passed away. Then, on one fateful night his son lost the entire garden on a bet.

The ownership of the Humble Administrator's Garden has changed quite often in the more than four hundred years since its creation. It was once divided into three sections. These became a private garden, an official garden and a public area. It wasn't until the 1950s that the three sections were reunited and the place once again called the Humble Administrator's Garden. The garden covers more than ten acres.

It can be divided into four parts: the east, middle, west and residential. The middle section is the major attraction and the essence of

The Humble Administrator's Garden

the garden. This section covers an area of about three acres, one-third of it being ponds. In the middle section, a number of structures surround the ponds and pools, such as lofty pavilions and elaborate terraces designed in accord with the elevation of the banks of the streams. Trees and hills set off one another, and emerald green bamboo is everywhere. With the vast ponds and flourishing forests, the scene is a sight to behold. The buildings facing the water are of varied architectural styles and random heights.

The western section, originally referred to as the courtesy garden, is the smallest part of the garden, with an area of two acres. In the western section the streams flow roundabout, and there is a condensed layout. Hills are on one side and water on the other, flanked by pavilions. Exquisite verandas encroach on the rippling waters of the snaking streams that run through the mountain gorges. This is an excellent example of the artistic brilliance of Suzhou landscape gardening. The major building of the western section is the Hall of Thirty-six Pairs of Mandarin Ducks, located near a building that was used for banquets and listening to music. The ornamentation inside the central hall is something to think about. The eastern section was once called Returning to the Fields Residence, after the minister, Wang Xinyi, returned there in the fourth year of Emperor Chonzhen's reign during the Ming Dynasty (1631). It occupies an area of about five acres. This part of the garden was long ago deserted and left barren, but it has since been rebuilt. It is designed to complement the flat ridges, faraway hills, pine tree woods, grasses, bamboo docks and roundabout streams in the area. In combination with mountains, ponds, pavilions and terraces, it forms a style that remains clear and bright. The major buildings are Snowy Orchid Hall, Lotus Terrace, Heavenly Spring Pavilion and Auspicious Clouds and Mountains Peak, which were all taken from other places and brought here.

Although the Humble Administrator's Garden has undergone reconstruction for generations, the builders preserved the style of architecture characteristic of the Ming Dynasty. The garden is naturally spaced and made up mainly of bodies of water, the quantity of which makes the landscape peaceful, simple, brilliant and natural. At the center of the garden are pools surrounded by lofty rotating pavilions with carved windows. Winding pathways cut through mountain boulders, ancient trees, green bamboo and other various flora and fauna, making for an elegant, serene picture.

The Ming Dynasty era was in fact quite an inspiration for art and literature. China's varied topography of lakes, pools and gullies fueled the artistic concepts of the classic poetry and paintings of the period that reveal the stark beauty as well as the realities of nature. One can appreciate the fish swimming below the lotuses in summer, the plum blossoms and snow in winter. Spring's sunny days entice flowers into bloom, and fall brings red to the lush reeds in the ponds. The passionate and poetic scenery is undauntedly implicit, the twisting paths revealing beauty every step of the way. Not only do the divisions in the Humble Administrator's Garden make use of and adapt to the natural environment, they are testament to great technique in the use of contrast that allowed for the creation of gardens within gardens, representative of typical gardens in the regions south of the Yangtze River. Some have referred to the Humble Administrator's Garden as the mother of all the gardens under heaven.

The Lingering Garden

The Lingering Garden is located on the outskirts of Changmen Gate in Suzhou city. It was built during the reign of Emperor Jia Qing of the Ming Dynasty (1522–66) and was the private residence of Xu Shitai. During the Qing Dynasty, in the fifth year of the reign of another emperor similarly named Jia Jing (1800), the garden belonged to Liu Rongfeng who renamed it Cold Mountain Villa. Since his surname was Liu, it was commonly known as the Liu Garden.

Sheng Xuren obtained the property in the second year of Emperor Guangxu's reign and renamed it the Lingering Garden. The Lingering Garden occupies five acres (some say more than eight acres) and can be divided into four sections: the middle, east, west, and north sections. In each there are distinct visual aspects of scenic mountains and rivers, pastoral landscapes, wooded areas and courtyards.

The middle section is famous for its aquatic scenery, which is the essence of the entire garden.

The eastern section is famed for its curved courtyards and winding corridors. There are more than ten structures, including the famed Worshiping Stone Pavilion, the Palace of the Spring, the Return-to-Read Pavilion, Cloud-Capped Pavilion and the Cloud-Capped Tower. Three rock mountains stand behind the pools in the courtyard, Cloud-Capped Peak being in the center, with Auspicious Clouds Mountain and the Mountain of the Cloudy Cave at its sides. The northern part of this section is pastoral landscape and newly developed potted plants.

The western section, in all its wildness, is at the highest altitude of the garden. It is unique for the ornate manmade rock gardens that are

The Lingering Garden

interconnected with the features of the natural landscape. The original construction in the north was destroyed. In recent times, bamboo, peach and apricot trees are being widely cultivated there.

The Lingering Garden features the most buildings of all the gardens of Suzhou. There are also dozens of courtyards containing halls, corridors, coral walls, arched doors, rock gardens, pools, flowers and trees. The landscaping of the Lingering Garden fully embodies the superb techniques and high intelligence of the ancient Chinese landscapers. It also features distinct artistic styles reminiscent of gardens in southern China.

In the Lingering Garden are three famous features. One is the Cloud-Capped Peak. Like the other so-called mountains, it is actually exquisite stones projecting from Lake Taihu. According to legend, the magical stones were relics of Hua Shigang of the late Song Dynasty. The stones in Taihu Lake are of four distinctive qualities: thin, wrinkled, porous and hollow.

The Redwood Palace Hall in the vicinity is named for the mighty Chinese cedar pillars that support it.

A fossil of a fish is preserved in a natural marble slab that is housed in the Celestial Hall of the Five Peaks. The central part of the face of the slab shows the fish surrounded by hills and overlapping cliffs. The underside depicts running water and flowing waterfalls, while above are graceful, flowing clouds. A white spot at the center represents the sun or moon. These features synergistically form an exquisite landscape portrait. The marble originated from Yunnan Province, each slab being about a yard in length and six inches thick.

RESIDENCES

China is a multiethnic country. The style and architecture of the homes here are rich and colorful. Among the most representative styles are:

The *Hutong*

Many visitors to Beijing often ask, "Where in Beijing can I find _____ *hutong*?" Indeed, there are a lot of alleys in Beijing. Some records tell us there were as many as several thousand by the Ming Dynasty, more than nine hundred of which were inside the city and more than three hundred in the suburbs. During the Qing Dynasty, the number had grown to more than eighteen hundred. During the Republic of China, residential alleys numbered over nineteen hundred. In the early days of the People's Republic of China, the total number of alleys topped 2,550 in Beijing alone.

Beijing's alleys originated in the Yuan Dynasty. The Mongolians referred to the streets of their capital as *hutongs*. It is believed that this word means water well in ancient Mongolian. People in Beijing generally refer to a road of south-north orientation as a street. Being relatively wide, these were used primarily by horse carts, so they were also known as horse roads. The east-west oriented streets are called alleys. These are relatively narrow and used mainly

Hutong

for foot travel. Along the sides of the alleys are courtyard residences. There are many *hutongs* with distinctive features in Beijing, such as the Banking Hutong, which is the shortest, only about 30 or 40 yards long. It lies adjacent to the Zhubaoshi District outside Qianmen Avenue.

The names of the alleys reflect the history of money exchange within the *hutongs*. In ancient China it was traditionally said that there were seven things to get when one stepped out of the house: firewood, rice, oil, salt, soy sauce, vinegar and tea. It is no surprise, then, that in Beijing there was a corresponding *hutong* for each: the Firewood Hutong, the Rice Hutong, the Oil Hutong, the Salt Hutong, the Soy Sauce Hutong, the Vinegar Hutong and the Tea Hutong. In this era, people placed great value on the five precious metals: gold, silver, bronze, iron and tin, and so there were *hutongs* named after each of these, as well.

Some believe that the *hutongs* were a product of the Yuan Dynasty. Their perfect relationship with the courtyard houses embodies the rulers' intelligence in residential planning and allocation. The *hutong* system is a work of urban managerial brilliance. The alleys are arranged in strict order along with the well-proportioned courtyard houses. *Hutongs* were used to divide residences, and they made Beijing look like a huge military camp. Some residential alleys are separated by dredging, as Beijing once housed several military camps for nomadic tribes. An anonymous wit made this analogy: the city of Beijing is like a large cube of tofu. There are streets and *hutongs* in the city, laid out agreeably from south to north and from east to west. Therefore, the inhabitants of Beijing must have a strong sense of direction.

Courtyard Residences

The courtyard is the traditional and most typical style of residence in Beijing and throughout northern China. It is made up of a central structure, an east wing and a west wing surrounding a central courtyard. This is the

Courtyard residences

oldest and most common among Chinese residential living traditions, due mostly to its connection with the Han, China's largest ethnic group. Some believe that courtyard residences have been around for more than three thousand years. As early as the Western Zhou Dynasty, the model had begun to take shape.

The gate of the courtyard residence is generally in the southeast or northwest corner. The main room in the northern courtyard is built on a stone-mortar foundation and is typically larger than the other rooms. The living room is reserved for the master of the house. The east and west wings embrace the two sides of the courtyard where the younger generations live. The corridors between the main room and wings are used for walking and resting. Windows on the street side in the enclosing walls and rooms are generally kept closed, and the courtyards are closed and secluded.

The courtyard residences of Beijing are famous throughout China and around the world. In Beijing there are various styles and sizes. Regardless of scale, such a house consists mainly of a courtyard with one-story residences on four sides. There is only one courtyard in the simplest residential areas, two or three in the more complex ones. Mansions occupied by the wealthy are made up of several courtyards side-by-side, with walls between. One distinctive feature of courtyard residences is the central structure and the symmetrically attached wings. What's more, the residences are multifunctional. The large ones can be imperial palaces or princes' mansions. The smaller courtyards are residences for common people. Both the splendid Forbidden City and suburban houses of the working class are designs in this same style of architecture.

Enclosed Residences

Because of wars and famine, the Han people, who occupied the Yellow River Basin, were forced to migrate to the south (from the Western and Eastern Jin dynasties to the Tang and the Song periods). During this time there were five large migrations, as successive populations emigrated to southern China. Since the flat area in the south was already inhabited, the newly arrived had no better option than to move to the northern mountains and hills. There is a saying from ancient times: where there are mountain peaks, there are guests. Where there are no guests, there are no mountains.

In those days, local officials would often register their residences as places for guests or travelers to stay. These were often called *keji* or *kehu*, giving rise to the word, *kejia*, to describe the Hakka ethnic group. In order to protect themselves from enemies and beasts, most Hakka people lived in groups, so the enclosed dragon house, walking horse residence, five-phoenix structure, warrior-surrounded building, and four-cornered house came into being. Among these, the enclosed dragon house is the oldest form and so the most famous. It is commonly referred to as the enclosed residence or enclosed Hakka House. Such structures also typify the architectural culture of the Hakka.

The enclosed dragon house originated in the Tang and Song dynasties and was popular throughout the Ming and Qing eras. The Hakka people primarily built the enclosed dragon house with one entrance, three halls, two side rooms and one surrounding wall. The enclosed houses of the Hakka are typically built similar to a military barracks surrounded by a square rampart. The enclosed house is fortified with a yard-thick wall that is fifteen yards high. It is built of earth mixed with lime (calcium oxide), cooked glutinous rice and egg white, with lengths of bamboo and wood pillars for strength. An ordinary enclosed dragon house covers an area of about 54,000 to 81,000 square feet. Larger houses can cover more than 215,000 square feet. Generally, it took five to ten years, and sometimes more, to complete a structure.

The enclosed dragon house is somewhat like the Hakka castle. It holds bedrooms, kitchens, various sized halls, wells, pigpens, henhouses, toilets and storehouses. An enclosed house can accommodate dozens, sometimes hundreds, lending itself to tight-knit, self-sufficient and enhanced social groups.

Regardless of the size of the structure, in front of the main gate there had to be a level area and half-moon pond. The level ground was used to dry harvested grains and to enjoy cool shade, among other activities. The pond served as a water reservoir and a place to raise fish and as protection against fire and drought.

Within the gate, there were upper, middle and lower halls and two or four wings at each side, commonly known as horizontal rooms. This type of room extends straight back. At the very end the enclosing wall was built to encircle the main rooms. A small enclosed dragon house could contain over ten rooms, with the larger ones including twenty or more spaces. The middle room of the enclosed dragon house was referred to as the dragon hall. Smaller-scale houses had one or two surrounding dragons, and four to six enclosed larger residences.

Enclosed residences

These structures are still in existence and can be found in the Fujian and Jiangxi provinces.

The Hakka's enclosed house, Beijing's courtyard residences, the dugout structures of Shangxi Province, the pole-house style of Guangxi Province and the carved homes of Yunnan Province are the five characteristic residential architectural styles of China.

BURIAL RITES

In ancient China, only the emperor's tomb was officially called a mausoleum. Numerous imperial mausoleums were built during all the dynasties. Most of these are now either submerged or destroyed, but many still stand.

The Mausoleum of the Yellow Emperor

The Mausoleum of the Yellow Emperor lies atop Qiao Mountain, north of Huangling County in Shanxi Province. It is the resting place of Emperor Huang Di, known more commonly as the Yellow Emperor. He is said to be the earliest ancestor of the Chinese and is regarded as a great leader of the last phase of primitive society. He was buried on the majestic Qiao Mountain, the base of which is surrounded by water. This mountain is refuge to more than eighty thousand cypress trees, many of which have been standing for over a millennium. Throughout the four seasons the area brims with lush and verdant greenery. The Mausoleum of the Yellow Emperor sits deep in a forest of old cypress trees near the peak of the mountain. It is 11'10" high and has a perimeter of 157 feet. It is a circular building of black brick and stones, with painted walls. In front of the mausoleum is a carved stele from the fifteenth year of the reign of the Ming Emperor Jiajing. The four Chinese characters *qiao shan long yu* (Qiao Mountain controls the dragon) are carved into the stele, marking the spot from which the Yellow Emperor rode a dragon to heaven.

Annual Sacrifice Ceremony at the Mausoleum of the Yellow Emperor

The Tomb of Yu the Great

The Tomb of Yu the Great is at the foot of Kuaiji Mountain in the southeastern city of Shaoxing in Zhejiang Province. Da Yu (Yu the Great) became a famous hero by governing the waters of ancient China to prevent floods.

The Tomb of Yu the Great is surrounded by mountains, with many peculiar peaks standing among eastward flowing streams, all of which enhances the magnificence and dignity of the mausoleum.

The mausoleum grounds are in three parts: the Tomb of Yu, the Temple of Yu and the Shrine of Yu. The tomb faces the Pool of Yu, in front of which stands a monumental stone archway. At the end of a 110-yard walkway is a stele pavilion carved with the words, "The Tomb of Yu the Great." The Temple of Yu stands in the northeast part of the grounds and faces south. This palatial building was started in the early stages of the Liang period during the Northern and Southern dynasties. The structures of the temple—namely the Reflecting Walls, Stele Pavilion, Meridian Gate, the Hall of Worship and the Main Hall—were designed with a south-north orientation and ascend the mountain. The Main Hall has rooftops with double eaves and rises beside the hills and towers majestically into the clouds. There are four Chinese characters, meaning "serene land under heaven," inscribed by Emperor Kangxi on the back wall of the hall, which is decorated with wisps of dragons and owls piercing the clouds. The Temple of Yu comprises two corridors and three rooms and is located to the left of the mausoleum. A serene mirrored pond reflects the temple and is known as the Liberating Life Pond.

The Mausoleum of Emperor Qin Shi Huang

The Mausoleum of Emperor Qin Shi Huang is located nineteen miles east of Li Mountain in Xi'an, Shaanxi Province. The towering ridges and peaks of the structure join with Li Mountain to form an unsurpassed harmonious unity. The size of the mausoleum park is quite imposing. It occupies 21.7 square miles. The mausoleum was originally made to be 380 feet high, but it is now 250 feet high. Inner and outer walls surround the grounds. The inner wall has a perimeter of 2.4 miles and the outer wall a perimeter of 3.9 miles. The historic ruins of both walls are now 26 to 33 feet high.

The burial mound is in the south of the grounds, and the Chamber Palace and the Hall of Expedience are in the north. The Mausoleum of Emperor Qin Shi Huang was built between 246 and 208 BCE and is the first imperial cemetery in Chinese history. Large in scale and holding many funerary objects, it is the precursor to all the mausoleums in the later dynasties. The mausoleum was modeled after the Qin capital city of Xianyan, according to the wishes of Emperor Qin Shi Huang as laid out in his will.

The entire layout of the mausoleum resembles the written character (*hui*, 回). The structures that remain are the Chamber Palace, the Hall of Expedience, the Temple Gardens and the ruins of the residences of minor officials. According to historical records, the tomb area is divided into two parts, the cemetery park and the imperial burial place. The tomb occupies approximately 21.7 square miles. It is 181 feet high and has a perimeter of 1.2 miles. The entire mausoleum covers an area of 85 square miles on which the large-scale palaces, pavilions and other structures stand. The imperial burial sites are surrounded by two walls, an inside square wall with a perimeter of 1.6 miles and a surrounding outside enclosure with a perimeter of 3.9 miles. The sheer scale of the mausoleum far exceeds that of the Egyptian pyramids. The Great Pyramid of Giza is regarded as the world's largest mausoleum above ground, but the Mausoleum of Emperor Qin Shi Huang is the largest subterranean tomb.

The Thirteen Ming Tombs

The mausoleums known as the Thirteen Ming Tombs house the remains of the emperors of the Ming Dynasty. It is located near the Mountain of Heavenly Longevity, at the foot of Mount Yan in Changping County of Beijing. It took over 230 years to build. Construction of the first mausoleum, named Changling, began in the fifth month of the seventh year of the Yongle period of the Ming Dynasty (1409). Construction of the mausoleums continued until the completion of the Si Mausoleum, built by Emperor Chongzheng of the Ming Dynasty. A total of thirteen mausoleums serve as the final resting places of thirteen emperors, twenty-three empresses, two princes, thirty imperial concubines and one court eunuch.

The Ming mausoleums are seated in a small basin and surrounded by foothills to the east, west and north, with a plain in the central region. A stream meanders in front of the mausoleums, adding to the delightful and picturesque scenery of green hills and clear waters. The Thirteen Ming Tombs are named after the thirteen emperors of the Ming Dynasty. They are the Chengzu Lead Tomb, the Renzong Tomb of Offering, the Xuanzong Tomb of Brightness, the Yingzong Tomb of Abundance, Xianzong's Luxuriant Tomb, the Xiaozong Tomb of Peace, the Wuzong Tomb of Health, the Perpetual Tomb of Shizong, the Muzong Clear Tomb, Shenzong's Tomb of Certainty, the Guangzong Tomb of Celebration, the Xizong Tomb of Ethics and the Sizong Tomb of Thought. The mausoleums, which were built in the east, west and north regions of the mountains, form a large, integrated system of majestic tombs. The Thirteen Ming Tombs, built between 1409 and 1644, may have a history of as much as five hundred years. The entire mausoleum development, which covers 15.4 square miles, is the largest in scale and contains the most imperial mausoleums in China and in the world.

Chapter 17

GO

The game of Go (also known as *weiqi* and *I-go*) is a game of strategy that originated in ancient China more than two thousand years ago.

It is said that, in ancient times, after Emperor Yao settled disputes among various tribes and brought peace and order, the capital of Pingyang saw an economic boom that was demonstrated by the prosperity of agriculture and social life. But one thing worried Emperor Yao: his adolescent son, Dan Zhu of Empress Sanyi, not only idled about and was reluctant to attend to his duties, he often started trouble and invited disaster. To help their son be more useful, the imperial Yaos racked their brains, but Dan Zhu held fast to his ways. They suggested that he practice archery or study other skills, but he had no interest whatsoever. When Emperor Yao saw that his son was not making any progress, he sighed, "I will make him learn stone chess to understand marching formations and strategic military positions. After learning stone chess from a master, he will be rather productive." As Dan Zhu learned of his father's intent, his views changed a little. He said, "It's so easy to learn how to play stone chess that I will understand it immediately." Thereupon he asked his father to teach him at once. Emperor Yao said to him, "You must practice something morning and night to master it, but if only you want to learn."

In giving this advice, he used an arrow to inscribe dozens of lines, forming a grid on a flat stone and then ordered the guards to gather a pile of stones and give half to Dan Zhu. As the ruling commander, he instructed Dan Zhu on the strategies of war by the placement of the stones, explaining the proper situations for advance and retreat. Dan Zhu seemed to get the idea and was patient. And so Emperor Yao taught his son the mechanics of Go until the sun set beyond the mountains. It was only at the urging of the guards that the father and son ended the first lesson.

In the following days, Dan Zhu took the

Go

game to heart, constantly learning and no longer strolling about idly. Despite this early interest, though, before long he had once again returned to his offensive behavior. All day long he made trouble and even conspired to steal Emperor Yao's title. On learning this, his mother, Sanyi, grieved endlessly, became ill and eventually died of remorse. Emperor Yao was also heartbroken and sent Dan Zhu to the South, never wanting to see him again. Moreover, he abdicated and gave the crown to Yu Shun, who was intelligent and had shown both ability and political integrity throughout Emperor Yao's three years of strict observation. After Yu Shun acceded to the throne, he taught his own son, Shang Jun, the strategies of Go to enlighten him as Yao had done for Dan Zhu. Later, the lines of Go appeared on pottery. The story "Emperor Yao Creates Go to Teach Dan Zhu" was also recorded. Go in ancient times was called *Yi* and became the precursor to chess. It now has a lifetime of more than four thousand years.

Go presents us with a vivid analogy to the black-and-white-contrasting world. It was a favorite entertainment in ancient China and has the longest history of all chess games. Thanks to its integration of science, art and skill, it allows for the development of intelligence and the cultivation of will as it forces a player to stay alert and strategic. As a result, the game has long been popular and has gradually developed into a culture of international competitions. There are now millions of Go competitors in Asia, and in Europe and the Americas there is no lack of people who enjoy playing the game. The rules of Go are simple, nevertheless it entails a vast arena of choices, which makes the game variable and dynamic and more complex than *Xiangqi* (Chinese Chess). For these reasons, there is an enduring fascination with Go. The time it takes for a round of Go can vary. A quick round may take only five minutes, while a slow round may take several days, although it's more common for match to last one or two hours.

There are nineteen pairs of equidistant horizontal and vertical intersecting parallel lines on the Go playing surface, which constitutes 361 intersections (generally called points). On the board are also several points called the star points. The middle point is called the heaven point or *tianyuan*. The round playing pieces are black and white. The optimum number of pieces is 181 black and 180 white.

Go is usually played by two. Before the game it is determined who will make the first move, and the players get their stones. Black moves first. The stones are placed one at a time, in alternating turns. The stones are placed on the points formed by the intersecting lines. After a stone is placed on the board, it cannot be moved. While the usual play involves alternating turns, either player can waive this privilege.

Playing Go sharpens the ability to calculate, remember, be original, think, exercise judgment and be attentive. Go is also used to help in the development of children, to cultivate their analytical abilities and improve self-control.

PRIMITIVE RELIGION: THE EXORCISING DANCE

The Exorcising Dance is also called the Big Exorcism and the Dancing Exorcism. It is also commonly known as ghost drama and Dancing with the Exorcism Face. Regarded as the foundation of a primitive cultural faith, the dance originated from the totems of the clans of ancient societies. As a part of a larger exorcism ceremony, this popular folk dance was used in ancient China to drive out evil spirits while offering sacrifices. The Exorcising Dance, which used to be used for sacrificing, is performed now during the traditional Chinese Spring Festival. Dancers wear hideous masks and dress up as a *Fangxiang*, a warrior who was sent by the gods to expel ghosts. They dance and shout, "*Nuo, Nuo!*" With one hand holding a halberd and the other a shield, the dancers jump and dance to every corner, searching for something inauspicious, to drive out the ghosts and pray for protection during the year.

The Exorcising Dance is still performed in the provinces of Jiangxi, Anhui, Guizhou, Guangxi, Shandong, Henan, Shaanxi, Hubei, Fujian, Yunnan and Guangdong. It is also called Jumping for Exorcism, Ghosts' Dance and Enjoying the Happiness in various parts of the country. There are two ways to perform this traditional folk dance. One involves four main performers wearing masks and fur and murmuring "*Nuo, Nuo,*" with a spear and shield in hand. The other type requires twelve people to wear red hair and painted fur and noisily crack long whips and shout the name of the deity who fights evil spirits and savage beasts. The performances are always accompanied by music.

The origins of the Exorcising Dance can be traced far back in Chinese history. It is recorded in the divination *ci* (a form of classical literature in China) of *Jia Gu Wen* (Oracle Words), sets of inscriptions on bones and tortoise shells found in the ruins of the Yin Dynasty. The Exorcising Dance was called national exorcism or big exorcism in the Zhou Dynasty and villagers' exorcism in the countryside. According to records in the *Analects of Confucius—Rural Party*, Confucius once wore the full

Exorcism Face

dress and stood reverently and respectfully to welcome the coming of an exorcism team. This folk dance was called villagers' exorcism by scholars after the Qing dynasty and was cited in local and temple epigraphs.

The custom of exorcising for sacrifice continued from the Qin and Han dynasties to the Tang and the Song Dynasties and continued to develop during the Ming and Qing dynasties. Although the Exorcising Dance has retained its own traditional meanings, it is also customarily performed for entertainment as a dramatic work and is locally called "exorcism hall drama" or "local drama." The traditional style of the Exorcising Dance has been preserved to this day, while new elements have been added in the provinces of Jiangxi, Hunan, Hubei and Guangxi, among others. For example, in the counties of Wuyuan, Nanfeng and Le'an of Jiangxi Province, the Exorcising Dance is performed to represent the deity who cuts the mountain in the legend of Pangu's creation of heaven and earth, "The Two Fairies of Harmony and Unity," and "Liu Hai Playing Gold Toad."

In the countryside, the dramas *Meng Jiangnu* and *The Legend of White Snake* are represented by the Jima dance. The making of masks and the performance style of the Exorcising Dance have the Sorcerer's Dance of the Zhuangs, Yaos, Maonans and Mulaos. All these dances have absorbed the cultural elements and the techniques of the Exorcising Dance but also developed new variations with characteristics reflecting particular nationalities.

The villagers' exorcism, recorded in *The Analects of Confucius—Rural Party*, has persisted as a ritual among the Chinese people. And it has evolved into various forms of exorcising dance and exorcising drama by combining elements of religion, art and custom. The dance is still popular in rural areas of China, mainly in the provinces of Jiangxi, Hunan, Hubei, Shaanxi, Sichuan, Guizhou, Yunnan, Guangxi, Anhui, Shanxi and Hebei.

The Exorcism Culture

Jiangxi is one of the birthplaces of the Chinese exorcism culture. The offspring of the Miaos, who inhabited the Basin of the Ganjiang River and Poyang Lake during the Shang and Zhou dynasties, created a splendid bronze sculpture in Jiangxi Province. The bronze mask of a deity with double angles, excavated in Da Yang Zhou of Xin Gan County, gives us information about exorcism in Gan (Jiangxi).

The earliest record of Jiangxi exorcism is Jin Sha's *Yus' Pedigree of a Clan: The Judgment Notes of Nuo Shen* (a god that is supposed to drive away pestilence) from Nan Feng County. It says that Wu Rui, the ruler of Changsha, was under orders to go on a punitive expedition to Min (Fujian Province). He camped with his troops on the military mountain of Nanfeng in the early years of the Han Dynasty. In order to avoid war, the villagers had been warned to practice exorcism to eliminate demons.

As the Tang Dynasty was at the height of its cultural splendor, the Kai Yuan Ceremony was a regular exorcism ceremony in prefectures and counties, which led to the spread of rural exorcism in eight prefectures and thirty-seven counties of Jiangxi Province. For example, exorcising temples were built and the *Nuo Shen* was sacrificed during the Tang Dynasty in the counties of Nanfeng, Pingxiang and Xiushui.

The economy and culture of Jiangxi Province were prosperous in the Song Dynasty, which led to a proliferation of Exorcising Dances. According to Jin Sha's *Yus' Pedigree of a Clan*, in order to find shelter from the turmoil of war the Yus migrated to Nanfeng from Yugan at the end of the Tang Dynasty. During the early stages of the Song Dynasty, they moved a statue of Er Lang Shen, a legendary character from ancient China worshiped by their ancestors, from Guankou of Xichuan to Kingsha (present-day Huansha in Zixiao County). They built a temple and burned joss sticks and candles before it each year. This practice was called *Qu Nuo* (the act of exorcising). Having flourished during the Ming and the Qing dynasties, exorcism in Jiangxi was recorded or practiced in more than thirty cities and counties. Nanfeng topped the others locales in the number of exorcism rituals in eastern Jiangxi. Exorcising classes were established in 180 villages from the end of the Qing Dynasty. Today, 113 villages still perform the dance, which is also referred to as jumping for exorcising, jumping the bamboo horse, jumping for harmony and dancing like the Eight Immortals. In Le'an County there are classes in rolling the *Nuo Shen*, playing the drums and enjoying happiness. In Yihuan County there is jumping for exorcism. In Guangchang there are Meng drama and jumping with the chief star. In Lichuan there are jumping for harmony and jumping the eight shelves. Of all the counties in eastern Jiangxi, Pingxiang has the most variations of the Exorcising Dance. The Exorcising Dance is called *Yang Nuo Shen* (admiring the exorcising god) and *Shua Nuo an* (playing the exorcism board). The exorcising dance, the exorcism temple and the exorcism mask are known as the three treasures. In Wanzai County there is *Tiao Xiao* (jumping mandrills) and *Ban An* (moving the case), and there are two types of dance: exorcising with mouth closed and exorcising with mouth open. These rural exorcism types were influenced by the Gan cultural groups and have Jiangxi characteristics.

As the Exorcising Dance spread to varied regions, its performance styles differ. There is civil exorcism, characterized by complicated scenes, elegant performance, vibrant styles and graceful postures. And there is acrobatic exorcism, characterized by a mighty and majestic momentum, a lucid and lively rhythm and powerful and vigorous movements. Such traditional types of Exorcising Dance are still popular in the stages, halls and farmlands in many counties, among these Dean, Wuning, Wuyuan, Nanfeng and Duchang of Jiangxi Province. Generally, the performers put on masks to represent the many forms of *Nuo Shen*. Some masks represent characters in mythology and others represent common people and major figures in history. One who takes off the mask is a common person; one who puts on the mask is a deity. The musical instruments used for the Exorcising Dance are simple, generally percussion instruments such as the drum and the gong. The organization formed by the dancers is called an exorcism class. A class has eight to ten or more participants and strict rules. The Exorcising Dance is performed during the climax of the exorcism ceremony. The performances are deeply rooted in the culture throughout the country and have more of an impact when combined with sacrifice.

The *Nuo Shen* temple is where the performers rest and the exorcising ceremony is held. There are seventeen such temples in Pingxiang County of Jiangxi Province and another seventeen in Nangfeng. The earliest recorded temple was built in Kingsha village during the North Song Dynasty. The temple in Ganfang village was rebuilt during the Yongle period of the Ming Dynasty (1403–24) and has been preserved well to the present time. Another temple, in Shiyou village, rebuilt in the *Xinchou* year of Emperor Qianlong's reign (1781), has the strongest folk flavor.

The exorcising ceremony follows a traditional performance sequence. The exorcism in Gan follows the old traditions, which includes several basic procedures: the start (opening the box, coming out of the cave, taking out the board), the performance (jumping for exorcism, jumping with mandrills, jumping the evil spirit), the expelling (searching and ridding, cleaning up the hall, processing) and the finish (sealing the box, blocking up the cave, putting away the case). The period of performance lasts from the first day in the first month of the lunar year to several days after the Lantern Festival (the minority exorcism troupes stop in February). To expel the ghost is the objective of the whole ceremony, during which the performer drives out the pernicious demons by putting on a wry mask and moving a weapon along the gate by the light of a torch. As a major artistic form, the Exorcising Dance is praised as a living fossil of Chinese dance. There are now over two hundred traditional programs, more than ninety of which are held in Nanfeng County.

Because of its long history and course of development, exorcism today embodies Chinese anthropology, sociology, history, religion, folklore, drama, dance, aesthetics and plentiful cultural details. Since the Chinese nation has always placed emphasis on the protection of its non-material cultural heritage, on May 20, 2006, the Exorcising Dance was put on the first list of national non-material cultural heritage by the State Council.

BEIJING OPERA

Beijing opera, also called *jingxi* and *pingju* (*xi* and *ju* meaning opera), National Opera and *Pihuang*, is the genuine quintessence of Chinese culture.

The creation of Beijing opera can be traced back to several ancient Chinese local operas. In the fifty-fifth year of Emperor Qianlong's reign during the Qing Dynasty, there were four local theatrical troupes from Anhui Province: Three-Celebrations Troupe, Four-Happiness Troupe, Spring-Publicity Troupe and Spring Troupe. These troupes went to Beijing to put on performances, and all the performances met with success. Beijing opera came into being as a result of classes from Anhui Province cooperating with artists with the Han accent from Hubei opera. The opera form absorbed the essence of such local operas as Kunqu opera, Shangxi opera, and Watchman's clapper, mainly in the Erhuang style of the Hui dialect and Xipi of the Han dialect. It is generally thought that Beijing opera originated in the Guangxu period of the Qing Dynasty, since the name *Beijing opera* was first seen in *Shen News* (*Shanghai News*).

Some say that Beijing opera was first seen mentioned in *Shen News* during the second year of Guangxu's reign (1876). Others believe that Beijing opera came into being during Daoguang's reign in the Qing dynasty. It became a popular form from the south to the north in counties and cities in China after its introduction. In fact, Beijing opera was the most popular type of opera in China, especially in the 1930s and 1940s when it was called National Opera. Today, it is still the quintessential Chinese art form that also has the greatest impact on the nation.

Beijing opera features well-developed roles, is mature in performance and has a magnificent and imposing manner. The form is representative of modern opera in China. It tops other dramas for the many productions, the great number of artists, the large number of troupes and the broad audience, which tells us the form has great impact across the country.

One reason for this impact is that Beijing opera programs are so abundant; there are more than a thousand traditional programs. The most widespread and famous are *The King Separating from His Lover*, *Gathering of Heroes Attacking the Zhus's Mansion Three Times*, and *The Junctions of Three Roads*.

Beijing Opera costume

Second, Beijing opera is a multidisciplinary performing art that integrates singing, soliloquy (reading), action (performing), acrobatic fighting, and dancing. It depicts the stories and portrays the inner lives of the characters using various forms of theatrics to express happiness, anger, grief, joy, surprise, fear and sorrow. The reason why Beijing opera is compared to Oriental opera is that both are similar in form, and both are special forms of theater that integrate song, dance, music, art and literature. Also, these two types of stagecraft that come from different cultural backgrounds have secured a traditional place within their respective cultural circles.

Third, the types of roles in Beijing opera fall into four categories: *sheng, dan, jing* and *chou. Sheng* is the positive male character, and *dan* is the female counterpart. *Jing* is the male supporting role, with a rough and straightforward disposition. *Chou* is either the funny role or the villain. All of these are quite appealing.

Fourth, each role in Beijing opera has its own distinct facial makeup and appearance. The audience recognizes the identities of the roles as soon as the characters appear. Facial makeup is used to paint colors on the face to indicate the disposition, quality, role and fate of the character. This is not only a major characteristic of the opera but also key to understanding the plot. Generally speaking, a red face has a positive connotation and denotes loyalty and bravery. A black face is neutral and stands for courageous wit. The blue and the green faces are both neutral and represent the uncultivated heroes. The yellow and the white faces have a derogatory aspect and represent malicious characters. Gold and silver faces are mysterious and stand for deities or demons.

In addition to the colors, the visages produced by the facial makeup also mean things. For example, the powdered face that indicates the crafty and sinister has two forms: the fully powdered face and the partly powdered face (only on the bridge of nose and around the eye sockets). The difference of coverage and where a color is painted on the face indicates the degree of cattiness and craftiness. Generally, colors indicate the dispositions of the characters, while facial makeup is used to show different degrees of disposition. In this way, the characters in Beijing opera show loyalty to evil, beauty to ugliness and righteousness to ferocity. There is an uncommon number of famous artists in Beijing opera, including Cheng Changgeng,

Yu Sansheng, Tan Xinpei, Ma Lianliang, Mei Lanfang, Yu Shuyan, Cheng Yanqiu and Shang Xiaoyun.

KUNQU OPERA

Few know of the town of Qianshan in Kunshan city of Jiangshu Province. But many are familiar with Kunqu opera. In fact, as early as over six hundred years ago, Kunqu opera's predecessor, Kunshan music, originated in Qiandeng town. Kunqu opera, an ancient Chinese type of dramatic music, was originally called *Kunshanqiang*. This was shortened to *Kunqiang* (*qiang* meaning opera). It has been called Kunqu opera since the Qing dynasty. These days it is also known as Kun opera.

Kunshanqiang arose toward the end of the Yuan Dynasty in Kunshan city of Jiangsu Province. At the time, *Kunshan* music was a branch of Southern opera. Before the reign of Wanli of the Ming Dynasty, it was only a kind of popular oratorio in Wuzhong. *Kunshanqiang* underwent innovation and development after the middle stages of the Ming Dynasty, that is, during the reigns of Emperor Jiajing (1522–66) and Emperor Longqing (1567–72). During this period, Wei Liangfu, a citizen of Nanchang of Jiangxi Province, came to Kunshan and devoted himself to composing southern-style music. He collaborated with artist Zhang Meigu, who was quite good at playing the *dongxiao* (a vertical bamboo flute). This led to great innovation and development in the music of Kunshan. Also known as the musical sage, Wei Liangfu summarized and developed the singing and performing techniques of Kunqu opera in use in the previous two hundred years using the original Kunshan song as foundation and the strong points of *Haiyan* and *Yuyao* music. He also integrated the singing methods of the northern traditions into his new form. This led to the writing and publishing of *The Water Millstone Song*.

The year 1543 was an extraordinary one in the development of Kunqu opera. It was then that Wei Liangfu published his historic work, *Southern Prosody*, which established a quality benchmark for Kunqu opera. Then the transition of Kunqu opera from singing to staged drama was triggered, in the Ming period, by Kunshan local Liang Chengyu's *Washing the Silken Gauze*. This brilliant writer of traditional opera was proficient in poetry and tonality in much the same way as the masters Zheng Sili, Chen Meiquan and Tang Xiaoyu, all of whom had excellent command of musical theory and combined folkloric literature and new operatic tunes with the performing arts to create work of substance. In the opera *Washing the Silken Gauze*, the legendary beauty Xi Shi is the main character. This was also the first time that Kunqu opera was performed on a stage, having matured and taken now a different form. The staging of *Washing the Silken Gauze* had a great impact on the Chinese theater circles of the time. Because it was what the poets had been striving for in the tradition, many artists turned to studying and producing works for Kunqu opera. This form, along with Yuyao opera, Haiyan opera, and Yiyang opera are referred to as the Ming Dynasty's four operas. Later, the styles diffused from Yangzhou into areas of Beijing and Hainan, even extending to Sichuan, Guizhou and Guangdong, among other areas, and so Kunqu opera became an influential national form.

The instruments used in Kunqu opera are mainly the flute, along with the bamboo pipe, reed mouth organ, zither, Chinese oboe and stringed instruments. The music of Kunqu opera belongs to a joint genre called *qu*, short for the *qupai* style, which is the basic unit of Kunqu music. According to rough statistics, there are over a thousand styles of *qupai* used in Kunqu opera.

Also, Kunqu opera had its own allure, the most prominent characteristic being the expression of deep emotion, exquisite acting, the integration of singing and festive dancing, and an emphasis on costumes, colors and facial makeup. The types of roles in this opera were based on the *sheng, dan, jing, mo, chou, wai* and *tie* traditions. But, using the drama of the Yuan Dynasty as a frame of reference, Kunqu opera had an additional five roles—*xiaosheng, xiaodan, xiaomo, xiaowai* and *xiaojing*—for a total of twelve different roles.

Of the long performance pieces, several collected works of Kunqu opera have survived, some of which have had great influence on theater. Commonly performed operas included Wang Shizhen's *Cry of the Phoenix*, Tang Xianzu's *Peony Pavilion, The Purple Hairpin* and *The Handan Dream*, as well as *A Dream Under the Southern Bough* and *Memories of a Chivalrous Man* by Shen Jing. In addition to these operas, there are also Gao Lian's *The Jade Hairpin, Mistakes of the Kite* by Li Yu, Zhu Sucheng's *Fifteen Strings of Coins*, Kong Shangren's *The Peach Blossom Fan* and *Longevity Hall* by Hong Sheng. Other famous Kunqu operas performed on stage included *Dreams of Wandering the Garden, Yangguan Pass, Three Drunks, Autumn River, Thinking of the Mundane* and *The Broken Bridge*. Most of these have become immortal masterpieces, especially *Peony Pavilion*, which was first produced during the period of great prosperity of Kunqu opera and was destined to be a great work handed down from generation to generation. For this reason, Tang Xianzu is viewed in the same light as William Shakespeare, as one of the world's greatest dramatists. Canadian professor Dr. Catherine Swatek spent fifteen years researching her ethnographic work, *Peony Pavil-*

ion Onstage: Four Centuries in the Career of Chinese Drama. This extensive account describes and analyzes performances throughout China and the world, as well as the history of the opera's adaptation for Western opera.

It is said that each nation has its own refined and exquisite performing art that symbolizes the spirit and aspiration of its people, like the tragedy of Greece, the opera of Italy, the ballet of Russia, and Shakespeare's dramas. As for China, this art is undoubtedly Kunqu opera, which has a history of over six hundred years and is praised as one of the three original forms of world drama. It is also the ancestor of all other types of operas and the mother of all theater in China. Many regional theater styles in China, such as Shanxi opera, Puzhou opera, Shandong opera, Hunan opera, Sichuan opera, Jiangxi opera, Guangxi opera, Nanning opera, Yue opera, Guangdong opera, Fujian opera, Wu opera and Yunnan opera, were all nurtured and influenced by the many artistic elements of Kunqu opera. Even Beijing opera, which is referred to as the quintessence of Chinese culture, inherited from Kunqu opera, and it utilizes its types of roles and styles of presentation.

As a modern representative of traditional Chinese culture, Kunqu opera now extends across national boundaries. During the 1980s and 1990s, opera troupes from all over China went abroad to stage performances. Their refined interpretations have been retained in Europe, North America, Hong Kong and Taiwan, and so Kunqu opera has planted its seeds in foreign countries. According to records, various Kunqu opera organizations have been established in countries including the United States and Japan. For example, the Kunqu Opera Association, founded by Zhang Huixin, is one of the most influential overseas opera associations. Founded in the United States in Maryland in 1995, this association attracts a number of returning audience members. And whenever the theater companies hold performances, many more join the associations. Kunqu opera has become a way for foreigners to understand China and its rich culture and history.

On May 18, 2001, Kunqu opera was selected the leading representative of the art of oral and non-material cultural heritage by UNESCO. On May 20, 2006, it was named a high-ranking non-material part of China's cultural heritage by the State Council of the People's Republic of China.

YU OPERA

Yu opera is also known as Henan clapper opera and Henan lofty tune. It is also called Henan ballad, as the early performers sang using distinct techniques of the throat and in falsetto when starting and ending tunes. They voiced the syllable *ou* (meaning ballad) at the ends of phrases. Yu opera performed in the western mountainous regions of Henan relied on the flat areas among the hills for production staging. So it is known in those regions as "roaring beside the mountain." Because Henan Province's term, *yu*, became popular to describe the style, this regional dramatic form was officially named Yu opera after the establishment of the People's Republic of China.

Yu opera originated between the end of the Ming Dynasty and the early stages of the Qing Dynasty. It was greatly loved and appreciated by the masses and developed rapidly. The origins of Yu opera are hard to verify from written evidence, which has given rise to several theories. One is that the art was formed by combining regional folk songs and music with the Shanxi opera and Puzhou clapper opera that had spread to Henan Province by the end of Ming Dynasty. Another theory is that the form developed directly from the stringed melodies of Northern opera. Some believe that Yu opera was formed on the basis of Henan traditional arts, especially the *xiaoling* (a short meter for poems that contains relatively few syllables), which was popular in the central plains during the middle and later stages of the Ming Dynasty. According to this theory, these characteristics, combined with the absorption of stringed melodic music, created the style. However it was influenced, Yu opera has a long history of development. During Emperor Qianlong's reign (1736–95) it was called *tubang* drama and *bianliang* opera and received great reviews.

Yu opera is prominent in the northern areas of the Yangtze River in Henan Province, and in other northwestern provinces, as well as in regions including Xinjiang, Tibet and Taiwan. The types of roles in Yu opera are *sheng, dan, jing* and *chou*. There are generally four of each. The performing troupe is formed by casting the four male roles, four female roles and four painted-face roles, as well as four soldiers, four generals, four maids and eight stagehands, plus two officers and four mixed roles. The four male roles are the old man, the lead red-faced role, the second red-faced role (military character) and the younger supporting male role. The four main *dan* female roles are *da jing* (black-faced role), the lead painted-face role, the second painted-face role and the third painted-face role (*chou*). There is yet another style that incorporates five female roles and five roles with painted faces. Performers generally specialize in one type of role, although some are adept at playing several roles. For example, they may play a main part as well as other characters.

There are more than a thousand traditional Yu opera scripts, most of which draw from historical novels or romances, such as the dramas *Granting Titles to Gods*, *The Three Kingdoms*, *Wagang Drama*, *Lord Bao's Drama*, *The Yang Family Drama*, *The Yue Family Drama* and other operas that deal with marriage, love and cultural ethics. The most famous operas are *Fighting with Short Spears*, *Three Times in the Sedan*, *Di Tang Ban*, *Catching the Thief*, *The Trial of Zha Mei* and *Twelve Widows Travel to the West*. Since the establishment of the People's Republic of China, many modern operas and newly edited historical operas have appeared, including *Chaoyang Ravine*, *Little Erhei's Marriage*, *Personal Joys and Blaring Horses*, *The Unlucky Uncle's Marriage*, *Testing Husband* and *The Ripening Apple*.

Yu opera focuses on the singing aspect and uses clapper vocal music, which is fluent and clear-cut in rhythmical arrangement as regards key elements of the plot. It is full of distinctive dialogue with merry and lively phrases, it has a unique artistic charm and is easy for audiences to grasp. Other attributes of Yu opera are that it is filled with bold and unrestrained passions of yang energy and is adept at expressing scenes of great moment and intense emotion; it has strong characteristics of regional culture, which are simple, unadorned and close to the daily life of the people; it uses clear and intense rhythms; the conflicts are sharply delineated, as the plots have distinct beginnings and endings; and, the characters are well developed.

The major types of Yu opera are the eastern theater and the western theater. The eastern theater is influenced by its counterpart, the Shandong clapper opera, in that the male voice is loud and sonorous, and the female voice is vivacious and pulsating and commonly used as comic relief. The western style is adept at tragedy and retains the charms of Shanxi opera, like the bleak, solemn and stirring male voice and lingering sweet female voice. Representative characters of Yu opera are the five famous female roles: Chang Xiangyu, Chen Suzhen, Cui Lantian, Ma Jinfeng and Yan Lipin, each with a distinct style. Other common roles with various distinct characteristics are the male roles: Xiaosheng, Zhao Yiting, Wang Sujun, Xusheng, Tang Xicheng, Liu Zhonghe, Liu Xinmin, Hei Lian Li Sizhong and Chou Niu Decao.

HUANGMEI OPERA

Huangmei opera, formerly known as Huangmei theater, originated in Huangmei county of Hubei Province and later developed in the Anqing prefecture region of Anhui Province. As early as the late eighteenth century, in the bordering areas of Hubei, Anhui and Jiangxi provinces, traditional performances were based on the local folk literature. The name "Huangmei opera" was formally proposed in *The Annals of Susong County* in 1921. With a history of over two hundred years, Huangmei opera has become a wildly popular form of opera among Chinese audiences, particularly in the last several decades.

Tactful and pleasant-sounding, the music of Huangmei opera falls into two categories: coloratura and tranquil verse. Coloratura is performed mainly in the form of short plays and is rich in traditional cultural songs and poetry. Tranquil verse, or *ping ci*, is the major vocal music for the original dramas and is used with many narrations and lyrics. It is euphemistic-sounding, extending beyond the lingering charm of floating clouds and flowing water. As a major form of vocal music, the place of *ping ci* has been further strengthened as it regards the narration and lyrical aspects of modern Huangmei opera. The innovation has broken through the restrictions of the coloratura by the use of particular operas, by absorbing the elements of folk ballads and other music, and by forming a new style of vocal and instrumental harmony. Huangmei opera relies mainly on the stringed accompaniment of the *gaohu*, coordinated with cymbals, drums and whatever other folk instruments are fit for expressing the themes of the works.

According to records, there are thirty-six full-length Huangmei operas and seventy-two different short dramas. The full-length dramas express major social themes, as in *The Story of Buckwheat, Lawsuit of the Grain Officer* and *Marriage of the Goddess*. The short plays mirror aspects of the daily life of laborers in the countryside, as depicted in *The Barley, Spinning Cotton into Yarn* and *Selling the Grain Baskets*. Since the establishment of the People's Republic of China, many traditional operas have been collected and adapted, among them, *Marriage of the Goddess, The Emperor's Female Son-in-Law, Handkerchief Tales, Zhao Guiying, A Kind Mother's Tears* and *The Three Searches in the Mansion of the Father-in-Law*.

Further, other operas have been adapted from myth, including *The Cowherd and the Weaving Maid*, as well as the historical and modern operas: *Warm Spring and Blooming Flowers, Early Spring in the Little Shop* and *The First Flower Blossoms*. Others, including *Marriage of the Goddess* and *The Emperor's Female Son-in-Law*, as well as *The Cowherd and the Weaving Maid*, have found success on the silver screen and have had great impact in China as well as on the rest of the world. Well-known performing artists include Yan Fengying, Wang Shaofang, Wu Qiong and Ma Lan.

YUE OPERA

Yue opera is a traditional form of Chinese opera prominent mainly in the Shanghai municipality, although it also familiar throughout the Zhejiang, Jiangsu and Fujian provinces. The origins of Yue opera can be traced to Shengxian County of Zhejiang Province's *luo di chang shu* (a genre of popular entertainment consisting mainly of dialogue and singing). In the spring of the thirty-second year of Guangxu's reign during the Ming Dynasty (1906), the form began to evolve into a form of theater staged on the rural grassland and was referred to as small singing troupes, *du* troupes, and *shao-xing* drama. The original performers were primarily males from the rural areas who were semi-farmers and part-time artists. And so in early times it was commonly known as male troupe theater. It wasn't until the start of female song troupes in Shi Jiatai of Shengxian County in 1923 that the style was renamed *shaoxing* female opera, as it was vastly popular for female impersonators to play male roles. From then on, the male actors gradually became teachers and workers. The name, Yue opera, first appeared in the advertisement section of Shanghai's *News Report* on September 17, 1925.

Yue opera focuses on expressing emotion, mainly by singing. The vocal tone is beautiful, exquisite and pleasant. The performances are vivid and moving, embodying the sentiments of Jiangnan (the area south of the Yangtze River). The golden era of Shaoxing opera was the 1950s and the early 1960s. Some of the most influential artistic treasures were created at this time, including *Butterfly Lovers*, *The Romance of the Western Chamber* and *A Dream of Red Mansions*, which received great reviews both in China and around the world. The most popular works—*Butterfly Lovers*, *Love Detectives*, *Chasing the Fish*, *The Jade Pin* and *Tales of Colored Buildings*—became the repertoire, and *Butterfly Lovers*, *Love Detectives*, *Chasing the Fish*, *The Jade Pin* and *A Dream of Red Mansions* have been adapted for film. By means of such propagation, Shaoxing opera has become ever more popular in all parts of China. Popular actors in Yue opera are Yuan Xuefen, Fu Quanxiang, Qi Yaxian, Fan Ruijuan, Xu Yulan, Yi Guifang, Wang Wenjuan, Zhang Guifeng and Mao Weitao.

THE ART OF DUNHUANG

Dunhuang is located at the intersection of China's Gansu, Qinghai and Xinjiang provinces. The Mandarin word *dun* means sincere, and *huang* means brilliance. The grand and majestic region of Dunhuang has a long history and splendid culture. The Dunhuang murals are not only rare orchids from a time-honored and unique culture but also an important part of Dunhuang study that has attracted worldwide interest.

The Dunhuang Murals are the frescoes painted in the Dunhuang Caves. The murals are found in 552 caves, among them the Mogao Caves, the Western Buddhist's Caves and the Anxi Yulin Caves. Substantial in content, grand in scale and exquisite in technical design, these murals from past dynasties cover over 538,000 square feet, the largest collection of murals in the world.

The Dunhuang Murals are substantial in artistic content and colorful. Compared with other religious art, they depict mainly the images and activities of deities and relationships among the deities or between deities and human beings. These images pacify the mind, as do those in the famous Mogao Grottoes.

The Mogao Grottoes, also referred to as the Dunhuang Caves and the Thousand Buddhas Grotto, lie at the foot of Mount Mingsha, sicteen miles southeast of Dunhuang County. The name is taken from their location near Mogao village. These are the largest and the most famous Buddhist art grottoes in China and are praised as the pearl of oriental art. The Mogao Grottoes are distributed throughout three or four levels of varying degrees in the cliffs of Mount Mingsha, for an overall length of one mile. Today there remain 492 caves with 2,100 painted Buddhist sculptures. The murals cover a total area of 484,375 square feet. The grottoes vary in size and the statues in height. The work in the larger caves is magnificent

and vigorous, while that in the smaller ones is so exquisite and ingenious that the profound attainment and rich imagination of the artists are clear. The murals often draw their content from Buddhist folklore and sometimes mirror the various traditions of agriculture, weaving, hunting, marriage, death and festivals. These painted frescoes exhibit great skill and exquisite artisanship, and so this treasured Buddhist art has been referred to by some as the acknowledgement of the dawn of a new era in civilization.

The Dunhuang Murals typically fall into the following six general categories:

Dunhuang fresco

1. Buddhist Art

Buddhist art is prominent in the Dunhuang Caves. It mainly depicts various statues from different eras, such as the third and seventh generations of Buddha as well as Sakyamuni, all treasured images throughout history. Various Bodhisattvas, such as Manjusri, Samantabhadra, Avalokites-vara and Shizi are depicted, too. Also represented are the Eight Dragons of the Heavens: Heavenly King, Dragon King, Yaksha, Flying Apsara, Gandarva, Gardua and Mahor-aga. Of these Buddhist depictions, the spirit of Avalokite-vara has great presence. The Mogao Grottoes are home to nearly 933 paintings dealing with Buddhist doctrine, and there are some 12,208 statues of Buddhist images with varied expressions.

Buddhist scripture murals mainly take advantage of the artistic modes of painting and literature to convey the profound Buddhist classics by means that are easy to grasp. Such ways are referred to as *bianjing*. Similarly, expressing the content of classical Buddhism through painting is commonly known as *bianxiang* and *jingbian*, while the written depiction of classic scripture is called *bianwen*.

2. Mythology

Paintings with the theme of traditional Chinese mythology are portrayed in the caves of the late Northern Wei Dynasty. Here we can also see the influences of Chinese Taoist thought. For example, on the top of cave number 249 of the Western Wei Dynasty, beside the lotus well in the center, there are paintings of Asura and Cintama on both the west and east walls, and the north and south faces depict the Emperor of the East and the Empress of the West traveling respectfully in dragon-and-phoenix chariots. On top of the chariots are high-hanging canopies, while at the rear of the chariots, gonfalons flutter in the wind. A warrior is depicted in the foreground hoisting a banner while leading the way. Behind is an enlightened mythical beast with a man's head and the body of a dragon. Also included here are the Vermilion Sparrow, the Black Tortoise, the Azure Dragon, and the White Tiger, distributed throughout the various levels of the frescoes. These paintings are quite vivid and animated. For example, in one Lie Gong, the god of thunder, furiously beats a drum while lighting strikes and splits a rock with a flash as rain pours from an endless mist. Such images graphically depict a strong, distinct sense of ethnic identity.

3. Benefactor Images

The benefactors are the people who provided the funds for the building of the caves. In an effort to show their piousness and leave behind a good reputation, these wealthy individuals had portraits of themselves, their families, their relatives and their servants painted on the walls when they hewed the caves. Such portraits are called referred to as benefactor portraits.

4. Decorative Patterns

Among the Dunhuang Murals there are many rich and colorful vignettes that were primarily used for decorating the cave walls, tables, crowns and vessels. The decorative patterns vary in form depending on the time period and so are ever-changing, but all painted with superb skill from abundant imagination. These decorative patterns are found mainly in paintings of geometric design, rafter patterns and precise edging motifs.

5. Story Paintings

Story paintings were aimed at attracting devotees and propagating Buddhist doctrine and scripture. To achieve this, the pictures needed to express the abstract and profound Buddhist classics in a simple and terse way, so that devotees would understand immediately and become inspired. And so they would also devoutly believe and pay homage. A large number of these pictures were painted in the caves to educate devotees unobtrusively and imperceptibly while they were being admired. Substantial in content and moving in plot, the story paintings show the strong artistic ability of their creators.

The story paintings fall into five categories:

a. The first category is that depicting the lifetime achievements of the founder of Buddhism, Siddhartha Gautama. Most of these involve legends and the folklore of ancient India. As Buddhism passed through the centuries, ever more importance was attached to the depiction of the Sakya-muni Buddha. Prevalent here are scenes of an elephant carrying a human baby and the story of jumping the wall at midnight. The eighty-seven pictures in Cave No. 290 of the Northern Zhou period tell the whole story of Siddhartha, from birth to his becoming a Buddhist. These are "read" horizontally, with every six pieces in sequence. Such an extensive and in-depth form of art is rare among Buddhist story paintings in China.

b. Paintings of Jataka stories, the second category, depict Siddhartha's charitable deeds. The pictures convey the Buddhist concepts of karma, bitter hardship and ascetic practice through benevolence by the vivid depiction of stories, such as those of a Bodhisattva Sa Chuina feeding the tiger by sacrificing his body, Prince Sattva rescuing a pigeon by cutting off his flesh, a nine-colored deer sacrificing itself to save others, or, Xu Geti supporting his parents by cutting off his flesh. Although the pictures primarily convey Buddhist concepts, they also retain more or less the inherent qualities of legends, mythology and popular folktales.

c. Story pictures of predestined relationships, the third category, mainly tell about delivering all living creatures from torment by Buddhist monks and nuns, Buddhist devotees and Siddhartha. These differ from the Jataka story pictures in that the latter describe only the affairs of Siddhartha during his lifetime, while the former tell the stories of followers of Buddhism and Buddhist devotees in both pre-existing and contemporary generations. These stories depict, among other things, "The Five Hundred Thieves Attain Enlightenment," "The Novice Monk Commits Suicide Abiding by the Disciplines," and "Prince Shanyou Seeks the Treasures of the Sea." The stories in this category are not only bewildering and complicated in plot but also rather dramatic.

d. The fourth category is pictures of historical events and facts of Buddhism whose content is drawn from written accounts. These include the holy deeds of Buddhism, influential stories, the achievements of eminent monks, pictures of auspicious images and depictions of monastic disciplines. Such work contains historical characters and events that recur in the annals of Buddhism. The historical pictures are painted mainly in secondary positions, including on the surfaces of paved paths and in the corners. Some of these, though, are also painted on the walls, as is Cave No. 323's picture of Zhang Qian being sent to the Western Regions on a diplomatic mission, Fotucheng (a Buddhist from the Western Regions) and Buddhist Liu Sae's depictions in Cave No. 72.

e. In the fifth category are metaphorical story pictures, mainly the stories told by Siddhartha to explain the profound in simple terms to Buddhist monks, nuns and devotees and so reveal the doctrines of Buddhism. These various stories are primarily from ancient India and Southeast Asia. As folklore and fairy tales collected by followers, they have been recorded in Buddhist scriptures that are preserved to this day. Typical of this category are *The Guard Elephant and the Golden Elephant* and *The Lion with the Golden Hair*.

6. Landscape Painting

Abundant in subject matter and diversified in form, the landscape paintings are dispersed among the Dunhuang Murals and throughout the grottoes. The paintings integrate scripture murals and story paintings as a whole but also for contrast. Also treated are famous landscapes that make reference to Buddhist scriptures. This imaginative form of art commonly deals with scenes of the dynamic paradise of Sukhavati (Pure Land of Buddhism), with its verdant hills and green waters, birdsong and fragrant flowers.

Other caves are independent of this style and contain only landscapes, like the painting of Mount Wutai in Cave No. 61. Except for the decorative patterns, the other six previously mentioned categories of murals encompass a general theme, especially the scripture murals and story paintings, which reflect largely social life. Such scenes include: the journey of a high official, banquets, trials, hunting, tonsure and Buddhist Dharma. Among the works about commoners' activity we see agriculture, hunting, fishing, pottery making, metallurgy, animal slaughter, cooking, construction and beggars. Also, many social activities and roles in society are treated, including marriage, attending school, military drills, performing arts and traveling merchants, as well as renditions of distinct ethnic groups and foreign ambassadors. As a result, the Dunhuang Caves serve not only the function of showing art but also the presentation of history.

In addition to the five main categories mentioned above, there are also paintings of architecture, vessels, birds, flowers and animals among the Dunhuang Murals, of precious artistic value. In general, the murals systematically mirror the historical physiognomy of China during various periods of artistic style, and historical involvement through artful renderings that pay attention to layout, sculpture, patterns and vivid colors.

JINGDEZHEN PORCELAIN

Jingdezhen, Jiangxi Province, is considered the birthplace of porcelain. It is located in the transitional region of Mount Huang, the foothills of the Huaiyu Range and the plain of Lake Poyang, where there is beautiful scenery surrounded by hills and rivers. In all four directions, lush green mountains embrace a small basin in the middle of undulating hills. Yet it is precisely in this inconspicuous region that the subterrain holds all the necessary raw materials for the manufacture of porcelain, including magnetite, glaze, kaolin, feldspar and limestone. These are not only found here in tremendous quantity and variety but they are also of superior quality. Pure as jade, thin as paper, bright as a mirror and rings like a bell, Jingdezhen porcelain has become a distinct cultural symbol of the Chinese nation. In English, the name China is used to describe the country as well as the porcelain that originated here.

History tells us that pottery was first made in Xinping County during the Han Dynasty. Since Xinping was the earliest name for Jingdezhen, it is claimed that in this place, pottery was born.

During the Song Dynasty, industry and commerce expanded vigorously and thriving cities prospered. The economy grew rapidly in the Yangtze River Basin and southeastern China, which facilitated the development of porcelain making in ancient times. During the late Tang Dynasty and the Five Dynasties era, artisans began firing the celadon and white porcelain of the Changnan district in Raozhou Prefecture. Later, the fine qualities of the two styles were combined to form the blue and white porcelain known as *raoyu*. Like mild smooth

Celadon porcelain vase from Jingdezhen

jade, the blue and white porcelain became popular throughout the world. Reproductions of this porcelain sprang up in large quantities south of the Yangtze River, based on the methods of the Jingdezhen-manufactured wares. And great amounts of porcelain products sold well abroad.

To date, the famous blue and white porcelain that has been excavated at archaeological sites around the world is quite commonly that of the Song Dynasty. Emperor Zhenzong of the Song Dynasty was so fond of this kind of porcelain that he would not let go of it. He issued an imperial edict that demanded ceramic royal tribute, with the symbols meaning "made in the year of Jingde" written on the bottom. He also gave the small porcelain-making mountain town the title of his reign, Jingde. So the distinct blue and white glazed porcelain became the only porcelain on which is bestowed the name of an emperor's reign.

In 1004, Changnan was renamed Jingdezhen and established itself as the production center for ancient porcelain. Jingdezhen ceramics flourished during Emperor Shenzong's reign of the Song Dynasty. In the fifth year and eighth month of Emperor Yuanfeng's reign (1082), the feudal authorities established the Porcelain Exchange Center in Jingdezhen to deal with the china trade and taxes for it. From then on, Jingdezhen gradually became the ceramics capital of China, triggering the development of a unique subculture with extensive knowledge and profound scholarship as to the methods for firing ceramics, selling them and managing the expenditures related to the trade.

During the Yuan Dynasty, a new kind of vitreous enamel was developed in Jingdezhen. It was lighter in hue than the traditional blue and white porcelain, with a combination of the gemlike glaze colors and shining white finish that resembled goose eggs. The development of such porcelain seems to have foreshadowed the emergence of the blue-flowered porcelain that became immensely popular during the middle and late periods of the Yuan Dynasty. This porcelain is spotlessly white, thick and heavy. The glazed surface is lustrous and perfectly clear. The colors of the flowers are verdant and gorgeous, with a dazzling brightness like that of a hibiscus flower in clear water. Unadorned, it is commonly referred to as the national color. From the Yuan period and over the six hundred years to the present, the blue-flowered porcelain has continued to be the highest artistic achievement in porcelain and it is in the mainstream of the manufacturing and export of ceramic wares. As a result, Jingdezhen porcelain has sold profitably all around the world, as people everywhere are introduced to China through its exquisite porcelain.

During the Ming Dynasty, Jingdezhen gradually developed the characteristics of a major center for ceramics. With the establishment of a porcelain factory by the imperial government in Jingdezhen, expert potters from all over the country came here, grandly known as artisans coming from all eight directions. Their finished wares were distributed around the world. Jingdezhen during the Ming era not only prospered from the government kilns but brilliance came from the civilian kilns as well.

After the middle period of the Ming Dynasty, colored porcelain was fired in large quantities. Red, green, yellow and purple were added to the blue of the flowered porcelain, generally referred to as the five great Ming colors. The most representative multicolored porcelain of the Ming Dynasty was produced during the reign of Emperor Chenghua, the Chenghua Doucai, a newly developed artistic creation based on flower blue and the red hues of the early stages of the period.

During the Qing Dynasty, the Jingdezhen ceramic industry reached a golden age of prosperity. The town boasted a six-mile street that was half kiln factories and half houses. Smoke blanketed the sky during the day and flames shone deep into the night, as the town worked to remain the ceramics capital of the world.

Three generations of emperors, Kangxi, Qianlong and Yongzheng, considered Jingdezhen porcelain the national ware, so attaching great importance to the ceramics industry. By this time, Jingdezhen porcelain art had reached epic proportions. Over fifty types of colored glazes had come to be produced and fired here, as well as numerous reproductions of famous ancient ceramic items. The blue flower-tinted wares retained their unique position though newer artistic forms emerged, as the five colors of Kangxi's reign, the mixed glaze, enamel colors and deep black pigments together pushed the Jingdezhen ceramic industry to a historic high.

In modern times, the original techniques for making Jingdezhen porcelain wares cannot be equaled. But there was a breakthrough, an eruption that told of the long-term accumulated influence of China's ceramics. The appearance of the flowing poetic ceramics of scholars and works such as those of the Eight Friends of Zhushan took Jingdezhen porcelain art to another realm.

In July 1965, Guo Moruo, vice-chairman of the Standing Committee of the National People's Congress, and other deputies conducted an inspection of Jingdezhen. After visiting the factories that were making exquisitely artistic porcelain, he wrote the now-famous line, "China is praised as a nation of fine porcelain, and the peak of the porcelain industry is this city."

Chapter 18

SCHOOLING

The earliest school in China was probably started during the time of the slave-owning society. From what we know, there had been schools during the Xia Dynasty, using a complete system of learning developed in the Western Zhou period. The schools fall into two categories: the Imperial Academy and the rural schools. Emperors in their capitals established the Imperial Academies during the period of the vassal states. All the academies—Biyong, Zhong, Dongxu, Chengjun, Guzhong and Shangxiang—taught the broad scope of the Five Studies: . Among these, the structure that housed Biyong was the center. It was surrounded by water on all sides. Compared to this style of architecture, subordinate universities built by monarchs were less complex in design, with only one of the buildings half-facing water. This style was referred to as *pan gong*.

In addition to imperial colleges, there were also schools throughout the rural areas established by administrative subdivisions. Because of the various sizes of the different regions, the rural schools were variously referred to with names like *lushu*, *dangxiang*, *zhouxu* and *xiangxiao*.

According to the records of Zhou Rites, the universities of the Western Zhou Dynasty educated students on the three virtues, the three behaviors of conduct, the six rules of etiquette and the six Confucian arts. Among these rich cultural aspects, the school of education stressed the concept of ethics. During the three periods of the Xia, Shang and Zhou dynasties, formal teaching was done by feudal officials. It wasn't until the Eastern Zhou Dynasty that the emperor's dethronement led to the poor management and decline of the official schools, which changed the direction of education with regard to region. The rising feudal states began to attract talented individuals, as the erudite officials blended in among the commoners and academics gradually became private study. Laodan, a historian of the Zhou Dynasty, the musician, Shixiang, of the state of Lu, and Confucius all recruited a range of disciples. It was the first time that the culture of education was felt by the general population. However, at that time there was no regular location for Confucius and the others to lecture and educate their students.

After the Emperor Qin Shi Huang unified China, he established the official system of court academia in order to move the trend away from private education. Although the doctoral officials received salaries from the government, they were called advisors and never participated in actual decision making. At the same time, they were obliged to recruit new disciples if they wanted to retain their scholarly status as court academicians.

The court system of doctoral officials wasn't abolished until early in the Han Dynasty. Huge changes occurred during the reign of Emperor Wu as he established the Imperial College, based on the doctoral officials' instruction of the Five Classics of Confucianism. At the Imperial College the students were referred to as doctoral disciples. Then, Emperor Wu of the Han Dynasty attempted to revert to the former tradition of the government-sponsored education of the Western Zhou Dynasty, so that subsidized education would no longer be just for aristocrats but also for commoners.

The emphasis on the system of education during the Western Han Dynasty worked to combine the cultivation of talent with a selection of worthy individuals. In other words, the institutes were mutually compatible with the recruitment process, thus the government officials of the Han Dynasty were all from the Imperial College. Compared with those of former regimes, the new institutions proved to be advanced. But the Imperial College gradually deteriorated for various reasons, among them a lack of interested students. The scholars who truly wanted to pursue studies returned to the private colleges. And so the system of private education was revamped.

After the Eastern Han Dynasty, political power disintegrated. During this period there emerged the two forms of family education and monastery education, the prominent scholars of the time coming from either wealthy families or monasteries. The Han Dynasty system of public education was revived with the unification of the Sui and the Tang dynasties. During Taizong's reign during the Tang Dynasty, many foreign students were sent to China from places like the three Korean kingdoms of Goguryeo, Baekje and Silla, as well as from Gaochang (Kharakhoja), and from the Tibetan kingdom of Tubo, such that the number of incoming students was at one point over eight thousand.

The Tang Dynasty implemented a system of examination apart from the schools. Going to school was relatively easy, but running for public office was painstakingly hard. Society highly regarded a *jinshi* (palace graduate) and attached little importance to the students of the Imperial College. Therefore, the state-run education of the time began to accomplish significantly less than formerly.

During the Tang Dynasty, an entrance examination was necessary, but there weren't the schools to cultivate the talent. Educating a student was dependent on monasteries and on family stature. While the talent cultivated in the monastery did not go into secular life, the candidates that came from upper-class families became less and less. Despite this, there were many palace graduates, yet they could merely recite poetry and compose poetic essays and had little practical ability. So there was no universal education at the time. A great majority of learned individuals went to the monasteries to lay the foundations for the Zen sect of Buddhism.

In the later years of the Tang Dynasty, the academy of classical learning emerged as the remnant of the wealthy family member education and thrived during the Tang Dynasty. In order to rectify the mistakes of Tang Dynasty education, the Song Dynasty implemented both public and private systems of education, with state-run colleges and private institutions. However, the Imperial College was riddled with political corruption and the results of educational shortcomings, so government-sanctioned education gradually lost the confidence of the people. Although the government of the Song Dynasty strived to promote education, the government-run schools still could not duplicate the achievements of the private schools, although educators such as Zhou Dunyi, Cheng Jing and Cheng Yi of the Northern Song Dynasty and Zhu Xi and Lu Jingshan of the Southern Song Dynasty gave lectures that were of great influence.

In the Yuan Dynasty, as the Mongolians occupied the Central Plains, Academies of Classical Learning were cropping up everywhere and flourishing even more than in the Southern Song period. The first Ming Emperor, Zhu Yuanzhang, even before he seized power established county schools in Wuzhou. When he was on the throne, he published an imperial edict to establish schools in counties all over the country. According to the statistics, there were then 4,100 educators in the prefectures, government offices, administrative divisions and garrisons across China, several hundred times more than the number in the Yunfeng years of the Northern Song Dynasty. The local students attended the national school, which was originally called Guo Zi Xue (Imperial School) and later Guo Zi Jian (Imperial College).

As the Ming Dynasty was established, the two systems of education and examination were merged. Unlike in the Tang era, when recruiting was done according to one's ability to compose poetry, during the Ming period selection was made through *jingyi*, which involved writing an eight-part essay. Nevertheless, the system ended up infected by malpractice, and so many public lectures were given in opposition. Wang Yangming and his disciples, as well as the scholars from the Dongling Academy, often amassed crowds to address the issue.

In the Qing Dynasty, state-run public schools and schools of the central authorities in all areas existed only in name, as the Academies of Classical Learning continued uninterrupted. The Academy of the Qing Dynasty focused mainly on contributions to library collections and inscription.

In 1905, the government of the Qing Dynasty comprehensively abolished the imperial examination, opened a great number of academies and established a central administrative authority so as to exercise control over education nationwide. Although it had made great progress in terms of historical significance, judging by its intrinsic attributes the educational system of China, whether in the teaching of philosophy, course content or administration, hadn't at the time fully left the nest of the feudal code of ethics. The educational system of the time remained within the classification of a semi-colonial and semi-feudal society.

In 1912, the Xinhai Revolution (led by Dr. Sun Yat-sen) led to the overthrow of the Qing Dynasty, ending over two thousand years of dominance by a feudal autocratic monarchy. After this, education in China entered a new phase.

THE IMPERIAL EXAMINATION CULTURE

The Imperial Examination was given to intellectuals of ancient China as a means of selecting insightful, talented individuals. It was an integral system from the feudal past of recruiting government officials. It was called keju (subject selection) since it adapted its selection methods based on a range of subjects. The system was implemented at the beginning of the Sui Dynasty and was in effect until the end of the thirty-first year of Emperor Guangxu's reign (1905) of the Qing Dynasty, more than thirteen hundred years.

The ancient Chinese Imperial Examination System arose during the Sui Dynasty. In the third year of his reign (605), Emperor Yang established the *jinshi* exam to select successful candidates for the highest level of imperial examinations. The system interconnected book study and testing and stressed official conduct, opening a new page in the annals of China's electoral system.

The emperors that followed used the talent recruiting system of the Sui Dynasty, taking it one step further. As a result, the Imperial Examination System gradually became complete. During this period, the imperial examination was usually composed of two main sections, *jieshi* and *xingshi*, the examination given by the Ministry of Rites. Anybody who passed the second phase was pronounced a *Jinshi*, or metropolitan scholar. But since the *jinshi* examination was so hard that few could actually pass, successful candidates generally went on to become elected officials. Those who ranked first among the candidates in the final examination were given the honorary title of *Zhuangyuan*. But the *Zhuangyuan* of the Tang Dynasty did not have the same priority as that of later periods. Also, the final examination of the Tang era was judged not only by the score but also by the prominence of the person who recommended the candidate. In 702, during this same dynasty, the *Wuju* examination was implemented to select military talent. Later, successive dynasties continued to use the system, eventually integrating it with the *jinshi* examination as one comprehensive test.

The Imperial Examination of the Song Dynasty was generally the same as that of the Tang Dynasty except it produced more successful candidates. Many individuals of common ancestry entered the bureaucracy through the examination system and participated in governing the country. The Song Dynasty decided that the examination was to be held once every three years and on three levels: the rural, the provincial and the court. Candidates who successfully completed the final examination immediately received a title without being checked by the board of civil office. *Jinshi* during the Song era was divided into three strata: *jinshi jidi* (the first level), *jinshi chushen* (the second level) and the third-level, Tong *jinshi chushen*. During the Song Dynasty, the *jinshi* of the final examination enjoyed a political superiority that lasted until the end of the Imperial Examination System.

In the Yuan Dynasty, the imperial examinations were held occasionally for the Mongolians. But during this time there first appeared a complete examination based on the contents of *The Four Books: The Great Learning, Doctrine of the Mean, Analects of Confucius* and *Analects of Mencius*. Further, the Yuan implemented a policy of racial discrimination against the Han as regards taking the examination.

The establishment of the Ming Dynasty brought about the downfall of the Yuan Dynasty. At this time, the Imperial Examination System entered a period of great prosperity. The authorities of the Ming Dynasty attached great importance to the system. The methods of selection became much stricter than those of any other past generation. Before the Ming Dynasty, the Imperial College was one of the ways to get candidates, but during the Ming Dynasty one had to enter through the Imperial Examination System.

During the Ming era, the examination was formally divided into three levels: *xiangshi* (rural), *huishi* (provincial) and *dianshi* (court examination). First-place candidates in the rural examination were called *jieyuan*; on the provincial test called *huiyuan*; and on the court examination, *zhuangyuan*. These were collectively known as the Three Yuan. As regards the court examination, in addition to the *zhangyuan* there was a second and third ranking for scholars, respectively known as *bangyan* and *tan-hua*. During the Ming Dynasty, the main content of the Imperial Examination included a specific eight-part essay. The examination questions came from the verses of *The Four Books* and the Five Classics and required candidates to expound on the principles of these classic texts. But the candidates were to answer the questions in the ancient style of writing and in a particular format. Also, the number of answer words was strictly limited and the syntax required an antithesis. The eight-part essay

The Imperial Examination Scene

caused great harm and seriously fettered the thinking of the candidates. Meanwhile, the Imperial Examination System led itself to a dead end.

During the Qing Dynasty, the Imperial Examination was generally the same as that of the Ming era. But the policy of racial discrimination persisted. The Manchu enjoyed various priorities, becoming officials without even taking the examination. And so the Imperial Examination System declined day by day, with more and more disadvantages coming to light. Particularly, the onslaught of foreign aggressors hastened its death. In the thirty-first year of Emperor Guangxu's reign of the Qing Dynasty, after the imperial examination was administered for the last time, it was officially terminated, in 1905.

In the over one thousand years of the Imperial Examination System, various other relatively comprehensive systems were set up. For example, in order to discourage fraud, there was an avoidance system—relationships of kin were to be avoided between examiner and candidate; there was a concealed name system—the names and other information of the candidates were hidden; and there was a transcription system that required that all completed examinations be transcribed in uniform handwriting by one official both to avoid deception and to create a clean copy. These systems had far-reaching influence and even play a role in modern China.

An important invention of ancient China, over the years the Imperial

Examination System has had great impact on the society and culture. Neighboring countries in Asia, including Vietnam, Japan and Korea, have all at one time or another introduced similar systems by which to select learned individuals. Sun Zhongshan believed the Chinese Imperial Examination System to be the world's oldest and most prestigious framework for assessing and selecting talented people.

COLLECTING AND ARCHIVING
BOOKS AND DOCUMENTS

There were four major systems of cataloging books in ancient China: official libraries, private libraries, academic libraries and monastery collections. The history of book collection can be traced back to the pre-Qin era, when people used *jiaguwen* (Oracle Bone Script) to record social, political, economic and military issues and established halls to house the various tortoise shell and bone inscriptions, which became the first archives of China. From this point on, China began its over three thousand-year history of library collections.

As the Zhou Dynasty came to power, the royal library, monastery and vassal libraries were beginning to take shape with the appearance of writing tools such as inscribed wooden tablets, bamboo slips and fine silk paper. During the Warring States Period, the social atmosphere of a hundred schools of contending thought had broken down the government's monopoly on information, and the tradition that only imperial historiographers could record oration and public affairs was left behind. This began a new chapter in book collecting as private libraries were established.

During the Qin and Han dynasties, the First Emperor Qin burned the books and buried the Confucians, and this was incredibly destructive. Huge numbers of historical documents and classical works vanished. Fortunately, some private collectors had protected their books with the upmost care, to preserve what they could for future generations.

Then, during the two periods of the Han dynasties (Western and Eastern), the book collecting culture was revived and further developed. According to documents, there were a total of twenty-two private collectors at the time, most of them nobles, officials in high position and families of learned scholars. The most famous collections are those of dignitaries such as Liu An, Liu Xin, Cai Yi and Zheng Xuan.

During the Wei, the Jin and the Northern and Southern dynasties, the general content of private libraries changed. For one thing, the invention of paper and the wide range of uses for it help slash the price of books. For another thing, book collecting was very popular at this time among the minister class. These officials circulated books among themselves and even donated volumes, so that a small number of commoners could join start collecting. The number of private book collectors had grown to over one hundred by then, and the quantity and quality of the libraries was improved.

The Sui and Tang dynasty period was the peak of Chinese feudal society. There was a great demand for books at this time and the writers were becoming prosperous. This can likely be attributed to the invention and use of block printing. Block printing not only increased the speed and efficiency of publication, it also broke down the system that books were the exclusive purview of the aristocracy and enabled commoners to read and collect literature. Further, the establishment of the Imperial Examination System propelled the book culture to a boom and prosperity, and this brought forth many official librarians within the palace.

During the Tang Dynasty, a new cataloging system came into being, the academic library. The Imperial Academy established an archive with abundant books. More than one hundred thousand volumes were collected during the period of recruitment at the Academy of Classical Learning in Luoyang. The academy's collections were regarded as a spiritual homeland for scholars as well as being an effective way of preserving traditional Chinese literary works and culture. It especially made an indelible contribution to the storage and protection of ancient books and records and spurred growth in document research, textual criticism and the publication of periodicals.

Throughout the Song and Yuan periods, great forward movement took place in collecting. During this time a new precedent was set for the collating and cataloguing of such things as bibliographies, annotated editions, textual criticism and studies on publishing. The quantity of works in the archives had the edge over that of the previous generation, and management practices during this period also became standardized.

During the Ming period, society was relatively stable and flourishing as regards politics, the economy and culture, and so the book culture continued to expand. The block-printing industry particularly prospered, and growth in the number of bookstores and individual sellers formed a favorable material base for the development of the book industry. According to records, during the Ming Dynasty there were 869 book collectors who had accomplished much more than the collectors of the Song and Yuan dynasties in terms of the management of materials. They were particular about the locations and the names of buildings where materials were stored, and they paid particular attention to the three protections: fireproofing,

Ningbo's First Hall Under Heaven

moisture resisting and insect deterring. At the same time, attention was paid to discouraging scattered and lost books. Ningbo city's First Hall Under Heaven was the leading archive of ancient book collections. The oldest private library in Asia, it is also one of the world's three earliest existing collections.

Throughout the Qing Dynasty, the growth in collecting literature was unprecedented. The government of the Qing Dynasty attached the utmost importance to the collections of the work of all the previous generations. In fact, the achievement of the Qing Dynasty surpassed that of all the previous generations with regard to the accumulation and archiving of books. In this period emerged the masterpiece edited by palace officials of the Qing Dynasty: *The Complete Collection of Four Treasuries*.

The Monastery Collections

In addition to the above-mentioned imperial, private and academic archives, there was yet another system of collecting and cataloging—the monastery system. This emerged alongside the introduction of Buddhism and Taoism during the period of the Six Dynasties of the Han and Wei. As early as the rule of Emperor Ming of the Han Dynasty, ambassadors had been sent to the Western regions by the imperial government to obtain *The Sutra in Forty-two Chapters*, and the White Horse Temple was built to store and protect it.

In the eleventh year of Yong Ping's reign during the Eastern Han Dynasty, in the holy land of Buddhism, at Mount Wutai, the Dafu Lingjiu Temple was built. This would become the model of ancient Chinese monastery book collections, as the circulation of literature was encouraged by the efforts of the devotees. During the last years of the Eastern Han Dynasty, Taoism emerged and was addressed in literary works, and these books were gathered into the temple collections.

In order to protect and preserve the ancient books and records from natural and man-made calamity, the devotees use methods of concealed storage, either carving storerooms into the cliffs of caves in remote mountainous regions or disguising them in private rooms and Buddhist pagodas. Since many temples were local cultural centers in ancient times and served universal education by preserving the Buddhist and Taoist canonical texts, other categories of books were also stored in the temples. The monastery collections were relatively stable and not as disturbed as others. Also, some philosophers were inclined to store their work in the temples.

The four major systems of book collecting worked together and this contributed greatly to the legacy of Chinese culture and tradition.

CONFUCIANISM

Confucianism refers to the doctrine of Confucian study that arose during the Spring and Autumn Period and then spanned an unbroken twenty-five hundred years. Emperor Wu of the Han Dynasty helped to integrate Confucian thought into Chinese culture. During this period, Confucian study expanded in content, forms and social functions in tandem with the development of society. Its progress can be marked by four stages:

Primitive Confucian study during the pre-Qin era was represented by Confucius, Mencius and Hsun Tzu.
The founding concepts of Confucian doctrine refer mainly to moral standards for cultivating people of virtue and principles for governing a country. People often refer to Confucian study as the study of benevolence, as a result of Confucius' conviction that benevolence is the fundamental moral standard required of a virtuous individual. *The Analects of Confucius* records many of his opinions as Confucius answered his students' questions about the idea of benevolence. This work contains various specific norms and principles to be followed in the conduct of mundane, practical activities.

Mencius went further with Confucius' idea that men's minds should be cultivated benevolently. He introduced the doctrine of a benevolent government, which has become the norm throughout the world. The requirements of benevolent governance were specific to the earlier work on benevolence. For example, it is written, "The conduct of a benevolent government should begin with the management of its borders." This so-called management of boundaries referred to the belief that farmland should be evenly distributed and a system enacted that allowed people permanent entitlement to their property. Although the norms and principles proposed by Confucius and Mencius were specific, they were much too idealistic and depended very much on people's realizing the innate nature of mankind. Therefore, Confucius did his utmost to emphasize self-restraint and self-cultivation. For his part, Mencius promoted the idea of kinship by nature and emphasized intuitive knowledge and the instinctive generosity of people.

Compared with Confucius and Mencius, Hsun Tzu was more inclined to realism. He not only gave priority over education to a sense of righteousness and morality but also stressed corporal punishment in the political and legal systems. Hsun Tzu proposed a theory of natural immorality, advocating that the intuitive nature of people should be educated and guided by a sense of righteousness and law so that their conduct would be in accord with the standards and requirements of social groups.

The original Confucian study was one of the prominent and earliest schools of thought on the idea of realism, making a great impact on society from the late Spring and Autumn Period to the Warring States periods. The idea of moral cultivation had a heavy influence on virtuous individuals. But ideal political and state-run systems were neither appreciated nor adopted by those in power, since they were not in touch with the social reality of vassals seeking hegemony and rival warlord regimes competing for parts of the country. And so the primitive Confucian study differs from the thinking developed later in that it was founded on the basis of then-current political and social systems and did not incorporate the original concept of moral cultivation with political ideals.

Politics- and religion-oriented Confucian study in the Han Dynasty

Rulers during the early part of the Han Dynasty made new policy, forming a streamlined administration, governing by non-interference and rehabilitating the people by reducing taxes and levies so they could recuperate financially from the destitution caused by tyrannical government and the turmoil of war in the later part of the Qin Dynasty. As well, they attached great importance to and advocated the Taoism of the Yellow Emperor. This continued until changes were made during Emperor Wu's reign during the Han Dynasty.

A renowned scholar named Dong Zhongshu, during the Western Han Dynasty, proposed that the authorities should pay supreme tribute to Confucianism and ban all other schools of thought, so as to accomplish national reunification. Emperor Wu liked this idea and so Confucian study entered political institutions and places of worship.

Dong Zhongshu studied the work of Gong Yang (Gong Yang Gao, a scholar of the Warring States Period), which was closely related to societal norms. Gong Yang expanded on *The Spring and Autumn Annals* ideals of the three systems (heaven, man, earth), the critical three months (periods of the lunar calendar) and the three eras (past, present, future). These ideals were aimed at expounding the establishment of the Han Dynasty, while the various virtues and established norms mentioned about these concepts could be emulated by the government of the Han Dynasty. *The Spring and Autumn Annals* is generally believed to have been written by

Confucius. Dong Zhongshu and Han scholars regarded Confucius as the Unadorned Emperor, namely, a ruler without a throne. Therefore, Confucian study was closely associated with the practical social-political system. It not only mitigated the uninvolved theories of morality, ethical cultivation and political idealism, it also functioned as articles of law for the social system. The religious orientation of Confucian study greatly influenced political institutions, so Confucius is praised as the King of Doctrine. The sociopolitical functions of Confucianism strengthened and developed as ideas about moral ethical cultivation and political ideals fell more and more out of favor.

As the later period of the Han Dynasty arrived, the governmental ethical code of Confucianism provoked fierce dissatisfaction among the masses, as it shackled and constrained people's natural emotions. It also became a means for hypocrites to fish for fame and compliments. The study of metaphysics and Taoist philosophy and religion took advantage of this negativity and replaced Confucianism as a cultivator of morals. After the periods of the Eastern Jin and the Northern and Southern Dynasties, the influence of Buddhism surpassed that of metaphysics and was of great interest to scholars interested in moral cultivation. Therefore, over the seven hundred years from the Wei, the Jin and the Northern and Southern Dynasties to the Sui, Tang and later part of the Five Dynasties, Confucian dogma, embodied by the political system, remained under the protection of the ruling authority.

The Confucian school of idealist philosophy of the Song, Ming and Qing dynasties

The doctrines of Buddhism and Taoism appealed to most scholarly officials when it came to self-cultivation, and this provoked dissatisfaction and uneasiness among the Confucians. It also sparked the revival of Confucian study. Wang Tong of the Sui and Tang dynasties started the movement and was followed by Han Yu, Li Ao and Liu Zongyuan during the middle period of the Tang era. (A more luminous view was presented during the Song Dynasty.) Moreover, these men strived to revive the main Confucian concepts of moral principles, ethics and character development as they hoped to give full play to its social functions and moral cultivation and return to the ideological fields that had been occupied by Buddhism and Taoism for the previous seven hundred years.

Confucianism was called the School of Principles during the Song and Ming dynasties, as well as the Yuan and Qing periods, because it differed greatly from the original Confucian theories. Generally speaking, early Confucian study told people the what and how of conduct in daily life, but it did not explain the why. Meanwhile, an ideological system involving cosmic principles and conscience arose along the lines of idealist philosophy, absorbing and amalgamating the theories of metaphysics, Buddhism and Taoism.

During the early part of the Northern Song Dynasty, Hu Yuan, Sun Fu and Shi Jie were known as the three teachers of the School of Principles. But it was actually Zhou Dunyi, Shao Yong, Zhangzai and the Cheng brothers who promoted the idealist philosophy. The work of Zhu Xi of the Southern Song Dynasty epitomized the thinking of this school and established a relatively complete objective idealist system, as he proposed that the philosophy existed before the creation of the universe. Lu Jiuyuan opposed Zhu Xi's subjective idealism and proposed that external reality is a product of consciousness. In the Ming Dynasty, Wang Shouren further developed the thinking of Lu Jiuyuan. He believed there is nothing and no reason outside the mind of man. He even asserted that the soul is the origin of the universe.

Confucian study in modern times

Neo-Confucianism emerged in the modern era as a result of the spread of Western culture into China and the collision of the philosophical ideas of the East and the West. The narrow approach of modern Neo-Confucianism points to the work of Liang Shuming, Xiong Shili, Ma Yifu, Qian Mu, Feng Youlan and He Lin. The broad approach of modern Neo-Confucianism embraces the doctrines of the Confucian innovations that emerged after the Opium Wars. The objective of the modern school of thinking was to promulgate the traditional cultural norms by means of modern interpretations so they could play a role in the cultivation of morals and the establishment of a nationalized ideology.

As an embodiment of Chinese culture passed down for over two thousand years, Confucianism is rich and profound in ideological connotations and has had extensive influence in China and East Asia. Meanwhile, as one of the main representatives of Oriental traditions, Confucianism is agreeable to Western cultures as well, being of increasing interest in the West with the passage of time.

TAOISM

Taoism is a school of thought that reflects ancient Chinese social, ideological and cultural values. Taking the *tao* (the way) as its core concept, it emphasizes the effortless and spontaneous laws of *wuwei* as well as human compliance with the ways of nature. Taoism was one of the Hundred Schools of Thought during the pre-Qin period and later expanded to include those who placed a premium on the doctrines of the scholars, Lao Tzu and Zhuang Tzu.

Because *tao* is the core of and the highest level of thought, Taoist scholars attach great importance to the concept. In general, *tao* involves several things: The *tao* is the source of many things in nature, is spontaneous without acting, is formless. The *tao* is omnipresent and timeless. As a genre of ideological and cultural thought, the essential characteristics of Taoism revered by Taoist scholars were those propounded by Zhuang Tzu, Lao Tzu and Emperor Huang. As the way of the *tao*, Taoism's ideological system speaks of the relationship between humans and all things under the heavens and the effortless and spontaneous ways of the cosmos and the acquiescence of humanity. Taoist scholars also treat worldly affairs with subtle and abstruse (metaphysical) language, such being the mindset of the recluse. Differing from the proponents of other schools of thought, Taoist scholars observe and record society by a more recollected, sober and profound means, while having the unique temperament of universal acceptance, transcending vulgarity, abandoning benevolence and etiquette and pursuing the more unassuming aspects of nature.

Taoism saw changes during the different periods of its evolution as it passed through three historical phases.

The focus of the studies of Emperor Huang and Lao Tzu in the Qin and Han dynasties was a school of philosophical political thought that emerged during the Warring States Period. In the term, "Huang Lao," Huang is a reference to the Emperor Huang and Lao to Lao Tzu. During the Warring States Period when the study of the Five Elements was popular, Emperor Huang considered himself not only one of the Five Elements but also the legendary ancestor of Chinese culture, and so he became an object of worship and relied on by military strategists, legal philosophers, the *Yin* and *Yang* school of philosophy and even the Confucians.

Moreover, Emperor Huang was described as a superior thinker in *The Way of Chuang Tzu*, a work that reflected the thinking of the Taoist master. In the late years of the Warring States Period, study of the ideas of Emperor Huang and Lao Tzu was rooted in a combination of Lao Tzu's influence in the state of Chu and the worship of Emperor Huang in the Central Plains area of China. It also marked an ideological trend for Taoism, which advanced to a new level. Writings by Emperor Huang and Lao Tzu are contained in *The Book of the Yellow Emperor* and *The Way of Lao Tzu*.

METAPHYSICS

During the Wei and Jin dynasties, metaphysics became a prominent school of thought. The Taoist classical works *The Way of Lao Tzu*, *The Way of Chuang Tzu* and *The Book of Changes* (collectively known as the Three Profound Theories) deal with a philosophy that integrates Confucian ideology with Taoist principles. The concept of *xuan*, meaning abstruse (the modern metaphysics), appears in the first chapter of *The Way of Lao Tzu*. "The abstruse is within the abstruse as the gateway to the multitude of the unfathomable." Metaphysics in the period of the Wei and Jin dynasties went through a development witnessed by the scholars He Yan, Wang Bi, Ji Kang, Ruan Ji and Guo Xiang. There was a transition from the ontology of valuing the idea of nothingness to theories dignifying existence.

After the decline in the study of metaphysics, the vestigial residue of Taoist thinking remained, which is clear from the many annotated editions of *The Way of Lao Tzu* and *The Way of Chuang Tzu* created from the time of the Sui and Tang dynasties. But not long after the Sui and Tang era, the existing forms of Taoism took on a new shape, and the philosophy prospered mainly within the religious realms. Taoist scholars began to put forth their own religious theories by interpreting and developing the thoughts of Chuang Tzu.

Nevertheless, Taoist philosophy and Taoist religion are two different things, similar in some ways, different in others, while the different times when the two emerged can account for the differences:

First, the philosophy of Taoism was founded by Lao Tzu in the last years of the Spring and Autumn Period, while the religion was established during the late years of the Eastern Han Dynasty.

Second, the ideas of the two are different. Even though the same person may have been writing, he was not the same personality in the view of the two practices. Leading the philosophical school of thought were Lao Tzu, Chuang Tzu and Lieh Tzu. The religion relied mainly on the teachings of Ge Hong, Tao Hongjing and Cheng Xuanying. Further, for example, Lao Tzu was a realistic ideologist and founder of Taoist philosophy, while later he was Supreme Lord Lao Tzu and a religious leader. Both schools of thought held him in high regard, but not in the same ways.

Third, in a strict sense, the philosophy of Taoism is a school only of ideology and culture, while Taoism as a religion not only functions ideologically but is also strictly organized and has religious activities. One obvious connection between the two practices is that the religion of Taoism is established on Taoist philosophical principles, but after the Han and Wei dynasties, no new scholars or schools of thought arose to support Taoist philosophy. Conversely, Taoism as a religion saw considerable growth during this time. Yet the philosophical school of Taoism did not completely vanish, one main reason being the continual growth and development of the religion. Moreover, since the religion employed the principles of the philosophy as its theoretical pillars, it conveyed philosophical thinking and continued to develop as Taoist religious scholars annotated the classic ideology of the writing of Zhuang Tzu.

As an indigenous religion, Taoism has contributed greatly to the development of traditional Chinese culture and is considered one of the Three Pillars (Confucianism, Buddhism and Taoism) of traditional Chinese culture. Moreover, given the serious environmental crisis we face today, the Taoist idea of the oneness of mankind, along with its wisdom about ecology, give rise to much-needed enlightenment and respect for the earth.

BUDDHISM

Buddhism emerged in India during the sixth century BCE. At that time, India was going through major turmoil and great change that resulted in continuous wars, social chaos, political corruption and no way to make a living. Some of the disheartened withdrew from social life and became monks known as *shramanas*. They lived in the wild, wore the bark of trees, ate acorns, drank with their hands, did not marry, bore no children and performed ascetic practices, not moving throughout the day.

The founder of Buddhism, Siddhartha Gautama, was born during this time. He had been in love with meditation from childhood and was deeply upset with the changes he saw in secular life, so he decided to leave it behind. At the age of twenty-nine, he abandoned the material life and left home late in the night, having shaved his head, to begin the life of a *shramana*. After years of penance and asceticism, at the age of thirty-five he finally reached the realm where all truths are realized, and so he became the Enlightened One, preaching across the land and widely recruiting disciples to advance his ideals. With the emergence of Buddhism, such Buddhist arts as pagoda building, sculpture and painted murals also appeared, which served to promote Buddhism through image and metaphor.

In the following centuries, Buddhism and its arts followed the Silk Road and diffused to the north, west and east. Around the first century BCE, they were introduced to China. After long-term development, a form of Chinese Buddhism was formed with distinct cultural characteristics.

Ultimately, there were three major sects of Buddhism in China, namely: Chinese Buddhism (the Mandarin system), Tibetan Buddhism (the Tibetan language system) and the Yunnan region's Theravada Buddhism (the Pali language system).

Chinese Buddhism

Buddhism is believed to have entered the Han regions of China in the Yong Ping years of Emperor Ming's rein during the Eastern Han Dynasty (58–75) after an envoy was sent on a mission to the Western Regions to obtain *The Sutra in Forty-two Chapters*. Buddhism spread from the centers of Chang'an and the Luoyang regions. The first temple built on Mainland China was the White Horse Temple, six miles east of Luoyang. During the Eastern Han period, the most of the Buddhist scriptures were translated.

During the periods of the Three Kingdoms, the Wei and the Western Jin dynasties, a major factor in the dissemination of Buddhist tenets was the translation of the sacred Buddhist literature. The Weiduo district of the ancient capital of Luoyang and the capital of Wu, Jiangye, were the centers of Buddhist propagation. Translation dissemination and research laid the foundation for the development of the Buddhist doctrine during the three periods.

Then, from the Eastern Jin to the Northern and Southern Dynasties periods, the popularity of Buddhism grew as it attracted believers from all social strata and as pagodas and temples were being built everywhere. The world-famous ancient Buddhist grotto art, including the Dunhuang Murals and Yungang and Dragon Gate, saw the start of construction during this time. Also, the scholar Kumarajiva (ca. 344–413) translated 384 volumes of sacred texts, and because they were accurate and concise translations, they made a substantial contribution to the spread of Buddhism. On a pilgrimage to the West in search of Buddhist scriptures, Fa Xian (337–422) toured more than thirty countries in the regions of India and Sri Lanka. The sacred literature and the travel log he kept have provided valuable information about the development of Buddhism in Chin as well as historical research on Central and Southern Asia.

Emperor Liang Wu of the Northern and Southern Dynasties period was a believer. During his fourteen-year reign, he entered the temple four times as a servant and held forth on the texts of Buddhism. He also composed scripture of his own. During the Liang Dynasty, there were 2,860 temples and more than 82,700 Buddhist monks and nuns.

During the Tang Dynasty, Chinese Buddhism saw a time of great prosperity. Having been helped by Buddhist monks to eliminate separation and turmoil in the land, Emperor Taizong issued an imperial edict establishing temples all around the country and setting up places for explaining Buddhist scripture. His actions served to cultivate a quantity of eminent monks and scholars. One of the most famous of these, Xuanzang, went on a long and difficult journey to India to acquire scripture. He translated seventy-five Buddhist scriptures, 1,335 volumes, and composed the *Great Tang Records of the Western Regions*. He was held in high esteem by Emperor Tang Taizong as the one who opened the gates to Buddhism and as the kind of person who appears only once throughout the ages. His life story was recorded in many books and eventually became the stuff of legends.

During the middle of the Tang period appeared the oral legends of Xuanzang. In the Song Dynasty, the Tang record *Xuanzang Obtaining the Scriptures* appeared. During the Ming Dynasty, Wu Cheng'en wrote the novel *Journey to the West*, which made the monk known to every household and loved and recognized by all the family.

The imperial government of the Northern Song Dynasty adopted a protective policy toward Buddhism such that Chinese and Indian monks came and went in an endless stream to share the tenets of their faith. In the fifth year of Emperor Tianxi's reign, Buddhism was at the zenith of its development, with nearly 460,000 monks and 40,000 temples in China. The imperial government of the Southern Song Dynasty was inclined to pacify the areas south of the Yangtze River, and so Buddhism was able to maintain its hold there.

Throughout the Yuan Dynasty, the Mongolians supported the Tibetan version of Buddhism while also preserving that of the Han nationality. Before the establishment of the Ming Dynasty, Emperor Zhu Yuanzhang was a monk. He proclaimed himself the Great Preacher of Daqing after being enthroned. He passed on to others the Buddhist doctrines, performing tonsures for the monks and even making use of the support of Buddhists to consolidate his newly established political power.

The imperial government of the Qing Dynasty practiced Tibetan Buddhism, while Chinese Buddhism prevailed among non-government factions. During the later stages of the Qing Dynasty, many Buddhist researchers emerged, including Yang Wenhui, Ouyang

Xuanzang

Jingwu and Da Xu. Also, modern thinkers such as Kang Youwei, Tan Citong, Zhang Taiyan and Liang Qichao were influenced by Buddhist doctrine and proposed various new ideas, which brought research into Buddhism to a new level.

Tibetan Buddhism

The Buddhism of Tibetan nationality is also known as the Buddhism of the Tibetan Language System, commonly known as *Lamaism*. *Lama* means "seat of honor" in the Tibetan language. Tibetan Buddhism arose in the middle of the seventh century, when the king of Tibet, Songsten Gampo, escorted his brides, Princess Bhrikuti Devi of Nepal and Princess Wencheng of the Tang Dynasty, both of whom carried Buddhist statues and scripture. Songsten Gampo was in turn converted to Buddhism under the influence of the two princesses and built Jokhang Monastery and Ramoche Monastery in Lhasa. By the middle of the eighth century, Buddhism had spread into Tibetan regions, channeled directly from India.

Tibetan Buddhism was formally organized in the latter half of the tenth century. It began to spread throughout Mongolia during the middle of the thirteenth century. In the more than three centuries since, all kinds of denominations with their own distinctions have arisen. The followers long ago generally practiced the teachings of Tantric Buddhism (Mantrayana). With the development of Buddhism in Tibet, lamas in higher positions gradually controlled local political power, which led eventually to the unique integration of Buddhism and government.

The most famous Buddhist building is Potala Palace, built for Princess Wencheng in the seventh century. The one we see today, however, was built during the seventeenth century.

Theravada Buddhism

Pali language Buddhism is popular among the Dai people in Yunnan Province, among the Bulang ethnic group and in other regions. The Buddhist traditions followed in these regions reflect those of the Buddhist countries of southern Asia, including Thailand and Myanmar. Around the middle of the seventh century, Buddhism spread into the Dai region from Myanmar. People there had upheld Buddhist traditions for centuries in accordance with the doctrines, disciplines and advanced teachings of the original Buddhism. As the males of the Dai nationality became of school age, they had to leave home to become monks. In the temples they studied until close to adulthood and then returned to secular life.

Chapter 19

A DREAM OF RED MANSIONS

A Dream of Red Mansions is also known as *The Story of the Stone*, *The Anecdotes of a Romantic Monk*, *The Treasured Mirror of Romantic Affairs*, *The Twelve Beauties of Jinling* and *Baoyu's Fate*. It was written in the age of Emperor Qianlong during the Qing Dynasty and is representative of the highest achievement of the novel form and one of the four greatest classical works of China. The book contains 120 chapters, eighty written by Cao Xueqin and forty believed to have been written by Gao E.

The authors use the four great families of Jia, Wang, Shi and Xue as background for the main story line, the love tragedy of Jia Baoyu and Lin Daiyu. The novel focuses on the descent from prosperity to decline of the Rongguo and Ningguo houses. It not only deals with multifarious life, it also makes specific references to colorful common customs and human relationships. The book is said to reflect the history of an era and to be an encyclopedia of late feudal society. The language in the novel is exquisite and vivid. A long and well-structured volume, the book is considered to be a high artistic achievement and one of the most substantial of the world classics.

The writer, Cao Xueqin (1715–63), was a novelist in the Qing Dynasty. His great-grandfather Cao Xi, his grandfather Cao Ying, and the elder Cao Yong and Cao Fu had been in charge of textile production in the Jiangning district for sixty years. They were all trusted by the Emperor Kangxi, and so Cao Xueqin grew up in a wealthy family. At the beginning of the reign of the Emperor Yongzheng in the Qing Dynasty, however, his family suffered from involvement in the internal struggles of the feudal ruling classes. Their property was confiscated, forcing the whole family to move to Beijing. After that, they lived in poverty and Cao Xueqin began to be concerned about the inconstancy of human relationships, which awakened in him a desire to understand feudal society. From then on, he lived without money. He could not only write poems but he could also paint. Being an excellent author, he set in to write *A Dream of Red Mansions* and worked on it for over ten years. Eventually, he produced a magnificent literary work known for its cultural

Jia Baoyu

Lin Daiyu

content, dramatic plot twists, philosophical thinking and exquisite artistic technique. The book is a masterpiece of realism. Tragically, in 1764 Cao Xueqin passed away, too poor to afford medical care.

A Dream of Red Mansions presents a picture of social norms by depicting society in terms of family relations and their transcendence over traditional ways of thinking and behaving. In the story, the Jia family is the essence of feudalism. The book talks about the rise and fall of four powerful families, but mainly the Jias. It also deals with the degradation of feudal marriage, morality, culture and education, and it presents a series of tragic emotional moments and images involving the roles of women.

The novel eulogizes the love between nobles who resist conforming to the feudal courtesy system. It also explores early democratic thinking and the individual pursuit of freedom, and it is deeply revealing of the social origins of marriage, which situation results in tragedy for the families of Jia, Lin and Xue.

This book has influenced generations of readers, transcending the boundaries of space and time. As a subject for study and research, *A Dream of Red Mansions* has never failed to interest scholars.

With regard to character development, *A Dream of Red Mansions* is felt to have attained perfection. The characters are all vividly portrayed, have unique personalities, and are three-dimensional, and this broke the mold of earlier styles of novels. It focuses on the distinctive psychological issues of the characters to create an atmosphere that reflects their inner emotions. Throughout the book, the imagery is conveyed via the characters:

Jia Baoyu is the protagonist. He is heir to the Rongguo Mansion, extremely intelligent and the much hoped for heir of the Jia family. But his thoughts and temperament induce him to forsake the family. The core of his nature embraces the equal treatment of others, a respect for individualism and the pursuit of freedom, and so he is rebellious toward feudal society despite his aristocratic background.

Lin Daiyu is an irreproachable noblewoman who indulges in self-admiration and is often depressed. Love what she would choose, but such love would not be tolerated in that it would destroy her aristocratic family.

Xue Bao Chai is a faithful woman who abides scrupulously by the laws of feudal society and is the wise and virtuous woman society expects her to be. At the same time, she is also a victim of the system.

There are roughly sixty versions of *A Dream of Red Mansions*, which has been translated into eighteen languages. It is a treasure of world literature and published throughout the world. Foreign scholars look to the "Red Study," study of the Oracle Bone inscriptions and study of the Dunhuang Murals as the three main fields of Chinese cultural research. And so the great work, *A Dream of Red Mansions*, belongs not only to China but to the world, as the spiritual treasure of people everywhere.

WATER MARGIN

Shi Nai'an wrote *Water Margin* during end of the Yuan period and the beginning of the Ming Dynasty. From childhood he had been clever and studious, surpassing others in insight and acumen and conducting himself in a righteous way when it came to others. When he was nineteen, he became a licentiate, and at twenty-eight years a provincial graduate of the Imperial Examination. At the age of thirty-six, he and Liu Bowen were listed as graduates with highest honors. He was an officer for three years in the Qiantang region (modern-day Hangzhou, Zhejiang Province), but, dissatisfied with officialdom and unwilling to deal with bureaucracy, he abandoned his government post and went back to the countryside. When Zhang Shicheng revolted against the Yuan Dynasty, Shi Nai'an took part in military exercises and later actively participated in Zhang Shicheng's conspiracy. Ultimately, though, Zhang Shicheng got greedy and was deaf to honest words, so Shi Nai'an, along with Lu Yuan, Liu Liang and Chen Ji, left the effort.

Soon afterwards, Zhang Shicheng died, imperiling the country. So Shi Nai'an began to roam. He traveled to such regions as Shandong and Henan Province, eventually living with the Xu family in Jiangyin, becoming their private teacher. Then he went back to the old white house, to live once again in seclusion. Witnessing the decay of politics, he wrote *Water Margin*.

Song Jiang

Later, he and a student, Luo Guanzhong, wrote *Romance of Three Kingdoms*. He was also quite talented in the arts of music and verse, but little has been preserved of his work in these areas. To avoid the conscription of the Ming Dynasty, he lived secretly in Huai'an, became sick, and died there at the age of seventy-five.

Most today consider Shi Nai'an to be the author of *Water Margin*, although some critics feel that he and Luo Guanzhong wrote it together.

Water Margin is based on the uprising led by Song Jiang in the final years of the Northern Song Dynasty. The Song Jiang revolt started in the first year of the Xuanhe period, in 1119, and ended in 1121. The art of storytelling flourished in the Song Dynasty. The tales of the outlaw Song Jiang and his thirty-six cohorts had been embraced as the fundamentals for creating folktales. *Water Margin* was written during the early part of the Xuanhe period of the Northern Song. By the time the Southern Song era had arrived, it had become a mainstay of oral folk literature.

At the beginning of the Yuan Dynasty there emerged a distinct literary form based on vernacular folk stories. *Matters of the Song Dynasty's Xuanhe Period* deals with the story of thirty-six people, including the well known Chao Gai and Wu Jialiang (Wu Yong), and reflects the gist of *Water Margin*. Over the years of the Yuan era, several variations of the work were produced as the untraditional Shi Nai'an constantly edited, recompiled and rewrote.

Water Margin gives us a vivid description of the peasant uprising against feudal society in China, led predominantly by Song Jiang. The social significance of *Water Margin* lies in its revelations about the decadent life of feudal society and the maliciousness of the ruling class. It tells us that the uprising was triggered by the government's treatment of the common people. With powerful artistic vision and vivid language, Shi Nai'an recounts several fascinating stories and paints many unique and heroic pictures.

The writer is passionate about the valiance of his characters, paying tribute not only to their spirit of resistance and righteous behavior but also to their outstanding martial arts skills and noble character.

The language of the characters is at a high level, disclosing not only the way the characters look but also how they think and feel. Family background is described by using the regional languages of the characters. In terms of the revealing language, for example, the disposition of Ruan Xiaoq's heart is impatient; the temperament of Wu Yong is resourceful; while the character of Song Jiang is modest. The vivid dialogue brings us into the very presence of the characters in the novel.

The novel gives us not only vivid plots but also rich description of detail. And, on the basis of oral folk language, it is written in a simple, terse style, full of expressive force.

After the novel was written, it spread far and wide. By the start of the 1920s, though, it had yet to be translated into English. One English-language version did eventually find its way into print as *Outlaws of the Marsh*.

Among many other versions, Pearl S. Buck's was the earliest translation. Her title, *All Men Are Brothers*, draws from expression in the *Analects of Confucius* that within the confines of the four seas, all men are brothers. Her book was published in 1933 as the first English translation and was a best seller in the United States.

There is now, however, a comparatively better English-language version, *Outlaws of the Marsh*, translated by the Chinese-born Jewish scholar Sidney Shapiro. He completed his translation during the Cultural Revolution. He remained faithful to the original work, and his reflects the energy of this masterpiece.

There is also a French version, translated by Jacques Dars as *Au bord de l'eau*, as well as several Japanese versions, including a comic book, a film and television adaptations.

THE ROMANCE OF THE THREE KINGDOMS

The Romance of the Three Kingdoms is China's first classic saga written with chapters that dramatize historical events. The author, Luo Guanzhong (ca. 1330–1400), was a noted opera writer of the late Yuan and early Ming periods. His *Romance* is the ancestor of the chapter-based novels yet to come. Before this, novels were short, and some even had dozens of characters.

The Romance of the Three Kingdoms is the first saga novel in China. Stories of the famous Three Kingdoms were widely popular among the people in ancient China. They were performed on stage during the Song and Yuan dynasties, and more than thirty different programs were performed during the Yuan and Jin dynasties. Luo Guanzhong combined folklore, opera and storyteller's scripts with Chen Shou's *Records of the Three Kingdoms* and with historical materials annotated by Pei Songzhi to create his novel. He wrote

Zhuge Liang

his book the way he saw the society and the norms of the late period of the Yuan era and in the wake of the Ming Dynasty. During the reign of the Emperor Kang Xi, in the Qing Dynasty, the father and son Mao Lun and Mao Zonggang edited the novel into the modern version of 120 chapters.

The Romance of the Three Kingdoms deals with the conflicts and battles among the political groups and military blocs of the three kingdoms of Wei, Shu and Wu, led respectively by Cao Cao, Liu Bei and Sun Quan. Based on broad social and historical background, the book affords a unique and complex look at the political and military conflicts reflective of the times. Moreover, it is the epitome of the great change in the historical epoch and the creation of all-conquering heroes, from the point of view of political and military strategy. The book even deals with their far-reaching effects in the afterworld. With regard to the history of the Three Kingdoms, the writer talks about the conflict between Liu Bei and Cao Cao, is in favor of Liu Bei's actions, and praises the main characters while making a supreme effort to also reprimand Cao Cao.

The Romance of the Three Kingdoms involves a vividly described cast of hundreds of characters, the most successful among them being Zhuge Liang, Cao Cao, Guan Yu and Liu Bei.

Zhuge Liang is the embodiment of the righteous minister. He has not only the virtue of integrity until his heart stops beating but also the lofty ideals and the great aspiration to recreate a time of peace and prosperity. The author endows him with the ability to devise superb stratagems.

Cao Cao is an unscrupulous careerist, his credo for life being, I would rather disappoint the masses than have the masses disappoint me. He is skillful and strategic but also brutal and devious. A cunning politician, his kind is all too familiar throughout history.

Guan Yu is a man of virtue and fortitude, but his righteousness is based on the premise of personal gratitude and resentment and not on the cardinal principle of the righteousness of the nation.

The author portrays Liu Bei as a humane monarch. He not only practices universal benevolence and shows respect for the wise, he is also a good judge of people and their abilities.

The main artistic accomplishment of *The Romance of the Three Kingdoms* is its treatment of war and the depiction of the characters. The novel is also adept at describing battles, each as having distinct traits. Many kinds of wars are addressed in this book. With this grand design and various prose techniques we are able to see clearly the gleaming sword and the crimson blood of conflict.

Scenes like the Battle of Guan Du and the Battle of Redcliff unfold one after another, with opulent and varied writing styles. While the battles are talked about, other activities are also described, including the prelude to war and the fortifications of armies. This technique is akin to the tension of the drawn bow and arrow, as well as the unstringing of the weapon in an attempt to sow discord—Guanzhong had wonderful narrative technique and skills, and made perfect fictional rhythm. For example, prior to the Battle of Redcliff, we read about the collaboration of the two families of Sun and Liu, the conflict between Zhuge Liang and Zhou Yu, the explorations of Cao Cao and about the allied armies of Sun and Liu and their strategies to lure the enemy in deep.

Hundreds of people populate *The Romance of the Three Kingdoms.* In writing about the characters, the author is adept at capturing their fundamental traits and prominent features, endowing each with vivid and unique qualities that bring them to life.

For example, everything Cao Cao does seems to be a scheme or an intrigue. Zhang Fei is quite forthright and outspoken, not naive to what is foreign and rude and impetuous in disposition. Zhuge Liang is calm and unruffled, has amazing foresight and believes that what the heart desires the hand can accomplish. There are also several chapters that include the famous stories of Guan Yu, including "The Wine Is Warm," "Hua Xiong Is Beheaded" and "Guan Yu Slays Six Generals Through Five Passes." Zhang Fei appears in the chapter "The Prestige of Chang Ban Bridge." Zhao Yun is described in "The Sole Rescue of a Child," and "Catching and Releasing Meng Huo Seven Times," involving Zhuge Liang.

Structurally, the story development is based on the main threads of the conflict of the Three Kingdoms, and so a plot is structured that is not only complex but also coherent. Moreover, each section is independent of the other, although all are artistically integrated into one complete work of art.

Throughout the book the language is neither profound nor extremely secular, yet is clear, concise and realistic and delivered with vigorous momentum. Its publication spurred an upsurge in the writing of Chinese historical novels.

The Romance of the Three Kingdoms is the highest achievement of classical

Chinese historical novels and one of the most influential. It has been widely circulated, its endless charm impacting a great portion of Chinese literary history as well as profoundly moving the masses throughout their daily lives.

JOURNEY TO THE WEST

Journey to the West is a traditional novel, folklore-based on the epics of the Buddhist monk, Xuanzang, and his quest to obtain the Buddhist sutras. It is written in a style similar to that of the Song and Yuan vernacular folk dramas.

The first seven chapters describe the monkey, Sun Wukong, entering the world. Then we find him following Xuanzang on his travels to the Western Paradise to acquire the scriptures. Along the way they subdue countless demons and surmount numerous difficulties.

The book thoroughly depicts Xuanzang, Sun Wukong, Zhu Bajie and Sha Wujing.

The author, Wu Cheng'en (ca. 1500–82), was a novelist in the Ming Dynasty. He was born into a small merchant family in decline; nevertheless he was quite fond of reading. As a child, he was intelligent and studious and an acute and well-read individual. He was extremely fond of ancient myth and folklore and wrote his masterpiece having in mind local culture.

The story of the journey of the Tang Dynasty monk in search of the Buddhist sutras has been told throughout history. Some thirteen hundred years ago, in 627, at only twenty-five, the monk Xuanzang left the capital of Chang'an with one of his disciples, planning to study on the Indian subcontinent. He returned to Chang'an in the year 645, bringing with him 657 Buddhist texts. With the help of Emperor Taizong of the Tang period, the Dayan Pagoda was constructed to preserve these scriptures. Xuanzang had spent nineteen years accumulating the sutras, making a legendary journey of thousands of miles, and this all caused quite a sensation at the time.

From then on, the story of the Tang Buddhist monk's search for the scriptures spread far and wide. Based on the vernacular folklore of the Song and Tang eras, as well as on traditional opera, in *Journey to the West*, Wu Cheng'en accomplished the creation of a monumental literary work by and large admired by the people of China. This work *entertains* the reader with the colorful world of the supernatural, and we marvel at the rich and daring artistic imagination of the writer.

Yet any literary work is also a reflection of the social environment in which it is created. In the novel's imaginary realms of demons we can see the projection of the reality of the society of the time in various places. For example, the ideals of the writer are entrusted to Sun Wukong. His unyielding struggle of the spirit and his dauntless battle with ghosts and demons represent the strength of righteousness, the display of conviction and the ability to deal with many difficulties. Another example is that along the way the fantasized demons (or catastrophes) become metaphors for the sinister powers that be. Moreover, in the pictures painted by the author of the Temple of Heaven ruled by the Jade Emperor and the Western Pure Land of Ultimate Bliss under the jurisdiction of the Buddha we are given a vivid picture of society.

TOP: The Monkey King (Sun Wukong); BOTTOM: Zhu Bajie

Journey to the West not only has deeply profound content; it is also a lofty artistic accomplishment. Coming from a very special creative imagination and containing great plotting, lifelike characters and humorous language, this novel is a unique and artistic setting for *Journey to the West*. But by far maybe the most remarkable achievement of all is the author's realization of the two enduring characters, Sun Wukong (the Monkey King) and the pig-like Zhu Bajie.

Sun Wukong is the protagonist of the novel, an extraordinary hero. He is endowed with boundless skill. His unyielding spirit fears nothing in the heavens or on the ground. He has the three traits of humanity, divinity and the nature of the monkey. He is witty, brave and has unusual tolerance. But he has one weakness: he likes to hear fair words. And it is known in every household that he can change into seventy-two forms and do a somersault of 180,000 miles.

Zhu Bajie's abilities are not as great as those of Sun Wukong, but he is similarly, starkly portrayed. His is a comic image, and he is possessed of strength and honesty and he is fearless in battling demons. He is Sun Wukong's right-hand man. He too has some shortcomings, though: he is fond of eating, he takes advantage of situations, he is fond of women and he is sometimes afraid of trouble and often retreats from it. He likes to tell lies. And from time to time he asks Xuanzang to recite the spell of incantation that tightened a band around Sun Wukong's head and caused him to suffer. Despite his faults, though, he still breaks through brambles and thorns in the pilgrimage west and makes nothing of the hardships he encounters.

And so he is not such a negative character, and readers are not disgusted with Zhu Bajie. On the contrary he is quite admired.

The characterization of Xuanzang is also executed in-depth, but it is not as extensive as those of Sun Wukong and Zhu Bajie.

The character Sha Wujing is given even less a visual and a mental description, and maybe this is one of the novel's shortcomings.

Nevertheless, the artistic achievement of *Journey to the West* is still astonishing. With their distinct personalities, Sun Wukong and Zhu Bajie are established in an immortal masterpiece of Chinese literature.

Journey to the West was written in the sixteenth century, during the middle period of the Ming Dynasty, and it was the best of the romantic saga novels of its day. Eventually, this sentimental epic affected the literature of the world as well.

The *Encyclopedia Americana* says, "the mythological novel boasts of sumptuous content and radiant ideas." And per the *Encyclopédie française*, "The entire story is brimming with humor and wit, giving the reader a deep sense of interest."

Since the beginning of the nineteenth century, this book has been translated into more than ten languages, including Japanese, English, French, German and Russian. There are various versions of the translation of the title. These include *The Pilgrimage of the Monk, A History of the Search for Buddhist Scriptures, The Monkey, The Monkey King* and *The Chronicles of the Monkey and the Demons.*

In other countries, the earliest story about the Tang monk's travels is the Korean version written in the early stages of the Ming Dynasty, but it is not entirely the same story as *Journey to the West*. The earliest formal version is the Japanese edition published during the middle of the eighteenth century. Sun Wukong, Xuanzang, Zhu Bajie, and Sha Wujing are also characters in such popular works as *Havoc in Heaven, Striking the White Bone Demon Three Times* and *Mountain of Fire*. Since it was written, *Journey to the West* has also been adapted to a variety of media, including Chinese operas, films, teleplays, animated cartoons and comic books. In Japan and other Asian countries, there are also a variety of works of art centered on the main character, Sun Wukong.

Chapter 20

THE NEW CULTURE MOVEMENT

In the early stages of the rule of the Northern Warlords (1912–27), the New Culture Movement erupted in China. It was like a bolt of lightning from dark and cloudy skies, advocating science as it did and opposing feudal superstition. It attacked the outdated feudal code of ethics, which had lasted several thousands of years.

The New Culture Movement was the result of the integration of economics, politics, philosophy and culture in a distinctive period of history.

After the failure of the Xinhai Revolution, the imperialists (or so-called Great Powers) supported Yuan Shikai as they encroached on China, establishing a secret intelligence. Meanwhile, the advanced intellects were in search of a way to change things for the better. As regards the economy, capitalism in China had further developed during the First World War as the bourgeois pushed for democracy so as to strengthen capitalism. Among philosophers, the idea of enlightenment was introduced to China within the newly formed schools and brought home by those studying abroad. The Xinhai Revolution influenced the ideals of a democratic republic and was supported by the people. Yuan Shikai's yearning to return to the ancient ways of Confucian thought was not compatible with democracy and was opposed by the intellectuals. These were the direct causes for the explosion of the New Culture Movement.

The journal *Youth* was first published in September 1915 by Chen Duxiu, in Shanghai. With the publishing of *Youth* (the name was changed to *New Youth* in September 1916, and the journal moved to Beijing in 1917), the New Culture Movement could attack feudalism under the twin banners of democracy and science.

The primary aim of the New Culture Movement was to promote democracy, science and a new morality, while opposing despotism, old superstition and feudalistic ideals.

Chen Duxiu published an article called "Advice to the Youth" in *Youth*, putting forward the mantra of democracy and science and attacking feudalism and its ideology. He promoted faith, economic growth, new societal norms and ethics and called on the people to fight China's old ideology with the weapon of democracy. As for science, he believed that anything is worthless if not fit for society though it may be cherished by the sages and advocated by the government. He called on the people to remain true to the scientific spirit so as to become the rulers and masters of nature.

Chen Duxiu was the first to advocate for the New Culture Movement. Other proponents, such as Li Dazhao, Lu Xun, Hu Shi and Qian Xuantong, quickly joined the movement.

The New Culture Movement not only defined a great ideological revolution but also a great literary insurrection.

In January 1917, Hu Shi published the article "Tentative Suggestions for the Reform of Chinese Literature." In it, he proposed a radical change in literature, arguing that vernacular Chinese should replace the classical and ancient styles. To do so, he proposed the following eight reforms:

1. To produce writings with substance.
2. Not to imitate the style of the ancients.
3. To respect grammar.
4. To refrain from the melancholy that results in unproductivity.
5. To eschew the old clichés.
6. To avoid comparing the present with the past.
7. To avoid using parallelism or couplets.
8. To use common words, characters and expressions.

In February of the same year, Chen Duxiu published "A Thesis of the Literary," written in clear opposition to the literature of the feudal period. He put forward the three revolutionary ideas of toppling aristocratic literature while constructing a new national literary style, doing away with the classics and embracing realism in literature, and abolishing the writing of feudal times with its obscure content about mountains and rivers and developing a literature that reflected society. These proposals waved the banner of revolution in literature.

Hu Shi's "Tentative Suggestions" marked the turning point of the Vernacular Movement, whose guiding principles saw a rapid response from Chen Duxiu.

In January 1918, writing in the vernacular was published in *New Youth*. May 1918 saw the publication of *Diary of a Madman* by Lu Xun, which was representative of the Vernacular Movement and became a crowning achievement.

Scholars who favored the classical style attacked the ideology of the Ver-

nacular Movement. But in 1919, the May Fourth Movement arose in opposition to imperialism and feudalism
and advanced the cause of the Vernacular Movement
by leaps and bounds. In 1920 the Education Ministry of
the Northern Qing Beiyang government decreed that all
elementary school textbooks from then on were to be
written in vernacular Chinese.

New organizations such as the Literary Research
Society then sparked the emergence of many new literary associations.

The publication of Lu Xun's novella *The True Story of
Ah Q* and the publication of a collection of Guo Moruo's
poems, *The Goddesses*, established a solid foundation for
vernacular literature. *The True Story of Ah Q* was the first
Chinese vernacular masterpiece to find world fame.

Youth Journal

The New Culture Movement was an unprecedented campaign for ideology, enlightenment and emancipation. It shook the foundations of feudal
ethical standards by pushing for the establishment of democracy and science.
The New Culture Movement also laid the foundation for the May Fourth
Movement, thereby paving the way for the spread of Marxism in China.

There were some inevitable limitations, though. New Culture proponents
did not introduce the Movement to the masses, limiting it to the circle of the
intellects. And evading the struggle of the warlord government at the time,
they did not directly oppose imperialism. Rather, they directly criticized
classical literature along with Western thought and literature.

HU SHI

Hu Shi (who styled himself Shi-zhi) came from Jixi, Anhui Province. A
famous modern scholar, poet, historian, writer and philosopher, he became
one of the leaders of the New Culture Movement, advocating a literary
revolution.

In 1910, Hu Shi went to United States to study under philosopher John
Dewey and was greatly influenced by experimental philosophy. In January
1917, he published "Tentative Suggestions for the Reform of Chinese Literature" in *New Youth*, which put forth eight proposals on literary reformation
aimed against traditional Chinese literature. These proposals dealt with some
fundamental problems of the literature, including content and form, social

Hu Shi

function, authenticity and the times. They became the first salvo in the literary revolution.

Hu Shi was an advocate not only in theory of the literary revolution but also in practice. He was the first to create free verse in vernacular Chinese. In February 1917, "Eight Pieces of Free Verse in Vernacular Chinese"—marking the beginning of a new verse style in Chinese history—was published in *New Youth* Volume 2, No. 6. From this verse, a new literary and stylistic revolution was born that was the forerunner for the reform of other literary styles.

In March 1920, Hu Shi published a collection of poems, *Collection of Attempts*. This was the first collection of free verse in vernacular Chinese produced during the New Literary Movement. The word *attempts* derived from Hu Shi's belief that success would come from the attempts made from ancient times. The collection is proof of Hu Shi's great desire to rescue China. *Collection of Attempts* agitated for "liberty of the poetic styles," smashed the shackles of the rules and forms of classical poetic composition, used understandable vernacular Chinese (common words and the language as it was spoken) and antithesis and rhyme.

Hu Shi proposed in fact that all former shackles of freedom should be smashed and that people speak freely. As far as poems went, Hu Shi declined to make a fuss and proposed to replace pedantic feudalism with democratic and humanitarian ideas. Some pieces in the collection, such as "The Old Crow," "Hope," "A Star," and "Up to the Hill," were poems that drew inspiration from the scene or from the senses, from events, using such techniques as direct description, simile and symbolism. Judged from the aspect of aesthetics, the artistic value of *Collection of Attempts* is less than its literary value. Hu Shi concluded, "When I look at my poems of the past five years in retrospect now (1922), it is just like a foot-bound woman watching as her feet become bigger and bigger, the smell of the blood left from the foot-binding still with her." So Hu Shi was a praiseworthy pioneer of the new free verse but not the founder.

Hu Shi served as a professor at Peking University, dean of the College of Liberal Arts at Peking University, professor and director at Furen University, Extraordinary and Plenipotentiary of the Republic of China in the United States, honorary advisor to the Eastern Division of the U.S. Library of Congress, president of Peking University, academician and dean at the Central Research Institute (south of Taipei Harbor), and librarian for the

Gest East Asian Library at Princeton University, among other posts. All his life he was greatly influenced by Aldous Huxley and John Dewey. He always claimed that it was Huxley who taught him to doubt and Dewey who taught him to think.

Hu Shi was the forerunner of liberalism in China. He advocated for freedom throughout his life. He proposed that the right way to approach academic study was to assume boldly, to demonstrate carefully and to make words proved conclusively. He focused his academic activities on history, literature and philosophy. His major works are *An Outline of Chinese Philosophy History*, *Collection of Attempts*, *A History of Literature in Vernacular Chinese* and *Hu Shi Literary Deposits* (four volumes). In his later years he devoted himself to textual research for an annotated edition of *Water Margin* but didn't get a chance to finish. He passed away in 1962 in Taipei.

LU XUN

Lu Xun was a great writer, thinker and revolutionary. His original name was Zhou Shuren, and he styled himself as Yucai. Lu Xun was the pseudonym he used when writing *Diary of a Madman*, published in the journal *New Youth*.

Lu Xun was born in 1881 to a downfallen feudal, scholarly bureaucratic family in Shaoxing of Zhejiang Province. In his youth the family fortunes declined because of his father's failing health. His grandfather was imprisoned as the result of a legal case as his father's illness was getting worse. In a flash, his family was plunged into a sea of financial difficulties and he anguished over the unfairness of life.

Lu Xun's mother was from the countryside, and so s a child he also came to know and understand rural areas and farmers.

In his early years of study, he was greatly influenced by the ideology of the revolution.

Lu Xun went to study in Japan on a state scholarship in 1902, at Kobun Institute in Tokyo. After graduating in 1904, his ideal of curing disease and saving lives took him to the Sendai Medical Academy. While there he found a mentor in a Japanese teacher named Dr. Fujino Genkuro. But many Japanese students discriminated against him. While abroad he was inspired by a slideshow about the war between Japan and Russia (1904–5). In the presentation, the Japanese army had captured a Chinese man believed to be a spy for the Russians. When the man was about to be beheaded by the Japanese army, a crowd of Chinese people gathered and bravely confronted the army. Lu Xun believed that "Medicine is not crucial. Even if an individual is healthy, many insignificant practices can lead to unnecessary illness. Therefore, the primary task is to change the spirit and advance the movement of art and literature."

In 1906, Lu Xun returned to Tokyo after leaving Sendai and started to write. Shortly after, he published some important dissertations, including, *The Annals of the Human*, *The History of Science*, *On Cultural Paranoia* and *On the Power of Romantic Poetry*.

In 1908, Lu Xun and his younger brother, Zhou Zuoren, worked together translating foreign short stories. They compiled *An Anthology of Foreign Stories*, which was published with help from cohorts. In 1909, Lu Xun left Japan and went home to China. He was soon a successful teacher in Hangzhou and then in Shaoxing. In 1911, he played an active role in the propaganda campaign when the Revolution of 1911 erupted. From 1918, he began to participate in the activities of *New Youth* magazine. In May, the journal published his first vernacular novel, *Diary of a Madman*, which had a significant impact on the history of modern literature in China because of its depth of expression and distinctive format.

Meanwhile, Lu Xun also published a great many essays in the column, "Random Thoughts," in *New Youth*. In addition to creating many literary works, he also organized the Not-Yet-Named Society (*Weiming she*) and the Yusi Society ("threads of talk"), which issued publications such as *Yusi*.

From 1925 to 1926, Lu Xun supported the mass struggle of the students in the Women Teachers Campaign at Normal University and the ideals that led to the March 18 Massacre. In October 1927, he settled in Shanghai and in 1930 established the Chinese League of Left-Wing Writers as a founder and leader. He died in Shanghai on October 19, 1936.

Lu Xun is considered the founder of modern Chinese literature. His radical new style found expression in several formats, including the novel, the essay, prose, poetic prose and the historical novel.

Tales in *Call to Arms* and *Wandering* are at the artistic peak of the modern Chinese short story. *The Diary of a Madman* is the first vernacular short story in the history of modern Chinese literature and reflects the writing style of the May Fourth Movement. The story described a man suffering from paranoia, and exposed the society's darkness, uncovered the essence destroying people of the feudal clan system.

In terms of ideology, *The Diary of a Madman* is the embodiment of anti-feudal sentiment. In terms of artistry it is both realistic and symbolic, making for a unique artistic effect.

The True Story of Ah Q is not only regarded a literary masterpiece in

China, it was also the earliest modern novel introduced to the world. Ah Q is such an image of a peasant that he is backward with psychosis. The most prominent trait of his character is his spiritualism. By the depiction of Ah Q, the writer is describing the souls of his countrymen, exposing the weaknesses of the people and achieving the effect of "reflecting the sickness to arouse the attention of the rescuer." Meanwhile, the author combines an exploration of the issues of the Chinese peasant with an analysis of revolution in China. He sums up the historical lesson of the failure of the 1911 Revolution in the form of Ah Q's fate.

Lu Xun

The essay was yet another important Lu Xun literary contribution. He was not only an ideologue but also a revolutionary. He fought his whole life. For him, the essay was the dagger, the javelin. He said that the essay was the inductive nerve "responding immediately to harmful things." His fifteen collections of essays are the phylogeny of ideology and culture, the faithful record of society from the May Fourth Movement to the mid-1930s in China.

As a writer, Lu Xun was concerned about people's reactions to major events and the changes in ideology, emotion and psychology as a result of major events.

He said, "The souls of the masses are reflected in my essays."

While writing the novels, *Call to Arms* and *Wandering*, Lu Xun also produced a collection of prose called, *Dawn Blossoms Plucked at Dusk* and an anthology of poetic prose, *Wild Grass*. In his later years he produced the short story collection *Old Tales Retold* (1936).

This collection of short stories talks about the mythology of ancient China, its folklore and historical fact. However, the author was not a stickler for formality in rendering the original stories, often adding his own interpretations and imaginative touches. His writing technique combined the ancient and modern styles of writing, using stark depiction to express solemn themes. This form of literature set a new precedent in the writing of historical short stories.

Lu Xun is referred to by many as the soul of the nation. Throughout his life he worked toward the survival and development of China. The verse, "Fierce-browed, I coolly defy a thousand pointing fingers; with my head bowed, I am an ox for the children." This exemplifies the artistic way in which he voiced his ideology.

Mao Zedong is quoted as saying, "Lu Xun has the hardest bones. He hasn't the slightest amount of subservience or flattery. This is a most treasured temperament of the people in a colonial and semi-colonial society." He also found the writer to be "... a great literary artist, thinker and revolutionary."

GUO MORUO

Guo Moruo was a famed writer, archaeologist, paleographic expert, ideologue and revolutionary. His birth name was Guo Kaizhen. Moruo was the pseudonym he used when he started publishing poetry in 1919.

Guo Moruo was born into a family of a landowners and businessmen in Leshan County, Sichuan Province. In the spring of 1914 he left to study in Japan. At first he studied medicine but later changed his mind and began to study literature. During this period, he read various foreign classical works, by Tagore, Heine and Goethe, among others. The writings of the Dutch philosopher Spinoza greatly affected him with its ideas about pantheism.

He was also inspired by the outbreak of the May Fourth Movement. He and some of his students in Japan worked together to form the Xia She, an organization that espoused opposition to Japanese imperialism.

He began publishing poetry in September 1919.

In 1921, various well-known writers including Guo Moruo, Yu Dafu and Cheng Fangwu founded an organization called the Creation Society. In August of that same year, Guo Moruo's first anthology of poems was published, entitled *The Goddesses*. This not only established his preeminent status in modern Chinese literary history but also ushered in a new era for Chinese poetry.

In 1921 and 1922, Guo Moruo returned to his motherland three times. But the reality and darkness of the life there shattered his ideals. His poetry collection *Starry Sky* contains many heartfelt poems.

In 1923, he went back to China after graduating from the Medical School of Kyushyu Imperial University. In China he continued to publish new work. At this time, his views on art, literature and politics took on a heterogeneous appearance. The prose anthology *The Forefront* is a unique record of ideological change during that era.

In 1924, the Creation Society met an early end because of differences between several key writers. Throughout

Guo Moruo

his trials and tribulations, he had gained an understanding of Marxism, reflecting a giant leap in thought.

In July 1926, Guo Moruo took part in the Northern Expedition, advocating for a proletarian revolutionary literary movement. The anthology *Restore* was his signature work of this period.

In February 1928, he left Shanghai for Japan, because of the change in the Chinese political environment, and stayed in Japan for ten years.

After war broke out against Japan, he returned alone to China and espoused resistance against Japanese aggression. He wrote six historical plays. Among them are the famous *Qu Yuan* and *Tiger Tally*. He also wrote much poetry, prose and a study of the historiography.

After the Chinese victory against Japan, Guo Moruo and vast numbers of progressive individuals participated in cultural work in areas including Chongqing and Shanghai, striving to create peace and democracy and standing bravely in the front ranks of the democratic movement.

After the founding of the People's Republic of China, Guo Moruo held leadership posts in the administration, in science and in culture. At the same time he was writing for variety of publications, including the poetry collection *Eulogy for New China*, and wrote the historical plays *Cai Wenji* and *Empress Wu Zetian*.

The Goddesses was not only Guo Moruo's first new anthology of poems but also a work of great significance in the history of Chinese modern poetry, setting the pace for new poetry styles. *The Goddesses* was a collection of the writer's major poems from 1919 to 1921. There were fifty-seven pieces altogether including the preface, which was written when the writer was studying in Japan.

Literary critics divide Guo Moruo's career into three phases. The first includes works such as "Rebirth of the Goddesses" and "The Flower of the White Poplar." The poems of the climactic May Fourth Movement are expressed in "Nirvana of the Phoenixes," representative of the second phase. The third phase involves major poems from the early years, including "The Temptation of Death." Other wildly popular poems include "Coal in the Grate," "Sunrise," "Earth, My Mother!," "The Sky Dog," "Good Morning" and "At the Edge of the Earth."

The Goddesses conveys the spirit of May Fourth. It focuses on the following:

First, *The Goddesses* is an intense reflection of democratic ideals and the birth of the new world.

Second, "Nirvana of the Phoenixes" is a solemn song of the era, filled with a strong rebellious spirit and yearning for social change. The writer is nostalgic and expresses dedication to the motherland through the metaphor of a phoenix rising from the ashes to symbolize the revival of new China. The story also expresses the poet's self-respect and appreciation of nature.

The celestial dog in the poem "The Sky Dog" breaks through the nets and destroys all things of old. It conveys an unbridled passion and supernatural force, embodying the quest for personal liberation that was sought after in that era.

In *The Goddesses* there are several poems about the beauty of nature. In Guo Moruo's heart, nature is not only the symbol of creation's force but also the joy of life.

Third, *The Goddesses* is a manifestation of the spirit that embodies bold innovation and the destruction of the old ways.

The poet shows reverence for the destructive forces and such creative powers as the sun, the mountains, the rivers, the oceans, birth, death, volcanoes and the deep of night. All are made to reflect the rebellious spirit of the May Fourth Movement.

In "Praise for the Revolutionaries," the writer pays tribute to those who fought against outmoded convention. It also sings the praises of those who took part in the political, social, religious, artistic, literary and educational revolutions. In this work he professes his belief that only through complete destruction can new creation arise.

In *The Goddesses*, the ideal of absolute freedom is championed. And its style of poetry is relentless and challenging.

Written from a vivid imagination, with supernatural references and using language of intense tone and elegant color, *The Goddesses* was the start of a new style of romantic poetry in China.

MAO DUN

Mao Dun was not only a famous modern novelist and literary critic but also an important cultural and social activist. His birth name was Shen Dehong; he used the pseudonym Yanbing. He was born of a well-educated family in Wuzhen, Tongxiang County, Zhejiang Province, on July 4, 1896. When he was ten years old, his father died, and so his mother primarily raised him.

In 1913, he was admitted to the preparatory school of Beijing University, but because of financial difficulties he could not continue his studies. So he went to work for the Shanghai Commercial Press, where he translated and compiled Chinese and foreign books. He also wrote articles for several publications, including *Student Magazine* and *Study Lamp*.

In the period of the May Fourth Movement, as an active advocate of and participant in the New Culture Movement, Mao Dun proposed literature for life.

In 1920, the Literary Research Society was founded and Mao Dun became the backbone. In that same year he became chief editor of *Fiction Monthly*, and under his leadership that publication took a firm position against feudalism.

Mao Dun

Mao Dun was also the earliest revolutionary intellectual and took part in the communist movement in China. In 1921, he became one of the first members of the Communist Party and participated in laying the foundations of the party. He was actively involved in the social struggle led by the party.

After battling through blood and fire on April 12, 1927, Mao Dun wrote the trilogy *Erosion*. This was his maiden novel. The pen name on the original manuscript was Maodun, meaning *contradiction* and reflecting the political mood of the time. Later, Ye Shengtao changed the name to Mao Dun. *Erosion* is a profound work about the mentality of intellectuals in a turbulent era. It consists of three volumes: *Disillusion*, *Indecision* and *Pursuing*.

In July 1928, Mao Dun went to Japan. One reason was to escape persecution by the Kuomintang reactionaries; another was because he was depressed. While in Japan he wrote the novel *Rainbow*, which explores the life of a young man taking a new path, in the context of a broad historical background. It depicts a generation of intellectuals from May 4 to May 30, 1919. The book is about the coming together of the masses and their bitter struggle to break free of their bonds.

In April 1930, Mao Dun returned to China from Japan, to take part in the work of the Chinese League of Left-Wing writers and to work with Lu Xun. This overall effort promoted the writing and popularity of left-wing literature.

The period from 1932 to 1937 was the high point of Mao Dun's career. His novel *Midnight* established him among the greats of modern Chinese literature.

The "rural trilogy" (*Spring Silkworms*, *Autumn Harvest* and *Winter Ruin*) and some of his short stories, *The Lin Family's Shop*, are proof of his creative vitality as a writer of revolutionary realism.

During the time of the War of Resistance (1937–45), Mao Dun traveled and visited Hong Kong, Xinjiang, Yan'an, Chongqing and Guilin, among other places. During his travels he produced many popular works, including the essays "On Landscapes" and "Tribute to the Poplar," long novels including *Putrefaction* and *February's Frosted Red Leaves Appear as Flowers* and the play *Days of the Pure Brightness*.

After the founding of the People's Republic of China, Mao Dun served as the vice-chairman of the literary association, the Minister of Cultural Affairs, and the chairman of the writer's association. He also served as vice-chairman of the Political Consultative Committee.

He died in Beijing on March 27, 1981.

Mao Dun donated 250,000 yuan to establish an award for writing that was later named the Mao Dun Prize for Literature. Established in October 1981, it is the first award for literature in China named for an author. It has since become one of the most prestigious prizes for literature in China and is awarded to a novel every four years.

The Works of Mao Dun consists of forty volumes and is a collection of all his writing. It has been in continuous publication, by the People's Literature Publishing House, since 1983.

Among the Works is *Midnight*, published in June 1933, at the peak of the author's creativity. This book shook literary circles in China, and its enormous influence is evidenced by the fact that the politician Qu Qiubai called this one particular year Mid-night Year.

Midnight paints a picture of Chinese society in the early 1930s. It is a comprehensive portrayal of the intense conflict between the national capitalist Wu Sunfu and the competing capitalist Zhao Botao. Because the novel deals with workers on strike and the rioting of the peasants, the reactionary authorities suppressed and destroyed the revolutionary movement. The government then annexed small- and medium-sized national industries, triggering a fierce fight for government bonds. Various businessmen struggled, and there was a great deal of fighting in capitalist families. By addressing these issues and diverse ways of life, the novel reconstructs the struggles of the second domestic revolutionary war and gives us a portrait of the typical national capitalist.

For more than half a century, *Midnight* has not only reached a wide range of readers in China, it has also been translated into several languages, including English, German, Russian and Japanese, and so it is of great international influence.

The famous Japanese literary researcher Hajime Shinoda recommended *Midnight* as one of the world's literary masterpieces of the twentieth century. He felt that *Midnight* can be favorably compared with such epic works as

In Search of Lost Time by Marcel Proust and *One Hundred Years of Solitude* by Gabriel García Márquez.

BA JIN

Ba Jin is one of the most influential writers since the May Fourth New Culture Movement. Modern Chinese literary circles have long known him to be a master artist. His original name was Li Yaotang; his courtesy name was Feigan. Ba Jin became his pen name in 1928, after he wrote *Destruction*.

Ba Jin was born to a feudal bureaucratic landlord family in Chengdu, Sichuan Province. He spent his childhood in the loving warmth of family life. His mother, Chen Shufen, was his first teacher, and her love for education was planted in the ground of universal benevolence, which played a significant role in her son's later ideological development.

Sickness took the life of his mother and father in 1914 and 1917, respectively, and this radically changed Ba Jin's life. The death of his father forced his once wealthy family into autocratic society. From the prison of hypocritical feudal ethics, he watched his brothers and sisters struggling and suffering, and this killed the love in his heart. And then he began to hate, awakened by the outbreak of the May Fourth Movement. Among the various ideas of the time, it was anarchism that first broadened his worldview.

In 1923, Ba Jin left his ancestral home of Sichuan for Shanghai and Nanjing to continue his studies.

In 1927, in an effort to further study anarchism, he went to a university in France. While living abroad there, he was moved by two major events. One was that the victory of the Chinese Northern Expedition was short-lived; the other was the execution of two Italian anarchists by the United States. Out of extreme pain and bitterness, Ba Jin wrote his first short novel, *Destruction*, creating the hero Du Daxin, who despised the workings of society and was desperate for love. This work marks the formal beginning of Ba Jin's literary career.

At the end of 1928, Ba Jin went home. Between 1929 and the end of 1949, he produced eighteen novels, twelve collections of short stories and sixteen volumes of essays, in addition to several translations. Among these, his epic novels became Ba Jin's main literary achievements prior to the founding of the People's Republic of China.

The Love Trilogy was Ba Jin's favorite among his early writings. It consists of three sections—*Fog, Rain* and

Ba Jin

Lightning—and is not only the summing up of intense and long reflection on the great social problem of revolution of his early years but also a vivid presentation of his early worldviews.

The Torrents Trilogy—*Family*, *Spring* and *Autumn*—is a representative collection of Ba Jin's works. In particular, the first book, *Family*, is of eternal artistic value.

In the preface to the Torrents Trilogy, Ba Jin writes, "What I want to convey to the reader is a picture of a past of more than ten years. This is naturally only a part of life. However, you can see the undulation of the torrents of life formed by love and hate, joy and pain."

This work deals with complications of the heart. On the one hand is the collapse of the feudal patriarchal system and a dying aristocratic ruling force frantically determining the fate of young lives. On the other hand, attracted by the idea of revolution, the younger generation sets out on the tragic path to realization in the wake of the struggle of revolution. Among the various characters in the Torrents Trilogy, Gao Juehui is the most significant. Out of sympathy for the worker and a distrust of the feudal system, he comes to embrace bourgeois reform and democracy, ultimately taking part himself in the social struggle.

Ba Jin's writing led to a new wave of thinking, awakening China at the beginning of the twentieth century and under the influence of the May Fourth Movement. He was not only a sharp critic of feudalism but also the enthusiastic and young revolutionary. Through his character, Gao Juehui, the author shares the ideology of the advanced intellectuals of China in the last hundred years.

Cold Nights, written in 1946, was not only Ba Jin's last novel but also another substantial work after *Family*, marking a new stage in the writer's artistic development. This novel discusses the tragedy of death and the destruction of the young functionary Wang Wenxuan. By means of this character the author reveals the fate of the righteous and virtuous intellectual while exposing the dark reality of the war of resistance.

By the time of China's victory in the war against Japan, Ba Jin was engaged primarily in translating, editing and publishing. After the founding of the People's Republic of China, he went twice to the Korean front and wrote there two collections of essays, *Living Among Heroes,* and *They Who Defend Peace.* Unfortunately, during the Cultural Revolution, Ba Jin was cruelly and unjustly persecuted.

After the Chinese Cultural Revolution, Ba Jin began writing *Random Thoughts*, which he worked on from 1978 until September 1986, producing 150 chapters and 420,000 words. Because of its profound ideological and cultural content and unique style, *Random Thoughts* has become one of the most important creative compilations of essays of the new period, marking yet another milestone in Ba Jin's literary career.

What moved people most was Ba Jin's spirit of consciousness and reorganization of the ego, reflecting an outstanding moral character and intellectualism. Combining personal introspection and the reflections of a nation, as well as personal and social criticism, his work marked a brilliant chapter in the annals of the intellectual and spiritual path of the Cultural Revolution and is of great importance in the history of ideology and culture.

LAO SHE

The birth name of Lao She was Shu Qingchun; his courtesy name was She Yu. He was born into a poor Manchu family in Beijing who lived in an alley that collectively domesticated lambs.

In 1918, he graduated from Beijing Normal University and assumed an administrative office at a primary school.

The democratic, scientific and liberating trends in thinking reflective of the May Fourth Movement awakened him from the mentality of the conscientious primary school official with its deference to the mother and the convention of marriage and parenthood. The prosperity of the new literary revolution enabled him, instead, to indulge in art and literature, and this was a fresh starting point in his life and career.

In 1922, Lao She worked as a Mandarin language teacher in the Nankai Middle School. That same year he published his first short novel, *The Bell*. In 1924, he went to England and served as lecturer of Mandarin in the School of Oriental Studies at the University of London. Apart from teaching, he read volumes of foreign literary works and started out on his own creative career. During this time he published three satirical novels describing the life of the people: *The Philosophy of Old Zhang*, *Zhao Ziyue* and *Ma and Son*, which attracted attention in literary circles.

In 1929, on is way home, Lao She decided to stay in Singapore for several months, and he wrote there a fairy tale in the form of a novel called *The Birthday of Xiaopo*.

After returning to the motherland and before the outbreak of the war of resistance against the Japanese, he taught at Qilu University in Jinan and Shandong University in Qingdao. Also, during this period he wrote six novels, one novella and three short stories. *Cat Country*, *The Divorce* and *Rickshaw Boy* are among his most famous works.

Lao She

Cat Country is a book about an outer space engineer who drifts off-course and ends up on Mars in a country ruled by cats. What he sees and hears there is analogous to the partisanship of the era, and the book is clearly political satire masquerading as science fiction.

Through the analogy of the family troubles of several section members of a public finance office in Beiping (modern Beijing), *The Divorce* criticizes the entire social system of old China and features characters rooted in a culture of urban living.

Rickshaw Boy has also had enormous impact. A rickshaw operator's whereabouts leads to a trail of clues in Beiping, and we see the incessant fighting between warlords and the dark rule of a country over the poor lower class. Here is the bitterness of city residents and the light in the center of a dark abyss. By means of the protagonist, the novel speaks of refusal to accept defeat, as well as dissolution, and also the acceptance of destiny. The book encourages city people to be their own masters and teaches that nobody can survive alone in a city.

Between the outbreak of the war of aggression to the liberation of the country, more than ten years passed. During this time, Lao She wrote the novellas *This Life of Mine* and *The Crescent Moon*, as well as novels including *Four Generations Under One Roof* and *The Drum Singers*.

The structure of *The Crescent Moon* is delicate and the storytelling precise. It is a critique of a dark world using the miserable life of a mother and daughter and their deterioration into prostitution.

Four Generations Under One Roof—including *Anxious and Perplexed*, *To Live Without Purpose* and *Famine*—was a milestone in the creative career of Lao She. Using the common alley as the epitome of the western district of Beiping and focusing on the circumstances of old-fashioned businessman Qi Tianyou's family of four generations, it reveals the pain of the souls of people suffering under the rule of foreign invaders. It shows us the closed, perfunctory and perplexing burden of the spirit. Moreover, it provides a reflection of the attitude of the people in the 1940s, conveying the quality of the national spirit and their psychological state.

Four Generations spans almost the entire time of the eight-year war against aggression, from the bombing of Pearl Harbor to the surrender of the Japanese. It makes its points both directly and indirectly. As regards geography, it touches on many places: the small alley in Beijing, the residential compound, the streets, the suburbs, the countryside, the square, the theaters, the execution grounds, the brothel, the schools. There is even a Japanese puppet official and the embassy. In terms of its breadth, depth and vigor, this novel affords a panoramic view in an imposing epic.

Lao She Tea House in Beijing

After the founding of China, Lao She wrote important works including the novel *Beneath the Red Banner*, the long report *The Nameless Highland Has the Name*, and the plays *Dragon Beard Ditch* and *The Teahouse*.

The Teahouse not only is representative of Lao She's dramas, but also is a modern Chinese classic. We are given a small teahouse (representing local and national characteristics) to vie with the whole of society in China. We see three eras and three societies: the late Qing Dynasty after the coup by the Dowager Empress Cixi; the society during the People's Republic of China and the civil wars begun under the rule of the warlords after the failure of the Revolution of 1911; and the Kuomingtang-controlled areas after the war of resistance. In this work the author puts forward the theme of burying the three old ages.

In reading Lao She's work, we see a basic premise that is obviously a reflection of and criticism of traditional culture.

In some ways, Lao She is influenced by Lu Xun's idea of national character. But in other ways he is his own man.

Lao She grew up among the urban Beijing population. Focused on the people of Beiping, his work has dense local atmosphere and the intense breath of life. He is therefore known to vividly depict city residents as well as sharply criticize the urban life of Beijing.

In 1951, the Beijing Municipal People's Government awarded Lao She the title "the People's Artist."

CAO YU

Cao Yu is a renowned playwright who made an outstanding contribution to the development of modern Chinese drama.

His original name was Wan Jiabao. He was born into a declining feudal bureaucratic family in Tianjin. His mother died of puerperal fever three days after giving birth to him. His mother's younger sister became his stepmother and raised him.

Cao Yu

His stepmother enjoyed the theater very much. In his boyhood, Cao Yu often went with her to see local plays—the Beijing opera, the Kunqu opera and the Hebei clapper opera, as well as the new cultural dramas popular at the time.

In 1922, Cao Yu started at Nankai Middle School in Tianjin. While a student he took an active part in theater. He played the protagonist in several plays, including Henrik Ibsen's *A Doll's House*.

In 1929, Cao Yu went to study in the Foreign Language Department at Tsinghua University. There he made an extensive study of the tragedies, from the ancient Greeks to Shakespeare, as well as the works of Anton Chekhov, Henrik Ibsen and Eugene O'Neill.

In 1933, on the eve of graduation from university, Cao Yu wrote a drama in four acts, *Thunderstorm*, which was published in 1934 and rapidly evoked an intense response. This was not only his maiden work but also a famous and representative work. *Thunderstorm* uses realism to deal with the tragedy of a distinguished family. The play takes place in one day and in two settings (the Zhou family household and the Lu family residence). It deals with thirty years of complex conflicts between the two families and is exquisitely structured.

Zhou Puyuan is not only the main character in *Thunderstorm* but also the root cause of various dilemmas. The author portrays the character by two means: First, the conflict between him and his wife, Fanyi, mirrors the internal dispute in the family. Second, the clash between him and the miner, Lu Dahai, reveals the contradiction between him and the workers. The two conflicts are closely related to the character Shiping, making up the complex discord of the drama.

Zhou Puyuan is depicted as a vicious and brutal capitalist and an autocratic and callous feudal patriarch. Cao Yu treats him as an actual living person and not as a product of his class.

The novel also features another important character, Fanyi. She is known for having a nature that has the manner of a thunderstorm. In the production notes, Cao Yu writes, "Her character has an irresistible, unreasoned drive that causes her to make reckless decisions. If she loves someone, she will love him intensely, like fire. While if she hates someone, she will use that fire to burn him."

Throughout the work, the author likens Fanyi's struggle to that of a caged animal because of a suffocating environment and the cruelest love interlaced with the most unbearable hate. She resists with despair and is filled with the blood and tears of an oppressed woman, showing bold contempt for and rebelliousness against the feudal forces and the moral values. Her thunderstorm passion not only destroys the order of the feudal family but also ruins her own life. The tragic image of Fanyi is one of the contributions made by Cao Yu to modern drama that conveys the May Fourth theme of anti-feudalism and the liberation of the personality.

In 1936 and 1937, Cao Yu published two major plays, *Sunrise* and *The Wilderness*.

During the war against the Japanese, he wrote *Peking Man* and adapted Ba Jin's novel *Family* for theater.

After the founding of the People's Republic of China, the major plays of Cao Yu were *Courage and the Sword* and *Wang Zhaojun*.

A year after publishing the *Thunderstorm*, Cao Yu created another work of realism in four acts called *Sunrise* whose backdrop is the semi-colonial and semi-feudal city of Tianjin in 1930s. There are two settings: the luxurious parlor of social butterfly Chen Bailu and the third-class brothel of Cui Xi. The play shows us two different living situations, of upper- and lower-class society, revealing the unreasonable truth of the harm created by abundance.

While *Thunderstorm* reflects the oppression and slaughter of feudal despotism, *Sunrise* exposes the poisonous, devouring and murderous people of a money-oriented society.

Cao Yu also turned his eye to the countryside and wrote the psychological tragedy of a farmer avenger under the mind control of a feudal clan in his third play, *The Wilderness* (a three-act play).

The three-act play *Peking Man* marks yet another artistic peak for Cao Yu. Here he once again returns to his familiar subject of the outdated family, in the process thoroughly criticizing feudalism. While *Thunderstorm* focuses on a critique of the relationship between ethics and morality, *Peking Man* is an in-depth analysis of feudal cultural traditions in which the Zeng family is depicted as the epitome of the weak feudal society after the era of prosperity has passed.

The only happiness Zeng Hao had was to repeatedly paint his own coffin, thereby symbolizing the death of feudalism. Meanwhile, the intelligent and benevolent feudal scholar Zeng Wenqing becomes a superfluous person and merely the hollow shell of a man, his spirit paralyzed.

Cao Yu opposed traditional culture and found the spiritual strength to show us a new way of life.

APPENDIX
A BRIEF CHRONOLOGY OF CHINESE HISTORY

Xia Dynasty			2070–1600 BCE
Shang Dynasty			1600–1046 BCE
Zhou Dynasty		Western Zhou	1046–771 BCE
		Eastern Zhou	770–256 BCE
		Spring and Autumn Period	770–476 BCE
		Warring States Period	475–221 BCE
Qin Dynasty			221–206 BCE
Han Dynasty		Western Han	206 BCE–25 CE
		Eastern Han	25–220
Three Kingdoms		Wei	220–265
		Shu Han	221–263
		Wu	222–280
Western Jin Dynasty			265–317
Eastern Jin Dynasty			317–420
Northern and Southern Dynasties	Southern Dynasties	Song	420–479
		Qi	479–502
		Liang	502–557
		Chen	557–589
	Northern Dynasties	Northern Wei	386–534
		Eastern Wei	534–550
		Northern Qi	550–577
		Western Wei	535–556
		Northern Zhou	557–581
Sui Dynasty			581–618
Tang Dynasty			618–907
Five Dynasties		Later Liang	907–923
		Later Tang	923–936
		Later Jin	936–947
		Later Han	947–950
		Later Zhou	951–960
Ten Kingdoms			891–979
Song Dynasty		Northern Song	960–1127
		Southern Song	1127–1279
Liao Dynasty			907–1125
Jin Dynasty			1115–1234
Yuan Dynasty			1206–1368
Ming Dynasty			1368–1644
Qing Dynasty			1616–1911
Republic of China			1912–1949
People's Republic of China			Founded October 1, 1949

POSTSCRIPT

After two years work on subject selection, writing, translation, illustration and editing, we finally bring to reality our conception of The Fundamentals of Chinese Culture. We rewrote and revised the draft several times, because we know a good book is the result of repeated language refinement. Particularly, this is a comprehensive survey of Chinese culture issued overseas for university students who are interested in China. In this sense, we are propagandists for Chinese civilization and facilitators of a cultural exchange between China and the West. And this has sharpened our awareness of the mission's value and urged us to be selective in terms of the compilation.

The Research Group of the Jiangxi Provincial Academy of Social Science undertook the writing task:

- **Liu Shuangqin:** Chapter 1: sections 1, 2, 3, 5 and 6; chapter 2; chapter 3: section 18; chapter 6: sections 1, 2, 4, 5; chapter 7: sections 7, 8, 9; chapter 9: sections 17, 19, 21, 22; chapter 13.
- **Li Qing:** Chapter 1: section 4; chapters 4, 5; chapter 8: sections 10, 12, 13, 14, 15; chapter 11: section 1; chapter 15.
- **Ni Aizen:** Chapter 3: sections 11–17; chapter 6: section 3; chapter 7: section 6; chapter 8: section 11; chapter 9: sections 16, 18, 20; chapter 11: sections 2–4; chapter 12: section 10; chapters 13, 15.
- **Xia Hanning:** Chapter 10; chapter 16; chapter 17: sections 4–9; chapter 19.

The teachers of Jiangxi University of Finance and Economics undertook the translation.

- **Wuke:** Chapters 1–5; collated chapters 1–5, 11–20.
- **Yuan Zhimei:** Chapters 11–15 (50,000 words).
- **Lin Ying:** Chapters 16, 17, 18 (32,000 words).
- **Yuan Zhen:** Chapter 19, sections 16–26 (18,000 words).
- **You Jiajuan:** Chapters 6, 7, 8.
- **Li Jian:** Chapters 19, 20.

Chinese culture is famed for a well-established and long-standing history, as well as an inclusiveness and profundity. So it is no easy job to cover the most representative components and present them in plain and concise language in a book of this scope and length. Despite our wholehearted efforts, inaccuracies and mistakes are probably unavoidable, partly due to our limited competence. We hope to receive criticisms and suggestions from our dear readers.

—Editorial Board of *From Moon Cakes to Mao to Modern China*

INDEX

A

abacus 66–68, 275
Abing (Hau Yanjun), 164
Academies of Classical
  Learning, 224, 225
acupuncture, 154
*Admonitions of the Instruc-
  tress to the Palace Ladies*
  (painting), 70
"Advice to the Youth" (Chen
  Duxiu), 251–52
All Men Are Brothers (Buck),
  183, 245
allegorical expressions, 4
*Along the River During the
  Qingming Festival* (paint-
  ing), 70
An Shi Rebellion, 53, 119
Analects of Confucius, The,
  94, 96, 108, 168, 201, 202,
  226, 231, 245
Ancient Literature Move-
  ment, 171
*Annals of Susong County,
  The*, 212
Annals of the Human, The (Lu
  Xun), 256
*Anthology of Foreign Stories,
  An* (eds. Lu Xun and Zhu
  Zuoren), 256
Anthology of Liu Hedong, The
  (Liu Zongyuan), 171
Anxi Yulin Caves, 77, 214. *See
  also* Dunhuang Caves
Anyang, 74, 140, 143
Ape Wine, 123
Arbor Day, 25
architecture
  courtyard residences,
    194–96
  enclosed residences,
    194–96
  hutongs, 192–93

palace, 144–46
  residential styles, 193–96
  temple, 147–49
archives, *see* libraries
Art of War, The (Sun Tzu),
  102–4
arts and crafts, folk, 136–39.
  See also embroidery; paper
Asian Chinese Chess Federa-
  tion, 156–57
"Asking Heaven" (Qu Yuan),
  26, 109
Au bord de l'eau (Dars), 245
autonomous regions, 55
Autumn (Ba Jin), 264
Autumn Harvest (Mao Dun),
  261
*Autumn in the Palace of the
  Han* (Ma Zhiyuan), 180
Autumn River (opera), 208
Autumn Thoughts (Ma Zhi-
  yuan), 180
Avicenna, 155
Aydingkol Lake, 85

B

Ba Jin, viii, 263–65, 269
Badaling, 78–79
Bai Juyi, 144, 174
Bai Pu, 180–81
Baitou Mountain, 85
"Ballad of Mu-lan, The"
  (poem), 46, 113
ballad singing, 161
bamboo flute, 162–63
bamboo *xiao*, 162
Ban Biao, 114
Ban Chao, 115
Ban Gu, 111, 114–15
Ban Jieyu, 70
Banpo archaeological site,
  1, 141
Barley, The (opera), 212

Beijing, 140, 193. *See also*
  opera, Beijing
Beiping (modern Beijing),
  266, 267
Bell, The (Lao She), 265
"Bells in the Rain" (Liu
  Yong), 177
Beneath the Red Banner (Lao
  She), 267
benevolence, 94, 231
bengbeng, see duets
Bhrikuti Devi, 240
Bi Sheng, 64
Bian Que, 155
Bianliang, *see* Kaifeng
Bingling Temple, 77
Bird Island, 86–87
Birthday of Xiaopo, The (Lao
  She), 265
Bonaparte, Napolèon, 104
Book, The, see *Book of His-
  tory, The*
Book of Changes, The (I
  Ching), 2, 29, 93, 108, 143,
  169–70, 236
Book of Chuang Tzu, The,
  92–93
Book of Han, The, 114–16
Book of History, The, 93, 108,
  168–169
Book of Mencius, The, 96, 168
Book of Music, The, 93
Book of Poetry, The, 93
Book of Rites, The, 93, 95, 108,
  168–69
Book of Songs, The, 75, 107–8,
  110–112, 168–169
Book of Tao, The, 88
*Book of the Grand Scribe,
  The*, 113
*Book of the Yellow Emperor,
  The* (Huang Di), 235
Book, The, see *Book of His-
  tory, The*

books, collections and
archives, *see* libraries
British East India Company,
122
Broken Bridge, The (opera),
208
bronze, 75
Buck, Pearl S., 183, 245
Buddha, *see* Gautama,
Siddhartha
Buddhism
Chinese, 238–40
Dunhuang Caves, 214–18
introduction to China, 141
libraries, 230–31
for moral cultivation, 233
origins of, 237–38
Pali language, 240
sites along Silk Road, 77
Tantric, 240
temples, 147–49
Theravada, 240
Tibetan, 149, 240
Zen, 121, 224
See also White Horse
Temple
Buddhist Thousand Beings
Society, 121
Bulang ethnic group, 240
Butterfly Dream (Chuang
Tzu), 92
Butterfly Lovers (opera), 213
"Butterfly Lovers, The" (leg-
end), 43–44

C
—————————————————

Cai Lun, 63
Cai Wenji (Guo Moruo), 259
Cai Xiang, 6
Cai Yi, 6, 228
Cai Yong, 111
calamus, 27
calendar
agricultural (lunar), 18–19
twenty-four solar terms,
19–20
Call to Arms (Lu Xun), 256
calligraphy, 5–7. *See also*
Oracle Bone Script
Cangjie, 1–3, 33

Canon of Medicine, The, 155
Cantonese, 10
Cao Cao, 52, 182, 246, 247
Cao Fu, 241
Cao Wei Dynasty, 141
Cao Xi, 241
Cao Xueqin, 184, 241–42
Cao Ying, 241
Cao Yong, 241
Cao Yu, 267–69
carriages, *see* horse and
carriage
Cat Country (Lao She), 265,
266
Catching the Thief (opera), 211
Celestial Hall of the Five
Peaks, 192
Celestial River (Milky Way),
41
Chan, Jackie, 159
*Changes of the Zhou, The,
see Book of Changes, The (I
Ching)*
Chao Gai, 244
Chaohu Lake, 85, 86
Chaoyang Ravine (opera), 211
characters, Chinese, *see* writ-
ing, Chinese
Chasing the Fish (opera), 213
Chen Duxiu, 251–52
Chen Dynasty, 53
Chen Ji, 243
Chen Meiquan, 207
Chen Peisi, 160
Chen Shou, 245
Chen Shufen, 263
Chen Zi'ang, 174
Cheng, Emperor, 70
Cheng brothers, 234
Cheng Changgeng, 206
Cheng Fangwu, 258
Cheng Jing, 224
Cheng Xuanying, 236
Cheng Yanqiu, 207
Cheng Yi, 224
Chengde Palace, *see* Moun-
tain Resort
cheongsam, see qipao
Chess, Chinese, 155–57
China
dragon as symbol of, 48–52

foundations of, 7–8, 33–34,
74–75, 119–20
trade with West, 76–77
*China—My Traveling
Achievements* (von Rich-
thofen), 76
Chinatown, Washington,
DC, 50
Chinese League of Left-Wing
Writers, 256
Chinese National Sport Com-
mittee, 156
Chinese New Year, 21–23, 31,
56–57, 124
Chirac, Jacques, 82
Christianity, 141, 147
chrysanthemums, 29, 30, 124
Chu State, 7, 53, 109–10, 150,
235
Chu Suiliang, 6
Chu Xiang, 109
Chuang Tzu, 88, 91–93, 235,
236. *See also* Lao Chuang
Philosophy
Cixi, Empress Dowager, 185,
267
Classic of Tea, The (Lu Yu), 121
Classic Rites of Da Dai, The,
169. *See also* Book of Rites,
The
Classic Rites of Xiao Dai, The,
169. *See also* Book of Rites,
The
clothing, 129–34
Cloud Ridge, 77
Cold Food Day, 24
Cold Nights (Ba Jin), 264–65
*Collected Works of Chang Li,
The* (Han Yu), 171
Collected Works of Jiayou, The
(Su Xun), 172
Collected Works of Luancheng
(Su Zhe), 173
*Collected Works of Ouyang
Xiu*, 172
Collection of Attempts (Hu
Shi), 254, 255
Collection of Musical Pieces
(Liu Yong), 177
Collection of Yue Fu Poetry,
46, 112

compass, 63, 65
Compendium of Materia Medica, 155
Complete Collection of Four Treasuries, The, 230
Complete Collection of Military Tactics Management, A (Ohashi), 104
Complete Collection of Song Poems, 176
Complete Poetry of the Tang, 174
Confucian Shrine, Nagasaki, Japan, 51
Confucianism, 57, 90, 92, 94–96, 99, 105–6, 124, 163, 170, 223, 231–34, 237
Confucius
  The Book of Songs and, 108, 169
  exorcism dance and, 201–2
  the Five Classics and, 107
  honoring of, 96
  Lao Tzu and, 88
  life, 93–96, 168
  Mo Tzu compared with, 99
  The Spring and Autumn Annals and, 170, 232–33
  as a teacher, 222
  See also Analects of Confucius, The; Confucianism
Confucius Educational Award, 96
Confucius Institutes, 96
Courage and *the Sword* (Cao Yu), 269
Cowherd and the Weaving Maiden, The (opera), 212
Creation Society, 258
Crescent Moon, The (Lao She), 266
Cry of the Phoenix (Wang Shizhen), 208
"Crying Ospreys, The" (poem), 107
cuisine
  Anhui, 128
  Fujian, 126–27
  Hui, 125
  Hunan, 128
  Jiangsu (Huaiyang), 127
  Lu (Shandong), 125
  Sichuan, 125–26
  Yue (Guangdong), 126
  Zhejiang, 127–28
Cultural Study, 8–9
currency, *see* money

D

Da Xu, 240
Da Yu, 34–35, 101, 196
Dafu Lingjiu Temple, 230
Dahe village, 144
Dahong Temple, *see* Humble Administrator's Garden
Dai De, 169
Dai ethnic minority, 54, 56, 240
Dai Sheng, 169
Dan Zhu, 199–200
dances
  Dragon, 31
  exorcism, 201–5
  Jima, 202
  Lion, 31–32
Daoguang, Emperor, 205
Dashan (Mark Rowswell), 160
Dawn Blossoms Plucked at Dusk (Lu Xun), 257
Dayan Pagoda, 248
Days of the Pure Brightness (Mao Dun), 262
derivative cognates method, of word formation, 3
Destruction (Ba Jin), 263
Di Tang Ban (opera), 211
dialects, 3, 4, 10–11, 109, 151, 160, 161, 183, 205
Diary of a Madman (Lu Xun), 252, 255, 256
"On Landscapes" (Mao Dun), 262
Divorce, The (Lao She), 265, 266
Doctrine of the Mean, The, 96, 168–69, 226
dogwood, 29, 30, 31
Dong Zhongshu, 232–33
Dongfang Shuo, 109, 113
Dongting Lake, 85, 86, 128
Double Ninth Festival, *see* Double Yang Festival
double yang cakes, 29–30
Double Yang Festival, 29–30, 56, 124
Dragon Beard Ditch (Lao She), 267
Dragon Boat Festival, 18, 25–27, 45, 50, 124
dragon boat race, 27
Dragon Dance, 31
Dragon Gate, 238
dragons, 48–52
Dream of Red Mansions, A (Cao Xueqin and Gao E), 184, 241–43
Dream of Red Mansions, A (opera), 213
Dream Under the Southern Bough, A (Shen Jing), 208
Dreams of Wandering the Garden (opera), 208
Drum Singers, The (Lao She), 266
Du Fu, 83, 144, 174, 175–76
Du Mu, 174
Du Shenyan, 175
duets, 161–62
Dujiangyan irrigation project, 86
Dunhuang Caves, 77, 213–18, 238, 243
Dust Sweep, 22
dynasties, overview, 52–54, 271

E

Early Spring in the Little Shop (opera), 212
Eastern Han Dynasty, 6, 52, 63, 74, 111, 112, 130–31, 141, 155, 223, 230, 236, 238. *See also* Han Dynasty; Western Han Dynasty
Eastern Jin Dynasty, 129, 142. *See also* Jin Dynasty; Western Jin Dynasty
Eastern Zhou Dynasty, 74, 141, 222. *See also* Western Zhou Dynasty; Zhou Dynasty
education, 222–28. *See also* Imperial Examination

Eid al-Azha, 56
Eight Classical Chinese Prose Masters of the Tang and Song Dynasties, 170–71
Eight Eccentrics of Yangzhou (Zhu Fushan), 7
Eight Friends of Zhushan, 221
"Eight Pieces of Free Verse in Vernacular Chinese" (Hu Shi), 254
Elder's Day, 29
"Embracing the Sand" (Qu Yuan), 26
embroidery, 138–39
    Chuan (*Shu*), 139
    Su, 138
    Xiang, 139
    Yue (*Guang*), 139
Emei Mountain, 147, 172
Emperor's Female Son-in-Law, The (opera), 212, 212
Empress Wu Zetian (Guo Moruo), 259
Encyclopedia Americana, 183, 250
Encyclopédie française, 183, 250
Epang Palace, 141, 144, 185
Erhai Lake, 86
erhu, 162, 164
Erosion (Mao Dun), 261
ethnic minorities, 54–56
Etiquette and Ceremony, 169. See also *Book of Rites, The*
Eulogy for New China (Guo Moruo), 259
Eurasian Continental Bridge, 144
Examination of Fuxi, An (Wen Yi-duo), 48–49
exorcism dance and culture, 201–5
Explaining Simple and Analyzing Compound Characters, 11

F

Fa Xian, 238
families
    filial piety, 57, 94–95
    genealogy, 58
    importance of, 56–58
    patriotism and, 58
    titles within, 15
    See also marriage customs
Family (Ba Jin), 264
Family (Cao Yu), 269
fan, folding, 134–36
Fan Ruijuan, 213
Fan Zhongyan, 172
Fang Bao, 173
February's Frosted Red Leaves Appear as Flowers (Mao Dun), 262
Feng Yansi, 176
Feng Youlan, 234
Festival of Ascending the Heights, 30
Fiction Monthly (journal), 261
Fiery Emperor, see Yan Di (Fiery Emperor)
Fifteen Strings of Coins (Zhu Sucheng), 208
Fighting with Short Spears (opera), 211
filial piety, 57, 94, 98, 99
firecrackers, 23
First Emperor, see Qin Shi Huang, Emperor
First Flower Blossoms, The (opera), 212
First Hall Under Heaven, 230
First International Symposium on Yangtze Culture and Chu Culture, 120
Five Classics, The, 107, 108, 168, 169–70, 223, 227. See also *Book of Changes, The* (*I Ching*); *Book of History, The*; *Book of Rites, The*; *Book of Songs, The*; *Spring and Autumn Annals, The*
Five Constant Virtues, 58
Five Dynasties, 53, 54, 65, 112, 129, 130, 142, 165, 166, 177, 219, 233, 271
Five Dynasties and Ten Kingdoms, The, 53
Five Sacred Mountains, 82–84
Five Studies, 222
food, see cuisine
Forbidden City, 145
Forefront, The (Guo Moruo), 258
Former Shu State, 53
Four Books, The, 96, 168–69, 170, 226, 227. See also *Analects of Confucius, The*; *Book of Mencius, The*; *Doctrine of the Mean, The*; *Great Learning, The*
Four Dreams at Linchuan (Tang Xianzu), 181
Four Generations Under One Roof (Lao She), 266
Four Great Classic Novels, 182, 184
Four Great Yuan Playwrights, 180
Four Sacred Mountains of Buddhism, 147
Four Talents, 174
fragrant pouch, 27
Frog Lake, 85
Fu Quanxiang, 213
Fu River, 85
Fujino Genkuro, 255

G

Gahai Lake, 86
games
    Chess, Chinese, 155–57
    Go, 199–201
Gan Dialect, 10
Gan River, 85
Gao E, 184, 241
Gao Gong, 144
Gao Lian, 208
Gao Zu, Emperor, 115
Gaozu Liu Bang, Emperor, 96
gardening, landscape, 185
Gautama, Siddhartha, 216, 217, 237
"Gazing at the Waterfall of Lu Mountain" (Li Bai), 175
Ge Hong, 236
genealogy, importance of, 58
Go, 199–201
Gobi Desert, 75
Gobi Sea, see Ulungur Lake

Goddesses, The (Guo Moruo), 253, 258, 259
Goethe, Johann Wolfgang von, 258
Golden Lotus, The (novel), 184
Gong Yang, 232
Granting Titles to Gods (opera), 211
Great Learning, The, 96, 98, 168, 226
Great Tang Records of the Western Regions (Xuanzang), 239
Great Wall, 8, 42–43, 52, 77–79, 86, 140
greeting styles
  body language, 14
  verbal, 13–14
Gu Kaizhi, 165
Guan Hanqing, 180, 181
Guan Yu, 182, 246, 247
Guangxi Zhuang autonomous region, 55
Guangxu, Emperor, 152, 186, 191, 205, 213, 225, 227
Guanzhong, 140, 182, 183, 244, 245, 247
Guangzhou Dialect, 10
gunpowder, 63, 64–65
Guo Maoqian, 46, 112
Guo Moruo, 221, 253, 258–60
Guo Xiang, 236
guqin, 163
guzheng, 163–64

H

Haihe River, 86
Haixin Mountain Island, 86
Haiyan opera, 208
Hajime Shinoda, 262
Hakka
  Dialect, 10
  ethnic minority, 194–95, 196
Hall of Supreme Harmony, 145
Han attire, *see* clothing
Han Dialect, 4
Han Dynasty, 29, 52, 58, 63, 77, 83, 107, 110–13, 114, 115, 129–31, 141, 150, 162, 167, 169, 203, 219, 223, 230, 231,

232–233, 271. *See also* Eastern Han Dynasty; Western Han Dynasty
Han Fei Tzu, 104–6. *See also* Legalist school of philosophy
Han Fei Tzu (book), 105
Han fu (poetry form), 110–11
Han Yu, 171, 174, 233
Han Yue fu (poetry form), 112–13
Hanaoka Seishu, 155
Handan Dream, The (Tang Xianzu), 208
Handkerchief Tales (opera), 212
Hangzhou, 142–43
Hart, Basil Henry Liddell, 104
Havoc in Heaven, 250
He Lin, 234
He Yan, 236
Heath, Howard, 79
Heine, Heinrich, 258
Hemudu culture, 118
Heng Mountain, 36, 82, 83, 84, 147, 148
hierarchy, social, *see* social hierarchy
History of Literature in Vernacular Chinese, A (Hu Shi), 255
History of Science, The (Lu Xun), 256
History of Song and Yuan Drama, The (Wang Guowei), 181
Hmong ethnic minority, 54, 55
Hodgett, Richard M., 104
Hong Sheng, 181, 208
Hongwu, Emperor, 79
Hongze Lake, 85, 86
horse and carriage, 72–73
Hou Baolin, 160
Hou Yi, 28, 38–9
Hsun Tzu, 231–32
Hu Shi, 252, 253–55
Hu Shi Literary Deposits, 255
Hu Yuan, 234
Hua Mountain, 33, 36, 82–83
Hua Shigang, 192

Hua Tuo, 155
Huai Su, 6
Huaihe River, 85
Huang Di (Yellow Emperor), 1, 12, 33–34, 66, 96, 113, 153, 196–97, 232, 235
Huang Lao, 235
Huang Tingjian, 7
Huangmei opera, 211, 212
Hui ethnic minority, 54, 55, 56, 125
Hui Dialect, 205
Huiji Mountain, 35
Huizi, 92
Hukou Falls, 85
Humble Administrator's Garden, 189–90
Hunan Dialect, 10
Hundred Schools of Thought, 235
Huo Yingdong, 157
huqin, 164
hutongs, 192–93

I

Ibsen, Henrik, 268
I Ching, see Book of Changes, The (*I Ching*)
ideogram, 3
ideogrammic compound, 3
idioms, *see* sayings, idioms and proverbs
"Idle Life" (Pan Yue), 189
Imperial Examination, 223–24, 225–28, 229, 243. *See also* education
Injustice to Dou E, The (Guan Hanqing), 179, 180
ink, black, 9. *See also* Cultural Study
ink stone, 9. *See also* Cultural Study
Inner Mongolia, 55
International Culture of Confucius Festival, 96
International Symposium on Sanxingdui Culture and Yangtze Civilization, 120
iron, 75
Islam, 141, 147

J

Jade Hairpin, The (Gao Lian), 208
Jade Pin, The (Yue opera), 213
Japan, 51, 68, 104, 108, 122, 129, 130, 136, 148, 154, 159, 209, 228, 250, 255, 256, 258, 259, 261, 264
Ji Chang, 52
Ji Fa, 52
Ji Junxiang, 181
Ji Kang, 236
Jia Jing, Emperor (Qing Dynasty), 191
Jia Yi, 111
Jiajing, Emperor (Ming Dynasty), 189, 196, 207
Jiang Kui, 176, 178
Jiang Kun, 160
"Jiangnu" (poem), 107
Jiangxi Dialect, 10
Jiangye, 238. *See also* Nanjing
Jiangzhe Dialect, 10
Jianhuai Dialect, 10
Jiayu Pass, 77, 79
Jie, Emperor, 52
Jima dance, 202
Jin Dynasty, 6, 30, 52, 54, 131, 140, 142, 180, 228–29, 271. *See also* Eastern Jin Dynasty; Western Jin Dynasty
Jin Sha, 202, 203
Jingdezhen porcelain, 218, 220, 221
Jiuhua Mountain, 147
Jokhang Monastery, 240
Journey to the West (Wu Cheng'en), 182, 183, 239, 248–50

K

Kai Yuan Ceremony, 203
Kaifeng (Bianliang), 70, 74, 75, 140, 141–42, 172
Kang Youwei, 240
Kangxi, Emperor, 54, 187–88, 197, 220, 241

Kind Mother's Tears, A (opera), 212
kinship appellations, 15
Kissinger, Henry, 81–82
kites, 25
Kong Shangren, 208
Korea, 68, 85, 104, 108, 129, 130, 134, 148, 154, 183, 228
kuai ban, 161
Kuaiji Mountain, 196
Kublai Khan, 53
Kumarajiva, 238
kung fu, 144, 157–59. *See also* martial arts
Kunqu opera, 205, 207–9, 268
Kunqu Opera Association, 209

L

lakes, 84–87
Lamaism, *see* Buddhism
Lantern Festival, 31–32, 204
Lao Chuang Philosophy, 91–92. *See also* Taoism
Lao She, 265–67
Lao Tzu, 88–90, 91, 92, 235, 236. *See also* Taoism
Laodan, 222
Lasha Shonton Festival, 56
Late Qin Dynasty, 140
Later Han Dynasty, 53, 142, 271
Later Jin Dynasty, 53, 141, 142, 271
Later Liang Dynasty, 53, 74, 142, 271
Later Shu State, 53
Later Tang Dynasty, 53, 141, 271
Later Zhou Dynasty, 52, 53, 74, 142, 271
Lawsuit of the Grain Officer (opera), 212
Lee, Bruce, 159
Lee Kuan Yew, 81
Legalist school of philosophy, 104–6
Legend of the White Snake, The (film), 46

legends and traditional stories
  about the abacus, 66–67
  about Anyang, 143
  "The Butterfly Lovers," 43–44
  on Chinese New Year origins, 21–22
  "The Cowherd and the Weaving Maid," 40–41, 212
  on the creation of earth, 35–37
  on the creation of humans, 37–38
  Da Yu and flood control, 34–35
  on Dragon Boat Festival origins, 26
  about dragons, 48–49
  on the formation of characters, 1
  about Go, 199–200
  "Hou Yi Shoots the Suns," 38–39
  on Lantern Festival origins, 32
  "Meng Jiangnu Weeps Down the Great Wall," 42–43, 78
  on Mid-Autumn Festival origins, 28
  Milky Way origins, 41
  Mu-lan, 46–47
  White Snake, 44–46, 202
  about wine, 124–25
  about Yan Di (Fiery Emperor), 33
  on zodiac animals, 17
Li, Jet, 159
Li Ao, 234
Li Bai, 83, 174, 175
Li Dazhao, 252
Li He, 174
Li Qingzhao, 176, 177–78
Li Sao, see "Sorrow for Departure"(Qu Yuan)
Li Shangyin, 174
Li Shimin, 53, 158. *See also* Taizong, Emperor

Li Shizheng, 155
Li Si, 105
Li Yu, 208
Li Yuan, 53
Liang Chengyu, 207
Liang Dynasty, 53, 271
Liang Qichao, 240
Liang Shuming, 234
Liang Wu, Emperor, 238
Liang Zhu (concerto), 44
Liao Dynasty, 140
libraries, 228–31
Lie Zi, 144
Lieh Tzu, 236
Light of the Buddha Temple, 148
Lingering Garden, 185, 191–92
Lion Dance, 31–32
Literary Research Society, 253, 261
literary tools, 9
Little Erhei's Marriage (opera), 211
Liu An, 228
Liu Bang, 52, 96
Liu Bei, 52, 182, 246, 247
Liu Bowen, 243
Liu Gongquan, 6
Liu Ji, 7, 53
Liu Liang, 243
Liu Rongfeng, 191
Liu Xiang, 109
Liu Xin, 228
Liu Yong, 176, 177
Liu Yuxi, 174
Liu Zhuang, 148
Liu Zongyuan (Liu Hedong), 171, 174, 233
Living Among Heroes (Ba Jin), 264
Longevity Hall (Hong Sheng), 208
Longmen (Dragon Gate), 77
Longmen Caves, 141, 143
Longqing, Emperor, 207
Longshan culture, 84
Lord Bao's Drama (opera), 211
Love Detectives (opera), 213
Love Trilogy, The (Ba Jin), 263

Lu Guimeng, 189
Lu Jingshan, 224
Lu Jiuyuan, 234
Lu Xun, 252, 253, 255–58, 261, 267
Lu Yu, 121
Lu Yuan, 243
Lu Zhaolin, 174
lunar calendar, *see* calendar
Lunar New Year, *see* Chinese New Year
Luo Binwang, 174
Luo Guanzhong, 182, 183, 244, 245, 247
Luoyang, 74, 75, 77, 140, 141, 147, 229, 238

M

Ma and Son (Lao She), 265
Ma Ji, 160
Ma Lan, 212
Ma Lianliang, 207
Ma Sanli, 160
Ma Yifu, 234
Ma Zhiyuan, 180, 181
Magpie Bridge Day, 41
Maiji Mountain, 77
mail delivery, 68–70
Manchu ethnic minority, 53, 54, 55, 132, 227, 265
Mao Dun, 260–63
Mao Dun Prize for Literature, 262
Mao Kun, 171
Mao Lun, 246
Mao Weitao, 213
Mao Zedong, 54, 258
Mao Zonggang, 246
March 18 Massacre, 256
marriage customs, 59–62, 123. *See also* families
Marriage of the Goddess (opera), 212
martial arts, 157–59, 244. *See also kung fu*
Marx, Karl, 63
Marxism, 253
Matters of the Song Dynasty's Xuanhe Period, 244

Mausoleum of Emperor Qin Shi Huang, 197–98
Mausoleum of the Yellow Emperor, 196–97
May Fourth Movement, 253, 256, 257, 258, 259, 260, 261, 263, 264, 265, 269
medical texts, 155
medicine, traditional Chinese, 33, 152–55
Mei Cheng, 111
Mei Lanfang, 207
Memories of a Chivalrous Man (Shen Jing), 208
Mencius, 96–100, 168, 231
"Meng" (poem), 107
Meng Jiangnu, 42–43, 78, 202
Meng Jiangnu (Jima dance drama), 202
Meng Jiangnu Temple, 43
metaphysics, 236–37
Mi Fu, 6, 166
Mi Heng, 111
Mi Youren, 166
Mid-Autumn Festival, 27–29, 57
Midnight (Mao Dun), 261, 262–63
Min Dialect, 10
Min State, 53
Ming Dynasty
  abacus in, 68
  agricultural calendar in, 19
  Buddhism in, 239
  calligraphy in, 7
  capital, 141, 142
  clothing in, 129, 130
  Confucianism in, 233–34
  education in, 224, 226–27
  embroidery in, 138
  folding fan in, 134–35
  gardens in, 189, 190, 191
  Great Wall, 78–79
  hutongs in, 192
  libraries in, 229
  literature in, 171, 173, 183, 239, 243–44, 248, 250
  medicine in, 155
  money in, 151–52

Ming Dynasty, *continued*
  opera and theater in, 181,
    207, 208, 210, 213
  overview, 53, 271
  paper cutting in, 137
  porcelain in, 220
  sedan chairs in, 71
  tea drinking in, 121–22
  temples in, 204
  Thirteen Ming Tombs, 198
Ming Taizu, Emperor, 84
Mingsha Mountain, 214
Mistakes of the Kite (Li Yu),
  208
Mo Tzu, 99–102
Modern Literary Group, 256
Mogao Caves, 77, 214, 215. *See
  also* Dunhuang Caves
Mohist School, 99, 101
Mondale, Walter, 82
money, 150–52
Mongolia, 55, 74, 77, 78, 187,
  240
Mongolians, 53, 56, 122, 193,
  224, 226, 239
moon cakes, 29
"Moon Festival, The" (Su
  Shi), 177
*Moon's Reflection on the Two
  Springs, The* (music), 164
Mountain of Fire, 250
Mountain Resort, 187–89
moxibustion, 154
mugwort, 27
Mulan (film), 47
Mulan II (film), 47
musical instruments, 162–64
"My Darling Slave" (Su Shi),
  177
Myanmar, 240

N

Nadam, 56
*Nameless Highland Has the
  Name, The* (Lao She), 267
names
  conventions for, 13
  surnames, 12–13
Namtso Lake, 85, 87
Nangchang sub-dialect, 10

Nanjing, 142. *See also* Jiangye
Nationalist Government, *see*
  Republic of China
natural resources, 55. *See also*
  lakes
Neo-Confucianism, 234
New Culture Movement,
  251–53, 261, 263
New Year Scrolls, 22–23
New Year's Day, *see* Chinese
  New Year
New Youth (journal), 251, 252,
  253, 254, 255, 256
Night of Sevens, 41
"Nine Elegies" (Qu Yuan),
  109
Nine Schools of Thought, 114
"Nine Songs" (Qu Yuan),
  26, 109
"Nine Thoughts" (Wang Yi),
  109
Ningxia Hui autonomous
  region, 55
Nixon, Richard, 79
North Dialect, 10
North River Dialect, 10
Northern Dynasties, 52–53,
  54, 129, 131, 151, 233, 238,
  271. *See also* Northern Wei
  Dynasty; Northern Zhou
  Dynasty
Northern Expedition, 259,
  263
Northern Han State, 53
Northern Song Dynasty, 64,
  71, 75, 137, 142, 151, 155, 166,
  171, 172, 173, 177, 224, 234,
  239, 244, 271. *See also* Song
  Dynasty; Southern Song
  Dynasty
Northern Tang Dynasty, 142
Northern Warlords, 251
Northern Wei Dynasty, 53,
  141, 148, 215
Northern Zhou Dynasty, 53,
  140, 216, 271. *See also* Wei
  Dynasty
Northwest Silk Road, *see* Silk
  Road
Not-Yet-Named Society
  (*Weiming she*), 256

novels, 181–84
Nuwa, Goddess, 37–38

O

Ohashi Takeo, 104
Old Tales Retold (Lu Xun), 257
On Cultural Paranoia (Lu
  Xun), 256
*On the Power of Romantic
  Poetry* (Lu Xun), 256
opera, 208, 209
  Beijing, 205–7, 209, 268
  Huangmei, 211–12
  kunqu, 207–9
  Yu, 209–11
  Yuan, 179
  Yue (Shaoxing), 213
Opium Wars, 234
Oracle Bone Script, 1, 6, 63,
  143, 228
*Orphan of the Zhao Family,
  The* (Ji Junxiang), 181
Ou Yangxun, 6
Outlaws of the Marsh (Shap-
  iro), 183, 245
*Outline of Chinese Philosophy
  History, An* (Hu Shi), 255
Ouyang Jingwu, 239–40
Ouyang Xiu, 171–72
Over the Wall on a Horse (Bai
  Pu), 181

P

paintings, 164–67, 214–18
Palace of Eternity, The (Hong
  Sheng), 181
Pan Yue, 189
Pan'gen, King, 143
Pangu, 35–37, 202
Pangu Ancestral Hall, 37
paper, 9
  cutting, 136–38
  making, 63–64
  See also Cultural Study;
    printing
*Pavilion of Moon-Worship,
  The* (Guan Hanqing), 181
Peach Blossom Fan, The
  (Kong Shangren), 208

"Peacock Flies Southeast, The" (poem), 113
Pearl and Jade Verses (Yan Shu), 176
Pei Songzhi, 245
Peiligang culture, 144
Peking Man, 117–18, 269
Peking Man (Cao Yu), 269
Peony Pavilion (Tang Xianzu), 181, 208–9
Peony Pavilion Onstage (Swatek), 208–9
People's Republic of China (PRC), 54, 152
Personal Joys and Blaring Horses (opera), 211
Philosophy of Old Zhang, The (Lao She), 265
phonetic loan method, of word formation, 3–4
phono-semantic method, of word formation, 3
pictogram, 2
Pingzhun Shu, 116
poems
    on the dynasties, 54
    on Mu-lan, 46, 47
    on the twenty-four solar terms, 20
Poems Composed at the Orchid Pavilion, 6
Poems of Jade (Zhou Bang-yan), 177
Poems of the Hills, 177
Poems of Washed Jade (Li Qingzhao), 178
poetry
    Song Dynasty, 176–78
    Tang Dynasty, 174–76
Poetry of the South, see Songs of Chu
Poets Day, 26
political ideology
    Confucianism and, 233
    Lao Tzu, 89–90
    Mencius, 97–98, 231, 232–33
porcelain, Jingdezhen, 218–21
Porcelain Exchange Center, 219
Portuguese traders, 122

post roads, 68
post stations, 69–70
Potala Mountain, 147, 149, 240
Potala Palace, 149, 240
Poyang Lake, 85, 202
PRC, *see* People's Republic of China (PRC)
prehistoric finds, 117–18, 141, 143, 144
Preparatory Committee of the Chinese Chess Federation, 157
printing, 63–64, 229. *See also* paper
propriety, 95
Prose of the Eight Masters of the Tang and Song Dynasties, 171
proverbs, *see* sayings, idioms and proverbs
Pu Songling, 184
Pure Brightness Day, 23–25, 27
Purple Hairpin, The (Tang Xianzu), 208
Putrefaction (Mao Dun), 262

Q

Qarhan Lake, 85
Qi Dynasty (Northern), 53
Qi Dynasty (Southern), 53, 142
Qi Yaxian, 213
Qian Mu, 234
Qian Xuantong, 252
Qianlong, Emperor, 54, 184, 185, 187, 188, 204, 210, 220, 241
Qiao Mountain, 196
Qin Dynasty, 271
    army, 80–71, 106
    capital, 74, 140, 141, 142
    clothing in, 129, 130, 131
    conflict with other states, 26, 109
    education in, 223
    ending of, 106, 232
    establishment of, 7, 52
    Great Wall, 78

legends and traditional stories about, 42
literature in, 108, 169
money in, 150
See also Qin Shi Huang, Emperor
Qin Eradicate the Six States Period, 7
Qin Shi Huang, Emperor, 7–8, 43, 52, 78, 80–81, 82, 83, 84, 108, 141, 150, 197–98, 223, 228. *See also* Ying Zheng
Qing Dynasty
    agricultural calendar in, 19
    Buddhism and, 239–40
    calligraphy in, 7
    clothing under, 132
    Confucianism in, 233–34
    education in, 22, 96, 225, 227
    embroidery in, 138
    exorcism dance in, 203
    folding fan in, 135
    hutongs in, 192
    libraries in, 230
    Lingering Garden, 191
    literature in, 173, 181, 182, 184, 241, 246
    money in, 150, 152
    Mountain Resort, 187
    opera in, 205, 210
    overview, 53–54, 271
    painting in, 166
    porcelain in, 220
    theater in, 160
    transportation in, 69, 71, 72
    Summer Palace, 185–86
    tea drinking in, 121–22
Qinghai Lake, 85, 86–87
Qingzhen Poetry (Zhou Bang-yan), 177
qipao, 132–34
Qu Yuan, 26, 109–10, 259
Qu Yuan (Guo Moruo), 259

R

Rain on the Paulowina Tree (Bai Pu), 181
Rainbow (Mao Dun), 261

Ramadan, 56
Ramoche Monastery, 240
Random Thoughts (Ba Jin), 264–65
Rao River, 85
Record of Art and Literature, The, 115
Record of Criminal Law, The, 115
Record of Geography, The, 115
Record of the Five Phases of Philosophy, The, 115
Record on Agriculture and Commerce, The, 116
Records of the Grand Historian, The, 113, 114–15, 162, 163
Records of the Grand Historian Post Biography, 115
Record of Washed Grievances, 155
Records of the Three Kingdoms (Chen Shou), 245
Redology, 184
Redwood Palace Hall, 192
reed pipe, 162
Rehe Traveling Palace, *see* Mountain Resort
relay stations, 68–60
Ren Zong, Emperor, 64
Republic of China, 54, 142, 152
Research Library of Changjiang Culture, 120
Restore (Guo Moruo), 259
rice wine, *see* wine
Rickshaw Boy (Lao She), 265, 266
Ripening Apple, The (opera), 211
roads, post, 68–70
"Roadside Mulberry, The" (poem), 113
Romance of the Three Kingdoms (Luo Guanzhong), 182–83, 244, 245–47, 244
Romance of the West Chamber (Wang Shifu), 181
Romance of the Western Chamber, The (opera), 213
Rowswell, Mark (Dashan), 160
Ruan Ji, 236

S

same-road-width policy, 8
Sanxingdui (Three Star Mounds), 118, 119, 120
Sanyi, Empress, 199, 200
sayings, idioms and proverbs, 4–5
  on children, 57
  on Chinese New Year, 21
  inspired by Da Yu, 35
  for double yang cakes, 30
  involving dragons, 50
  on elders, 57
  on emperor's authority, 50
  on family, 56, 58
  on filial piety, 57
  on firecrackers, 23
  on Great Wall, 79
  on Hangzhou, 143
  on Hunan cuisine, 128
  on Jingdezhen porcelain, 221
  on moon cakes, 29
  for newlyweds, 62
  for Pure Brightness Day and Dragon Boat Festival, 27
  on Sichuan cuisine, 126
  on West Lake, 143
Scholars, The (Wu Jingzi), 184
School of Principles, 233–34
sedan chairs, 70–71
Seiji Ozawa, 164
Selling the Grain Baskets (opera), 212
Seven Ancient Capitals of China, 74
Seven Warring States, 7
Seven Works of Dongpo (Su Shi), 172
Sha Wujing, 183, 248, 250
Shan Tianfang, 161
Shang Dynasty
  bronze in, 75
  capitals, 74, 141, 143, 144
  carriages in, 72
  clothing in, 130
  cultural relics from, 118–19
  education in, 222
  money in, 150

Oracle Bone Script, 1, 63
  overview, 52, 271
Shang Jun, 200
Shang Xiaoyun, 207
Shang Yang, 105, 106
Shanghainese, 10
Shanglin Garden, 185
Shangtang, Emperor, 52
Shanhai Pass, 77, 79
Shangxi opera, 205
Shao Yong, 234
Shaolin Temple, 84, 144, 158–59
Shaolin Temple (film), 158
Shaoxing opera, 213
Shapiro, Sidney, 183, 245
Shen Buhai, 106
Shen Dao, 106
Shen Jing, 208
Shen Quanqi, 174
"Sheng Min" (poem), 108
Sheng Xuren, 191
Shennong's Herbal Classic, 155
Shi Jie, 234
Shi Nai'an, 183, 243–44
Shixiang, 222
Shong Yu, 109
shramana, 237
Shu State, 52
Shun, Emperor, 35
Siling Co Lake, 85, 87
silk, 76–77
Silk Road, 69, 76–77, 79, 141, 237
"Silk-Washing Brook, The" (Yan Shu), 176
Sima Qian, 113, 114, 162, 163, 173
Sima Xiangru, 111
Sima Yan, 52
Six Disciplines, 99
Six Dynasties of the Han and Wei, 142, 230
Six Teachings, 99
social hierarchy
  according to Mencius, 97
  in Confucianism, 95
  within families, 15–16
  sedan chairs and, 71
Social Soup, 121
Song Ci, 155

Song Dynasty
  Buddhism in, 239
  calligraphy in, 6
  capitals, 142, 143
  clothing in, 129, 130
  Confucianism in, 233–34
  cuisine, 125
  education in, 224, 226
  enclosed residences in,
    192–93
  exorcisms during, 203
  folding fan in, 134, 136
  gunpowder in, 65
  legends and stories in, 44,
    46, 244
  libraries in, 229
  literature in, 46, 75, 112,
    170–71, 172, 173, 176–78,
    182
  medicine, 155
  money in, 151, 152
  overview, 53, 271
  paper cutting in, 137
  porcelain in, 219
  sedan chairs in, 70
  tea drinking and, 121
  See also Northern Song
    Dynasty; Southern Song
    Dynasty
Song Dynasty (Southern
  Dynasties), 53
Song Jiang, 244, 245
Song Mountain, 36, 82, 84,
  158
Song Sui, 7
Song Yu, 109
Song Zhiwen, 174
Songkrang Festival, 56
Songs of Chu, 109–10, 111
Songs of Jiang Baishi (Jiang
  Hui), 178
Songshan Mountain, 144
Songshan Scenic Area, 144
Songsten Gampo, 240
Songyang Academy, 144
"Sorrow for Departure" (Qu
  Yuan), 26, 109, 110, 113
South Meditation Temple, 148
"Sound, Sound, Slow" (Li
  Qingzhao), 178
Southern Dynasties, 52–53,

54, 129, 130, 131, 228–29, 233,
  238, 271
Southern Feng musical style,
  110
Southern Han State, 53
Southern Ping State, 53
Southern Prosody (Wei
  Liangfu), 207
Southern Song Dynasty, 65,
  96, 142, 151, 155, 168, 169,
  170, 177, 178, 224, 234, 239,
  244, 271. See also North-
  ern Song Dynasty; Song
  Dynasty
Southern Tang State, 53, 142,
  176
Spinning Cotton into Yarn
  (opera), 212
Spinoza, Baruch, 258
Spring (Ba Jin), 264
Spring and Autumn Annals,
  The, 93, 108, 168, 170, 232–33
Spring and Autumn Period,
  25, 26, 52, 54, 63, 72, 88, 89,
  93, 102, 107, 108, 110, 115,
  129, 130, 150, 168, 169, 170,
  231, 232, 236, 271
Spring Festival, see Chinese
  New Year
Spring Silkworms (Mao Dun),
  261
Starry Sky (Guo Moruo), 258
Story of Buckwheat, The
  (opera), 212
storytelling, 160–61
Strange Tales of a Lonely Stu-
  dio (Pu Songling), 184
Striking the White Bone
  Demon Three Times, 250
Student Magazine, 261
Study Lamp (journal), 261
Su Dongpo, 143
Su Shi, 6, 171, 172, 176, 177, 178
Su Xin, 177, 178
Su Xun, 172
Su Zhe, 172–73
Sui Dynasty, 6, 53, 74, 129,
  130, 131, 140, 141, 142, 176,
  225, 229, 233, 271
Summer Palace, 140, 146,
  185–87

Sun Fu, 234
Sun Quan, 52, 182, 246, 247
Sun Tzu, 102–4. See also Art
  of War, The (Sun Tzu)
Sun Wukong (Monkey King),
  183, 248, 249–50
Sun Yat-sen, 54, 79, 142, 152,
  225
Sun Zhongshan, 228
Sunrise (Cao Yu), 269
Suspended Temple, 147, 148
Swatek, Catherine, 208–9
swinging, 25

T

Tagore, Rabindranath, 258
tai chi chuan, 157, 159
Tai Mountain, 36, 82–83
Tai Shi Gong, 113
Taihu Lake, 85, 86, 192
Taiping Heavenly Kingdom,
  142
Taizong, Emperor, 84, 223,
  239, 248. See also Li Shimin
Tales of Colored Buildings
  (opera), 213
Tan Citong, 240
Tan Xinpei, 207
Tang Dynasty
  Buddhism and, 148–49,
    238–39, 240, 248
  calligraphy in, 6
  capitals, 74, 140, 141
  clothing under, 129, 130,
    131
  Confucianism in, 233
  Double Yang Festival
    and, 29
  education in, 223–24, 226
  exorcisms during, 203
  legends and stories in, 46
  libraries in, 229
  literature in, 170–71,
    174–76, 182
  money in, 150–51
  overview, 53, 271
  painting in, 165, 167
  paper cutting in, 137
  porcelain in, 219
  printing in, 64

Tang Dynasty, *continued*
  sacrificial ceremonies during, 83
  sedan chairs in, 70
  Shaolin Temple in, 158
  Taoism in, 236
  tea drinking and, 120–21
Tang Shunzhi, 173
Tang Xianzu, 181, 207, 208–9
Tang Xiaoyu, 207, 208
Tao Hongjing, 236
Tao Yuanming, 30
Taoism, 82, 83, 88–89, 90, 215, 230, 232, 233, 234–35.
  See also Lao Chuang Philosophy
tea, 83, 120–22
Teahouse, The (Lao She), 267
Temple Fair, 31
Temple of Heaven, 146
"Tentative Suggestions for the Reform of Chinese Literature" (Hu Shi), 252, 253
terracotta warriors, 80–82, 141
Testing Husband (opera), 211
Thatcher, Margaret, 79
theater
  folk musical, 159–62
  Yuan mixed, 179–81
Theravada Buddhism, 238, 240
"Thesis of the Literary, A" (Chen Duxiu), 252
They Who Defend Peace (Ba Jin), 264
Thinking of the Mundane (opera), 208
Thirteen Ming Tombs, 198
This Life of Mine (Lao She), 266
Thousand Beings Society, 121
Thousand Buddhas Grotto, *see* Dunhuang Caves
Three Cardinal Guides, 58
Three Drunks (opera), 208
Three Hundred Tang Poems, 174
Three Kingdoms, The (opera), 211
Three Kingdoms Period, 6, 31, 52, 54, 113, 120, 129, 238, 247, 271
Three Kingdoms Sacrifice, 96
"Three Officials" (Du Fu), 175

Three Pillars, 237
Three Profound Theories, 236
Three Searches in the Mansion of the Father-in-Law, The (opera), 212
"Three Separations" (Du Fu), 175
Three Sovereigns, 7, 74, 84, 120
Three Times in the Sedan (opera), 211
Thunderstorm (Cao Yu), 268–69
Tianchi Lake, 85
Tianti Mountain, 77
Tibetans, 56
Tibet, 55, 85, 87, 117, 149, 210, 240
Tiger Tally (Guo Moruo), 259
Tomb of Yu the Great, 35, 196–97
tomb sweeping, 24–5. *See also* Pure Brightness Day
Torch Festival, 56
Torrents Trilogy, The (Ba Jin), 264
traditional stories, *see* legends and traditional stories
transportation
  horse and carriage, 72–73
  post roads, 68–70
  sedan chairs, 70–71
Treatments for Typhoid and Other Complicated Diseases (Zhang Zhongjing), 155
tree planting, 25
Trial of Zha Mei, The (opera), 211
Tribute to the Poplar (Mao Dun), 262
True Story of Ah Q, The (Lu Xun), 253, 256–57
Turpan Depression, 85
Twelve Widows Travel to the West (opera), 211
Tzu Chang, *see* Sima Qian

U

Uch-Turpan Monastery, 77
Uighur Autonomous Region, 55, 87

Uighur ethnic minority, 54, 55, 56
Ulungur Lake, 85, 87
UNESCO, 77, 81, 84, 96, 164, 209
Unlucky Uncle's Marriage, The (opera), 211

V

Vernacular Movement, 252–53
von Richthofen, Ferdinand, 76

W

Wagang Drama (opera), 211
Wandering (Lu Xun), 256
Wang Anshi, *171*, 172, 173
Wang Bao, 109
Wang Bi, 236
Wang Bo, 174
Wang Chong, 7
Wang Guowei, 181
Wang Linchuan Anthology (Wang Anshi), 173
Wang Shaofang, 212
Wang Shenzhong, 173
Wang Shichong, 158
Wang Shifu, 181
Wang Shizhen, 208
Wang Shouren, 234
Wang Tong, 233
Wang Wei, 165
Wang Wenjuan, 213
Wang Xianchen, 189
Wang Xinyi, 190
Wang Xizhi, 6
Wang Yangming, 224
Wang Yi, 109
Wang Zhaojun (Cao Yu), 269
Warm Spring and Blooming Flowers (opera), 212
Warring States Period, 7, 25, 52, 54, 65, 72, 77–78, 88, 91, 93, 94, 96, 99, 104, 105, 109, 110, 129, 130, 138, 142, 150, 152, 155, 163, 168, 169, 228, 232, 235, 271

Washing the Silken Gauze (Liang Chengyu), 207, 208
Water Margin (Shi Nai'an), 182, 183, 243–45, 255
Water Millstone Song, The (Wei Liangfu), 207
Way of Chuang Tzu, The, 235, 236
Way of Lao Tzu, The, 88, 235, 236
Wei Dynasty, 74, 131, 228–29, 238
Wei Liangfu, 207
Wei State, 7, 52, 142
Weiming she (Not-Yet-Named Society), 256
Wen Tingyun, 174
Wen Yi-duo, 48–49
Wen Zhengming, 7, 189
Wencheng, Princess, 240
West, contrasts with greeting styles, 14
paintings, 167
West Lake, 143
Western Buddhist's Caves, 214. *See also* Dunhuang Caves
Western Han Dynasty, 52, 77, 96, 109, 111, 115, 120, 130, 223, 232. *See also* Eastern Han Dynasty; Han Dynasty
Western Jin Dynasty, 129, 140, 141, 238. *See also* Eastern Jin Dynasty; Jin Dynasty
Western Wei Dynasty, 140. *See also* Wei Dynasty
Western Zhou Dynasty, 54, 63, 72, 74, 107, 141, 169, 185, 194, 222, 223, 271. *See also* Eastern Zhou Dynasty; Zhou Dynasty
White Horse Temple, 141, 147–48, 230, 238
Wild Grass (Lu Xun), 257
Wilderness, The (Cao Yu), 269
wine, 122–25
Winter Ruin (Mao Dun), 261
woodblock printing, *see* printing
Works of Mao Dun, 262

World Chinese Chess Championship, 157
World Heritage Records, 79, 81
World Wildlife Fund, 85
wormwood, 27
writing, Chinese, 1–7. *See also* calligraphy
writing brush, 9. *See also* Cultural Study
Wu, Emperor, 83, 84, 113, 114, 223, 231, 232
Wu Changshuo, 166
Wu Cheng'en, 183, 239, 248
Wu Dialect, 10
Wu Jialiang (Wu Yong), 244
Wu Jingzi, 184
Wu Qiong, 212
Wu Rui, 202–3
Wu State, 52, 53, 142
Wu Yue State, 53
Wu Zetian, Empress, 83, 259
wushu, see kung fu; martial arts
Wulie River, 187
Wutai Mountain, 147, 148
Wutai Mountain, 147, 148, 218, 230
wuwei, 89, 91, 235

X

Xi Hongdu ruins, 74
Xia Dynasty, 52, 70, 74, 84, 141, 144, 222, 271
Xia She, 258
Xi'an, 74, 76, 80, 83, 140–41, 197
Xiang Dialect, 10
Xiang Yu, 52
xianghe, 112
xiangqi, see Chess, Chinese
Xianyang, 74, 114, 141
Xiaoshan, 109
Xin Qiji, 176, 177, 178
Xin River, 85
Xinhai Revolution, 152, 225, 251
Xinjiang, 55
Xiong Shili, 234
Xiu River, 85

Xu Da, 53
Xu Shitai, 191
Xu Yulan, 213
Xuan Tong, 152
Xuanhe period, 244
Xuanzang, 183, 239, 248, 249, 250
Xuanzang Obtaining the Scriptures, 239
Xuanzong, Emperor, 83, 84, 198
Xun Tzu, 104

Y

Yamdrok Lake, 85, 87
Yan Daocheng, 118
Yan Di (Fiery Emperor), 33–34
Yan Fengying, 212
Yan Jidao, 176, 177
Yan Shu, 176, 177
Yang, Emperor, 225
Yang Family Drama, The (opera), 211
Yang Guang, Emperor, 53
Yang Jian, 53
Yang Jiong, 174
Yang Wenhui, 239
Yang Xiong, 111
Yangcheng, 84
Yangguan Pass (opera), 208
Yangshao culture, 84, 118
Yangtze River, 85, 86, 117–18, 122, 188, 219
Yangtze River culture, 117–20
Yao, Emperor, 34, 199–200
Yao Nai, 173
Yarlung Tsangbo River, 87
Yellow Emperor, *see* Huang Di (Yellow Emperor)
Yellow Emperor's Internal Classic, The, 153
Yellow River, 34, 74–75, 83, 117–20, 141, 194
Yellow River culture, 119–20
Yi ethnic minority, 56
Yi Guifang, 213
Yi Luo, *see* Luoyang
Ying Zheng, 7–8, 105. *See also* Qin Shi Huang, Emperor

Yiyang opera, 208
Yongle Period, 135, 198, 204
Yongzheng, Emperor, 54, 187, 188, 220, 241
Yongzi Eight Ways, of calligraphy strokes, 5–6
Young Lady's Departed Soul, A (Zheng Guangzu), 181
Youth, see New Youth (journal)
Yu Dafu, 258
Yu Erniang, 181
Yu Mausol*eum, see* Tomb of Yu the Great
Yu opera, 209, 210, 211
Yu Sansheng, 207
Yu Shinan, 6
Yu Shun, 35, 200
Yu Shuyan, 207
Yuan Dynasty
  Buddhism and, 239
  calligraphy in, 7
  capital, 140
  clothing in, 129, 130
  Confucianism in, 233–34
  education in, 224, 226
  hutongs and, 193
  libraries in, 229
  literature in, 243–44
  money in, 151
  music, 182
  overview, 53, 271
  opera and theater, 179–81, 207–8
  painting in, 166
  porcelain in, 219, 220
Yuan River, 26
Yuan Shikai, Emperor, 152, 251
Yuan Xuefen, 213

Yuan Zhen, 174
Yuanfeng Leigao, 173
Yuanmou Man, 117–18, 269
Yue Dialect, 10
Yue Family Drama, The (opera), 211
Yue fu, 112, 113
Yue opera, 209, 213
Yungang, 238
Yus' Pedigree of a Clan (Jin Sha), 202, 203
Yusi (journal), 256
Yusi Society, 256
Yuxi River, 86
Yuyao opera, 208

Z

Zen meditation, 121. *See also* Buddhism
Zeng Can, 168
Zeng Gong, 172, 173
Zhang Fei, 247
Zhang Guifeng, 213
Zhang Guolao, 84
Zhang Heng, 111
Zhang Huixin, 209
Zhang Meigu, 207
Zhang Qian, 76, 77, 141, 217
Zhang Shicheng, 243
Zhang Taiyan, 240
Zhang Xu, 6
Zhang Zhongjing, 155
Zhang Zi, 6
Zhangzai, 234
Zhao Benshan, 160, 162
Zhao Guiying (opera), 212
Zhao Kuangyin, Emperor, 53, 121
Zhao Mengfu, 6

Zhao Yi, 111
Zhao Yun, 247
Zhao Ziyue (Lao She), 265
Zheng Guangzu, 180, 181
Zheng Sili, 207
Zheng Xuan, 228
Zhengzhou, 144
Zhenzong, Emperor, 84, 219
Zhongyue Temple, 144
Zhou, Emperor, 52
Zhou Bangyan, 176, 177
Zhou Dunyi, 224, 234
Zhou Dynasty, 23, 52, 53, 72, 97, 107, 108, 129, 140, 169, 201, 202, 222, 228, 271. *See also* Eastern Zhou Dynasty; Western Zhou Dynasty
Zhou Yu, 52, 247
Zhou Zuoren, 256
Zhu Bajie, 183, 248, 249–50
Zhu Da, 166
Zhu Fushan, 7
Zhu Ke, 7
Zhu Sucheng, 208
Zhu Xi, 96, 168, 169, 224, 234
Zhu You, 171
Zhu Yuanzhang, Emperor, 53, 224, 234
Zhu Yunming, 7
Zhuang ethnic minority, 55
Zhuang Tzu, 235, 237
Zhudi, Emperor, 135
Zhuge Liang, 52, 182, 246, 247
Zi Chan, 144
Zisi, 169
zither, 162, 163–64, 208
zodiac, 16–17
zongzi, 26
Zu Yuanzhang, 224